D1371720

From
the Library
of
Margaret Listar

Margaret Listar

TEACHING HOME ECONOMICS

TEACHING HOME ECONOMICS

Second Edition

Olive A. Hall
Counselor, El Camino College,
Torrance, California

Beatrice Paolucci
Professor, College of Home Economics,
Michigan State University

JOHN WILEY & SONS, INC.
New York · London · Sydney · Toronto

Library of Congress Catalogue Card Number: 73-109432

SBN 471 34288 2

Printed in the United States of America

10 9 8 7 6

Preface

Change is the word that most aptly describes what has taken place in home economics education since our first edition was published. In keeping with trends in education as a whole, home economics teachers have been developing a structure emphasizing the concepts and generalizations that are fundamental if students are to understand the subject matter of home economics. Our profession has moved forward considerably in organizing intellectual content. This trend is reflected throughout our book, but particularly in the chapters dealing with program planning.

Taxonomies of educational objectives are now available which help direct our attention to some of the less tangible, but very important, objectives. Both the affective and psychomotor domains have been included in our revision. We want to commend Elizabeth Simpson for her contribution in developing the psychomotor domain.

Along with a more systematic approach to the teaching of home economics has come a change in the curricular emphasis. As the roles of family members are different in our technological society, home economics is now stressing preparation for human development, managerial, and consumer roles. In addition to offering the programs designed for family living, home economics is training students for gainful employment. Suggestions for such programs have been included in this revision.

One of the new chapters (Chapter 11) discusses special needs of individuals who are slow learners, gifted, underachievers, culturally diverse, disadvantaged, disturbed, or physically handicapped. Other chapters give increased attention to individualizing instruction so that all students will find their needs and interests fulfilled to a greater extent. Another area that has been expanded is that of the home economics teacher's role as adviser for student activities.

We are extremely pleased with the warm reception our first edition received. It is impossible for us to mention individually all of the individuals who helped us to set the tone of this revision, but we want to express our appreciation to the following persons for their helpful suggestions: Marilyn Adix, Jane Bemis, Ellen Champoux, Aleene Cross, Viola Herington, Sister M. Jamesine, Beth Jordan, Isabella McQuesten, Ruth Pestle, and Sister M. Alban Schramm.

OLIVE A. HALL
BEATRICE PAOLUCCI

Los Angeles, California
East Lansing, Michigan
October, 1969

Preface to The First Edition

This book is intended primarily for the preservice preparation of home economics teachers. However, the book should also be helpful to those who are already teaching home economics in junior and senior high schools, to teachers of adult classes, to home demonstration agents, and to supervisors responsible for in-service home economics education programs. Our objectives in writing this book have been (1) to provide descriptions of home economics programs in a variety of school situations; (2) to help define the role of the home economics teacher; (3) to examine the various aspects of the home economics teacher's job; and (4) to provide specific aids for successful teaching. We speak directly to the in-service teacher and to the future teacher, and we attempt to point out the means for arriving at a functioning philosophy of home economics education, as well as some ways for implementing this philosophy.

We have approached our subject through the student teaching experience because, for the prospective teacher, this is a crucial experience—the climax in a series of experiences toward which she has exerted her efforts over a considerable period of time. Student teaching is an emotionally charged experience in which the possibilities for learning are more than usually significant. The period is crucial, too, because it is one in which important attitudes toward teaching are crystallized and initial patterns for operation are established. We have aimed to build confidence and security and to dispel the notion that student teaching is a "proving ground."

The book should find its greatest application at the preservice level—in the classes on teaching methods that precede student teaching, during the student teaching experiences, and in the classes and seminars that follow these student teaching experiences. In a less formal manner, the book may be used as a guide during other growth experiences, such as individual and group projects, work experiences, and a variety of observation and participation experiences.

A large part of the information in the book could be applied by the home economist on the job—that is, by the teacher, the extension worker, the adult educator, and the mass-media communicator. This information includes basic concepts of program planning and development, as well as a variety of experimental techniques. The beginning home economist should find that the book helps her especially in overcoming her self-consciousness and in establishing a functioning philosophy to assist her in answering questions, solving problems, and making decisions that arise in her daily work experiences. A teacher who has been out of the field for a time, but who wishes to return to active service, will find the book helpful in bringing herself up-to-date in both philosophy and practice.

We have also tried to include material that will be valuable for in-service education, particularly in study groups and by supervisors working with teachers. Many of the techniques described can be applied in teaching home economics at the elementary and adult levels as well as at the secondary level. In less formal situations outside the classroom, the home demonstration agent and the home economist in business may also find these techniques useful in their teaching.

Our underlying philosophy, during the writing of this book, has been that home economics education is important for all age groups, and for men as well as women. The reader will note that many of our discussions of classroom techniques and activities have been based on the assumption that boys, as well as girls, will be students of home economics.

We have placed special emphasis on using an interdisciplinary approach in the preparation of the reader's guide to selected references. Because home economics is a field of study that draws from many areas for its subject matter, teachers benefit from familiarizing themselves with the reading and research in a number of disciplines. Much good material is being developed continuously in home economics at local, state, and national levels. Problems of sharing this material, as well as problems in the intelligent use of such material, are numerous. We have faced these problems by referring primarily to books and periodicals that are generally available. Where possible, we have secured permission to incorporate, in the text, useful materials that are not generally available. In all cases, our emphasis has been on ways of utilizing these materials.

We wish to express our deep appreciation to our present and former students and professional colleagues who have provided many helpful suggestions and examples that have enriched our discussions, as well as continual encouragement. We especially want to acknowledge Dr. Marie Dirks, Head of the Home Economics Education Division at Ohio State

University, whose intellectual stimulation, ideas, and questions were significant in making this project a reality.

OLIVE A. HALL
BEATRICE PAOLUCCI

Los Angeles, California
East Lansing, Michigan
August 1961

Contents

TEACHING

HOME

ECONOMICS

PART I

The Nature of Home Economics Education

1

A Look at Student Teaching

You are at the threshold of student teaching. Those of us whose job it is to help you become a teacher have observed how greatly college students vary in their readiness to begin teaching and how important this factor is in teaching success. Some of you are eager to begin, confident of your ability and assured that in teaching you will find the satisfactions you have anticipated. A few of you dread the experience and approach it fearfully, not sure that you really want to teach after all. In between are others, hopeful that teaching will be a happy experience, yet approaching it with varying degrees of uncertainty and anxiety.

Some feelings of hesitancy and inadequacy in the face of a new experience are to be expected. A certain measure of these feelings may actually be helpful in that they serve to stimulate you to greater effort and help you guard against overconfidence. The important thing, when you take over as a regular classroom teacher, is that you be sufficiently certain and confident, so that you can achieve and maintain the positive and constructive approach essential to success in teaching. It is with this in mind that we provide student teaching experiences as part of the program in teacher preparation.

You have been building confidence and abilities for teaching through a succession of experiences in a wide variety of class and out-of-class activities. Student teaching constitutes but part of a broad program of professional growth experiences extending on a continuum through preservice preparation and beyond, into actual teaching. Student teaching is crucial in this series of experiences because it provides the opportunity for you to try on the role of the teacher under the guidance of experienced teachers who are ready to help you make the necessary alterations so that the role may fit you.

BECOMING ACQUAINTED WITH THE ROLE OF A TEACHER

There are a number of ways in which you can get an idea of what will be expected of you when you become a home economics teacher. In your home economics courses you will have an opportunity to extend your contacts with children, youth, and adults in school and family settings through guided observation, participation, and student teaching experiences.

In some institutions prospective home economics teachers have an opportunity to participate in what is known as a school-community experience. During this time, students observe and sometimes participate in a school situation during a period when public schools are in session but when the college or university is not. At this time you can get a picture of what is involved in starting a new school year, be in on some of the initial planning for the year, observe how teachers and students get acquainted with one another, and participate in helping the regular teacher get the physical setting organized for teaching.

Just what this kind of experience can do for you was described by Dirks and Albanese this way:

> As illustrative of the type of experiences students have, that of Carolyn H. might be described. Her purposes were to gain more insight into what she would be doing as a teacher and what students would expect of her, to see what the home economics program was like in a rural community school, and to observe the planning and methods used. Carolyn spent eight days in the school . . .
>
> Among a variety of experiences, Carolyn starred as especially helpful the following: a study of the community and attendance at such community functions as the band ice-cream social and 4-H Achievement Day; assistance with lesson planning and preparation, laboratory classes, extracurricular activities, and evaluation of teaching; conferences with administrator, some parents, and students; and in addition, the opportunities afforded for first-hand observation of students' attitudes and interests, variation in levels of work, student participation in planning, and teacher-pupil conferences. To quote Carolyn in her summarization of the experience:
>
>> This has been more than a worth-while experience for me, it was a necessity! Now I am beginning to realize just how much more I need to know and to be able to do in order to be a good student teacher and teacher.[1]

At some time during your professional training, as a part of your work relative to a particular area of study or in an especially designed seminar, you may have the opportunity to work with special agencies that serve families, visit in homes that are quite different from those you have known, or take a summer job that will give you practice and security in

[1] Marie Dirks and Naomi Albanese, "Enriching the Student Program in Home Economics Education," *Journal of Home Economics,* **49**: 726–727, November 1957.

an area of home economics where you feel the need for more training. This kind of field experience is a part of the university program in teacher education in a number of institutions.

Typical of such experiences are those of two seniors who assisted with two well-child conferences sponsored by the Columbus Public Health Department and Instructive Nursing Association. One conference group was composed entirely of children of Negro families, the other of Negro and white families. Both represented lower income levels. Students visited each of the assigned centers one day a week throughout the quarter and spent approximately three hours at each session. Children with whom they worked ranged from 16 months to school age. Activities supervised included finger painting, reading to children, play activities, and reassuring children who were frightened or shy. Opportunities to work with mothers included visiting with them individually as they waited to have physicians see the children and teaching lessons to them in groups on some phase of child development.

Students had access to family records which gave background information regarding educational level and social and economic status of those with whom they worked. Following each conference period they also had an opportunity to discuss with the nursing staff possible reasons for a child's behavior. Arrangements were made for each of the students to visit the home of a particular child so that they might better understand the neighborhood, the type of housing, and the standard of living of families represented. Values derived from this type of experience are best seen through the students' own words:

> I feel this experience is good for every college student who may become used to his own surroundings and not recognize that teaching does not always involve upper and middle class children . . . I have a better knowledge of the influence of family attitudes, status, and cultural patterns on the child as a person.
>
> My home visits were experiences I will never forget . . . I feel that the three families I visited allowed me to see homes of three different economic levels with three different kinds of parental attitudes . . . Talking with nurses before going to the homes and then our discussion following the visit helped me to see it is necessary to keep an objective point of view if you are going to help those who need guidance.
>
> My third adult class was the best one I taught . . . I've decided that it takes experience and that no matter how much you read about teaching in a book or listen to it in a lecture you don't really get the full meaning until you do it . . . I found that for this group 15 minutes was a good time to allow for a lesson . . . After that time they were ready to socialize . . .[2]

[2] Ibid., page 727.

There will be a number of opportunities for you to observe, and, perhaps, to participate in actual teaching situations—if you recognize this as a worthwhile experience. Some of your professional education courses arrange such kinds of experiences for you. When you see actual classrooms in session, the theory that you read, study, and discuss in your college courses becomes more meaningful to you.

One prospective home economics teacher kept a diary of her observations-and-participation experiences in a junior high school. You will note that she was able to draw some conclusions from her experience that facilitated her ability to be a more secure and confident student teacher and teacher.

Diary

My participation experience consisted of five two-hour sessions at ________ Junior High School. I visited the school once a week and observed in Miss ___________'s home economics classes.

Tuesday, February 11, I merely became acquainted with the teacher, the classroom and its activities, and the school. The teacher had a somewhat dramatic appearance; she was effervescent, enthusiastic, and very artistic. I found the classroom very attractive and modern, decorated in tones of beige and dark green, with coral accents. It seated approximately thirty students comfortably; however, the seventh-grade class which I observed had twenty-five students.

Each day I visited from 12:00 until 2:15 P.M. The class was held from 12:38 until 2:04, twice a week. At this particular time these seventh graders were studying child care. They were organizing and compiling the kind of information that was needed when caring for one-to-five-year-olds. The teacher assisted by raising questions, summarizing, and helping the students relate the information to questions the seventh graders raised in relation to children they knew . . . Although there was no other activity except class discussion during the period, I noticed that the students were very attentive, alert, and responsive. Their assignment for February 13 was to read in their text and in bulletins the teacher helped them to find. Through their reading they were to discover what "authorities" believed to be physical growth patterns of children.

I noted that the classroom had a number of books and bulletins available for the students to use. The teacher was especially pleased with a book especially written for seventh grade students. I noted that it was interestingly written, and had illustrations and examples that should help students with varying socio-economic and ethnic backgrounds identify with the situations.

After class that day, conferred with the principal to learn more about the school, the curriculum, the community, and especially, his view of the home economics program. He gave me a booklet that explains how home economics fits into the entire curriculum for grades seven through twelve. The principal emphasized a point made in the booklet—that home economics is required in the seventh grade and may be elected from then on. In high school, home economics is specialized. Mr. __________ also gave me a written version of the school's philosophy for the purpose of telling me of their general education approach. When I asked about the home background of the students, he stated that the students came from a wide range of homes—some large, some small; some with no other children in the family, others with five or six siblings living at home. A number of students came from one-parent families. Although most of the students in the school were white, there were a number of black students. The principal indicated that home economics classes were especially helpful to the students in his school because "they offer the students an opportunity to learn about everyday living, to appreciate the importance of the home environment . . . , and to understand ways of living that may be different from their own."

The following Tuesday, February 18, I concentrated on learning names of students. I used the teacher's grade book and tried to identify each student as she participated in class discussion. I made a seating chart as I went along. I was interested in noting at the end of the hour how involved most of the class had been. Somehow, I'd had the impression that the teacher did most of the talking. She did ask important questions now and then, but mostly that day, she discussed the out-of-class activity she wanted them to complete before Thursday. Each student was to observe a child between the ages of two and five years and write down specific observations of the child's play activities—what he did, what toys or equipment he used, and who played with him. If a student did not have a brother or sister at home, or if he knew no children of that age in his neighborhood, the teacher agreed to make arrangements for the student to observe children in a local Head Start program.

Before class that day, I talked with the teacher concerning her other activities outside of actual classroom teaching. She is president of one professional organization and treasurer of another. Teaming this with PTA and teachers' meetings, classroom projects, and some extracurricular social activity, she is busy nearly every night of the week. Miss __________ is an extremely active person and quite devoted to her profession.

The following Tuesday, February 25, I taught the class. For days before I worried about that—wondering if I knew enough about child care to be able to teach it. The class members were to bring children's toys that they thought would fill certain developmental needs—social, mental or physical. Prior to class, Miss __________, the regular teacher, looked over my lesson plan and made suggestions. What I was hoping to accomplish that day was to have the students learn to select toys "appropriate for preschool children at various developmental stages." Briefly, through discussions, the students identified the developmental purposes of toys, and a few examples were cited. We also reviewed, very briefly, the social and physical characteristics of the different age groups of children.

On the board I drew a chart, formed through their discussion. We listed the developmental areas vertically, and the age groups horizontally, thus creating squares, in which we listed the appropriate toys. I showed them possibilities for using kitchen utensils as toys. Then we discussed the characteristics necessary in a good toy, from the standpoint of safety, interest, and money. Finally, they divided themselves into three groups, each group taking for study a share of the toys brought to class. After five minutes, each chairman and her group had categorized the toys according to "safe" and "unsafe," and according to age group. Place cards were provided to make the chairman's report easier. The reports and discussion took approximately 15 minutes. Miss __________ again took over the class during the last five minutes, and the students planned for Thursday's class.

The next Tuesday, March 5, these students had a test covering the entire unit on child care. I brought questions to cover the material I had taught. While the students were taking the test, I read the cumulative records on one of the students, a girl named Rusty. Afterward, I observed the displays on the various home economics units, which the students had set up for the school's Open House. The child care unit was represented by several booklets on baby-sitting. The class members had brought the toys they had started collecting the previous Thursday and completed for March 5. They discussed the characteristics of each of their toys, and then the class selected a few toys for the display. Among the toys were sock puppets, bean bags, stuffed animals, strings of spools, and paper hats.

I feel that this experience was very good for me. It was the first time I had ever planned and taught a class, and it certainly helped give me some confidence, which I needed very much. However, I felt that this class was really no problem. The students were interested, responsive, and presented no discipline worries. Although I had neglected to tell them to be sure to return the toys I had brought from home, they placed every toy on the teacher's desk as they left the classroom. I felt that most of them did learn something in this class experience, and my feeling was borne out by the way they carried out Thursday's toy activities.

Conclusions I Drew

First of all, I discovered how responsive and enthusiastic junior-high students can be. They love activity and seem to want to please. Although I was aware of the common characteristics of students at this age level, I was unaware of how "individual" each student really is!

Second, I discovered that each class must be planned very carefully in order to take full advantage of the time allowed. The teacher is responsible for doing this. I learned how important proper planning is to teaching.

Third, I realize more clearly that students relate everything to situations outside of class and particularly to their own homes. I think this would be a very good device for the teacher to use deliberately, as it seems to hold the student's interest best.

Fourth, I found that cumulative records are helpful, but may be very incomplete. The home economics teacher could probably add quite a bit of information by noting some of the comments the students make about their homes and families.

My overall conclusion is that, although nearly all of this has been covered in classwork throughout college, the theory and book learning becomes a part of you when you gain actual experience. I think this is necessary for developing into a really effective teacher.

THE CHALLENGE OF STUDENT TEACHING

No two student teaching experiences can be identical even for students from the same institution; and from one institution to another, student teaching programs vary widely. There are differences, for example, with respect to the length of the student teaching period, whether full time is devoted to student teaching or other college courses are carried at the same time, whether the student teacher goes off-campus to teach or continues to be resident on campus, and whether she is assigned to handle a particular situation alone or shares the assignment with others. There are also differences in the kinds of growth opportunities afforded, depending on the type of school in which the student teaching is done, the way in which the home economics program is organized, and whether the student teacher participates in but one phase of the program or has contact with the total program.

One student teaching experience can only introduce a prospective teacher to the many facets of the home economics teacher's task, provide an opportunity for her to observe or teach in several related areas of home economics, and enable her to work with some of the various age groups for which home economics education may be provided. This is one of the reasons why many institutions provide observation and participation experiences in a variety of situations, and in some instances, more than one student teaching experience. The programs of some institutions are flexible enough to allow a person to select a student teaching situation that will provide experiences to meet her particular needs and interests.

The Purposes of Student Teaching Programs

In spite of the many variations in the patterns of student teaching, these programs tend to provide a more or less common core of experiences that afford opportunity for the student teacher to establish herself in a new situation, which means not only creating a favorable impression but also gaining the liking and respect of others. Thus, she can add to her understanding of human behavior and achieve new skill in human relationships. There is also the opportunity to establish herself in the teacher role—to learn to look the part as well as to feel what it means to be a teacher, to perform comfortably and without self-consciousness in the teacher role, and to be accepted by others as a teacher. In every student teaching experience there are constant challenges to growth in relationships with students in and out of the classroom, in ability to work with the supervising teacher, in professional activities with other teachers, and in contacts with parents and others outside the school.

One of the primary purposes of student teaching is, of course, to build competency in the actual process of teaching. Many of the activities in any student teaching situation are planned with this purpose in mind. You will be faced with innumerable illustrations of how individuals differ with respect to patterns of growth and development and in terms of individual needs and interests. If you have an opportunity to work with several age levels and with boys as well as girls, your understanding of the developmental needs that are characteristic of particular groups will be strengthened. Despite their many differences, you will be impressed by how alike students are in their needs for affection, recognition, and security. To learn to look at their behavior in these terms and to be able to mold the methods and materials of instruction to meet their many needs and aspirations are two of the worthwhile achievements of teaching. Student teaching can do no more than start you on the road to the accomplishment of such goals.

As a home economics teacher, you will be particularly interested in the needs of students as they relate to home and family living and in the ways in which home economics instruction is adapted to meet these needs. Although the basic needs of students may vary little from one locality to another, their more immediate needs may vary considerably, depending upon such factors as whether the community in which they live is predominantly urban or rural; the kind of occupations in which their families are engaged; whether mothers as well as fathers work; the mobility or permanency of residence; the ethnic or religious composition of the community; the economic levels at which people live; the kinds of equipment and facilities characteristic of their homes; and whether the majority of students marry soon after graduation, enter some kind of work, or are college bound. Every home economics teacher, in one way or another, takes these and other factors into consideration as she plans learning experiences. Two of the most interesting opportunities you will have in student teaching are discerning the kinds of learning experiences that will be most meaningful to your students, and planning in accordance with these experiences.

Overall Planning

Unless you enter your student teaching at the beginning of the year, or at the beginning of the semester, much of the overall planning will probably have been done. The fact that the situation you enter is an ongoing one, and that at best you see but a segment of the year's work, is one of the limitations of a student teaching experience. Nevertheless, overall planning is but a flexible framework within which teacher and students plan as the work progresses. Most student teaching situations offer some opportunities for cooperative planning with students on a problem basis and many opportunities in connection with day-by-day class activities. It will be necessary for you to familiarize yourself as thoroughly as possible with the work that has preceded your coming and to be sure you understand how the work that is being covered while you are there contributes to overall goals and fits into what will follow after you leave.

Selection of Methods and Materials

Those aspects of planning that most excite the imagination and creativeness of some teachers have to do with the selection of the methods and materials of teaching. These may provide more than the usual amount of challenge when factors over which the teacher has little or no control threaten to limit her choices. In this category might fall periods that seem too short, classes that are extremely large, rooms that are equipped inadequately and arranged inefficiently, and budgets that restrict the resources needed for effective teaching. There are situations in which it is exceedingly difficult to create the informal atmosphere and to employ the individualized instruction and small group activity that have been so characteristic of home economics teaching. Every situation, however, requires some adaptation in the use of methods and materials. One of the most valuable things you may gain from your student teaching is to see how your supervising teacher works around, and often turns to advantage, such limitations as there may be in her particular situation. The numerous opportunities you will have to vary the use of methods and materials may well prove to be among the most interesting aspects of your student teaching experience.

Teaching and evaluation go hand in hand. Not all teachers see evaluation as a continuous and integral part of the teaching process, serving initially as the basis for setting goals, and subsequently, for measuring progress toward these goals. Evaluation must be concerned with appraising the total growth of the student and not only with the acquisition of knowledge and skills. This implies the need to employ a variety of techniques and procedures. There will be many opportunities for you in student teaching to learn more about evaluation and to experiment with evaluation procedures, both in relation to student learning and with respect to your own growth and development.

A STUDENT TEACHER'S EXPERIENCES

Thus far you have seen that student teaching is intended, as are your other college classes, to be a growth experience—one that will be satisfying and worthwhile. The following is a description of an actual student teaching experience in a small, somewhat rural, midwestern community high school. Although your own student teaching experience may be very different in some ways, this description illustrates some opportunities for growth that may be possible in any student teaching experience. As you read it, you may wish to look for the kinds of opportunities in this situation of which the student teacher took advantage.

> For some time I had looked forward to this, my off-campus student teaching experience. From my friends who had already done their student teaching, I had had glimpses into what this experience might be like. My teachers and classes in home economics education, too, helped me visualize what I might expect. However, to be perfectly frank, I really did not know what to expect. I was eager to begin but there was a little place inside me full of questions, doubts, yes, even fears. Questions like these kept creeping into my mind: Will it be fun? Will I be lonely? Will they like me? Will it be hard? Where will I live? And the *big* question, do I have the ability to teach?
>
> Now I realize that no one can tell you exactly what your student teaching experience will be like, for each is as individual as the student teacher herself. In discussing student teaching with my friends, I found that, while we each had had an entirely different experience, we all had experienced some things in common. I would like to share with you some of the aspects of my student teaching, not because it was outstanding, but, rather, because it was typical.
>
> I arrived in my student teaching community in the late afternoon. I was met on the walk by a small boy who accompanied me to the door of my new home. His mother greeted me and showed me my room. I was pleased because it looked comfortable and had a place where I could study. We visited while I unpacked, and she told me where I might do my laundry, made suggestions of places to eat, gave me some ideas about what I might find interesting to do while in the community, and told me I could entertain my friends in the living room. I was already beginning to feel at home.
>
> I went to school early that first morning. My supervising teacher met me and introduced me to the principal. He welcomed me to the teaching center and introduced me to other faculty members and students. With my supervising teacher, I went to the home economics room. Immediately I was made to feel I belonged, for there was a special place just for me—a drawer for my materials, a packet containing schedules, special forms used by the school, and other helpful information. As students came into the room, I was introduced to each one. I found it hard to connect names and faces, but each day it became easier. Prior to student teaching I had been concerned about

whether I would get along with my supervising teacher and how I should act around her. My worries were for naught, for she accepted me right from the start and treated me as a colleague!

During the first days I explored the home economics department, became familiar with the school program, and found myself helping in a number of ways. As I helped students with projects, group work and reports, and jotted their ideas on the chalkboard during a class discussion, I realized that I was already involved in teaching. Helping members of the Future Homemakers of America plan a three-dimensional bulletin board to describe the objectives of their organization, working with the Home Economics III class as they prepared for a nutrition unit which they were going to teach the first graders, and accompanying a student as he made arrangements for a resource person for the family living class offered many opportunities for geting to know my students better.

One of the things I enjoyed most was talking over the classes my supervising teacher taught. It was fun to help her plan lessons, observe her teaching, and later discuss what happened and why. It also made it easier for me when we did the same thing with classes I taught.

One of my first responsibilities with students outside the home economics classes was the supervision of a small study-hall. It was here that I first experienced the difference between the hum of industry and the chatter of idleness. I found I was called upon to answer questions about English, social studies, algebra, and computer sciences. Needless to say, I often did not have the answer.

The Future Homemakers of America chapter in this school plays an important part in the home economics program. Working with this organization was one of my most valuable student teaching experiences. I attended an initiation ceremony and a number of chapter meetings. Often, I met with the advisory council to help plan activities for our chapter. Attending a section meeting was a good way to learn what other schools were doing in their chapters.

I wrote my home economics teacher-educator at the college to keep her informed about my teaching. She visited us at regular intervals. With my supervising teachers, we discussed my progress. Together we looked at ways I might enrich my experience and discussed new methods and materials we could try. I described with her what I had done that was of particular interest. For example, I let her listen to a tape recording we had used with a family living class in analyzing one of the class discussions. I appreciated the bits of news about friends who were teaching in other centers and about what was taking place on campus.

My principal was very helpful in giving me any background information that might be necessary in order for me to understand the problems being discussed at faculty meetings. Occasionally he asked my opinion and I felt that he really wanted it. For example, when we were using the norms from a statewide testing program, he asked me to help interpret them, since I had recently had some study and experience with testing.

The home economics classes at the freshman and senior levels included both boys and girls. Working in small groups in these and other home economics classes helped students learn to give and take ideas as one must do in a family. I tried out a variety of teaching methods and techniques. I felt the need for more experience in working with small children so I made arrangements to participate in the preschool program. This was of real assistance later on, when I began helping a class to plan for a play group in connection with a child development unit.

When the music teacher learned that my particular interest, in addition to home economics, was music, she asked me if I would like to play the piano for the glee-club practice. I also had the opportunity to work with the girls' ensemble, which was entering the district contest for the first time. (I might add, they received a first-division rating!) In these small ways, I was able to contribute to more of the school's activities. I believe I would enjoy helping with some vocal work when I begin teaching next year.

Much effective teaching is done outside the classroom. All communities have valuable resources if we look for them. In a housing unit I taught, we visited several different types of homes in the community. I also took students to the locker plant to see a meat-cutting demonstration. These activities not only improved my teaching, but also helped me to know the community better.

I thoroughly enjoyed making home visits. Meeting my students and their families in their homes gave me a better understanding of them. I always received a warm welcome and sometimes refreshments. Before I made a visit, I asked if I might come. Of course, what is even better is to have a student invite you to the home, and this happened frequently in our department.

While I was student teaching, I had many conferences with students, some planned and some spontaneous. Usually we dealt with class projects, but sometimes students came for special help with a personal problem. I felt that, through such conferences, I was able to help a few students whom I would not have been able to reach otherwise.

I found that demonstrating certain things saved energy and materials and utilized time more efficiently. Demonstrating flower arrangements enabled me to show all of the girls a number of art principles with the few flowers that were available to us. I used the demonstration method of teaching, because that was one method with which I felt I needed experience. Of course, I realize that students, too, gain competence through actual practice; so, as I gained confidence, I encouraged them to participate more and more in the demonstrations I gave.

Teaching adult classes was a great challenge to me. Our adults seemed to have a special interest in new equipment. With the help of the supervising teacher and a member of the adult advisory council, I planned a series of lessons on the use and care of small electrical equipment. We borrowed some of the equipment from the local utility company. I believe I learned as much teaching these classes as the adults did. My adults helped me to understand better the homemaking practices in the community; in turn, I helped them to understand better the high school home economics program, for they often commented on how much the program had changed since they were in school.

Near the end of my student teaching experience, I had a conference with my supervising teacher, my college teacher-educator, and my principal. We discussed my experiences and the particular things I had gained from them. We also discussed ways in which the student teaching experience might be improved.

I thoroughly enjoyed my off-campus student teaching experience. I believe I have a good picture of what teaching home economics will be like. It seems to me that only by actually going to a new school and new community can you see a school situation as a whole. I saw how home economics fits into the total school program; it cannot be considered a thing apart from the rest of the school and community. Teaching home economics has a wide range of possibilities in methods, techniques, resource materials, and subject matter. It is up to the student teacher to make her experience as broad and as meaningful as she can. You get from student teaching largely what you put into it. My student teaching experience has made me eager to begin my career in teaching home economics.[3]

What Was Gained from These Experiences?

For the student teacher in this story, student teaching offered many challenging opportunities that greatly strengthened her interest in teaching and her desire to teach. One of your major responsibilities as a teacher will be to help your students draw from their learning experiences some generalizations that will have meaning for them in new situations. Drawing generalizations is equivalent, in effect, to saying: "What did I learn from this experience that will be applicable elsewhere?" As she thought back over her experience, this student teacher was able to pull from it some of the things she considered to be most important and why. Table 1 shows a sample of what she did.

What the student teacher did in the illustration in Table 1 was to sort from her many experiences some from which she had derived new understandings that she recognized as meaningful for future teaching. We suggest that you try her technique in connection with some of your observations and other prestudent teaching experiences. Generalization, as used here, means to draw from an experience new understandings that you have gained, or to reformulate old understandings that may have taken on new meanings or may have reflected a greater breadth of application. Later chapters contain further discussions about generalizations and the way in which they relate to learning. They *are* important in the teaching-learning process.

[3] Adapted from script written to accompany slides taken by a home economics student from Illinois State Normal University, during her student teaching experience.

TABLE 1 Generalizations Drawn from My Student Teaching Experiences

Some of the things I thought most important:	I thought them important because:
I found it helpful to talk to student teachers who had already done their student teaching, to visit several student teaching centers, to talk with teachers, and to consider student teaching in education classes before I went out to teach.	Knowing what is expected of one makes it easier to adapt to a new situation.
I appreciated the nice place I had to stay and the way the landlady and her small son greeted me the day I came; also, everyone's friendliness at school and the efforts they all made to help me get acquainted, the special place Miss ________ provided for me to keep my things, and the many ways she and the students found for me to be of help while I was getting acquainted.	It is important to feel that we belong.
I especially liked the way Miss ________ brought me up-to-date on what the classes had been doing before I came and the time we took to block out a tentative plan for nine weeks in the center, early in my teaching period.	A feeling of security comes with a sense of direction.
The conference I had with my supervising teacher and the college teacher-educator in which we talked over my progress always gave me ideas for new things I could try, such as using the tape recorder with my family living class.	Continuous evaluation of progress toward goals provides the basis for planning new goals.

Summary

You might look also at the student teacher's story in terms of what it tells about the home economics teacher's job and about the home economics program. First, it indicates that the teacher may work in different ways with various age groups—at the elementary level in helping with special units; at the secondary level, in home and family-living classes; and with adults, through formal classes and by giving help in informal ways. Next, the teacher may use a wide variety of resources, some of which are at hand within her own department and school, while others are drawn from the community. Further, she may use a great variety of methods, both formal and informal—demonstrations, field trips, projects, bulletin (or tack) boards, conferences, group work, reports, discussions, tape recordings, play schools, home visitation, and resource persons. So that she may use these human and material resources wisely, she finds it necessary to study her community, its homes, and its families.

In her planning, the home economics teacher enlists the cooperation of others—parents, students, and other community members. In addition to carrying on the activities of her own department, she contributes to the total school program. She works with student club groups such as the Future Homemakers of America. She may help with music or other all-school activities if she has an interest in and the talent needed for such participation. She also takes part in professional activities of the faculty.

During your various prestudent teaching experiences and in student teaching, you will want to learn as much as you can about such things as how the teacher secures the information she needs about homes and families, the techniques she uses for identifying needs and interests, how she carries on cooperative planning, from what sources she secures teaching aids, and how she judges the effectiveness of her teaching. These constitute the know-how of teaching.

As you will recall, the student teaching story described a home economics program in one type of situation—a community school in a somewhat rural area. One of your first major decisions relative to your role as a teacher will be that of deciding where you would like to teach. The following chapter describes representative programs in other types of schools and communities, and indicates how these programs vary.

Selected References

Brown, Thomas J., *Student Teaching in a Secondary School* (2nd ed.). New York: Harper and Row, 1969.

Houston, W. Robert, Frank H. Blackington III, and Horton S. Southworth, *Professional Growth Through Student Teaching*. Columbus: Charles E. Merrill, 1965.

Reilly, Howard E., *Student Teaching: Two Years After*. Cedar Falls, Iowa: State College of Iowa, Association for Student Teaching, Bulletin No. 24, 1965, pp. 1–24.

Steeves, Frank L., *Fundamentals of Teaching in Secondary Schools*. New York: The Odyssey Press, 1962.

2

A Look at Today's Home Economics Programs

Today, home economics education is an integral part of the public schools in the United States. Boys and girls, men and women are recognizing increasingly that the complexity of living demands that they have some formal training if they are to solve the problems of family life with a greater degree of ease and satisfaction. Home economics education at all levels is dedicated to the task of helping individuals learn better those behavior patterns and skills that will enable them to fulfill effectively their roles as family members.

Families are not the same everywhere. They differ from one locale to another, and even in the same area there may be wide variances in family values, patterns, and practices. A large measure of the success of teaching home economics is dependent upon recognizing these basic differences among families. When such factors as actual home situations, existing family practices and values, and knowledge and abilities deemed important, have been considered in developing a home economics program, that program becomes unique for the people it serves.

There are, however, many similarities among families. All are affected by social and economic changes. All persons grow, learn, and develop in much the same manner. All strive for fulfillment of the basic physical, social, and psychological needs. The application of knowledge concerning socio-economic trends, psychology of learning, and human growth and development gives all home economics programs, no matter where they are located, a commonness of purpose and procedure.

Each of us is a product of our experiences. We are who we are, and we act as we do because we have been exposed to a particular set of behavior patterns—at home, at school, in our play groups as children, and in a variety of social and work situations as adults. Repeatedly you have noted that you seem to fit into and enjoy some situations more than others. Usually this is because the situation contains some elements of the familiar for you. Most of us operate with a greater degree of efficiency and satisfaction if we know what to expect in a given situation and what is expected of us.

TYPICAL HOME ECONOMICS PROGRAMS

The first and perhaps the most crucial decision you will make in your teaching career will be that of deciding *where* you will teach. In many ways your choice will color all other decisions you will make in teaching, for, in a sense it will determine *who* you will teach, *what* you will teach, and in most instances, *how* you will teach. Since home economics programs do vary from one setting to another, you will need some basis for selecting the kind of position that is most interesting and challenging for you. This section contains descriptions of a few widely different, yet typical, home economics programs. Each description illustrates only part of the teacher's planning and activities in a typical day. As you begin to make decisions concerning what and how to teach, you may want to re-examine these descriptions to note how the particular situation patterned to some degree what and how each home economics teacher taught.

Midwest Consolidated School

Located a few miles from the outskirts of town, sprawled in what was once the middle of a cornfield, is Midwest Consolidated School. The teachers—commuters all—pull up outside the school at about 7:50 A.M., generally driving their own cars. They spend the next half-hour picking up mail and announcements from their boxes, exchanging greetings and plans with colleagues, and making last-minute preparations for classes. Promptly at 8:20 A.M., just 10 minutes before classes are scheduled to begin, the familiar yellow school buses roll up to the side entrance, discharging the exuberant student population. From the neighboring towns come the "town kids"—a bit sleepy-eyed, having gulped a bit of breakfast and hopped on the bus some twenty minutes earlier. From the outlying areas and the farms come others—some fortunate enough to have traveled only a short distance, while others have been on the bus for nearly an hour. Jostling, laughing, exchanging the latest news about who's dating whom, planning the day's activities, and occasionally discussing their studies, they pour into the quiet building and scatter to their lockers.

At the end of the wide corridor, with its attractive display cases that are currently depicting career possibilities in home economics, is the attractive, functional, and flexible home economics room. This is indeed a busy room, inhabited during the course of a day by a wide range of personalities—among them girls and boys in regularly scheduled classes, adults seeking information, teachers gathering for a meeting, and students seeking special help or working on a particular project.

In the few short minutes before the students arrive, the home economics teacher attempts to review the day's agenda. Today the "family living" class will be viewing a movie; it has arrived and been previewed, and the student operator has been contacted. The one detail the teacher must remember is to have the members of her Home Economics I class —who today are having a panel discussion with the parents—rearrange the room after the class so that the movie can be viewed more comfortably. The Home Economics II students will be in the unit kitchens for the preparation of their first meal today. Last night before she left school she ordered the groceries, but at the moment she is a bit apprehensive as to whether they will arrive in ample time for her class. What to do in case the groceries do not arrive in time will take some real thinking. If all goes well—that is, if study hall is really quiet for a change —she can get some planning done during that period. She must try to think of some way to insure this needed quiet. Then there is the note from the principal that was in her box this morning; she will have to find a few moments during the day when they are both free to smooth out a few of the details concerning the curriculum meeting that is their joint responsibility. One thing has really been well planned and should follow through with relative simplicity—that is the snack preparation laboratory for her eighth graders. Yesterday they discussed the part food plays in entertaining friends, and worked quite hard on the planning details for a "nutritious snacks laboratory," so today they may be sure they will get everything completed during their class period. The conference period today is to be devoted to an executive council meeting with the Future Homemakers. Tonight the leader plans to leave school as soon as possible, since she needs to get a few household tasks done before returning to school to attend a parent meeting. She hopes Mrs. G., Mary's mother, comes to the meeting, as she is eager to talk with her about the progress Mary and she are making on the planning for taking over management of the home for a week while Mrs. Green goes to visit her ailing mother. This is a part of Mary's home experience. If all goes well and there are not too many interruptions during the day, the home economics teacher will be able to look back on her day with the realization that she has accomplished a good deal; and, to say the least, it will not have been a routinized day.

Farmville School

The hub of Farmville is the local school; the major educative, social, and political activities of the village and surrounding countryside are centered in the school. Everyone in the community shares in the pride of the new elementary-school annex that stands out in bold relief against the old two-story brick building. Throughout the community, people look forward to the time when they can remodel the high school so that it will be as bright, cheerful, and functional as the "new school."

The people of Farmville, because of increased rural-urban interaction and broader social relationships due to mass communication and transportation, are well aware that life for their children will be much like that of their city cousins. Hence Farmville School must assist its youth to live in and understand both the rural and urban worlds.

Farmville's youth come to high school in their own cars, on bicycles, by foot, and, in many cases, by school buses. The teachers live in Farmville or in neighboring communities.

Much activity is underway long before school begins. Students tend to come early; some are quite serious about getting extra help and participating in school activities, while others come because they have nothing else to do. It is not unusual to schedule a student committee meeting or to participate in a ping-pong tournament—all before classes start.

Mrs. Smith, the home economics teacher, arrived early on the scene this morning. The girls in her Home Economics I class are involved in a food preservation unit. Today they are working with peaches and are planning to get their learning experience by freezing home-grown peaches. Mrs. Smith wanted to be at school when the farmer's wife brought the fruit. While readying the room in preparation for the preservation laboratory, she chats with the farmer's wife about their joint responsibilities as part of the refreshment committee for the Parent-Teacher Association. Jane, a girl whom she had in class last year, stops by to get some suggestions on the kind of interfacing she might use in a suit she is making. The biology teacher stops to remind Mrs. Smith that most of the sophomore class will be gone for the day on a field trip he has planned. As she makes a mental note of her day's activities, her thoughts are organized something like this:

Home Economics I. Will want students to see possibilities of various containers available for freezing. Also help class to see other ways of preserving peaches, i.e., canning, drying, jams.

Freshman-Sophomore Physical Education. Field Hockey. Must remind the girls to bring notes of parental permission if they plan to attend out-of-town field meet.

Advanced Home Economics. I need to work on some ways of keeping the class interesting and challenging for all the girls during this child-development unit. It is hard to gear the class to such an age range—the group has sophomore, junior, and senior girls. Remind the girls of Thursday night's PTA meeting, since they have promised they will baby-sit that night for parents attending the meeting.

Check with the school lunch manager about a time for meeting. We must be clear about what we both can contribute when we meet with the principal concerning the school's proposed venture into job preparation for some of our students in the area of food service.

Check with Jim, the junior class president, about plans for a class meeting.

Mrs. Smith can expect, during the day, to participate in many other activities which, in her morning mental joggings, she has not anticipated. These may include listening to a personal problem of a student who has come to her for help, "disciplining" a couple of boys who were scuffling in the hall, or replacing all her afternoon activities due to an unscheduled assembly.

Suburbia High

The last word in modern school construction; building scarcely finished but already overcrowded; curriculum a hot issue because families are highly mobile, both physically and socially—this is Suburbia High. By public transportation, in a station wagon, or under his own steam, the sophisticated and well-dressed teenager comes to school. The outside casual observer looks at him and notes that he is loaded with books because homework is a part of the school pattern; usually he displays the symbols of courtesy because this is a parent expectation; he acts somewhat bored and tends toward in-groupishness as a part of the peer code. The teachers of Suburbia High are highly trained—a large number of them have advanced degrees or are aspiring toward them. They are active community members, loyal and dedicated to the school organization, and they participate actively in in-service professional groups. Preschool and postschool workshops and teacher study groups are parts of the pattern.

The home economics teacher, upon arrival at school, goes to the home economics department. It is a multi-room department that is used concurrently by several home economics teachers. Modern in decoration and functional in purpose, the rooms reflect the character of the home economics program. There is a large-group instruction room well equipped for use of instructional media such as overhead projectors, video and audio tapes, and films. Nearby are smaller rooms with flexible furniture that can be used for discussion purposes. A multipurpose flexible laboratory is available for independent or group work in special areas such as food preparation, home nursing, clothing construction, motion studies, laundering, and interior design. The home economics department operates a preschool for children two to four years of age. Here, under the supervision of a qualified preschool teacher, students from home economics classes have an opportunity to learn firsthand, through observation and participation, about child growth and development.

At some time during his or her high school life, every single Suburbia teenager will have a class in this room, because home economics is a part of the general education program of the school.

The following telescoped scenes depict a typical day for one of the home economics teachers:

First Scene. Common Learnings—Home Economics, Section 1.

The first class is part of the "common learnings" program, designed by the school to help students acquire the knowledge, skills, understandings, and attitudes that are required by all in order to live together effectively as present and future citizens. This program is included in many secondary schools on a "block" basis—that is, two or more consecutive modules form a large block of time during which the students study personal, social, and community problems.

Today, thirty-five energetic ninth-grade boys and girls are working in family groups—making plans for the supper they are going to prepare and serve. Decisions are being made concerning how much money can be spent from their total budget, choices of foods that meet nutritional needs, yet are acceptable to the variety of likes and dislikes represented, and division of labor for shopping, cooking, serving, and cleanup. The process of arriving at an acceptable decision, although not formally analyzed, is being practiced as alternatives are first proposed and investigated, then rejected or accepted.

Second Scene. Home Economics I, Section 2.

The twenty-four sophomore girls are actively engaged in learning about some of the new fibers that are being used in their clothing. Through the reading of their textbooks, of articles in current professional and popular magazines, and of literature secured from manufacturers, the girls are discovering some of the reasons why certain laundering procedures are preferred. At home and at school they will try out some of these procedures as they care for their clothing.

Third Scene. Home Economics II, Section 3.

Twenty-two junior and senior girls are in the process of examining how much time it takes to perform some of the typical homemaking tasks. Today they are reporting to the whole class the results of some time studies they had carried on at home. Comparisons are being made concerning the length of time required by the various methods of dish-washing, to clean up the dishes after an average supper. The students will be challenged to recognize the importance of time norms.

Fourth Scene. Family Living, Section 1.

The senior boys and girls are evaluating yesterday's trip to a home for the aged. They are discussing the various ways in which senior citizens express their need for affection and security. The conclusions reached by these students reflect some insights into human behavior and a sense of social responsibility.

Fifth Scene. Common Learnings Committee Meeting.

The teachers who are involved in teaching the common learnings core are meeting to discuss shifts in the groups. Special progress and needs of individual groups are discussed and plans are made for the learning experiences of the students as they shift among the home economics, music, and typing groups.

Sixth Scene. Supper Meeting—Elementary Curriculum Consultant.

Some ways of introducing home economics into the elementary school curriculum are examined. The home economics teacher offers to sit in on some curriculum meetings with the elementary teachers during the winter.

Seventh Scene. Adult Class, Registration.

Tonight the home economics teacher is helping with the registration of adults in the adult home economics program that is offered several nights a week. Although in this case she is not responsible for the actual teaching, she does help to organize the classes and select competent instructors. On occasion, if she so desires, she may teach an adult class.

Metropolitan Junior High

Crowded playgrounds, the flow of city traffic, and the convergence of over a thousand energetic preteens—all identify the location of Metropolitan Junior High. Students and teachers generally walk to school or take a public conveyance. Transportation in private cars is unusual—the students are too young to drive and parking spaces are too limited for the teachers. Teachers are asked to arrive about a half hour before the students; they assume monitoring duties in halls and rooms as soon as the school is open to the students.

One year of home economics is required of all girls attending Metropolitan Junior High. There are several home economics teachers; each works in a particular area, usually foods and nutrition, clothing, and family relationships. Except for a chance meeting in the teacher's lounge, at the cafeteria, or at a planned committee meeting, contacts with other teachers are limited. During a large part of the day, the home economics teacher's realm of operation is her room. As an example of one teacher's day, some of the activities of a clothing teacher are described:

Period 1. Thirty seventh graders are each engaged in the construction of a simple skirt. The goal for the day is learning to mark and put in a hem. The teacher demonstrates the process, identifies the pages in the textbook where the procedure is discussed and photographed, and places a model of the completed process on a bulletin board. During the 55 minutes of class time she answers questions, checks progress, and sees to it that the class ends on time and with the room in readiness for the next group.

Periods 2, 3, and 4. A new group of girls. More skirts, similar problems, different demonstration—putting in a zipper.

Period 5. Twenty-five ninth graders, whose goal for the day is selecting appropriate accessories for school wear and for employment. In small groups the girls are experimenting with putting together sweaters, colored scarves, necklaces, pins, and collars. In a few minutes each group will report its decision of the most appropriate combination and point out the principles they used in making their selections.

Period 6. Still another group of thirty girls. Same room, lesson similar to that for the fifth-period class.

Period 7. Home room, with forty seventh-grade boys and girls. Attendance is taken. Home room chairman reads announcements and conducts business affairs of the day.

After school the home economics teacher meets with a student committee whose responsibility it is to help set up appropriate standards of dress for boys and girls attending Metropolitan Junior High.

RELATION OF HOME ECONOMICS PROGRAMS TO SCHOOLS AND COMMUNITIES

The foregoing descriptions and the analysis that now follows are intended to help you see that, despite many basic similarities, home economics programs vary in different schools and different communities. Although the names of the schools whose programs have been described are fictitious, the programs themselves are typical of home economics programs that do exist throughout the country. The characteristics of the Farmville School, Midwest Consolidated School, Suburbia High, and Metropolitan Junior High, like those of their respective communities, may be recognized in a number of places throughout the country.

You should become familiar with as many different programs as possible because the program in which you teach, and whether it meets your expectations, may mean the difference for you between satisfaction and dissatisfaction with teaching as a profession. The subject matter you teach, the personalities and characteristics of your students, the involvement of you as the teacher in the total school program, the variety or repetitiveness of the day's activities—these and other factors may influence, in large measure, your reaction to your job.

Furthermore, it is important for you to learn to look at the home economics program and the school in relation to the community in which they exist because the community exerts a very real influence on the way in which a program is organized. How well your program is organized to meet your school and community needs is determined by the interests and needs of students in the classes, the expectations of the parents, the attitudes of others in the community with respect to home economics, and the resources and facilities with which the teacher has to work.

As you look at the differences between the programs that have been described, you might try to analyze reasons for these differences. Some of the distinguishing features pertain to the nature of the school and the community, while others are in terms of the teacher's job.

In analyzing the nature of rural and urban communities, you will notice the effects of certain basic facts: (1) urban communities have a complicated task of trying to predict which of the many possible roles young people will assume as adults; (2) urban communities are confronted with the task of trying to provide specialized curricula that will meet the widely varying needs of individuals and groups; (3) cooperation between the home and school is difficult to achieve but is a necessary part of urban education; (4) rural communities are recognizing that the small high school with few teachers cannot provide a quality program —hence, consolidation becomes a must; and (5) urban education, because of high land and construction costs, high salaries necessary to attract teachers, and special needs of large numbers of culturally deprived children, may be more expensive than suburban or rural education.

Rural and Small Communities

Farmville is typical of the rural and small town community, where the school is centrally located. Teachers and students live within easy walking distance, or they drive from the surrounding countryside. Ten, 12, or 20 miles in any direction is another small town with another high school. Thus, circumscribed and with little possibility for further growth of the community through industry or new business, Farmville High has continued to operate with a few hundred students and a limited number of teachers. The population of the community has remained fairly stable. Increasing numbers of young people continue to drift to urban areas upon graduation.

Most people in the community make their living either by farming or by working in some occupation allied to the farms, in small businesses providing goods and services for community members, or in the various professions. With increased mechanization the number of small farms has decreased, sometimes being absorbed by neighboring farms, occasionally by outside financial interests. Displaced owners have in some instances become tenants; others have become involved in allied services, become part-time farmers and factory workers, or moved to other communities. On the surface, however, these changes are not very obvious. The population is relatively homogeneous. Newcomers are few and they are absorbed readily into the community. Although differences do exist in material assets and some distinctions are made with respect to social class, these are not marked. Contrasts, if any, between students who live in the country and those who live in town, are negligible. They enjoy substantially the same advantages, and they vary little in the matter of appearance or in the interests they pursue.

Teachers, students, and townspeople all know each other relatively well, and their lives touch each other at many points. They share many common interests, and the school and its activities provide a common meeting ground. Civic groups frequently make use of school facilities, and the school, in turn, draws heavily upon the resources of the community members for assistance and support. Integration of home, school, and community activities is a part of the tradition.

In some rural and small-town areas local citizens and educational leaders have recognized that, by pooling resources, programs might be expanded to provide richer and more varied instruction, better facilities, higher salaries for teachers, and increased educational opportunity for more people. In communities such as these, consolidation is taking place. The picture then shifts to become more like that presented by Midwest Consolidated High. There is likely to be a new school, larger and considerably better equipped than any one community might afford, with larger enrollments, more teachers, and a more diversified program. Often it is located in the open country as nearly central as possible to the two or more schools comprising the unit. The fleet of school buses shuttling back and forth tends to regulate the nature of the school program in rather specific ways. Activities, for example, which once were allocated to after-school or evening hours, have had to be worked into the regular school day or be eliminated. Teachers, who once resided in the school community and participated actively in its affairs, may live some distance away and drive a number of miles to and from school each day. The teachers' time for preparation before the school day begins or after classes are over in the afternoon is limited, as is their time for working with students outside of class on make-up work or extra-curricular activities.

For the most part, students from neighboring schools who have been brought together through consolidation, have learned, after a brief period for overcoming old rivalries and building new loyalties, to work together harmoniously. In some instances the school is less a center for community activities than it once was, although in others, the unification of school districts has been the means of extending community boundaries. Where divergent religious and ethnic groups or communities with strong self-interest have been brought together, growth of understanding or a new appreciation of social and cultural differences have sometimes resulted.

Suburban Communities

Just as consolidation represents an innovation in the educational program for rural America, so Suburbia marks a new trend in its development in more densely populated and urban areas. Suburbia stands at the crossroads of town and country. Land once rural has been absorbed by rapidly expanding urban populations. In some cases Suburbia's population is composed of a heterogeneous mixture of farmer-turned-factory-worker; city dweller in search of fresh air and a small plot of ground to call his own, as well as an escape from the problem of the center city; and the ever-present newcomer. Or, Suburbia may be surprisingly homogeneous—a completely new community, specifically designed, as its housing will clearly indicate, to meet the needs of a particular economic and social group. They may, for example, be primarily the workers of one or two outlying plants. Or the community may be somewhat higher on the economic scale, composed of the junior executives who are an important link in the rapidly expanding chain of industrial enterprises.

The school is one of the factors providing cohesiveness in this fast-growing community. Even if it is a new school, it may already have proven inadequate. Or, as it stands, it may represent but one unit in a master plan designed to provide for expansion as the population inevitably increases.

In some suburban communities, families are predominantly young, highly transient, and upwardly mobile. Many find themselves enmeshed in a pattern of living that is fraught with insecurities, not the least of which involves the shouldering of civic responsibilities for which they are ill prepared. Furthermore, they find themselves almost totally without the counsel of more mature adults who, in older and more established communities, are likely to assume such responsibilities.

Providing adequate schools for rapidly increasing numbers constitutes one of the most challenging of their responsibilities as citizens. Likewise, they have great concern as parents—partly, as some sociological studies would seem to indicate, because they recognize education as the avenue of their own upward mobility and want to assure their children of the same opportunity, or because, in such institutions as the school and the church, they identify the stabilizing influences and commonality of values they seek for themselves and their children. As a consequence, matters pertaining to the school often become important issues, and men and women alike demand an active role in decisions concerning school affairs.

Teachers in a community such as this face a constant challenge. Because traditional and well-established patterns are lacking, the conflicting points of view of various civic and social groups make the establishment of consistent school policy difficult. The continuous financial pressure needed to provide additional facilities for rapidly expanding school populations places the faculty as well as the administration, and those otherwise responsible for the conduct of the school, in a vulnerable position with respect to public attitudes. Teachers are expected to be progressive in their methods but, at the same time, to adhere to the basic fundamentals and to instill in students time-honored virtues. Even the environment provided for teaching—classrooms with flexible furnishings, snack bars, solariums, family living centers, and the like—carries with it a challenge to new methods and a new philosophy of education.

Urban Communities

Another of the distinctive types of school situations in which you, as a beginning home economics teacher, may find yourself today is represented by the term "Metropolitan Junior High." At one time, teaching positions in city schools were not open to the beginner but, as the critical shortage of teachers has developed, and as senior teachers turn to suburban areas where salaries may be higher and problems appear simpler, younger people who hold degrees but have had little or no experience have been employed increasingly. In some cities, positions are more likely to be open at the junior high than at the senior high school level.

For teachers with distinctly rural and small-town backgrounds, the typical city school with its large numbers of students, diverse racial and ethnic groups, routinized procedures, and more or less impersonal atmosphere, represents a distinct change—one for which they need to be prepared if such is the locality in which they wish to teach. Of course, the reverse is true also—a teacher from an urban background must be prepared to make adjustments for living and teaching in a small community.

If the city is industrial and supports a number of businesses and professions as well, the homes from which students come vary as to social and economic level and in the attitude of families toward the school and toward education. Leadership in matters pertaining to the school frequently rests in the hands of those who determine policies in relation to the community affairs generally. Traditionally, individuals representative of the upper and middle social and economic classes have assumed such leadership and exercised such control; consequently, value patterns of these socio-economic classes have tended to be dominant. Studies have shown, moreover, that the expectations of the community are such that teachers tend to hold and teach the same value patterns. In cities where the influx of persons with diverse backgrounds and values has been unusually large, however, the stability of old and established patterns is severely threatened, and conflict situations within the school or among those determining school policy have arisen.

In many cities, the building of schools has not kept pace with rapidly expanding populations, and schools are overcrowded. In large urban areas school buildings tend to be decrepit and in need of repair. Equipment may be outmoded. The schools are woefully overcrowded, classes too large, and special services, especially important because of the inadequacy of home backgrounds, inadequate housing and limited health facilities, far too few.

With increasing pressure on schools to solve the social ills of the inner city, more formally organized patterns of administrative control have become necessary. Procedures have become more routinized, and there may be less opportunity for individualization. Within the schools, larger numbers of teachers and students may mean less opportunity for close personal contacts. Teaching loads may be such that teachers have time for little more than their immediate teaching responsibilities. Association with other teachers may be limited to those whose work is directly related, to those whose rooms are in close proximity, or to those who share the same lunch period or monitoring duties. Furthermore, once outside the school, teachers' interests may prove so diverse and their paths lead in such widely separated directions that they seldom converge.

Teachers and students may find it equally difficult to know each other well, especially if classes are large and there is little opportunity beyond the classroom for them to work together. Contacts between teachers and parents may be almost nonexistent. The teacher in the urban school has less opportunity for visiting students' homes, and, as a rule, the school does not serve as a center for community functions as it does in rural and small-town areas. PTA meetings or Open House programs probably afford the best opportunities for teachers to meet parents, but, unfortunately, many parents do not attend these events when they are held.

Although the current situation in urban schools is critical, the opportunities for teachers who desire to be on the cutting edge of the future are limitless. It is the belief of many citizens and politicians alike, members of black and white communities, that the city is today's frontier and its school is a bastion of hope. They contend that, with appropriate support and dedicated and understanding teachers, profound reforms and innovations are possible in urban education. These changes will lead to a better education with resultant new hope and opportunity for the presently disadvantaged youth of the inner city.

ROLE OF THE HOME ECONOMICS TEACHER

One of the things that may have occurred to you as you read the descriptions is that, in small schools like Farmville, your schedule might include subjects other than home economics, such as general science, social studies, girls' physical education, or English. This is important to some teachers, and may be a factor which you will want to consider in deciding where to teach. While home economics teachers in consolidated, suburban, and city schools may teach subjects other than home economics, larger enrollments mean more potential entrants for home economics classes, so that the school may require a home economics teacher who teaches no other subjects. But even in a large school, enrollment in home economics may fluctuate from year to year and thereby provide occasional opportunity for a home economics teacher to teach another subject. You may, as a student, already have given some thought to this matter of teaching in a second field, since certification laws in most states require college preparation for such teaching.

In many small schools, such as Farmville, practically all of the girls in school, and even some of the boys, take home economics. In this situation, the teacher may give her full time to teaching home economics classes. Where double periods are allocated to the classes, as is sometimes done, she will have time for little more than one, or at the most two, classes beyond the basic courses for Home Economics I and II. In vocational home economics programs, which are supported in part by federal and state aid, in addition to local funds, only the home economics classes can be reimbursed. Therefore, the teacher is likely to devote full time to home economics.

The supervision of a study hall may be one of the responsibilities of the home economics teacher in the smaller school. Or, she may be asked to take charge of the school lunch program—supervising the planning of menus, the buying of food, keeping of accounts, and the preparation and serving of meals. Often, her responsibility is only one of general supervision, and the actual operation is left to several experienced and competent women in the community who serve as cooks.

Contacts may extend into the elementary school, where the home economics teacher may serve as consultant to the teachers as they plan simple nutrition units, or where she may supervise high school home economics students who assist the elementary teachers with such units. A home economics teacher may give demonstrations or provide simple laboratory lessons for the children.

At the adult level, there may be formal classes for the women in the community or for both men and women, if such topics as family finance or child development are chosen. Although the home economics teacher may not choose to teach these classes herself, she can help to make the necessary arrangements to provide them as a part of the home economics program in the community and give them general supervision. Many other contacts with adults will, of course, come about informally, as the teacher works with the parents of her students, as parents are invited to the department for special occasions, and as parents are brought in as resource persons in connection with class activities.

There are, on the other hand, teachers who would much prefer to confine their activities, as far as possible, to regular classroom teaching, concentrating their attention on such responsibilities as may be directly related to their own area. Home economics programs in larger schools, such as Suburbia High and Metropolitan Junior High, are more likely to permit this kind of concentration than are those in small schools. Classes may be large and scheduled in such close succession throughout the day that there is little time for participation in other types of school activities. In addition, large enrollments may justify the hiring of persons who are qualified by professional education to supervise special activities. Under these circumstances, the home economics teacher's contacts with persons outside of regular day classes may be limited to hall duty or home rooms, if such are part of the school pattern.

If there are several teachers in the home economics department, one teacher may give full time to working at but one level or in one subject area. For example, she may have all ninth-grade sections; or she may do all of her teaching in one aspect of home economics, such as the foods-and-nutrition program. Organization of courses along subject-matter lines is quite characteristic of the high school program in metropolitan areas, whereas in the smaller schools, and in those that are reimbursed with vocational-education funds, courses are more likely to be comprehensive in nature, giving attention to all aspects of home economics, including education for employment in occupations involving home economics knowledge and skills.

Boys are being brought into the program at the junior-high level in some city schools. There is an increasing number of mixed classes for boys and girls at the seventh- and eighth-grade levels. Somewhat less frequently, but increasingly, one finds schools offering family living classes for boys and girls together at the upper class levels. The 1960 Golden Anniversary White House Conference for Children and Youth, however, recommended that increased attention be given to family-life education at the secondary level. The current sexual revolution, brought about in part by the availability and acceptability of contraceptives, as well as by increased independence of youth and feelings of alienation that are alleviated in part by turning to intense personal relationships, has placed a resurgence on the need for sex education at all levels of education. A number of states have appointed special commissions to study the needs of sex education in public schools. Home economics leaders serve on these commissions, for sex education and the study of sexuality are integral parts of family life education.

Integrating her work with the elementary program may prove difficult for the teacher in the city school, since elementary schools are often quite widely separated from secondary-school buildings. Although adult classes may be offered regularly, special teachers are often employed to teach them, so that there may be little or no connection between these classes and the day-school program. Home visitation and parent conferences are often handled by persons especially delegated to those responsibilities, rather than by regular classroom teachers.

Since the passage of the Vocational Education Act of 1963, and the Vocational Education Amendments of 1968, schools in suburban and urban areas have placed increased emphasis on preparing young people for gainful employment. Home economics programs have offered courses and/or units aimed at assisting young people with information and understanding of those personal traits and habits that make for employability. In addition, they have provided knowledge and skill in particular occupations such as child care and food service.

In many respects, the home economics program in schools such as Midwest Consolidated is similar to that of the rural, small-town school, except that, in a school with a larger enrollment, the job may be shared with a second teacher. The builders of new schools frequently provide facilities for several teachers, anticipating an expansion of the program even though at the time there may be but one teacher. In such cases, several rooms, designed to accommodate the teaching of all areas of home economics, may be provided. If there are two teachers in the school, teaching responsibilities may be divided along subject matter lines. The extent to which there will be opportunities for working with teachers and children at the elementary level, for bringing boys into the program, and for providing instruction for adults, may depend somewhat upon how readily such groups may be brought into the program, as well as upon how broadly the teacher interprets home economics and the functions it may serve in that particular school and community.

In many sections of the country, the consolidated and the rural, small-town schools are those most likely to have vocational home economics programs. In such programs teachers regularly allocate a portion of their time to home visitation, to related home and community experiences growing out of classroom instruction, to the programs of the Future Homemakers of America, and to special courses that prepare youngsters for paid employment.

This does not mean, of course, that all such schools have vocational home economics programs, or that vocational programs are not to be found in suburban and metropolitan high schools. Nor does it mean that vocational programs are the only ones enriched through home visitation, related home and community experiences, and Future Homemakers of America programs. Although these may not be formally organized parts of the program, every home economics teacher should find ways to acquaint herself with the homes and families of the community, so that she can better adapt her instruction to the particular needs of those with whom she works, and can, in every way possible, relate what is taught to the various activities of everyday home and community living.

The home economics teacher's job in Suburbia is, in some instances, like that of the teacher in a more rural, consolidated school, while in others it more nearly resembles that of the teacher in a city school. Whether Suburbia represents the expansion of an older and established community or is a completely new development will probably be reflected in the school program. If it is the latter, teachers are very likely to find themselves involved in trying out a variety of forward-looking ideas and procedures. A part of the home economics teacher's time, for example, may be devoted to participating in a core or common learnings family life program, where she will have a chance to adapt home economics instruction to meet the needs of general education. More than the usual amount of attention may be given, in this type of school, to experimentation with organization, new approaches, and variety in teaching methods. Although part of her program may be carried on in a more or less traditional manner, the home economics teacher will need to be experimental in her approach and continuously alert to the need for keeping her program in accord with the times. When home economics is interpreted narrowly, in terms of a few of the specialized skills of homemaking, which are rapidly diminishing in importance, it is out of date anywhere, but is particularly so in communities that reflect rapidly changing social and technological conditions.

In general you will note that home economics learnings are introduced into the curriculum in the elementary schools as a part of the general learning of all boys and girls. The first separate courses are usually offered in the sixth or seventh grade. These introductory courses include study of the various areas of home economics. The curriculum of home economics at the secondary level proposed by Simpson and others includes [1] (1) comprehensive course in education for homemaking and family life, (2) courses in education for employment in occupations involving home economics knowledge and skills and (3) pre-professional courses in home economics where the student may pursue through independent study, depth in problems related to some phase of home economics.

Some teachers have full-time home economics positions, and have interests in music activities, sports, dramatics, art, and/or writing, as well. These teachers find outlets for their additional interests by working in the extracurricular program of the school—helping with the chorus group, working with the intramural volleyball and basketball teams, working with the student government organization, helping coach a play, planning costumes, or supervising the school paper or yearbook. In small schools, such as the one in Farmville, most of the teachers help with school activities in one way or another, if these are part of the school program.

Involvement in activities outside their own departments, and working with students other than those in their own classes, attracts many teachers to the profession. Teachers enjoy an environment, in the school as well as in the community, in which they know everyone and can engage in a variety of activities. Their departments may be almost continually in use by different groups. Classes may include both boys and girls—in mixed classes at the junior-high level and in senior family-living classes, in separate classes for boys, or in exchange units with classes in agricul-

[1] Elizabeth Simpson, "Projections in Home Economics Education," *American Vocational Journal*, **40**, 41–43, November 1965.

ture and industrial arts. Through serving as a class sponsor and otherwise helping with the extracurricular program, a home economics teacher may have opportunity to work with boys as well as girls.

In the large schools, where special teachers are available to direct the students in dramatics, music, and publications, the home economics teacher is likely to find herself engaged in activities that are more directly connected with her own teaching. She may, for example, be working in committee to develop objective examinations for home economics students that will be used in the entire home economics program. Other possible areas of activity for the home economics teacher in a large school are: televising home economics programs and lessons, giving demonstration lessons for beginning teachers, serving as a guidance counselor, and doing special work with social agencies.

This chapter has presented an overview of home economics programs, and the ways in which they vary, depending on the nature of the school and community of which they are a part. Other factors, however, also influence the nature of the program. Very important among these factors is the teacher herself—her beliefs about home economics in general, what she sees as the function of the home economics program in her particular school and community, how she defines her role as a home economics teacher, and how she sees herself in relation to this role. The following chapters will help you to look at the role of the teacher in relation to the home economics program.

Selected References

Bloom, Benjamin, Allison Davis, and Robert Hess, *Compensatory Education for Cultural Deprivation.* New York: Holt, Rinehart, and Winston, 1965.

Brookover, Wilbur B., et al., *A Sociology of Education.* New York: American Book, 1964.

Clark, S. D., *The Suburban Society.* Toronto: University of Toronto Press, 1966.

Conant, James B., *Slums and Suburbs.* New York: Signet Books, 1961.

Gist, Noel, and Sylvia Fava, *Urban Society.* New York: Thomas Crowell, 1964.

Havighurst, Robert J., *Education in Metropolitan Areas.* Boston: Allyn and Bacon, 1966.

Michael, Donald N., *The Next Generation.* New York: Vintage Books, 1965.

Moore, Bernice, and Wayne Holtzman, *Tomorrow's Parents—A Study of Youth and Their Families.* Austin: Hogg Foundation for Mental Health, University of Texas Press, 1965.

National Committee of Home Economics Educators, "Home Economics in the Secondary School," in *The Bulletin of the National Association of Secondary-School Principals,* Vol. 48, No. 296, December 1964.

National Society for the Study of Education, *The Educationally Retarded and Disadvantaged.* 66th Yearbook. Chicago: The National Society for the Study of Education, 1967.

National Education Association, *National Conference on Contemporary Issues in Home Economics Education.* Washington, D.C.: National Education Association, May, 1965.

"Problems of Urban Education," *Phi Delta Kappan,* Vol. 48, No. 7, 1967.

PART II

Needs of Individuals and Families

3

Knowing Your Community

You can give realism to a home economics program if you are aware of the many components that go together to make up your particular teaching community. Communities exist because groups of people have chosen to establish homes in a particular area. This grouping came about because the area provided for them a means of making a living and rearing their families. It is here that they educate their children, house their families, and in varying degrees find their consumer, educational, religious, health, and recreational needs met.

The community at large, but more particularly the subcommunity or neighborhood, exerts a considerable force in shaping the basic personality structure of individuals. It is here that those norms that become patterns of living for families take shape and are felt. As a home economics teacher whose major goal is to help individuals and families live more effectively, you are obligated to be aware of these various community forces and their influences. You must be familiar with information about community backgrounds, attitudes, industries, practices, and resources, if the home economics program in your school is to function.

The teaching of home economics at any level is concerned with learnings relative to specific subject matter areas. These are: the feeding, clothing, and housing of the family; the managing of family resources in such a way that the family is able to achieve the way of life it wants within the limits of its resources; and the understanding of the growth, development, and relationships between and among family members. A keener understanding of those community forces that impinge upon individuals and their families will increase your ability to put over your subject matter in such a manner that it will "take."

REASONS FOR KNOWING YOUR COMMUNITY

The students, the community, and the home economics teacher all benefit when the teacher takes a sincere interest in knowing her community. Among the reasons for understanding the community in which you teach are the following:

1. IF YOU KNOW YOUR COMMUNITY, YOU CAN MORE READILY ADAPT THE PROGRAM IN LIGHT OF COMMUNITY NEEDS. For example, a home economics teacher, who knew that, in her school community, over 70 percent of the young people between the ages of 14 and 20 were married and had established families, would plan short courses on preparation for marriage. These sessions would be open to both boys and girls and would be offered to both freshmen and seniors. If the enrollment were limited to girls or to seniors, many of the youth of that community might have been denied an educational opportunity. Knowing the above-mentioned statistic would give the home economics teacher many cues for her teaching. Child development units could be placed in the curriculum at earlier times; money management units could be geared to planning for families soon to be a reality; housing could be viewed with an eye toward preparing the student who might be actually planning on a specific house choice.

Knowing the average number of family members as compared to the average number of rooms in the houses of a neighborhood or community can influence your way of teaching home furnishings, management, and family relationships. The home economics teacher can, for instance, plan home-furnishing activities so that they tie in with what exists in the community. Where families are large and housing space is minimal, she might help students to utilize better the space in the home so that it might serve many purposes more efficiently. Seeing the possibilities for using the kitchen as a place for eating, preparing food, entertaining, sleeping, and doing homework, and, at the same time having it attractive, offers real challenges for teaching.

There is some evidence that, when the learning experiences of students are closely related to practices in the home, there is an increase in interest on the part of the students, and they are made to feel that what they learn is practical for use in their own homes.[1] In a Michigan school, one teacher attempted to build her classroom food-preparation and serving units around the practices girls used at home. Little emphasis was given to the more formal ways of setting a table, or to the use of table linens, centerpieces, and the like. Instead, the girls practiced passing food along the table; they utilized disposable "linens"; and learned to make centerpieces that consisted of food to be used in the meal—fruit, cake, and the

[1] Mary Lee Hurt, "A Study of the Effect on Attitude toward and Home Carry-Over of Homemaking Education When Teaching Is Keyed to Lower and Middle Class Values and Practices." (As abstracted in *Journal of Home Economics,* **46**, 198, March 1954.)

like. Special emphasis was given to foods for special celebrations—Thanksgiving, Christmas, birthdays—because, in the families from which her students came, these occasions were customarily celebrated by serving special foods, and by using the "best dishes and linens." At this point, however, the teacher should proceed with a bit of caution. Schools are not committed to maintaining the status quo. In this ever-changing world, young people can be almost certain that the families or communities in which they will be living will not be just like the ones in which they were reared. Therefore, the school is committed also to introducing students to a variety of patterns of living, so that they might make more intelligent choices as to modes of living. For this reason, this teacher in Michigan also planned activities in which students prepared and served meals in a variety of ways, using different kinds of service, varieties of food, and varying table appointments. Hence, these girls were familiar with the ways in which people in different situations lived and they had a number of alternatives for decision making.

In one particular community, there was a great demand for the services of baby-sitters among the teen-age group, but there was concern on the part of parents who hired baby-sitters about the way the sitters disciplined the children. Here, the home economics teacher based her child-development units upon the objective of gaining a better understanding of youngsters. The members of the class used, as their point of departure, the actual discipline problems they encountered. The ways in which baby-sitters had handled discipline problems were analyzed, discussions were held as to other possible ways of handling the same discipline problems, and conclusions were reached regarding the consequences to the child of the different methods discussed. In this way some understanding of child development was brought into a problem situation.

2. KNOWING THE RESOURCES AVAILABLE TO YOU IN YOUR COMMUNITY WILL HELP YOU TO ENRICH THE LEARNING EXPERIENCES OF YOUR STUDENTS. There will be times when you can move your classes out of the schoolroom into the community. Trips to various housing areas, to social service agencies, to shopping centers, and to particular industrial locations will bring life to textbook readings and classroom discussions. A field trip to a credit bureau helped give one group some insights into the kinds of financial information gathered by a business organization about the families living in the community. Students were amazed to learn that an individual's pattern of paying for goods, his employment record, and the number of charge accounts he had were all part of a record—a record that tended to follow him from community to community!

It is also possible to move the community into the classroom, so to speak. Home economists from the utility companies, case workers from the social agencies, doctors, family lawyers, and the clergy—these and a host of others have information and knowledge that can add new dimensions to the learning of your students. One teacher invited to class a panel of home economists from business, education, and social agencies, in order to help her students get some perspective of the expectations of their jobs, thus opening new possibilities for careers in home economics. Another teacher brought in the local psychiatric social worker to help her group learn about the kinds of family problems that existed in this particular community. This first-hand information about the real problems families were facing in their own environment gave the students an impetus to preparation for solving or avoiding similar problems in their own lives. Meeting the various community resources in this manner helps young people to become sensitized to the world in which they live. As you use community resources, the students can identify your techniques for securing information and can utilize these methods for ferreting out information on their own. Needless to say, learning will make sense, for it is no longer just "stuff" read in the textbook; rather, it becomes an observable part of real life.

In the larger communities, where a number of professional groups and personnel are available and eager to help in the schools, the teacher can call upon them for a number of services. These could include government workers who might explain the Social Security laws and benefits, economists with accurate information on economic trends as they affect the community, and sociologists who can vividly describe the social setting. The harassed teacher has available, merely by using the telephone, literature from health agencies, libraries, and industry. These helps serve the dual purpose of enriching classroom teaching and acquainting students with the resources of their community. This knowledge should serve them in good stead at the moment as well as in the future when they will no longer belong to formal educational groups. Learning to be careful observers, to be able to analyze the printed word that presents a particularized point of view, to be able to seek out specific persons for help in special problems, and to be able to go to authoritative sources for answers to questions are important learning experiences. Becoming involved in using the community while they are students prepares young people for mobilizing community forces to meet their problems when they reach adulthood—a learning experience of special importance for youngsters in culturally limited areas.

3. RECOGNIZING SOME OF THE PREVAILING ATTITUDES AND PRACTICES OF A PARTICULAR COMMUNITY CAN MAKE THE TEACHER MORE ACCEPTING OF THE WAYS OF LIFE OF HER STUDENTS. Every community has a background and traditions that give it a special feeling and tone. Older communities

have built a number of traditions which, to some degree, tend to be maintained and which may even influence many of the existing practices. Some of these influences are ethnic in origin, stemming from the nationalities and religious backgrounds of early settlers. At times these traditions create an undertone of resistance to change; on the other hand, they may build a local pride that serves as a valuable stability factor in the people of the town. Other communities, young in relation to organization, are often composed of mobile, younger families who may visibly reflect an acceptance of change, even to the point of making radical changes without thinking through long-time consequences, and hence building feelings of insecurity.

The ways families arrive at decisions, their attitudes toward the dual sharing of homemaking activities, their patterns of food preferences, and their child-rearing practices, are often a reflection of the modes and mores of the community. A community does not usually institute a particular family living practice; nevertheless, because the community is composed of persons who share similar sentiments and who chose to settle in a particular area, it then tends to reflect and perpetuate a way of life that is considered acceptable by those living there. Understanding this process of feedback, the observant teacher can begin to see the importance of the community and its influences. As she uses the community, and as her students, in turn, operate in the community, the real aims of her home economics program are realized. The pattern of life of a community is part of the experiential background of all of your students; if learning is to be achieved readily, the school and community need to reinforce one another.

It is difficult to know exactly why any specific community attitude or pressure prevails, since the existence of such attitudes and pressures result from and are perpetuated by a tangle of forces. These may be related to economic factors, geographic location, racial and ethnic mores, and perhaps even to a historical or catastrophic happening. That communities do differ in attitudes and practices, however, is undeniable. One of your responsibilities is to be aware, as much as possible, of the kinds of attitudinal influences that are prevalent. This awareness can help you bring about the kinds of changes in behavior that you desire, for you will be working with, rather than against, the tides that can either hinder or enhance the possibilities for learning.

Here are some illustrations of how being aware of community attitudes helped the home economics teacher become more accepting of the ways of life of her students.

Illustration 1. In one home economics class, the teacher observed that, when her students described the ways they disciplined their younger brothers and sisters, they generally spoke in terms of the use of harsh talk, threats, and often physical punishment. They tended to laugh at the ways suggested in their textbook readings and attested that those ways would not work with the children they knew. The teacher began to appreciate the feelings of her students after she learned a few things about the conditions in which they lived. The crowded living arrangements, limited incomes, and harassed parents who worked in noisy factory situations, created atmospheres where loud talk and force achieved compliance in short order. The methods of disciplining that these students understood were the methods that were used with them. With this bit of insight the teacher used a number of ways during the year of helping her students to better understand why they acted as they did and to seek out and examine some alternate methods of behaving that might help them to be acceptable when living and working with others.

Illustration 2. The class was examining the costs of clothing for a family. One group, made up of students who were concerned with planning for a low income family, had spent the money it had allotted for clothing in a manner which the teacher thought was unwise. No allowance had been made for nightwear and the shoe allowance seemed inadequate for quality as well as number. At the same time, the sum allowed for "first communion dress and shoes" seemed all out of proportion. When the teacher recognized that these students, through the way they used their money, were expressing the value they placed upon some of the symbols of their religious faith, she was able to understand their ways of behaving.

Before a teacher can embark upon a home economics program geared toward improving, changing, and emphasizing homemaking practices, she needs to be cognizant of the attitudes and beliefs her students hold. When she has some understanding of what particular attitudes and beliefs mean to the persons holding them, she becomes more aware of the underlying values inherent in the practices she observes, and hence has some basis upon which to make intelligent decisions concerning her program.

4. RECOGNITION OF THE PREVAILING HOME PRACTICES CAN BE IMPORTANT IN HELPING YOU DETERMINE WHAT SHOULD BE TAUGHT IN SPECIFIC SUBJECT MATTER AREAS OF HOME ECONOMICS. Because the subject matter of home economics deals with experiences that, in varying degrees, are parts of the home living of all, students can readily detect whether the things they are learning will make sense in their lives outside of school. For this reason, you will want to be aware of the home practices that prevail in your community. The answers to the following and to similar ques-

tions will help: How much sewing is done at home? How much time does the family spend together as a group? Where in the home are family meals eaten? How much canning and preserving is done in the home? Who in the family is responsible for the preparation of food, for housekeeping, for shopping, for laundry? What kind of household appliances do most families possess? How many women are employed outside the home? How many families are one-parent families? What you teach in your home economics classes will be determined partially by the answers you find to these questions. If you find that few families in your community do any home sewing and that a very small proportion of your students have sewing machines available to them in their homes, you might eliminate or greatly limit the amount of garment construction in your classes.

At the same time, schools are not obligated to perpetuate all existing home practices. In fact, schools might well supply the information and knowledge that could result in changes in home practice. A large measure of the success of teaching home economics should be observable in the actual changes that have raised the levels of living of families. Home economics classes ought to be the *avant-garde* for instigating changes within families that contribute to improved family living.

5. A STUDY OF THE FEASIBILITY OF A PARTICULAR OCCUPATIONAL PROGRAM CAN HELP YOUR STUDENTS AND GRADUATES LOCATE SUITABLE EMPLOYMENT. Extreme poverty in the midst of our affluent society has caused Americans to undertake various programs designed to improve the living conditions of many disadvantaged individuals and families. Recognizing that a handout does not attack the root of the problem, government leaders have encouraged the development of training programs so that any person who is capable of working will be able to hold a job. Day-care centers for preschool children enable mothers to participate in job training or to hold a job. The idea of family assistance, rather than welfare, provides an incentive for families to stay together and to work toward meeting their own needs.

Training for a specific job is of no lasting value unless the individual can locate employment upon completion of the training program. Documenting the present and future needs of business and industry in your community is an important step prior to establishing a program in occupational education. Relating these data to the needs and interests of your students or prospective students can help determine the feasibility of a wage-earning program.[2]

[2] Examples of feasibility studies related to food service, child care, and clothing occupations may be found in "Action and Innovation," *Illinois Teacher for Contemporary Roles,* Vol. 12, No. 1, Fall 1968–69.

6. BEING AWARE OF THE POWER STRUCTURE IN THE COMMUNITY WILL FACILITATE YOUR SUCCESS IN IMPLEMENTING AND INTERPRETING YOUR HOME ECONOMICS PROGRAM. Every community has persons who are considered by others in the community to be key individuals or leaders in particular areas. These people, because of special knowledge, position, or authority, exert a considerable amount of power or influence in particularized areas of the community. They can exert a definite influence on the kind of home economics program it is possible for you to achieve. In a large measure, this power structure tends to control, by direct or indirect means, what the school or segments of the school can do. This can be illustrated in the following way. The local school board members are a part of the power structure of the school. The administrative staff, and in some instances certain students also, are a part of this so-called power structure. If these people see home economics as an important subject-matter area in the school, they will support the program both directly and indirectly. The school board may allow funds for effectively carrying out the program; the administrative staff may arrange schedules so that they are conducive to the free election of home economics by a large number of students; and the most popular students themselves may elect home economics. On the other hand, these power figures could, through direct or indirect methods, undermine the home economics program. Funds for classroom operation could be greatly curtailed; the administrative staff could discourage students from enrolling in your classes; leaders of the student groups could indicate by action and word that home economics is a "snap," "for the birds," and "O.K."

Outside the school, other key community leaders may be influential in controlling the kind of home economics program you will have. These might include individuals who have special interests in home economics—such as extension personnel, leaders of women's groups, personnel of social agencies, and parents of children in your school. If you know who these persons are, you can work with them in establishing the kind of program you desire. By working with them, you can more easily interpret home economics as you see it, and they, in turn, can help you to see their interpretation of your subject-matter area. Implementation will be more possible when the program is understandable to them, when it meets their expectations, and when it, in a measure, reflects some of their basic beliefs.

Here is how one teacher successfully gained assistance from the key persons in her community when she initiated the adult home economics program. She invited a representative group of persons whom she had identified as being power leaders to serve as an advisory council. In this case the persons chosen were the president of the school board, the program chairman of both the junior and senior Women's Clubs, the county home-demonstration agent, a mother of one student from each of her home economics classes, a representative from the women's groups of the local churches, and the school superintendent. She presented her idea for organizing adult home economics classes and, together with the group, explored the possibilities for such a program in the community. The advisory council members volunteered to survey their particular groups and friends to find out (1) if a need for such a program existed, (2) what areas of home economics could best be studied, and (3) the kind and number of persons who might be likely students of the adult program. In this instance, the advisory council was instrumental in organizing and planning a series of adult home economics classes. By word of mouth, by organized surveys, through newspaper writings, and, in a few cases, by coming to class themselves, they were directly responsible for the interpretation and implementation of that adult program.

When you are aware of just what the term "home economics" signifies to the influential persons in your community, you can operate with greater intelligence. If their ideas of what a home economics program should accomplish are similar to yours, you can move forward successfully to implement the kind of program you desire; if they hold ideas that are quite different from your own, you can take measures for more effectively interpreting the program to these people.

COMMUNITY DATA

As a beginning teacher, you will need to make specific plans for gathering information about the community in which you teach. Some school administrators prefer that you spend a few weeks prior to the opening of the school year becoming acquainted and established. In any event, you will find that your job is eased considerably and your program strengthened if you make the effort to become familiar with information that is pertinent and relative to adapting the home economics program so that it is functional and realistic for your community. Not all information about a community is collected in one grand sweep before school opens. More likely, you will find that getting to know your community has no designated stopping point. A home economics teacher gathers and compiles information, interprets it, and then continually makes adaptations in her program in light of her findings as long as she teaches. Because communities are dynamic, her information needs to be kept up-to-date through continuous study—only in this way can a teacher prevent her teaching from being static and make it dynamic.

Where does a teacher start to gather data about communities? What does she look for concerning community attitudes and backgrounds? How does she quickly compile information about local resources? Is there a simple means for detecting community homemaking practices? How does she find out what needs to be emphasized in a particular community if family living is to be improved? Are there particular sources to be tapped when a teacher wants to identify key persons? Having available some alternative sources for finding answers to these questions will make it possible for you to compile pertinent data concerning your community no matter where it is located or what limitations of resources you may encounter.

Community Backgrounds and Traditions

As a new person in a community, you can learn a good deal about the background and prevalent traditions by doing some reading. Any local library will have material on the history of the county, township, or city. In this material, there will be such items of information as who the early settlers were, a bit about ethnic or racial backgrounds, and the establishments of business and industry. You can note the progress a community has made, its general trends, and many of the bases for its traditions, as you delve into its past. The courthouse in many a small town or rural area has available considerable background information about the area —either in the printed word or as transmitted by word of mouth through the years by the "old-timers" who have held county positions for years.

Interviewing older members of a community is a means for securing information on background and traditions. You may choose to interview some of the older community members personally, as you become established and accepted, or you may ask your students to seek answers about the background and traditions of their home town. One teacher learned a good deal about the origins of wedding customs in her community by having her students interview their grandparents. Customs, which at first glance seemed to have no relationship to modern living, took on new meanings when she saw them through the eyes of older persons who had experienced the customs in a different setting. For instance, a wedding celebration of eating, dancing, and hilarity lasting several days appeared quite different when she understood the limitations of travel and communications of earlier days. Even though both travel and communication had changed in the particular community, the wedding celebration traditions, although slightly modified, had persisted.

A walking tour of various sections of a community will reveal much of its current background. If you are a discriminating observer, you can grasp a wealth of information by merely looking and listening. Note such factors as the kind and condition of houses, number and denomination of churches, and availability of social and educational facilities.

One prospective teacher chose to take a walking tour of three distinctly different residential areas. Uppermost in her mind as she walked and observed was the question: How does living in this area affect the behavior of the youth who live here? She looked for such factors as: kinds and sizes of dwellings; evidences of sanitation standards; size and condition of yards; symbols of material acquisitions such as automobiles, television sets, and outdoor play equipment; condition of streets and sidewalks; evidences of fire and police protection; and accessibility to schools, parks, shopping areas, and commercial recreation. Because she wanted to keep a record of her findings for future reference, she recorded her observations. A written account of some of her findings is included because it indicates what pertinent information a teacher can obtain through careful observation of various segments of a community.

Low Income: October 14

This house (address noted) typifies, to me, low income housing. However, the neighborhood surrounding the house was not what I would consider a slum area.

It is possible that the children could play in the back yard; yet the equipment provided for the children was extremely meager—consisting of only a small tricycle and a swing, broken beyond repair. Several small boys were playing ball in the street and some little girls were walking along a crack-ridden sidewalk. Teenagers clustered around the steps of an apartment dwelling nearby.

The shingled house was tiny, and comprised about four or five rooms. There were screens on about a third of the windows. I saw at least three children, who, I surmised, lived in the house, along with their parents.

Families appeared to meet some of the needs of the children. Their clothes were not elegant, but they looked clean and neat. The youngsters also appeared to be quite healthy as evidenced by their vitality in active play. I was struck, however, by the number of children and older persons I saw on the streets.

As far as I could tell the house appeared to have heating facilities, and it was wired for electricity, as I was able to distinguish a light in what appeared to be the kitchen. I am fairly certain that the lady of the house did not have an automatic washing machine or dryer. Although there were no clothes hung out, there was a clothes line toward the rear of the house.

I believe it is safe to assume that the house was large enough to accommodate a small bathroom. At any rate, I saw no outhouse. Several garbage cans were near the house entrance, filled. I assumed that garbage was picked up weekly in the neighborhood.

Right next door to the house was a building that had been converted into a Methodist Church. There were services for both English and Spanish-speaking peoples, according to the posted placard.

I noted a few indicators that the community provided some protection.

About a block down the street was a fire hydrant; in another direction a fenced, asphalt covered play-yard with a few swings provided a play-space for children.

I realize that my observation of a low income area is limited. From news releases on television and my travels I recognize the wide range of deprivation that can exist in rural slums and urban ghettos. I can see that my conception of low-income living situations was far too narrow in scope. Now I understand better the limitations that inadequate community facilities, overcrowded and unsanitary housing, and limited incomes can place on families.

Middle Income: October 17

I chose this house because it appeared to be one of the best-kept houses on the block. The surrounding neighborhood was neat and kept in good condition, although many of the houses were old.

Enclosing the back yard of the house were both a hedge and a small wire fence for protection. There were two tricycles in the driveway. In the back yard was a large gymnastic set complete with swings and a slide.

About two blocks from the house was the ________ elementary school. Annexed to the school and close to the medium-income neighborhood was a very large, fenced-in playground.

The house itself was a white wood-shingle construction, with freshly painted brown shutters, door, and porch. Although it was difficult to estimate the number of people inhabiting the dwelling, the house looked roomy and comfortable. It appeared to have about seven rooms plus a basement and a single-car garage.

The house probably had central heating and was wired for electricity. Apparently the lady of the house had no dryer, as there were several lines of clothes hung in the back yard.

As far as protection goes, at the end of the block was a fire hydrant, and the entire back yard was fenced in. Streets and sidewalks were well paved, and lawns well cared for. No garbage cans were visible.

Because my family belongs in the middle-income group, I do not feel that the observations I have made have proved very startling to me. All of my life I have lived with and associated with people from the middle-income bracket. Therefore, it was difficult for me to be as objective in my observations of this group.

High Income: October 20

The house I observed was one of the largest homes in the area and seemed typical of high-income housing. Obviously the surrounding neighborhood was extremely well-kept, although not all of the houses were so large. However, they were not bunched in together as were the houses in the medium and especially the low-income groups.

Although the back yard was very large, I could not see any play equipment for the children. I decided that there was probably a recreation room or playroom inside the house.

> It is safe to assume that the house supplied all of the living needs of the children who inhabited it. Looking through a large bay window in the front of the house I could distinguish a number of books and a piano.
>
> The house was of red brick, with white shutters and trimming. The lawn was painstakingly landscaped, as evidenced by the trees, shrubs, and flowers of various kinds surrounding the house. There were at least nine or ten rooms plus a basement or recreation room and a two-car garage.
>
> Obviously the house had heating and lighting. Probably the laundry facilities—automatic washer and dryer—were located in the basement. There was no clothes line in the back yard.
>
> In the middle-income neighborhood there were many signs of outward physical protection, such as fences and fire hydrants. Yet in the high income area none of these signs was outwardly visible—except for the screened-in porch on many of the homes. However, the houses are located on quiet, less-frequently traveled streets, and probably the need for fences is not essential. Also, most of the homes have special areas within where the children can play safely.
>
> While observing the middle-income group, I noticed many children playing together in groups, and mothers standing around chatting back and forth. I saw no evidences of this in the high-income neighborhood.

The writings of this prospective teacher are obviously circumscribed by her perspective, experience, and knowledge. However, they do at least show that she has broadened her understanding of the impact of neighborhoods on persons. Inherent in her increased awareness should be cues for enhancing the learning potential, and understanding the limitations of students in her home economics classes.

Prevalent Attitudes

Becoming an alert reader of a local newspaper will help you to discover and keep informed about a number of attitudes that are prevalent in your community. The kinds of activities reported, the amount of space devoted to school news, sports, local society, crime, politics, or world events are keys to community attitudes. Progressiveness or conservatism can be detected by analyzing the editorial pages, particularly if the people have an opportunity to respond in a "letters-to-the-editor" section. As a home economics teacher, you will want to notice the location and amount of space given to write-ups about school affairs, adult education programs, social issues, and problems involving youth and families.

Making personal contacts and participating in community activities will give you some insights into the attitudes that are held by groups within the community. As you work and play with the local citizenry in church, club, and social groups, you will learn to discern many of the prevailing attitudes and underlying values. You will come to understand their real feelings and attitudes much more easily as you visit with people after a committee meeting or participate in voter registration projects.

Student records and writing are yet another source of community attitudes. As you look through the cumulative records of students and take note of particular factors that seem to be dominant, you can make some generalizations about attitudes of a large number of persons in your community. For example, if you note that a high percentage have been members of youth groups, you can assume that the community in general has tended to support and reward organized activities for youth. The educational levels of parents and notations concerning parental attitudes relative to school attendance, grading, or student behavior are keys for helping you to understand the kinds of attitudes that exist in your community.

Community Practices

One of the more commonly used techniques for becoming familiar with the homemaking practices of students is that of conducting informal surveys. These can be quite simple check lists designed to secure information about a particular type of homemaking practice, or they may be a more complicated kind of interview schedule designed to get at a number of kinds of homemaking practices. One teacher used a series of simple check lists before starting the various units in a home economics class and, on the basis of her findings relative to the kinds of home experiences the students in her class had had, built her classes from that point, thus avoiding needless repetition and providing for new learning experiences.

One teacher was concerned with knowing more about the money practices in her community. She devised a check list to secure the following information:

1. Where the Family Gets its Money:
   Does the family depend on
   a. wages or salary of
      (1) both parents?
      (2) father only?
      (3) mother only?
      (4) parents and teenagers?
   b. welfare?
   c. gifts from relatives?
   d. pensions, interests, rentals?
2. How the Family Does Financial Planning:
   Does the family have
   a. a plan or established way for spending most of the family income?

   b. a few simple things to remember such as a set amount weekly for groceries or savings?
   c. no plan at all?
3. How the Family Handles Money:
   Does the family
   a. have a common purse?
   b. have a bank account?
   c. let one member of the family control the money, and have the others ask?
   d. keep household accounts?
   e. give children money to go to movies, church, and the like?
   f. give children money to shop for the family?
   g. allow children to use charge account or write checks on the family's account?
   h. encourage children to earn their own spending money?
4. Experience of Students in Deciding to Buy and in Buying:
   Does each one
   a. talk with parents before buying something for the family?
   b. decide between two different things for self?
   c. decide Christmas presents to buy?
   d. decide other gifts to buy?
   e. go with parents to pick out gifts?
   f. shop alone when picking out presents for others?
   g. decide on clothing for self?
   h. choose clothing for self?

Depending on the findings of a survey designed to get answers to the existing money practices, can you see how the home economics teacher might adapt the way she teaches money management to her students? Just as she needed information for adapting money management teaching, so will she need information when she adapts other home economic units. Simple surveys to reveal housekeeping practices, foods prepared and eaten, kinds of household equipment owned, ways families use time, ways of rearing children and caring for the sick or aged, and knowledge of other home practices will be helpful to a teacher.

Developing a keen ability to *listen* will also be valuable in identifying practices that exist in your community. The questions and comments your students make in class are often keys to existing practices. What home economics teacher is not continuously informed: "My mother does it . . ."? Rather than become irritated at comparisons made between what is practiced at home and what is done in the classroom, the wise teacher capitalizes on this information to help bridge the gap between home and school for her students. At the same time she increases the opportunities for all of her students to learn.

This technique is highlighted in the following observation of one student teacher. The student teacher was showing a filmstrip that depicted the importance of timing wash loads when using nonautomatic laundry equipment. The students insisted that the time periods suggested by the filmstrip were much too short, since their mothers "let the clothes run in the washer at least one half hour." In her attempt to explain why timing was important, this student teacher learned much about the laundry practices prevalent in that community: the kinds of clothes that were washed, frequency of washdays, kinds of detergents used, location of laundry areas, and temperature of water used. After that class, the student teacher modified the teaching of the rest of the laundry unit in an effort to help the class to conduct simple experiments on laundering in order to arrive at principles that would help them solve laundering problems intelligently and efficiently.

Besides a sharp ear, a discerning eye will also be an aid in detecting community practices. In your daily round of living in the community, you can learn much about prevailing community practices by observing purposefully what others are doing. What kinds of things do people load into their grocery carts? Who does the family shopping? Do you notice people using charge plates more frequently than cash in the department stores? Are the parks filled with whole families picnicking during nice weather, or are parks rarely used except by the very old or very young? Merely watching from an automobile in the shopping area on a Saturday afternoon will reveal a number of family practices to the discerning teacher!

Community Resources

Much of the information concerning what community resources are available to you can be found by consulting the telephone directory. Here are listed the locations of churches, of social and health agencies, of industries, of business organizations, and the like. By merely being cognizant of the data presented in the telephone directory, you can secure a fairly accurate knowledge of the many resources that will enrich your teaching.

One of the most helpful sources for securing accurate information concerning a particular community is the census. Some time spent in reading and interpreting data from the census is one of the most helpful means you have for securing pertinent information for adapting your classroom teaching to the local community. Census statistics include population data on such facts as the number of persons of varying ages in a particular area, the number and sizes of families, the proportion of white and nonwhite persons, the educational levels of various age groups, and the sources and amounts of incomes in the community. The housing census is full of information concerning the homes in a community: number of owners and renters; types of dwellings; number of rooms in dwellings; methods of heating; toilet facilities; number of telephones, television sets, radios, and household equipment; and the like. Going to census statistics as a first source of information about your community is one of the best ways of securing the kind of information you need for adapting your program to community needs.

By becoming familiar with the census data in her community, one home economics teacher learned in a few hours the important factors that would influence the ways she would teach about money management: average size of income, size and composition of families, location of families (rural-farm, rural-nonfarm, and urban), stage in the family life cycle, occupations of breadwinners, employment of homemakers, and educational levels of varying age groups. To trace down this information independently via observations, home visits, informal surveys, and personal contacts would have taken countless numbers of hours. The information so gleaned, in all probability, would not have been as accurate as that available in census compilations.

Identifying human community resources is a bit more difficult than casual listening and observing, or even the reading and interpreting of community census data. You can receive guidance in ferreting out those persons who will be most helpful, as classroom resources or as members of advisory and planning committees, from personal contacts and planning conferences with your administrator who, because of his training and position, has had more experience and opportunity for knowing the key persons in a community. As you become more familiar with a community and its network of communication between and among the varying power structures, you will find it increasingly easier to identify and use the human resources available to you for vitalizing your home economics program.

COMPILATION AND USE OF COMMUNITY DATA

The many types of information about your community will take on significance as you begin to classify what you learn and to organize it in a manner that is meaningful for you. A simple guide sheet for compiling data can suggest the kinds of information that you desire as well as provide a quick, convenient form on which to indicate your findings. If your information is well organized and easy to use, you will find yourself referring to it many times when you are confronted with decisions about what to teach, at what grade level to include certain problems, and how to make your teaching realistic and interesting for your students.

Compiling Community Information

Some of the information that you secure about the community in which you teach you will choose to carry around "in your head," so to speak. Other information, to be most useful to you and to others in the planning and implementing of a home economics program, ought to be compiled, recorded, analyzed, and filed in such a manner that you can locate and use it with relative ease.

In the foregoing pages some of the possible sources of community information have been identified. The next task is that of compiling information in a workable form. Some teachers keep folders on community information. In these folders, they place summaries of their findings concerning community practices, local beliefs about home economics education, statistical information about population and families, and a listing of key persons and other community resources. In some states, the departments of education provide forms for compiling community data. Some Ohio teachers, working alone or as parts of teacher teams, have used the following form (Table 2) for compiling information that is pertinent to the home economics program in suburban and small town communities. Adaptations will be necessary if your school is located in an urban area.

TABLE 2 Community Data Sheet (For Use in High School Home Economics Programs) *

General

Name of school ____

Location of school ____

(town or city) (county) (state)

Enrollment of school: elementary _____; junior high _____; high school _____; total _____

Total number of pupils who live in town _____

Total number of pupils who live in country _____

Population of town or city _____

Community Background and Traditions

1. Ancestry of early settlers: German _____; Swedish _____; French _____; English _____; other ____________________________
2. Ancestry of majority of present inhabitants ____________________________

* Adapted from teaching materials distributed by the Home Economics Education Division, School of Home Economics, Ohio State University, Columbus, Ohio.

TABLE 2 *(continued)*

3. List any historical events which occurred in or near this locality: ______

4. List any traditions which are observed by the community as a whole: ______

5. List any traditions which are observed by minority groups: ______

6. Does the observance of tradition in the community detract from the progressiveness of the community as a whole? ____ If so, in what way? ______

7. What is the attitude of the community as a whole toward change? ______

Community Industry

1. Occupations, types of:

Occupations, types of:	Percentage of population engaged in:	Average income:
Farming	______	______
Factory	______	______
Small Business	______	______
Office	______	______
Managerial	______	______
Service	______	______
Professional	______	______
Unskilled	______	______
Other	______	______

2. If farming is one of the major occupations, indicate the type of farming by placing a check mark in the correct blank: dairy ____; general ____; truck ____; stock and grain ____; others ______
3. If factory work forms a major occupation, list the kinds of factories located in the community: ______
4. What percentage of mothers work outside the home? ______
5. What type of work do they do? ______

Influence of Nearby Cities upon Community

1. List any important cities within a radius of 50 miles, the distance to the city, and size: ______

TABLE 2 *(continued)*

2. List the factories or other sources of employment available in these nearby cities: ____
____
____

3. Estimate the percentage of people in the community who are engaged in employment outside the community: ______
4. Resources in the community or in adjoining cities which will be of value to you as a teacher of home economics:

	Location
Special factories	____________________
Laundries	____________________
Hospitals	____________________
Day Care Centers	____________________
Lawyers	____________________
Social Workers	____________________
Trained Home Economists	____________________
Health and Welfare Agencies	____________________
Radio and Television Stations	____________________
Others	____________________

Shopping Facilities Available to the Community

1. Does the shopping center of the community take care of its needs, or do the people go to nearby communities for shopping? ____________________
____
____
2. Are the stores up-to-date? ____________________
3. What percentage of the people buy from mail order houses? __________
4. Are shopping facilities available for persons who do not have automobiles?
____

Facilities for Educational Welfare

1. School (list names of schools of each type that are located in the community)
public ____________________
private ____________________
preschools ____________________
community colleges ____________________
2. Adult education (check those available): evening classes ______;
day classes ______; television classes ______
3. Churches (list names
Protestant ____________________
Catholic ____________________
Jewish ____________________
other ____________________
4. Libraries (check types available): public ______; rental ______; other (describe)
____

TABLE 2 *(continued)*

5. Community clubs (list names)
   civic ____________________
   social ____________________
   others ____________________
6. Museums (list names and indicate specialization, if any): ____________________
   ____
7. Is there a Cooperative Extension or Community Action program functioning in the community? Explain ____________________
   ____
8. Approximately what percentage of the community's high-school graduates are now attending college? ____________________
9. Do the schools tend to be progressive or traditional? ____________________
10. Are the churches a strong influencing factor? ____________________
11. Is the community dominated by any ethnic or racial group? ____________________
12. What is the community attitude toward education? ____________________
    ____

Facilities for Recreational Welfare

1. Parks (list number available): public _____; private _____
2. Playgrounds (list number available): supervised _____; unsupervised _____
3. Places for swimming (list number available): public _____; private _____
4. Tennis courts (list number available): public _____; private _____
5. Commercial recreational enterprises (list number of each available): movies _____; dance halls _____; bowling alleys _____; liquor-dispensing agencies _____; ball parks _____; skating rinks _____; other types (list and describe) ____________________
   ____
6. To what extent does the community provide for recreation within the home?
   ____

Housing

1. Approximate percent of families in community owning homes (check one): majority _____; some _____; none _____
2. Types of housing (fill in approximate percent of each): one-family _____; two-family _____; multiple-family _____; mobile homes _____
3. Ownership of housing: private _____; public _____
4. Conveniences (list approximate percent of homes equipped):
   a. Facilities: electricity _____; natural gas _____; artificial gas _____; running water _____; bath _____; central heating _____; inside toilet _____
   b. Appliances: television set _____; freezer _____; sewing machine _____; telephone _____; automobile (one) _____, (more than one) _____; washer _____; dryer _____; air conditioner _____
5. Sanitation
   a. garbage-disposal methods: electrically operated disposal _____; collection _____; other methods (describe) ____________________

TABLE 2 *(continued)*

b. sewage disposal: adequate ____; inadequate ____
c. water supply: source ____; adequate ____; safe ____

Community Service

1. Local government
   a. type: mayor ____; city council ____; sheriff ____; marshal ____
   b. functions of government: in what way is provision made for social welfare?
   ____
2. Local services provided (check those available):
   police protection ____; fire department (regular or voluntary) ____; courts (permanent or circuit) ____; legal aid ____
3. Food-and-drug inspection:
   a. meat: government inspected? ____
   b. milk: pasteurized? ____; certified? ____; other? ____
   c. restaurants: properly inspected? ____
   d. drugs: inspected? ____; certified? ____
   e. other: ____
4. Health services: number of doctors in locality ____; number of public-health nurses ____; number of hospitals (public) ____; (private) ____
5. Are there any health and sanitation regulations? (Explain briefly.) ____
   ____
6. Does the community approve of quarantine and vaccination? ____________
7. Are well-baby clinics available? ________________________

Transportation

1. Is the community accessible? ________________________
2. Main highways (number): north-south ____; east-west ____
3. Rail transport: number of terminals in community ____; names of rail lines operating ________________________
4. Air transport: number of airports within community ____; If none in community, how close is the nearest? ________ Names of airlines serving area
   ____
5. Bus transport: number of bus terminals ____; names of bus lines ________
   ____
6. Local transport (check means available): buses ____; taxi cabs ____

Communication

1. How many local daily newspapers? ____; weekly? ____
2. What out-of-town newspapers are available? ________________
   ____
3. Do most families subscribe to a daily newspaper ________________
4. Are current magazines found in the homes? many ____; few ____; none ____
5. List percent of homes having: telephone ____; radio ____; television ____

Few home economics teachers have the time to compile all the information suggested on the community data sheet. However, every teacher has the responsibility for gathering the information that will have very direct bearing on her day-to-day teaching. She should add each year to the collection of community data and bring up-to-date those aspects of the data that shift as the community changes. If each teacher would see it as a part of her professional responsibility to keep up-to-date the descriptive record of a community, in a short while, without a particular hardship on any one person, each home economics department would have, as a part of its teaching materials, information that would be invaluable in helping to make that program more functional.

Using Community Data

The collecting, organizing, and interpreting of data about a community are neither routine chores nor ends in themselves. They are dynamic tools for helping you to direct your home economics instructional program to the actual conditions that exist and, at the same time, to have available for yourself and others those facts that are pertinent to long-time program planning and organization. Using community data in this manner helps make home economics realistic for the people it serves, for it gives a base for predicting and directing change. In a large measure the gap between theory and practice, ideals of what ought to be taught and what is taught, is bridged.

Let us look at the ways in which a teacher might use intelligently the knowledge and information about a particular community as a sound basis for making decisions relative to the teaching of home economics. This involves a four-step process: (1) identifying a particular community factor; (2) seeking out and identifying the facts concerning this factor; (3) interpreting these particular findings in relation to implications for the teaching of home economics in a particular school; and (4) adapting specific day-to-day home economics teaching to the implications.

Suppose one of the community factors you have identified is the number of high school graduates who had married within a year of graduation. The finding was that among the graduates of the last 5 years, 70 percent had married within a year of graduation. One of the implications for the instructional program might be that advanced home economics instruction ought to prepare students for establishing and maintaining a home and family. In light of this fact, what could you, the home economics teacher, do in your day-to-day instructional program? Might you help your students recognize the kinds of problems they will be solving in a short while? Might you adapt each of the subject-matter areas of home economics so that students might seek out and examine possible alternative solutions to these problems as they relate to their establishment of a family? One home economics teacher adapted her subject-matter areas to this one finding in the following ways:

1. MONEY MANAGEMENT. Each girl who was engaged was assisted by the person whom she was going to marry in defining the long-term as well as the more immediate goals they would like to achieve for their new family. These included such items as: help husband finish his apprentice training, furnish our apartment, start a life-insurance program, make a down payment on a house, buy a car, and see that we have an adequate diet and the right kind of medical care. Next, the students prepared net-worth statements (listings of their assets, including human abilities, and listings of their liabilities) and made estimates of the amounts of money they would have for the following year. On the basis of their stated goals, and with the estimated incomes as the limitations, each girl worked out with her intended marriage partner a plan for spending for the following year. In order to be able to make sound decisions about the amounts of money to allot for various items, the class needed to acquire considerable information and knowledge. Independently, in small groups, in teams, and as a class, students investigated many aspects of the family financial plan—the cost of credit; how much food money would be needed to provide an adequate diet; the cost of home furnishings; ways of paying for goods; purposes and costs of insurance programs; and the like. Those in the class who were not planning to marry within the year made plans for the use of their money for the next year; some of them planned how they would manage the salaries they would earn on their first jobs, while others planned how to use their shares of the family dollars as they continued their education and remained economically dependent upon parents.

2. FOODS AND NUTRITION. The instructional program in this area was geared toward helping the students with meal planning and preparation in relation to providing an adequate diet for two persons. Consideration was given to eating "out," both in relation to cost and as a means of providing some of the essentials of an adequate diet. Nutrition, as it was related to the mother and child in the prenatal period, was also examined.

3. CLOTHING. Clothing needs of a new husband and wife were discussed, and a survey was conducted among a selected group of newly married couples to find out what their clothing-buying practices were during the first year of marriage. Building the clothing wardrobe prior to marriage, changing clothing-buying practices, and deciding how much and how to pay for clothing for the family—all of these are representative of the problems these students examined.

Can you identify how you might adapt a home economics instructional program in the areas of family relationships, home furnishings and housing, or other areas in light of the finding we have described? You may want to try your hand at identifying a factor in a particular community, ferreting out the finding relative to that factor, drawing an implication as it relates to a specific instructional area in home economics, and seeing what you might suggest as a means for adapting the day-to-day teaching in home economics. One college student found the following schematic outline helpful in doing this:

Community Factor	Related Finding	Implication for Instructional Program	Ways to Adapt Daily Teaching

All home economics teachers make decisions as to what and how they will do their daily classroom teaching. In this realm of decision making, they find that pertinent information about a community is an important factor in helping them to make an intelligent decision as to what and how to teach. Although home economics administrators, such as state and city supervisors or the local school administrators, generally make the decisions concerning the kind of home economics program that will exist in a particular school or community, the home economics teacher is usually in a position to assist in making some of the decisions concerning the long-term program planning and organization. Whether decisions are made by administrators or home economics teachers, effective home economics programs will exist only if some thought is given to specific community factors and their implications for home economics education in that particular school setting. Reviewing and analyzing the important findings relative to home economics education for a particular community is the first step to intelligent decision making in the organization and long-term planning of a home economics education program. By using community data, teachers, school administrators, and advisory councils have a sound basis for organizing the instructional program in the schools, for determining the kind of home economics programs which would best serve youth beyond high school, and for establishing adult home economics education programs. For example, in one city it was found that over a hundred students 14 years of age had dropped out of school during the preceding year before they finished the seventh grade. Since most of these dropouts were married, the school decided that some home economics instruction might be offered to pupils in grades 1 through 7, that a class for out-of-school young people might be organized, and that part-time instruction on a half-day basis might be made available to meet the needs of some of these young people. When the people responsible for making the decisions about the organization of home economics education in a community are cognizant of the community factors that have implication for that program, a more successful program can be planned, tax money can be spent more wisely, and families can be helped to meet their day-to-day problems more effectively.

Selected References

Champoux, Ellen M., and Burl Hunt, "Draw on Community Resources to Improve Your Curriculum," *Illinois Teacher of Home Economics,* IX: 97–99; 1965–66.

Gans, Herbert J., *The Urban Villagers.* New York: The Free Press of Glencoe, 1962.

Goodlad, John, *The Changing School Curriculum.* New York: Fund for the Advancement of Education, 1966.

Havighurst, Robert, *Education in Metropolitan Areas.* New York: Allyn and Bacon, 1966.

Herritt, Robert E., and Nancy H. St. John, *Social Class and the Urban School.* New York: John Wiley and Sons, 1966.

Recommendations: Composite Report of Forum Findings. Golden Anniversary White House Conference on Children and Youth. Washington, D.C.: United States Government Printing Office, 1960.

4

Knowing the Homes and Families of Your Students

From experiences in your own family, from observations in your home community, from contacts with the families of your friends, and from your readings and studies in home economics and related fields, you have come to recognize that there are differences as well as similarities in the way families think, feel, and act. These family characteristics are vital influences in the formation of every individual's basic personality structure. Differences in family background and training helped to mold the individual personalities you will meet and with whom you will work in your home economics classes. What people eat and how they eat it, what they wear, the houses in which they live and how they are furnished, their occupations, the amount of money they have and how they choose to spend it, the ways they rear their children, their entire repertoire of manners—all these mundane facts differ from family to family.

THE INFLUENCE OF FAMILY BACKGROUND ON HOME ECONOMICS STUDENTS

Each of your students comes to your home economics class with his own particular backlog of family experiences that helps him to see and interpret his class work in a somewhat different light than you or any of his classmates view it. To illustrate, one student may set a table for a class meal with confidence and security, approaching the task routinely and with no inner conflict as to whether what he is doing will be judged in terms of correct or incorrect. Another may be completely insecure in the task, unfamiliar with the materials he is using, and hesitant as to how to get help in solving his problem. Some students may look upon the job as unnecessary and a waste of effort, since their chief concern is to get on with the business of eating without the falderal of setting a table.

Yet another may want to gain practice in setting a table in a variety of ways to suit a number of different occasions. The possible facets of a single learning situation for each student are innumerable and are dependent upon the individual's past and present experiences.

If you are to make home economics classes meaningful for your students, you will need to be concerned about understanding the homes and families from which your students come. You will find that what each individual learns in his family experience is basically similar. It is in the ways that the family teaches the individual what his world will be like, what and who he is, and what he must do to become a functioning member of his society that families differ. These differences and similarities exert an influential force in making every individual unique, yet very much like others; self-directed, yet subject to the biases of his particular family environment. The many differences in the ways families live have become increasingly of concern to the home economics teacher, whose purpose in teaching is to help individuals live more satisfying personal lives and to make worthwhile contributions to their present homes, as well as to sift out those values and practices that will become foundation stones when they establish their own future families.

The Working Mother

As you strive to make home economics classes fruitful for each individual, you will achieve some measure of success if you are aware of the conditions under which each particular family is living. Today an increasing number of women are a part of the labor force; well over 35 percent of the labor force was comprised of women in 1968. A number of children are expected to care for themselves if mother works outside the home. Often the mother is the only worker in the family; the one-parent family is a real part of family life in the United States.

If a large number of your class members represent one-parent families or families where both parents work outside the home, you could help your boys and girls see how they might assume a larger share of home responsibility. Practice in working within the time limitations that are present in the classroom situation can help them acquire skills in performing homemaking tasks in other situations where time is limited. These limitations, which may, in the beginning, appear to stand in your way, can in reality become important aids for effective teaching. Short-cuts in food preparation and in accomplishing household tasks can be emphasized, so that values held important by the family may be achieved, rather than pushed into the background by routine household tasks.

At the same time, some students may see in the performance of the everyday homemaking tasks an opportunity to develop some fundamental family values. In today's home, where many tasks are accomplished by mechanical devices, opportunities for developing a sense of worth, achievement, and responsibility become scarce. It is in the family setting that the means for mediating these values take on increased importance. Your home economics students can become aware of the many opportunities in everyday household tasks for perpetuating important family values.[1]

Family Size

The kinds and sizes of families from which your students come will loom important in helping to determine what to teach. For example, the girl who comes from a family in which each member has a private or almost private room, is faced with different problems and concerns in a housing unit than the boy who represents a family in which all members share a common bedroom. The families of your students may vary, too, in ethnic background, religious beliefs, patterns of right and wrong, numbers and ages of persons sharing a common abode, and the responsibilities each member is expected to assume. A knowledge of these family factors will help you gear class activities to the lives of the boys and girls you teach.

Cultural Background

One teacher, who worked with Mexican boys and girls, thought it important that they learn to prepare the typical breakfast of fruit, egg, cereal, and beverage. Because she felt it important that these children find means of getting more milk in their diets, she stressed cooking cereal with milk. The children listened to her directions, watched her demonstration, and then proceeded to prepare their class breakfasts, but neglected to cook their cereal in milk. Distressed by what appeared to be a lack of learning, the teacher questioned the group as to why they were not following directions. They calmly explained that her method might be "all right for home economics class," but they didn't like cereals cooked in milk, and besides, they never used milk in that way at home because if they did, "no one would eat the food." Ethnic and religious family differences have a marked influence on family patterns of food consumption. An important fact to remember is that helping people meet basic nutritional requirements is more important than stressing particular kinds of foods or dishes to be prepared or preferred meal patterns.

Once you recognize that family factors are closely akin to the effective-

[1] Dorothy Lee, *Freedom and Culture, A Spectrum Book,* New York: Prentice-Hall, 1959, pp. 27–38.

ness of your teaching, you will find yourself besieged with questions concerning the means for learning, interpreting, and implementing these facts. You will raise such questions as: Are the differences in the ways of living of the families of my students as varied as they appear to be? What are the basic similarities and differences among the families of my students? What methods will be most helpful to me in discovering these similarities and differences? How can I use this information to make my home economics classes challenging for each person? The answers to these questions will give you a basic background for guiding student growth and development.

LEARNING TO RECOGNIZE AND UNDERSTAND THE WAYS FAMILIES LIVE

There are a number of ways of learning about the families of your boys and girls. These entail familiarity with existing records and first-hand contacts with families and homes, as well as ardent study and an experimental attitude. The methods you choose will be determined by school practices that are established already, your personal beliefs and abilities, and the resources available to you.

School Records

One of the more accessible sources of family information for the home economics teacher is the material kept in school records. Most schools have some type of cumulative records in which can be found varying amounts and kinds of information about the family background of a particular boy or girl. Generally, the home address, the parents' names, the marital status of parents, the parents' occupations, and the number of children in a family are recorded. From such information the home economics teacher can gain perspective as to the sizes and kinds of families from which her students come. The marital status of parents and the number of brothers and sisters, as well as the parents' occupations, provide her with insights into the common problems and concerns of an individual student.

Depending upon the number as well as the philosophy of guidance personnel within a school system, available school records may give more or less pertinent information concerning a student's family environment. Some records contain data concerning family income, religious beliefs, ethnic background, parents' educational levels, and other social information. Most home economics teachers find that they can save themselves much effort if they go to school records as first sources of family information. No amount of pertinent information, however, serves a practical purpose unless it is utilized intelligently. You may want to transfer the particular information you need from school records to your own home economics class records in a form that will be more directly usable to you. For example, you may want to allow space in an over-all class profile for specific family data, or you may wish to set up a card file or folder for each of your students. Utilizing records that are already available is a wise procedure from two standpoints: (1) it helps you in organizing and interpreting generally accepted information for your particular use in program planning, and (2) it avoids duplication of effort on the part of both students and teachers in gathering information. Few practices are more irritating to boys and girls than the duplicate gathering of the same information by a number of teachers.

Home Visits

Home economics teachers have long used home visits as one way of gaining insight into the ways families live—their problems, concerns, values, attitudes, beliefs, taboos, aspirations, and practices. Visiting the adolescent and his family in their home can help you secure a better understanding of an actual home situation. When you see that Mary's home expresses a standard of cleanliness markedly different from the standard accepted and practiced at school, you can understand better the dishwashing procedures she uses and make plans for helping her choose desirable and satisfying standards for herself. Learning to recognize the ways families live is easier to accomplish if good rapport exists between you and the families of your students. When families come to know, accept, and like you as a person, they are more likely to share with you their thinking, more willing to let you see them as they really are, and more apt to seek your help in arriving at solutions to their common problems and concerns. Home visits can provide an excellent means for helping you build this kind of rapport.

Many of the class and home experiences that boys and girls choose to pursue make home visiting imperative for you, for they necessitate your seeing, understanding, and participating in the experience on the "home front." For example, one of your students may want to help his family utilize better the working space in the home kitchen. You will need to see the actual kitchen arrangement and know something of the pattern of living of the family if your help is to be most effective. As the student, his family, and you work together in the home, an agreeable kitchen plan for that particular family can be evolved. Comparable results would be difficult to achieve without home visiting. Working with the student and his family at home gives them an opportunity to understand you better and to realize that you are a person who is interested in their problems and who has special training and abilities for helping them achieve the results they desire. Home visiting helps you become cognizant of the needs of an individual student as well as the limitations he faces in solving problems related to his family living. In this manner you become more effective in helping students to select, carry out, and evaluate class experiences so that they can function more efficiently in their particular home environment.

Few beginning teachers face the task of home visitation free of doubt and apprehension. Frequently they are confronted with questions concerning how to get into a home, whether parents and students will welcome them, what to do when making a visit, how to observe and interpret significant factors, how to share what they learn with other teachers, what items are pertinent and how to record them, and on what bases to make the crucial decision of whether a home visit is necessary. These doubts and apprehensions are normal whenever a person is confronted with a new situation or experience. Most concerns can be alleviated if (1) the solving of the problem is based on the process of thinking through a number of alternate solutions and arriving at the particular solution that will best meet the specific need; and (2) the solution arrived at is reasonably likely to be pleasant and successful. If you firmly believe that the actual visiting in the home of a student will give you insights and understandings you could achieve in no other manner, you will choose to make home visits.

On the other hand, circumstances may limit the possibilities for home visitation. This may be especially true in urban areas and in widespread consolidated regions. If this is the case, you may need to rely on other ways to learn of the home situation of students. Some of the alternatives may be to visit representative homes; to visit only those homes where there are students who need help with special problems; or to rely on the information gleaned from other school personnel.

No two teachers follow the same procedure for contacting and visiting homes. Having in mind a few basic cues helps you to make the experience professionally helpful and enlightening. Sharing with your boys and girls and their families the reasons for wanting to know more about them and their families can help them to accept your visit. When someone understands the reasons for an undertaking, he is apt to look at it with a more wholesome point of view than if he is uncertain as to the purpose of the endeavor.

Although emphasis has been given to discussing the actual visiting of the student's home, we need not assume that this method is the "best" or "preferred" way for every teacher to get to know homes and families. Sometimes, using this method is undesirable or impossible because of the large number of students enrolled in home economics classes; the miles to be traveled; the number of mothers working; or the intangible personal attitudes of parents, teachers, or students toward home visiting. It is still essential, however, that you employ some technique for *knowing homes and families* if you expect to develop a realistic home economics program.

Informal Contacts with Families

Another means for getting to know families is to invite the parents of a particular group of students to school. This could be a formally arranged meeting but, more commonly, teachers find it easier to operate in an informal atmosphere. As parents and teacher sit around in informal groups, they can share with one another what they are doing and planning for their children. The teacher has the opportunity to discuss the purposes of home economics, special class projects, and various problems and ideas in a direct and informal manner. As parents and students begin to understand that it is necessary to know homes in order that the disparities between home and school not be too great, they are happy to share information usable to the teacher. More security, less tension, and fewer strains for all concerned result when the home and school operate as a team to bring the ideal patterns of school and the actual patterns of home practices nearer one another.

Planning Sessions

Gaining parents' assistance in the planning and evaluating of the home economics program can give you cues for a better understanding of families and their practices. Getting parents to come to the school takes careful planning, a friendly approach, and encouragement on your part, plus the established understanding of your students. If possible, hold the planning session at a time when most parents can find it reasonably possible to attend. One teacher met and got to know a large number of the parents of her boys and girls when, after completing the first unit of work and prior to beginning a new block, she invited the parents to an informal coffee hour. This gave the parents a chance to discuss with the teacher and the students what they felt their children and their families had gained (or not gained) from what had transpired and to give their points of view on possibilities for future class activities. In one such an evaluating-planning session, the teacher learned that her emphasis might well have been given to helping boys as well as girls learn to make intelligent shopping decisions, since a good deal of the family food buying in those particular families was done by the men and the boys of the family.

Special School Events

Special events sponsored by the school offer still more opportunities for becoming acquainted with the families of youth. Often whole families attend local athletic events, music affairs, or special home economics programs. Noting which parents attend and making an effort to talk with and get to know family members gives some insights into a student's family experiences. Seeing the whole family at a school function gives a live photograph of the family—the way each member looks and dresses, the span of ages in family members, and even more important, the actions that denote more loudly than words the family relationships.

Classes for Adults

The ingenious teacher avails herself of every opportunity for knowing families better. Working with parents in study groups or adult classes offers excellent opportunities. In an adult class on preparing family meals, one teacher learned of the concern a group of mothers had about the dietary habits of their daughters, particularly in the area of weight reduction. The teacher was able to capitalize on the information given her by the mothers; she used it for building food preparation units that were interesting to teenagers, yet met with the approval of anxious parents.

Resource Persons

Asking qualified parents to come to school to help in the actual classroom teaching is another means for getting at similarities and differences in families. One teacher employed this technique in a number of situations. In a unit on child development, she brought parents in as panel members to give their points of view as parents of baby-sitters. In this manner, the teacher as well as her class learned that a baby-sitter's parents have concerns about their children, although they differ in degree from the concerns held by employers of baby-sitters. Through such a panel the teacher can glean many of the mores of adolescent behavior as well as some of the points of conflict in those families where the pangs of economic and personal independence are first being suffered. On another occasion she invited a trio of Swedish women to demonstrate the making of traditional Christmas ludefisk. Utilizing parents and other family members in this manner can give a teacher many understandings of family celebrations and traditions, and religious and ethnic backgrounds. Chapter 9 contains suggestions for the effective use of resource persons in home economics classes.

Casual Community Contacts

Casual contacts with parents and other family members of your students in the community offer still more avenues for knowing families. You can learn a great deal about family values and school expectations as you involve yourself in community affairs. Often you will meet parents as you do your shopping, attend social functions or church services, and engage in your other daily rounds of community life. These unplanned, casual meetings can be utilized by the observant teacher. For example, such seemingly trite items as what the family loads into the shopping cart at the supermarket or who accompanies a youngster as he shops for clothing are cues for teaching home economics. Through one such casual contact, a teacher overheard and observed a mother and daughter make a decision on a dishwashing compound; the teacher thereby learned that it might be important to some students to receive guidance and help in the wise purchase of cleaning supplies.

News Items

Although face-to-face contacts may be more fruitful in giving cues to family living, indirect means may prove to be the most efficient ones in some situations. Careful reading of the local newspaper can help you see many facets of a family's life: the tragedies, as depicted in illness, death, divorce, and disaster; the happinesses, as portrayed in births, marriages, parties, and social events; and the accomplishments, as told in promotions, graduations, and honors. Knowing some of these factors at the right moment can help you turn a rather dull day into a rich, meaningful, teachable moment for a particular boy or girl. Such a red-letter school day came about for one boy when his home economics teacher called the attention of the class to an item concerning family hobbies that featured a special "bucket-barbecue pit" which the boy and his father had made for their family. It was with real pride that the boy was able to share with his classmates a project that he and his father had originated.

Student Writings

Many teachers have found it helpful to learn about families through student writings. Autobiographies and themes written by adolescents concerning their families, how they feel their home has influenced them, the desires and ambitions they believe parents hold for them, special family celebrations, kinds of home responsibilities, and feelings toward siblings and others sharing the family home, are all possibilities for acquiring family data. It was through such a device that one teacher learned that older members of families, such as grandparents, were resented by her boys and girls; hence, she made plans for helping them face this problem realistically and honestly.

Classroom Activities

Any teacher can learn about families by developing keen eyes and ears in the classroom. Specific kinds of activities may be planned to reveal pertinent information concerning family attitudes and problems. These include a variety of projective techniques such as free-response writings and role playing. These techniques and their use are described in Chapters 9 and 12.

The home economics teacher has an unusual opportunity to gain insights into family practices by observing the ways boys and girls work in the home economics laboratory. The habits acquired at home speak for themselves in telling a student's family background story. The way a person sets a table, how he goes about the job of preparing to work in the unit kitchen, the kinds of foods he chooses to prepare when he has a choice, how he gets along in his work group, and the ways in which he solves a problem as it arises—all of these provide the observant teacher with some insights from which she may begin to draw generalizations concerning an individual's family background. By the ways your students behave, by the things they say, by the references made to home and family, and by the actual sharing of family experiences, boys and girls present a living kaleidoscope of family events. The individual in your class is representative of his family's environment. When he comes to school, he brings the influence of his family with him!

COLLECTING AND INTERPRETING INFORMATION ABOUT HOMES AND FAMILIES

Several means available to you for gaining pertinent information concerning the homes and families of your boys and girls have been presented. This information can be useful to you only as you see its implications for teaching home economics. Few teachers have the time to originate their own devices for the collection of important family data; most teachers, however, can adapt existing instruments for their own use. On page 77 is a check list (Table 3) for securing family information, which you may find helpful. It can be modified so that it can be utilized whether the information is secured as the result of a home visit or by the other, less direct means that have been discussed.

The check list in Table 3 can serve as a mental guide as you make a home visit or as a kind of record after a home visit. Can you see how

TABLE 3 Knowing Homes and Families

Name of family ______________________
Address ______________________
Telephone ______________________
Date ______________________

Persons living in the home:
_____ Mother _____ Grandparent
_____ Father _____ Grandchildren
_____ Daughter(s): ages __________
_____ Son(s): ages __________

I. Appearance of outside of house
size: _____ large; _____ medium; _____small
condition: _____ good; _____ average; _____ poor
type: _____ apartment building; _____ single dwelling; _____ duplex
_____ converted house or business structure
_____ makeshift housing, such as boxcar
_____ mobile home
_____ public housing

II. Area lived in
_____ very exclusive section of town
_____ better suburb or apartment house area
_____ good location on farm or "in country"
_____ strictly residential area; space for yard
_____ average residential area; no deterioration evident
_____ area beginning to deteriorate
_____ considerably run down area; no yard space; semi-slum
_____ crowded; slum; streets and housing badly in need of repair

III. Furnishings of the home
floor plan:
_____ dining room; _____ dining area in living area; _____ dining area in kitchen
_____ sleeping areas in living room or dining room
_____ facilities for outdoor living
equipment and facilities:
_____ running hot and cold water
_____ bath
_____ central heating
_____ air conditioning
_____ closed kitchen storage space
_____ electric or gas range
_____ electric or gas refrigerator
_____ home freezer
_____ sewing machine
_____ laundry facilities
furniture and floor coverings:
_____ well selected and conveniently arranged
_____ in good condition
_____ include accessories that add to room attractiveness
_____ comfortable chairs
use and care:
_____ room appears clean and orderly
_____ room appears bare and unused

TABLE 3 *(continued)*

cultural features:

_____ television; _____ radio; _____ record player

_____ piano

_____ books; _____ magazines; _____ newspapers

IV. Personal appearance of members of the family

_____ neat; clothing attractive and clean

_____ careless in appearance

_____ clothing dirty and in need of mending, pressing, etc.

V. How family members get along with one another

_____ happy family experiences

_____ experiences that indicate family friction

_____ attitudes of family friendly and pleasant

_____ attitudes of family unfriendly and constrained

VI. Family's attitude toward home economics classes

_____ strong beliefs and convictions about program

_____ see home and school as cooperative team

_____ indifferent toward home economics

_____ unhappy about school situation

_____ see home economics as unimportant

VII. Home responsibilities student is expected to assume

_____ large share of housekeeping duties

_____ large share of child care duties

_____ large share of food preparation duties

_____ some financial responsibility

_____ care and responsibility of personal belongings

_____ little home responsibility

_____ no home responsibility

VIII. Observations and comments _______________________________________

____

it might also be used or adapted for securing or recording information about a family one might see at an athletic event or other community function?

Some of the information desired on the above check list can be gathered by actually visiting in a home, some can be collected from already existing school records, and some can be secured through a questionnaire which you may want to administer. Can you see how a walk or drive through a number of residential areas in your school community may give you some insights into the families from which your students come?

Information is helpful only to the extent that it is used. For the information to have optimum value, some kind of record must be kept. As teachers learn to keep and share records, the burden of record keeping for an individual teacher can be minimized. An important point that cannot be overemphasized is that the teachers should seek out and record only the information that has a direct bearing upon helping her adjust the home economics curriculum to her particular boys and girls. To glean information and not use it is wasteful of your effort, as well as professionally unethical. If the teacher exercises care in reporting what she sees, without making personal value judgments concerning homes and families, the information can be useful to other teachers who are also concerned with understanding the impact of family factors on a particular individual.

What type of records you keep is dependent upon the ultimate use to which you will put the information. Some information is valuable to all members of a school staff; other information can be utilized best within the scope of the home economics department. Information concerning the facets of a family situation, responsibilities students are expected to assume, kinds of home economics equipment typically used by families, and special aspirations parents hold for themselves and their children might become part of the record. What facts home economics teachers share with other teachers and how they choose to share these facts are often dictated by school policy and personal beliefs; nevertheless, if the school is to help each individual become a more effective citizen, some sharing of information is advisable.

A careful study of existing records should provide the teacher with a knowledge of overall patterns of family living that can serve as a guide for curriculum planning. For example, such facts as that the majority of students live in houses without dining rooms, a large percentage of mothers work outside the home, or many families do not own sewing machines, are indicators for possible meaningful learning experiences.

Records need to be analyzed to find common factors as well as to indicate individual differences in family patterns. Your home economics classes can be enriched and your teaching can be more challenging and stimulating as you learn to collect, record, interpret, and analyze pertinent information about homes and families.

Selected References

Bailard, Virginia, and Ruth Strang. *Parent-Teacher Conferences.* New York: McGraw-Hill, 1964.

Educating the Teenager in Human Relations, Management of Resources. Washington, D.C.: American Home Economics Association, 1966.

"Government Policy and the Family." *Journal of Marriage and the Family.* **29**, 6–17, February 1967.

Hess, Robert D., and Gerald Handel, *Family Worlds.* Chicago: University of Chicago Press, 1959.

McGrath, Earl, *The Changing Mission of Home Economics.* New York: Teachers College Press, Columbia University, 1968.

Moore, Bernice M., and Wayne H. Holtzman, *Tomorrow's Parents.* Austin, Texas: The University of Texas Press, 1964.

Moynihan, Daniel, *The Negro Family.* Washington, D.C.: United States Government Printing Office, Office of Planning and Research, Department of Labor, March 1965.

Report of the National Advisory Commission on Civil Disorders. New York: Bantam Books, 1968, pp. 251–274.

5

Knowing Your Students

What are they *really* like, these expectant young people who face me now on this first day I meet my home economics classes? There is Mike, surrounded by boys, expounding on his summer exploits, gesturing madly as he lets the gang in on his wrangling experiences out West. Then Sue, a well-groomed girl, with the latest hairdo and expressions, is surveying the situation to see just what potential new friends the class holds; she'll enjoy it more if the boys are in the majority, I'll wager! Here comes Tom Smith, son of the mill owner, headed for an Eastern prep school come next fall. And there is Mary Brown, daughter of a mill spinner, whose parents are divorced and who must find an after-school job so that she can help supplement her mother's income. Then there is Sandy—popular, bright, pretty, friendly with both boys and girls, Student Council president, cheerleader, and a real joy to have in class. In contrast is June—quiet, a diligent worker, alone most of the time, wearing her usual worried look—a girl whom I attempted to help last year but with whom I felt I made such little progress. These and thirty other eager faces, each curious about me, sizing up the situation, trusting me to help them make this class and this school year meet their varying expectations and aspirations—from particular home economics learnings and skills to just plain fun. Will I meet their hopes? Will I enjoy working and learning with them? Is it possible for me to get to know each of them as individuals? I can make snap judgments about them, a bit as I'm doing now, but experience has taught me that so often this way of getting to know others can lead to dead-end streets. There must be a line of attack that I can use to gather useful information that will be helpful to me as their home economics teacher. And surely, there must be some means of getting this information so that it won't be an insurmountable hurdle in an already crowded teaching day!

This could well be *your* soliliquy on the first day you meet your classes, whether you are a beginning teacher or an experienced one. Each home economics teacher is concerned with getting to know her students as individuals so that she might understand them better and gear her classes toward helping them face and solve their personal and family problems more realistically.

Where do you begin on this quest for learning to know students as individuals? Each of you already has developed a way for getting to know persons from living with and learning from them over a period of years. Capitalizing on the backlog of knowledge gained from your past experiences is your first key to understanding others. A bit of self-analysis, including such questions as the following, would be helpful. Ask yourself: "How do I usually operate when I meet a stranger? What do I tend to note about that person first—the way he looks; what he says; what he does? Over a period of time, have I found that first impressions were lasting impressions? What techniques have I used to delve deeper into another's background? Have I relied on talking and working with that person? Have I tended to get information about him through family connections and friends? Have I attempted to see him in a variety of situations?" Answers to these questions might serve as indicators of your already-established patterns of observing and learning about others. Although reliable in many instances, you must be continually aware that your own behavior, beliefs, and attitudes color your interpretations; your ways of judging conduct and of expressing acceptance or repulsion, like the behavior and attitudes of your students, are learned and traditional, neither universal nor axiomatic, but, rather, dependent upon your cultural background.

Your professional training is geared toward sharpening your perspective for understanding people. In your college human-development classes, you have been exposed to the most recent research and development in the ever-widening field of human growth and development. Through these classes you have come to understand the general growth patterns of development for people of varying ages. Allied disciplines of guidance, psychology, cultural anthropology, and sociology have broadened your perspective of the why's and how's of basic personality structures. This professional training has given you a theoretical framework for appraising individual personalities; now you must develop the ability to apply these learnings in actual practice.

Although it is impossible to view an individual out of the context of his environment, that is, his home and family background, his community, and the increasingly interdependent outer world, concentrating your attention on viewing an individual as a person in relation to these factors can give you insights for understanding him better. This chapter explores some means that may prove helpful for a better understanding of individuals. Because each situation is unique, these techniques are not to be taken as prescriptions for what is to be done in a particular situation, but rather as stimulators for the development of guides and processes for experimentation on your part in developing ways for better understanding the boys and girls in your school setting.

HOW TO OBTAIN DESIRED INFORMATION

A home economics teacher needs to know enough about each individual in her classes to help each make day-by-day decisions and to formulate patterns for optimal learning. Generally, information in the broad categories of home and family life; health; personal and emotional life; social adjustment; past school history; abilities, talents, and interests; and purpose, aspirations, and life values is very useful. There are a wide variety of techniques, procedures, or methods you might employ that will contribute toward a better understanding of the individual, and, if properly used, can lead him toward better development and adjustment. Among the techniques are observation, self-reports, and sociometric and projective devices; these techniques are explored in this chapter in the context of the home economics teaching situation.

Observation

The technique most commonly used for learning about persons is that of observation. Each day of the school year a teacher views the student in action. She can observe the way he looks and acts—vibrant with health or sluggish, well or poorly dressed, responsible or irresponsible in fulfilling class requirements, a leader or a follower, accepted or rejected by his peers. These views can be spasmodic or recurring; a teacher needs to be continuously aware of whether she is allowing a *single* sample of behavior to determine her concepts of an individual or whether she is basing her judgments on an adequate sampling of a student's behavior that gives a more objective means for appraising him.

Anecdotal records and rating scales are among the techniques that have been developed for acquiring a more objective and systematic view of student behavior. Although these can be employed for every student in the classroom, home economics teachers usually have to be more realistic and keep them only for selected students—those who present a special problem, those who have been referred to the home economics teacher by another teacher or by the guidance staff, or those who are representative of "typical" groups of students whom the teacher is attempting to know better.

Anecdotal Records

Randall described the anecdotal record as:

> . . . a record of some significant item of conduct, a record of an episode in the life of a student; a word picture of the student in action; the teacher's

> best effort at taking a word snapshot at the moment of the incident; any narrative of events in which the student takes such a part as to reveal something which may be significant about his personality.[1]

One home economics teacher kept the following time-sampling record of a boy in a seventh grade home economics class in which the group was engaged in preparing simple snacks.

Place Observed: Unit kitchen, home economics laboratory
Student's Name: Robert Smith
Date: 1/12/70
Incident: Group project, meal preparation; group—two boys, two girls
Time: 10:40 A.M.

Washed several utensils; dried them. Chatted with girls on left and boy on right. Smiled several times. Commented about the salad: "At least our fruit hasn't turned brown." Laughed when other boy, who was cutting an apple, dropped it on the floor. Said: "Pick it up and rinse it off and put it in the salad." Collected and stacked used knives and bowl. Washed them; another boy wiped them. Moved aside to let a girl get water; smiled at her; suggested to another girl that she ". . . put the lid on the sugar canister before it gets all wet . . ." Picked towel from floor, folded it, and hung it on towel rack.

Time: 10:50 A.M.

Walked to range; stood near oven; when oven door was opened, he jumped up and down with excitement at seeing the cookies. Put his hands up to his eyes and said in a loud voice: "They're burning!" Called to boy in neighboring unit: "Hey, Sabil, look." Did this twice, but was ignored each time. Saw girl shake hand as she took cookies from oven and placed them on counter. Said: "Did you burn yourself?" Chatted with the girl as she removed cookies from sheet, took several, and put them in his mouth whole and hot.

Time: 11:00 A.M.

Ate meal with group without contributing to the table conversation. Used utensils in an accepted manner; finished eating before the rest of the group. Said: "Any of you guys want the rest of these cookies?" (Three left on plate.) "O.K. then, guess I'll take them and eat them in homeroom." Put them in his pocket.

Time: 11:10 A.M.

Back at sink. Busy rinsing it with spray. Other group members had walked away. Said: "Come on, you kids, help or we won't get done on time." (No response from group.) Wrung out dishcloth, left it on sink; dried hands on a paper towel. Sat down. Noticed he had on an apron. Stood. Took it off and hung it in apron closet. (Bell rang.) Ran from room, darting between classmates and out the door.

Assuming that this was but one of a series of time-sampling anecdotal records kept of Robert, what significant indicators for understanding

[1] John A. Randall, "The Anecdotal Behavior Journal." *Progressive Education,* 13:22, January 1936.

Robert can the teacher glean from the record? Are there any indications of his work habits? Are there cues to his interaction with other group members? Are there any indications of his home training? Is there evidence that his behavior is typical or unusual? What clues for adjusting the teaching of home economics for that particular group can be found?

An occasional sampling of student behavior in a variety of home economics class activities can give the teacher insights into the behavior of particular students and help her to adjust the classroom situation to meet special needs. In certain instances a home economics teacher may want to record incidents of behavior of a student in a variety of situations in which she has an opportunity to observe him so that she might find clues for understanding him more thoroughly. These situations might include observations in the school halls, the cafeteria, at school functions, at parties or dances, in his home, or on the street. In any case, the following cues for observing and writing anecdotal records might well be kept in mind.[2]

1. The anecdote must be based upon a significant item of conduct.
2. The incident reported upon must be personally observed by the teacher.
3. The incident must be written as clearly, concisely, and accurately as possible, and immediately after the incident has occurred.
4. If possible, conversations should be quoted exactly as heard.
5. Significant conduct that is favorable should be reported as well as that which is unfavorable.
6. Only such data as helps one to understand the student better should be reported.
7. An anecdote should always be dated.

The anecdotes collected on a particular student are of limited value until interpreted, and interpretation is never an easy matter. The facts presented in all anecdotes must be sifted objectively and studied in relation to other factors. Contradictions must be detected to see if they represent consistent or inconsistent behavior patterns. Unique and recurring situations and unusual and repeated patterns need to be interpreted in light of what appear to be principal problems or personality characteristics. After facts have been studied, clues to their meanings may be detected more easily. If adequate and accurate observations have been made and interpreted in an orderly fashion, the clues of personality characteristics that are discovered can be invaluable guides for develop-

[2] Adapted from guide developed by the staff of the Department of Guidance and Counselor Training, Michigan State University, East Lansing, Mich.

ing home economics activities that will help the individual make more satisfactory and realistic progress in your classes.

Behavior Descriptions and Rating Scales

Another technique for learning about the boys and girls in your home economics classes is to use a variety of behavior descriptions and rating scales. These devices differ from the anecdotal record in that anecdotal records describe a particular set of incidents, whereas the rating scale attempts to give a generalized picture of an individual. In using a rating scale, the person doing the rating makes a general estimate of another's personality characteristics based on observable evidences of specific kinds of behavior in a variety of situations. When an individual makes an estimate of himself on a rating device, the device is usually called an "inventory"; when the judgments are made by others the device is usually termed a "rating scale."

A home economics teacher may develop her own rating scales for particular situations. One teacher found that a rating scale she developed with the help of her students was of special help to her group. During a class discussion on "What We Like About Our Classmates," she sifted the significant factors as expressed by the class and developed a behavior description device that she had the class use for rating one another. This is the way it appeared in its usable form:

Observation: Behavior Description Device
Senior High School

WHO ARE THEY?

Most of us are interested in improving ourselves, but sometimes we do not know our strong and weak points. How well do our opinions of ourselves agree with those opinions of us held by our classmates? This is an attempt to find out what other students think of you. Short paragraphs have been written about some of the things which may be considered important in the development of an all-round interesting person. A summary of the opinions about you by other students may help to draw your attention to certain things that will make you a more pleasing person. This is to help you, not to discourage you.

Directions: Attached is a sheet with numbers and names of each person in our class. On the following pages are descriptive paragraphs that may remind you of a person in our class. Read each paragraph carefully. Look at the names of the students in our class. At the right of each paragraph write the number of the student or students which this paragraph seems to bring to mind. Be as fair as possible, yet be willing to say what you honestly think because only in that way can we be helpful to each other. Rate only those students whom you think have the characteristics described; it may be one or a number of students; perhaps no one in our class fills the description. Do not discuss these paragraphs with others; depend upon your own judgment. Do not sign this paper.

Here is an example:

Some students are very talented musically. They sing well. They may play one or more musical instruments. Do we have any people like that in our class? Who are they?

Student: 6, 10, 3

Number	Name
1	Jane Brown
2, etc.	Bob Smith, etc.

Student

1. Do we have any students who are considered good sports? They are willing to do their share. They don't become angry if they lose or if the joke is on them. They are good losers, and do not blame others if they do not win. For example, they don't say that the referee was against them if the game is lost. Who are they?
2. Do we have students who are poor sports? They become angry if they can't have their way. They are poor losers. They "gripe" about unimportant things. They blame others for their mistakes. Who are they?
3. Which students rate at the top in friendliness? They always speak to you whenever and wherever they see you and sometimes they stop and chat with you. They seem to get along well with young and old, boys and girls. They know many people. Who are they?
4. Do we have people in or group who never speak first? They consider themselves better than anyone else. They associate with only a few people. Who are they?
5. Which students are full of energy and pep? They are interested in activities. They are not afraid to work. They do not tire easily. They like to do things. You see them really working for their class without griping. Who are they?
6. Do we have any lazy students in our group? They always try to get out of work. They never volunteer to give an extra report or to serve on a committee. They don't have time, they say, to sell tickets for a play or to clean up after a party. Who are they?
7. Do we have students in our group who always respect other people's property? They never mark school or public furnishings. You never find their names on things that don't belong to them. If they borrow, they return things promptly and in good shape. Who are they?

8. Do we have people who always borrow? What is yours is theirs. They never have their own pencils, paper, books or pins. They never return what they borrow. Who are they?
9. Do you know folks in our class who always know what to do? They feel at home in any group. They know the right things to do and say. Who are they?
10. Do we have students in our class who are never sure of themselves? They are always asking others about the correct thing to say, the right clothes to wear, the proper thing to do. They act uncomfortable around strangers. Who are they?
11. Who really has ability to do and try something different and original, such as designing an article of clothing, writing a clever skit for an assembly, or drawing a striking cover for the school paper? He looks for ideas and tries them out. Who are they?
12. Which students have the reputation for copying everything they see—from your algebra paper to the way you wear your hair? They have few new ideas of their own. Who are they?
13. Which students enjoy doing many things—crafts, sports, music, reading and other things; they want to learn about new things; they are seldom bored with life because they enjoy doing so many things. Who are they?
14. Which students seldom know what is happening around them; they take part in few sports; they can't do things; they don't like to read; they are not interested in trying new and different ideas. Who are they?

Summary Sheet

HOW DO YOU RATE?

Desirable Characteristics:	Undesirable Characteristics:
Good sport	Poor sport
Friendly	Snobbish
Energetic	Lazy
Respect for property	Chronic borrower
Socially adequate	Socially inadequate
Creative	Not creative
Wide range of interests	Few interests

The same characteristics that were covered in WHO ARE THEY? have been prepared in the form of a graphic rating scale on which the teacher or students might rate an individual:

Observation: Graphic Rating Scale
Senior High School
(Rating same characteristics as are rated in Who Are They?)

Rating of ____________ Rated by ____________________ Date _______

Directions: Check space that best represents your rating. If you feel that you have no evidence to check individual for a particular characteristic, leave it blank.

1. | | | | | |

Good sport; doesn't become angry if he loses or if joke is on him; willing to do his share.

Poor sport; becomes angry if he can't have his way; poor loser, blames others for his mistakes; gripes about unimportant things.

2. | | | | | |

Friendly; always speaks to you whenever and wherever he sees you; seems to get along well with people—young, old, boys and girls; knows many people.

Snobbish never speaks first; considers himself better than others; associates with only a few persons.

3. | | | | | |

Energetic; full of energy and pep; interested in activities; not afraid to work; doesn't tire easily; likes to do things; you see him working for the class without griping.

Lazy; always tries to get out of work; never volunteers to give an extra report or to serve on a committee; doesn't have time, he says, to sell tickets or clean up after a party.

4. | | | | | |

Respect's other's property; never marks school or public furnishings; never find his name on things that don't belong to him; if he borrows, he returns things promptly and in good shape.

Borrows all the time; what is yours is his; never has his own pencils, books or papers; never returns what he borrows.

5. | | | | | |

Socially adequate; always knows what to do; feels at home in any group; knows the right thing to do and say.

Socially inadequate never sure of himself; always asks others about the correct thing to say, the right clothes to wear, the proper thing to do; acts uncomfortable around strangers.

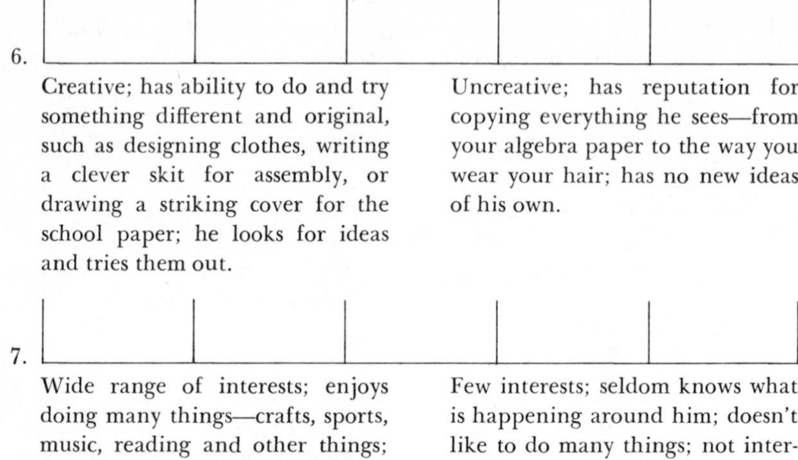

6. Creative; has ability to do and try something different and original, such as designing clothes, writing a clever skit for assembly, or drawing a striking cover for the school paper; he looks for ideas and tries them out.

Uncreative; has reputation for copying everything he sees—from your algebra paper to the way you wear your hair; has no new ideas of his own.

7. Wide range of interests; enjoys doing many things—crafts, sports, music, reading and other things; wants to learn about new things; is seldom bored with life because he enjoys so many things.

Few interests; seldom knows what is happening around him; doesn't like to do many things; not interested in trying new and different ideas.

A similar technique was prepared by another teacher. The difference, and strength, in this device, lies in the necessity for supporting choice with evidence (see Table 4).

The behavior-description and rating-scale devices will give you insights into the behavior of your students. They should offer cues for helping you adapt the learning situation for a particular individual or for the group in general. If there is to be student participation in a class setting in developing or filling in these devices, it must be within the context of what is being taught. For example, behavior-description devices might be developed by you and your class for getting at characteristics that are significant in developing interpersonal competence within a family group. More frequently, the home economics teacher uses the data that are collected via these devices by the guidance staff to deepen her understanding of students. In some schools, where she may carry responsibility for both counseling and teaching, the teacher can use these techniques for collecting data that will be useful in guiding individuals toward alleviating classroom and personal problems.

Self Reports

The student himself is the source of a good deal of information concerning himself. Technically, all standardized tests that he takes are, in reality, self-reports. The tests administered in a local school are an in-

TABLE 4 Who is Described?

Student's name ______________________ School ______________

During the semester, there will be a number of activities in which class members may take part. Your ideas will help in the selection of people for each activity.

Read each description and write down the names of the class members whom you think the description fits. Tell why you think this is a description of the person you have named.

Write as many names after each description as you think belong there. You may name the same person as many times as you think he or she is described. Put your own name down when you think the description fits you. If you can't think of anyone whom the description fits, go on to the next description.

Use this plan for writing your answers:

Description	I think this describes (write name)	I think this description fits her/him because
1. This person would do well on a committee that is to design a club program.		
2. This person would be good at helping write a newspaper article or at being interviewed about something that the class has been studying.		

3. This person would be good at selling someone or some group on an idea that the class wants to carry out.
4. This person would be good at getting information about equipment that the class is selecting for the department.
5. This person would be good at being in charge of fixing up the home economics rooms for a party that the class is giving.
6. This person would be good at leading a committee that is having a hard time agreeing on how to accomplish its work.
7. This person would be good to work with in taking notes at a meeting where you and he/she are both recorders.
8. This person would be good at helping others in a group talk, make suggestions, and feel at ease.
9. This person would be good at bringing people's ideas together in a plan for a class project.
10. This person would be good at leading a committee that has to work steadily at a job in order to get it done well and on time.
11. This person would be good at helping a group see whether it is working cooperatively and that it is staying on the beam.

valuable source of objective information concerning that student. Depending upon the testing program of your school, this information may be concerned with general mental abilities, special aptitudes, interests, and perhaps even personality inventories.

Students' scores are readily available to the teacher in the cumulative records that are kept on each individual in the school record office. Guidance personnel or a person in your school who is especially trained in testing can help you with test interpretations that will enable you to know your students in a more objective manner. As a home economics teacher you can use this information to adjust the curriculum for a particular student or for groups of students with specific needs or abilities. Seen in relation to other factors such as age, school grades, and home background, test scores are indicators for interpreting student behavior and for predicting future behavior of boys and girls.

The home economics teacher may also use, as parts of her regular classroom procedure, a number of reports written by students in which they give information about themselves. These may be questionnaires aimed at getting information concerning home responsibilities or family practices, autobiographies geared toward the youngsters' views of themselves as family members, free writings aimed at discovering their life values and aspirations, daily records or diaries which may reveal their dietary habits or use of time, and various evaluation devices where the individuals take objective looks at what and how they are learning in your class.

The ingenious teacher finds a number of ways to gain information about individual students by employing any one or a number of these techniques in her day-to-day teaching. For example, she might ask a student to keep a daily record of activities for a specified period of time. One girl kept such a record so that she might get a more objective view of the use of her time. On the basis of her findings she made more specific plans for use of time so that some of her leisure-oriented goals might be achieved. The record, as she kept it for one day, appears on page 93.

Does this daily record reveal anything of that girl's pattern of living? Does it give you any insight into her life values in terms of how she uses her time? Does it give any indications of health habits? Does it show a balance of activities? If this record were typical of the majority of days for a particular student, what generalizations concerning her way of living might you discern? Such daily records, if kept for a specified time, give a variety of indicators for a better understanding and knowledge of students. For example, if the home economics teacher found that the daily record of a student showed inadequate eating patterns, she might plan experiences relative to improving eating habits.

Daily Record of ______________________ Date __________

7:00 A.M.	Got up; bathed; dressed.
7:20 A.M.	Ate breakfast: peach; two slices toast with peanut butter.
7:25 A.M.	Made bed; hung up my clothes; played with my little sister; combed my hair.
8:15 A.M.	Gathered up my books; called Jane to tell her I'd be by in a few minutes; started the walk to school.
8:20 A.M.	Stopped and called for Jane.
8:25 A.M.	We arrived at school; went to our lockers; chatted with the kids we met.
8:30 A.M.	Homeroom.
9:00 A.M.	Spanish class.
10:00 A.M.	Study hall: studied my algebra.
11:00 A.M.	Home economics class.
12:00 noon	Lunch in cafeteria: vegetable soup, hamburger, carrot sticks, milk, ice cream.
12:30 P.M.	Special meeting for play cast.
1:00 P.M.	Algebra class.
2:00 P.M.	English class.
3:00 P.M.	Glee Club practice.
4:00 P.M.	Future Homemakers of America meeting.
5:00 P.M.	Walked home with Jane; stopped by to hear her new records.
5:45 P.M.	Got home, helped mother with dinner; set the table, dished up dessert.
6:05 P.M.	Ate dinner: meat loaf, peas, baked potato, gelatin salad, milk, canned plums.
6:30 P.M.	Helped stack the dishes; changed into slacks; fixed up for the basketball game.
7:00 P.M.	Tom picked me up; we went to the high school basketball game.
10:15 P.M.	Stopped on way home for a coke; then we walked home.
10:45 P.M.	Back home.
11:00 P.M.	Undressed; put up my hair; decided what to wear tomorrow.
11:15 P.M.	Read my assignment for English class.
11:45 P.M.	Turned off the light.
7: 00 A.M.	Got up; bathed; dressed.

Sociometric Techniques

Through observation and a variety of self-report techniques, the home economics teacher can learn about how the individual perceives himself and his interpersonal relations. She becomes cognizant of his self-image. A teacher also needs to know to what extent the student is accepted by his peers—the reputation he has among his age-mates and his position and status in the various groups of which he is, or is aspiring to be, a member. Be careful to avoid giving the impression that personal worth is dependent upon popularity.

Sociometric information is particularly important to the home economics teacher for two reasons: (1) one of her responsibilities is to help each student learn to become an effective member of a family group; and (2) some of the classroom activity in home economics is planned on the group basis. A recognition of the current group position and status of a particular student can assist the teacher in placing him in those situations that will help him achieve effective growth in group interaction and interpersonal competence. The sociometric techniques devised by Moreno[3] and adapted for classroom situations by Jennings[4] probably provide the most usable techniques yet developed for studying patterns of acceptance and rejection and the social structure of groups.

Sociogram

A sociogram is a graphic picture of the interrelationships among the individuals within a particular group, based upon the choices of those individuals for a *specified activity or situation.*[5] It portrays the status and role position of each individual at a particular time. A sociogram is made on the basis of a sociometric question that permits a student to reveal his choice concerning the group members with whom he prefers to be or work in a particular situation. For example, one home economics teacher asked her youngsters to jot down on a sheet of paper the three persons, in rank order, with whom they would like to form a family group for a three-week unit on the preparation and serving of family meals. From this information she plotted the sociogram shown in Fig. 1.

This sociogram portrays in graphic form the choices made by the boys and girls in one home economics class for the purpose specified. The results are usable because the students had confidence that their choices would actually be used in determining those with whom they would work in their family groups. A sociogram reveals a number of factors concerning the interrelations of group members: a pattern of mutual choices can be discerned, persons most frequently and least frequently chosen can be identified, youth who are completely isolated or rejected by their classmates can be selected, cliques and cleavages can be

[3] Jacob L. Moreno, *Who Shall Survive?* (rev. ed.). New York: Beacon House, 1953.

[4] Helen H. Jennings, "Sociometric Grouping in Relation to Child Development," in *Fostering Mental Health in Our Schools,* Association for Supervision and Curriculum Development. Washington: American Council on Education, 1948.

[5] Detailed information for collecting data and constructing a sociogram is presented in Ruth Cunningham and Associates, *Understanding Group Behavior of Boys and Girls.* New York: Bureau of Publications, Teachers College, Columbia University, 1951, pp. 154–171.

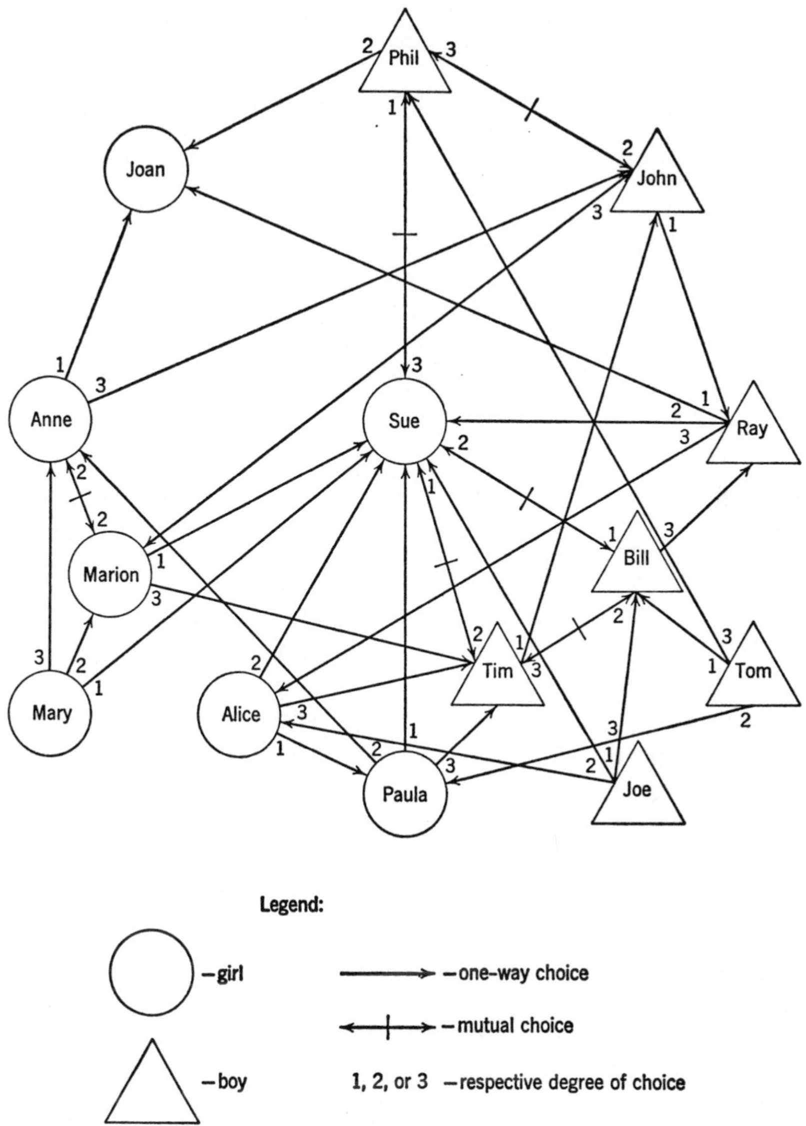

Figure 1. Sample sociogram: an illustration of graphic presentation of choice patterns.

noted, and choices between boys and girls can be discovered. When seen in relation with other factors, a sociogram provides a number of keys for shaping groups so that individual students can be helped to achieve satisfactory and satisfying group membership.

A home economics teacher might ask herself questions similar to these in making a first analysis of a sociogram:

1. What appears that I had expected to appear? On what evidence am I basing my judgment?
2. What appears that I have not expected? What are some probable reasons?
3. Are there small groups whose members chose each other but who were not chosen by those outside the clique?
4. As I view the structure as a whole, can I think of any arrangement (such as assigned seats in this class or in other classes) that might have been a factor in the general patterning of the sociogram?
5. Are there any procedures in the home economics classroom routine and arrangement that might have affected any patterns in the sociogram as a whole?
6. What trends seem to be present in the way or direction in which the students are making choices?
7. What cleavages, if any, appear in this sociogram? (A cleavage is defined here as the absence of choices between individuals who are in two or more subgroups.)
   a. boy-girl?
   b. economic?
   c. nationality or racial background?
   d. religious background?
   e. academic ability?
   f. after-school employment?
   g. prestige?
8. Does the structure of the group as a whole seem to be as integrated as would be good for class morale and individual growth for each member?

The most immediate thing to do with the findings of a sociometric technique is to carry out the agreement made with the students when the test was given. The object is to provide for each individual the best possible placement from *his* point of view. New relationships cannot be forced; they must be built gradually. The following simple rules, which have grown out of experience in using student's choices, seem to give each individual the maximum satisfaction compatible with similar treatment for everybody else:

1. Give any person who is unchosen or rejected his first choice to help fulfill his need for security. By placing him with the ones he feels most comfortable with, he may be encouraged to expand socially. *Example*: Joe chooses Sue first, Alice second, and Bill third. No one chooses Joe. Joe is placed with Sue.

2. Give any individual who is mutually chosen the highest reciprocated choice from *his* point of view; his first choice, if this is reciprocated; his second choice, if this is reciprocated and his first is not; his third choice, if this is reciprocated, and his first and second choices are not.

3. If a student was chosen only by persons he has not chosen, give him his first choice.

4. If rejections have been secured, try to place rejected persons apart from the ones who reject them.

5. Be sure every student has at least one of his choices fulfilled.

6. Try to reduce cleavages by placing in the same subgroups members of different segments, even if it means ignoring first choices and using second or third choices.

Classroom Distance Scale [6]

A technique that is used sometimes to extend understanding of individuals as they interrelate in a group setting is the classroom social distance scale, illustrated on p. 98. The purpose of this instrument is to discover the social tone of a group as a whole and the degree to which individuals and subgroups are accepted by the group and accept others in the group. It is devised to extend the usual sociometric approach, which allows a limited number of responses (that is, three choices), to include an opportunity for every student to give a reaction to every other in the group. Because the responses requested are of a highly confidential nature, which is *true of any sociometric device,* this instrument is valid only if honest responses are given. It should be used only in situations where the teacher has achieved a high degree of rapport with the group. If there is resistance on the part of boys and girls either to using the instrument or to signing their names, the device should probably not be used. Obviously, it should be used only by teachers with a professional point of view and a genuine interest in knowing more about students in order to provide a more adequate home economics program for them. If the teacher has good rapport with the group, she will have little difficulty in introducing it. Her explanation may be that she is interested in knowing how people in the group feel about each other in order that she may know how to help the group members get along with, work and learn with, and enjoy each other. The teacher's name may be inserted as a group member, in the appropriate alphabetical position, if she so desires.

Examining the responses from the classroom social distance scale is

[6] Ibid., pp. 171–174, 401–406.

just a beginning toward increasing the home economics teacher's understanding of boys and girls, not the end. Perhaps the greatest value in an examination of results is that attention is directed to certain aspects of interpersonal relations that lead to further observation of individual and group behavior. Such observations, carefully reported as anecdotes by home economics teachers who are sensitive to problems of group relations, can make contributions to knowledge in this area. At the same time they can help the teacher make intelligent class groupings that ought to enhance the potentials for learning for her students.

Projective Tests

The basic idea of projective tests is that a person reveals his personality characteristics by the manner in which he responds to a structured situation in which he is permitted a relatively free response. Generally, the use of such techniques and their analyses are not within the scope of training of beginning home economics teachers; they are jobs requiring a high degree of training and skill. Probably the typical high school student has not taken a projective test.

The more commonly used projective tests include the Rorschach, which is based upon an individual's responses to a series of inkblots; the Thematic Apperception Test, which involves telling a story about a series of ambiguous pictures; and a variety of verbal-association projective tests, commonly called word-association and incomplete-sentence tests. From the point of view of the authors, projective techniques have

Classroom Distance Scale *

Name ______________________________ Date ______________
School ______________________________ Class ______________

We don't like all of our friends in the same way. Some we like more than others. There may be some people we don't like at all.

The checklist that follows will give you a way of telling how close an acquaintance you would like to have with other members of your home economics class.

Copy the names from the list in alphabetical order, in the vertical spaces at the top of the scale. Then, below each name, put a check in the space opposite the statement that most nearly describes your feeling about that person.

When you come to your own name, check the statement that describes how you think most of the students feel about you.

No one in class will see your paper except your teacher.

* Adapted from "Classroom Social Distance Scale," Horace Mann-Lincoln Institute of School Experimentation. In Ruth Cunningham and Associates, *Understanding Group Behavior of Boys and Girls.* New York: Teachers College, Columbia University, 1951, p. 405.

Checklist

Fill in the names of your classmates in the squares																
1. Would like to have her as one of my best friends.																
2. Would like to have her in my group but not as a close friend.																
3. Would like to be with her once in a while but not often or for long at a time.																
4. Don't mind her being in our classroom but I don't want to have anything to do with her.																
5. Wish she were not in our classroom.																

limited usefulness in helping beginning home economics teachers know their students better, since effective use of such techniques demands the use of specially trained personnel, such as clinical psychologists, psychiatrists, and psychodiagnosticians. Findings from projective tests, however, are useful to the teacher who works with exceptional students.

Use of the Conference Period

The conference period, which is sometimes a part of a home economics teacher's daily schedule, offers many opportunities for getting to know individual students. Through the professional use of a large number of the techniques discussed previously in your day-to-day teaching, you will come to recognize the individual differences in your students. Paolucci illustrated their use and the conference period as follows:

> An alert teacher is constantly aware of individual differences and helps the pupil operate within his own abilities and limitations. During the conference period individual help can be given. Because of the nature of their classes, home economics teachers are in a position to counsel their pupils personally. The conference period provides school time for the teachers to help the pupil with his personal problems. For example, one teacher was able to help a boy who was rejected by classmates become more socially acceptable to his peer group. She first became aware that he was an isolate through sociogramming the class. In an individual conference, she learned that he felt left out. He attended few school functions, for he had no real friends who cared whether he was there. He seemed to be compensating by always pushing himself to speak up in class, and to do assignments faster and better than his classmates. Through a series of conferences, he was helped to analyze his problem and try out some ways for solving it. He learned to work cooperatively rather than competitively with his classmates. Although progress was slow and not consistently smooth, the boy was helped to adjust to his peer group—for the adolescent this is of major importance.[7]

Often other teachers or the guidance staff in a local school refer students to a home economics teacher if they feel she has special abilities for helping a particular boy or girl. Chapter 11 discusses in detail ways of working with these students.

Whether you are working with an individual in a conference situation concerning personal or family problems or a discipline problem, or in terms of helping her make vocational choices, you may find the following guides to interviewing helpful: [8]

[7] Beatrice Paolucci, "A Look at Today's Homemaking Program." Bulletin of the National Association of Secondary-School Principals, *Home Economics in the Secondary School.* Washington, D.C.: Volume 37, Number 196, October, 1953, p. 13.

[8] Adapted from outline developed by staff of the Department of Guidance and Counselor Training, Michigan State University, East Lansing, Michigan.

1. Provide an atmosphere for the interview that is private, comfortable, warm, and informal.
2. Be friendly, personal, relaxed, and natural.
3. Do something to put the person at ease. If he finds it difficult during the beginning conversation, introduce a topic of mutual interest or discuss something of pride and accomplishment.
4. Exhibit a keen interest in the student and what he has to say. Find out what *he* considers important. Give him ample opportunity to tell his own story.
5. Help him to see his own problem. Try to help him focus his problem in proper perspective. Help him to become more objective about his statements.
6. Inquire regarding the steps he has already taken in attempting to solve his difficulties. Determine, if possible, how much interest he has in wanting to find better solutions.
7. Judge his actions objectively, if they have to be judged at all. Relate these attitudes to the student's standards and welfare.
8. Keep a friendly, sympathetic, and helpful relationship, but don't assume the responsibility for finding solutions to the student's problems.
9. Lead the individual to develop a definite plan of action for himself. When appropriate, suggest some possible next steps. Assist him to choose those plans that may prove most helpful, but leave the final decision to him. It is his life and he should have freedom to make his own choices. You can help him foresee the consequences of particular action steps.
10. Mention by title and location such books and other printed materials as might be helpful.
11. Curb the desire to preach, to moralize, to judge, or to make decisions.
12. Stimulate the student to think for himself and to develop his own plans.

THE HOME ECONOMICS TEACHER AS A TEACHER-COUNSELOR

Because of your background of professional education, and because of the informal nature of home economics, you are likely to be called upon to serve on the guidance committee in your local school, to act as a homeroom teacher, or to assume the responsibility of teacher-counselor. The informality of the home economics teaching setting provides a close contact with individual students. Because you know the student in his home and community setting as well as in the classroom, you are able to gain significant evidences of his behavior that should be indicative of his unique pattern of personal characteristics. To put this insight and knowledge to effective use, you can take action in two specific ways:

(1) you can use this background of understanding to adjust both the content and methods of your teaching so that it will harmonize with each individual's level of readiness; and (2) you can share with other professional persons the information you have gained concerning individual students. It is perhaps in this latter role that you can make one of your most pertinent contributions to the total guidance program in your local school. To the extent that you share with others significant evidences of a student's behavior, the major objectives of the school's guidance program can come closer to being achieved. Only as teachers share their perceptions regarding the needs of a particular youth and appreciate that some needs require concerted effort on the part of all teachers will they be fulfilling their guidance role of helping each individual become self-understanding and self-directing.

As a home economics teacher you have three very specific channels through which you can function in the guidance role—your classroom, home economics department club groups, and home visits. In your classroom you have an opportunity to get to know each student well. This personalized contact often puts you in a position for opening up opportunities for a youth to receive help in understanding and solving his problems. During the conference period you can personally guide him in those areas where you are particularly competent. Through such personal contacts with students you may find realistic avenues for referring those who need special help to the guidance personnel.

As you work with your students in promoting and implementing school and departmental club activities, both they and you gain knowledge of and interest in each other. In the chapter organization of national groups, such as Future Homemakers of America, you can help an individual find a niche in a peer group that will provide a natural outlet for many psychological and social needs. Youth needs to belong; these organizations offer opportunities to belong to an organization whose members are working toward a common goal—better home and community life for all. Youth needs to feel important and wanted; these organizations help a young person develop leadership qualities and learn ways of working with others. Youth has a desire for gregarious activity, ritual, and symbolism; these groups provide opportunities for such ceremonies. Members can participate in small-group activities as well as those that involve the entire national organization.

The primary source of information concerning the home economics program in a particular school is the home economics teacher. Both the guidance staff and you can profit by an exchange of factual information and ideas concerning that program and the potential it has for both boys and girls.

Opportunities for vocations and avocations in the field of home economics should be well known to you as a home economics teacher. You are the one most familiar with the resources in the home economics area to which both you and the guidance staff or other teachers may go for certain types of specific aids for helping people solve personal, family, and vocational problems. You are aware of the educational offerings and opportunities in the field of home economics which certain students may wish to pursue after completing high school, and you are in a position to suggest institutions of higher learning that might meet an individual's needs for further study in the home economics field. The combined efforts of you and the guidance staff are needed if others are to be informed concerning the place of home economics in the total school program and the values that are inherent in the program for different students.

Your primary responsibility as a home economics teacher is to teach home economics well. You should be responsible, however, for carrying out those aspects of the guidance program that are basic to effective instruction.

Selected References

Barry, Ruth, and Beverly Wolf, *Motives, Values, and Realities*. New York: Teachers College, Columbia University, 1966.

Coleman, James S., *The Adolescent Society*. New York: Free Press of Glencoe, 1961.

Combs, Arthur W., and Donald Snygg, *Individual Behavior*. New York: Harper and Row, 1959.

Gordon, Ira, *Studying the Child in the School*. New York: John Wiley and Sons, 1966.

Gronlund, Norman E., *Sociometry in the Classroom*. New York: Harper and Row, 1959.

Jennings, Helen H., *Sociometry in Group Relations* (2nd ed.). Washington, D.C.: American Council on Education, 1959.

Kelley, Earl C., *In Defense of Youth*. Englewood Cliffs, New Jersey: Prentice-Hall, 1962.

Kovar, Lillian C., *Faces of the Adolescent Girl*. Englewood Cliffs, New Jersey: Prentice-Hall, 1968.

PART III

Deciding What to Teach

6

Bases for Program Planning

A good home economics program does not just happen; it is the result of considered decision on the part of many persons. Its perspective for decision making is three-dimensional—its background is the tradition and foresight of the pioneers of the home economics movement; its broad purposes stem from the current social scene and the thinking and research of leaders in home economics and allied disciplines of the sciences, arts, and philosophy; and its emphasis and focal point is the particular individuals and families whom it purports to serve.

All decision is based on values; these evolve into our basic goals—our precepts for daily operation. We express these quite simply when we say, "I want . . . ." Since the birth of home economics as a field of study, a number of persons have expressed those basic beliefs and concerns which they felt would enrich the lives of family members. They believed that if man was to achieve the "good life" during his days on this earth, he needed to have the opportunity to lead a satisfying and productive life in his family group. To achieve this, most men needed help; the avenue for securing this help was through the educative process. The field of home economics was built upon the basic premise that man could realize his potential for effective individual and family living more easily and satisfactorily if three conditions were fulfilled: (1) a concerted effort was made to utilize all known information and to focus it on the needs and functions of the family; (2) a pin-pointed search for new knowledge was made to illuminate and alleviate blocks to gratifying home life; and (3) productive means for communicating this knowledge were found.

You, as the home economics teacher in a particular school setting, are the *crucial* factor in implementing the basic beliefs of home economics. You are the decision maker in your realm of operation—the daily round of class activities and the face-to-face contact with students and the families they represent. It is both your obligation and privilege to plan your home economics program so that each day your students will learn something that will enrich their lives as individuals as well as family members.

This is not an easy challenge; however, it is not as formidable as it might at first appear. The classroom teacher is responsible for planning and implementing a home economics program for a particular school situation; she is not, however, responsible for creating this program out of thin air, so to speak. She has available to her a number of resources to which she might turn; in fact, there are some sources to which she is obligated to turn. How then will you, the home economics teacher, plan a program that will meet those purposes of home economics education to which you are dedicated? What do you need to know to be able to plan a program on a sound basis? Where do you turn for help? From what specific background of experience, information, and knowledge can you draw? How can you expedite the procedure and at the same time not become overwhelmed or frustrated by the job you are outlining for yourself? The purposes of this chapter are (1) to help you see the importance of structure in home economics (including concepts, generalizations, and problems) in providing a common element for all home economics programs; and (2) to outline some bases for program planning that should help you develop a home economics program tailor-made for *your students* and *your community*.

Educational programs are built on a somewhat common foundation. This common foundation is composed of the structure of a particular field of study; research and thinking concerning the social relevance of a field; and research and thinking concerning the growth and development of those individuals for whom a particular educational program is designed. You have had, through your professional education, insight into why these particular building blocks are essential to the establishment of a firm foundation for an educational program. Now your job becomes that of relating this generalized background of knowledge to the formation of a home economics program. Although you may have an opportunity, as you work with community or state groups, to formulate overall plans for home economics education, more likely you will be concerned with understanding how the broad overall pattern came to be and how you will tailor it to your situation. Those responsible for planning the overall program for states, cities, and communities have considered certain specific criteria and made decisions that have resulted in a proposed plan from which you will build your program. Understanding the bases upon which home economics programs are built will help you develop and implement your program on the local level.

THE STRUCTURE OF HOME ECONOMICS

All fields of study periodically undergo considerable scrutiny in an attempt to discover the best way to transmit knowledge and solve problems. With the vast increase in knowledge and the many ways for disseminating it has come the increased responsibility for educators to select that particular knowledge which is most relevant for the schools to teach. In the past decade, especially, home economics educators have been concentrating upon examining and defining the field so that they might plan educational programs more logically and meaningfully. Their efforts have been directed toward attempting to determine the structure of home economics. Structure of an area of study is a way of classifying and categorizing concepts (ideas) so that one can more easily see relationships among concepts and draw generalizations that will make knowledge useful, and give it meaning. Knowing the structure of a field helps one to (1) see how one concept is logically related to another concept, thereby making an area of study comprehensive and meaningful; (2) understand the interrelationship of sets of concepts, thus facilitating the development of generalizations that make transfer of learning from situation to situation possible; and (3) identify levels of concept formation, thus making it possible to plan *logical sequences of learning.*[1]

One way to determine the structure of a field is to formulate a theoretical framework comprised of concepts, operational definitions, assumptions, hypothetical relationships, and empirical data, and then to use these to explain an aspect of reality. Recent national projects aimed at curriculum reform in home economics have used this approach.[2] Examples of the concept approach will be found in the next section of this chapter.

Another approach to the structure of a field is that of identifying those competences needed by individuals to solve problems. This approach integrates the knowledge (concepts) from diverse disciplines, interpreting and communicating these concepts in such a manner that specific prob-

[1] For further discourse on the functions of structure see G. W. Ford and Lawrence Pugne (ed.), *The Structure of Knowledge and the Curriculum.* Chicago: Rand McNally and Co., 1964; Jerome S. Bruner, *The Process of Education.* Cambridge, Mass.: Harvard University Press, 1962; and Asahel D. Woodruff, *Basic Concepts of Teaching.* San Francisco: Chandler, 1961.

[2] See *Concepts and Generalizations: Their Place in High School Home Economics Curriculum Development.* Washington, D.C.: American Home Economics Association, 1967; and *Home Economics Seminar,* A Progress Report. French Lick, Indiana, July 24–28, 1961.

lems can be solved. Home economists have a long history of structuring the field in this manner.[3]

We shall discuss each of these approaches briefly because each has relevance for assisting you in determining what to teach and in planning your home economics program.

Concepts and Generalizations Approach

This approach is based on the assumption that home economics is a discipline with its own body of knowledge, composed of given concepts, definitions, assumptions, and hypothetical relationships from which one can make generalizations that help in understanding and explaining the everyday behavior of individuals as they function in the family setting. Operating from this premise, home economics leaders have identified specific concepts and organized them into content areas.

Concepts

Mallory has defined concepts as follows:

> Concepts are abstractions used to organize the world of objects and events into a smaller number of categories. They have many dimensions and meanings and constitute the recurrent themes which occur throughout the curriculum in a cumulative and overarching fashion.[4]

Chart 1 identifies five subject matter areas: human development and the family; home management and family economics; foods and nutrition; textiles and clothing; and housing. Concepts fundamental to each area have been listed. With these concepts, teachers can help students formulate and understand certain concepts, discover the relationships that exist among concepts, and draw generalizations that will help them explain the real world. Obviously the listing is subject to change as new knowledge becomes available.

[3] See *Home Economics: New Directions.* Washington, D.C.: American Home Economics Association, 1959; *The Field of Home Economics—What It Is.* Washington, D.C.: American Home Economics Association, 1964; Elizabeth J. Simpson, "Projections in Home Economics Education." *American Vocational Journal,* **40**: 41–43, November 1965; and Paul L. Dressel, "Organization in Higher Education, With Special Relevance to Home Economics." Paper delivered at meeting of National Association of State Universities and Land Grant Colleges, Chicago, Illinois, May 1968.

[4] Berenice Mallory, "Curriculum Developments," *Bulletin of the National Association of Secondary-School Principals,* **48**: 56, December 1964.

CHART I Outline of Basic Areas and Concepts in Home Economics

Human Development and the Family
- I. Universality of individuals and families
- II. Uniqueness of individuals and families
- III. Development and socialization of the individual
- IV. Challenge and creative possibilities of change

Home Management and Family Economics
- I. Environmental influences on individual and family management
  - A. Societal
  - B. Economic
- II. Managerial processes
  - A. Decision-making
  - B. Organization of activities
- III. Effective elements in management
  - A. Resources and their utilization
  - B. Values, goals, and standards

Foods and Nutrition
- I. Significance of food
  - A. As related to cultural and socioeconomic influences
  - B. As related to nutrition
  - C. As related to physiological and psychological satisfactions
- II. Nature of food
  - A. Chemical and physical properties
  - B. Factors effecting change in properties of food
- III. Provision of food
  - A. Production
  - B. Consumer practices
  - C. Protective measures
  - D. Management of resources

Textiles and Clothing
- I. Significance of textiles and clothing to the individual in society
  - A. Interrelationship of clothing and culture
  - B. Social and psychological aspects of clothing
  - C. Clothing as a medium for artistic perception, expression, and experience
  - D. Textiles and clothing in the economy
  - E. Physiological aspects of clothing and textiles
- II. Nature of textiles and clothing
  - A. Textiles
  - B. Garments
- III. Acquisition and use of textiles and clothing
  - A. Selection
  - B. Use and care
  - C. Responsibilities of consumers

CHART I *(continued)*

Housing
- I. Influence of housing on people
  - A. Physical and psychological
  - B. Social
- II. Factors influencing the form and use of housing
  - A. Human
  - B. Environmental
- III. Processes in providing housing
  - A. Designing
  - B. Selecting
  - C. Building
  - D. Financing
  - E. Furnishing and equipment
  - F. Managing
  - G. Maintaining *

* *Concepts and Generalizations: Their Place in High School Home Economics Curriculum Development.* Washington, D.C.: American Home Economics Association, 1967, pp. 25–52 (excerpts).

Generalizations

Mallory's definition of generalizations is:

> *Generalizations* express underlying truth, have an element of universality, and usually indicate relationships. Generalizations help give meaning to concepts. They are based on objective data, on experience, or on theory accepted by specialists in the field.[5]

The distinction between concepts and generalizations can be observed in the full report from which the list of concepts was drawn. For example, under the concept of "Managerial Processes," the following generalizations have been suggested:

1. Decision-making reflects varying degrees of rationality.
2. Decisions are affected by the interaction of factors which influence managerial behavior.
3. Rational decisions represent choices resulting from logical analyses of the elements of situations.
4. The decisions of individuals and families reflect differences in the perception of goals and goal achievements.
5. Satisfactory decisions may involve family members in different ways at different times.

[5] Mallory, op. cit., p. 56.

6. Disadvantages as well as advantages are usually inherent in the alternatives involved in a decision or choice.
7. Risk and uncertainty in decision-making vary with people and situations.[6]

Hoover has shown that three levels of development can be identified in the generalizations written by college students:

1. Definition, description, or classification; e.g., empathic ability is the process of projecting oneself into the role of another person and observing why he acts and feels as he does. It is also differentiating between the role of another and oneself.
2. Relationship among ideas; e.g., a child develops a self-concept as family members give their evaluations of him.
3. Explanation, justification, interpretation, or prediction (seeing cause-effect relationships and predicting consequences); e.g., communication promotes growth of healthy personalities; problem-solving is easier; needs and desires can be met if they are known; and understanding is at a peak when communication is productive.

Implied in this generalization is an understanding of the value of communication in personal development and in resolving conflicts and promoting understanding among individuals.[7]

You have, during your lifetime, been developing concepts in the subject matter of home economics through a variety of formal and informal experiences. In your college career in home economics you have had courses in each of the subject matter areas. These were oriented toward providing experiences that would assist you in formulating concepts and generalizations about human development and the family, home management and family economics, foods and nutrition, textiles and clothing, and housing. Your role in teaching home economics at a level lower than the college level will not be exactly the same as the role of the college teacher of specialized subject matter in home economics. The college teacher is concerned primarily with preparing professional persons in home economics; you are concerned primarily with orienting your teaching toward making contributions to better family life through the various areas of home economics for persons who are, in the large part, not going to be specialists in the field, but who are going to be using what they learn in their day-to-day living as family members. The basic concepts of the subject matter areas are essentially the same, however, for all levels—college, high school, elementary school. Therefore,

[6] *Concepts and Generalizations: Their Place in High School Home Economics Curriculum Development,* op. cit., p. 29.

[7] Helene M. Hoover, "Levels of Conceptual Understanding," *Journal of Home Economics,* **59**: 90–91, February 1967.

understanding the structure of a field—its concepts, the interrelationship among its concepts, and resultant principles and generalizations—is of major significance. This structure provides an essential base for determining educational objectives, the bedrock of effective learning.

Problem Approach

Knowledge can also be structured by determining problems that need solution. Fields of knowledge structured from this premise are termed "derivative fields" rather than "basic disciplines." These areas of study draw knowledge from particular related disciplines and integrate this knowledge in a new way, thus synthesizing new concepts and generalizations that are useful in explaining unique problems and communicating the new concepts so that particular problems can be solved. Nolan sees home economics as a derivative field that focuses on problems facing families; on "realities of living rather than on an organized set of thoughts, concepts, and principles derived from application, e.g. medicine focuses on the health of the individual, home economics on the well-being of families." [8]

Home economics from its beginning has been structured around problems. Home economics as a field of study came into existence because a group of farsighted individuals were concerned with such everyday problems as health, sanitation, nutrition, housekeeping, economy, and child care. As a result of their belief that scientific knowledge should be used to alleviate these problems, home economics was born. Early leaders defined the field as "the study of laws, conditions, principles, and ideals which are concerned on the one hand with man's immediate physical environment and on the other with his nature as a special being and especially of the relationship between these two factors." [9]

Present day home economists use essentially the same definition for the field but define the environment and man's social being more precisely. They view the crucial aspect of home economics as the particular relationship or interaction that exists between man and his near environment." [10]

Through the years, as a problem orientation has been used to structure the field, there has existed a more or less agreed upon focus—concern for the well-being of individuals in the family setting. The central

[8] *The Field of Home Economics—What It Is,* Washington, D.C.: American Home Economics Association, 1964, p. 55.

[9] Lake Placid Conference on Home Economics, *Proceedings of the Fourth Annual Conference,* Lake Placid, New York, Sept. 16–20, 1902, p. 71.

[10] Creekmore, Anna, "The Concept Basic To Home Economics." *Journal of Home Economics,* **60**: 93–102, February 1968.

problem to which home economists have purported to address themselves has been that of assisting the individual to find satisfaction and fulfillment through a viable home and family life.[11]

Home economics educators whose primary concern has been that of developing programs for the pre-college level have placed emphasis upon problems that have been "family-centered." They believe that what the student learns in home economics ultimately is used in a family—whether this is his own present family in which he is a child or teenage youth; the family in which he is a parent or adult member, if he is a student in an adult class; or the new family that he will establish when he marries.

McGinnis has identified the family-centered teaching program as one that: [12]

1. relates all phases of subject matter to the entire life cycle of the family.
2. takes account of the cultural level or background from which family members come as well as the one to which they now belong.
3. is based on knowledge of the conditions under which families are living today.
4. emphasizes the changing roles of men, women, and children within the family group.
5. relates all subject matter to costs in terms of personal or family resources.
6. increases student's ability and confidence in making decisions and learning to accept the "rightness" of her own judgment in choice making.
7. enhances the worth and dignity of each member of the family and decreases guilt feelings.
8. develops competencies in the performance of routine homemaking tasks in ways which lead to enhanced respect for oneself and one's job.
9. fortifies individual families to be free to set their own goals and make their own choices.
10. emphasizes decision making wherein unity, rather than conflict and bitterness, results from differences.
11. provides practice in group processes.

[11] Many persons question whether the field in reality holds this unified purpose. An examination of programs and/or courses indicates a lack of clarity of central purpose. For discussions on this point see Marjorie Brown, "Values in Home Economics." *Journal of Home Economics,* **59**: 769–775, December 1967; *The Field of Home Economics—What It Is.* Washington, D.C.: American Home Economics Association, 1964; and Paul L. Dressel, *College and University Curriculum.* Berkeley, Calif.: McCutchan Publishing Corp., 1968, pp. 125–127.

[12] Esther McGinnis, "Family Centered Teaching." *Journal of Home Economics,* **44**:9–12, January 1952.

12. includes learning experiences with children—from infancy through adolescence.
13. provides help for young people who are disturbed or upset about their family backgrounds and experiences.

Making your teaching family centered is a matter of structure and adaptation of learning experiences in the light of that structure. To be able to do this, you will need an appreciation for and understanding of the families with whom you will be working. Structuring your home economics program around problems of these families will make your program unique.

One prospective teacher of home economics tested her ability to make a particular area of study family-centered by putting her thinking into writing prior to planning learning experiences for high school students. It appeared thus:

> It is important that the home economics teacher teach students to maintain an adequate diet. Many teenagers do not realize the necessity of proper foods. Therefore, one goal of my foods class will be to teach the students how to plan, prepare, and maintain an adequate diet for themselves and their families. They can practice planning nutritionally adequate diets; they can incorporate this learning into their present families; and they should be able to feed their future families properly.
>
> This goal should be attainable in the program for advanced high school students. Both boys and girls ought to be included because the role of the male is changing; nowadays, the male accepts some of the responsibilities of the home, including responsibilities centering around feeding the family. Through actual class participation, boys and girls will be able to accept and practice this trend by working together in groups.
>
> The general topics to be studied will be: principles of nutrition; management of work, money, and equipment allocated toward feeding the family; marketing; and skills for preparing and serving food. Emphasis can be placed on solving the particular managerial problems related to food that arise from limitations of time, materials, and money. Since my chief goal is adequate nutrition, the main portion of time will be spent acquiring knowledge about adequate diets. Preparing and serving food will be worked in with this phase. First, the principles of nutrition will be taught in relation to the students' needs. They will be shown how to determine the needs of their own families. While they are learning about diets for their families, they can also be taught to see the different nutrition requirements for differing chronological ages of the various members of the family. We might also explore feeding patterns in other cultural groups.
>
> An important aspect of family-centered teaching is pointing out to the students the importance of time and energy use. Time and energy utilization will be taught along with planning diets and preparing foods. It is important for me to consider the cultural background of my students and relate this to

the teaching of budgeting. Students should be realistic about food costs, and this will be brought out while planning diets. Cost analysis can be included with the diet analysis, so that students will become familiar with the actual cost of feeding a family. They will also be able to practice this in their own buying of foods. They can compare food prices when studying purchasing. The school lunch room will be an ideal place for them to evaluate food and food prices. They can keep track of what the lunch costs and then see what the nutritional values amount to. Although the main goal is to teach adequate nutrition, some marketing will be included. The topic of school lunches may be studied for several days. In class we can consider the types of food available, preparation, techniques needed, and resources used. The students can figure nutritional value of several different lunches and then prepare a typical lunch.

As the teacher, I will have the responsibility of determining beforehand the socio-economic level of my students. I should know the emphasis that each family puts on food, so that I will then be able to gear my teaching toward the particular family. The students will gain practice in food selection, and will thus become more secure about planning, preparing, and selecting adequate diets. Each person should be able to plan diets suited to his or her own needs and those of the family. The students should be encouraged to plan diets which the individual family will accept. Toward the end of the learning experience, I should be able to see a marked change in the student's eating habits. I will listen for evidence that these food practices have been accepted in the students' homes.

One of the mental steps you will want to take before deciding upon a particular experience for your class is that of checking to see if the experience meets some of the criteria for family centeredness. This is one way of assuring yourself that the learning will have meaning for your students and that it has potential for improving family living. One danger in stressing family centeredness is that a program can become too narrow—you must avoid placing so much stress on the learner's own family that he forgets his responsibility to other families in the community and around the world. Particularly in the study of nutrition, you have real opportunities to expand the social awareness and concern of students who live in a country of surplus food, and who have had little or no opportunity to observe the serious nutritional deficiencies that are common in other countries.

Spafford and Amidon have identified the purposes of a home economics program at the secondary level as guiding those it teaches to

. . . establish values which will give greatest meaning to their personal, family, and community living.

. . . create a home and community environment conducive to the healthy growth and development of all the members of the family.

. . . achieve wholesome and satisfying interpersonal relationships within the school, home, and community.

. . . use their resources to provide the means for satisfying needs, developing interests, and using capacities to attain the values and goals considered most worthwhile for the individual, the family, and the community.

. . . develop mutual understanding and appreciation of differing cultures and ways of life and cooperate with people of other cultures who are striving to raise their level of living.[13]

For the fiftieth anniversary of the American Home Economics Association in 1959, the Philosophy and Objectives Committee formulated the following statement concerning the structure of home economics:

Home economics is the field of knowledge and service primarily concerned with strengthening family life through:

educating the individual for family living

improving the services and goods used by families

conducting research to discover the changing needs of individuals and families and the means of satisfying these needs

furthering community, national, and world conditions favorable to family living.[14]

This same committee pointed out the direction toward which home economics programs should move:

We believe that the clearest new direction for home economics is to help people identify and develop certain fundamental competences that will be effective in personal and family living regardless of the particular circumstances of the individual or family.

Fundamental to effective living are the competences to:

establish values which give meaning to personal, family, and community living; select goals appropriate to these values

create a home and community environment conducive to the healthy growth and development of all members of the family at all stages of the family cycle

achieve good interpersonal relationships within the home and within the community

nurture the young and foster their physical, mental, and social growth and development

make and carry out intelligent decisions regarding the use of personal, family, and community resources

[13] Ivol Spafford and Edna P. Amidon, *Studies of Home Economics in High School and in Adult Education Programs 1955–58*. Voc. Div. Bull. No. 286, H. E. Ed. Series No. 32. Washington, D.C.: U.S. Department of Health, Education, and Welfare, Office of Education, 1960, p. 3.

[14] *Home Economics—New Directions: A Statement of Philosophy and Objectives*. Washington, D.C.: American Home Economics Association, 1959, p. 4.

establish long-range goals for financial security and work toward their achievement

plan consumption of goods and services—including food, clothing, and housing—in ways that will promote values and goals established by the family

purchase consumer goods and services appropriate to an overall consumption plan and wise use of economic resources

perform the tasks of maintaining a home in such a way that they will contribute effectively to furthering individual and family goals

enrich personal and family life through the arts and humanities and through refreshing and creative use of leisure

take an intelligent part in legislative and other social action programs which directly affect the welfare of individuals and families

develop mutual understanding and appreciation of differing cultures and ways of life, and co-operate with people of other cultures who are striving to raise levels of living.[15]

Given that changes in the functions of the family have occurred since 1959, necessitating identification of new competences based on new concepts, then structuring a field around relevant problems and competences needed to alleviate them is a fruitful approach.

Dressel has suggested using a structure for organizing home economics in higher education that begins with a problem and identifies essential concepts that lead to the solution of the problem. He says that such a college would

> be concerned with relationships between people and their environment, and would study these in order to improve living conditions and assist each individual and family to achieve his and their fullest potential. Such a college would be concerned with three things:
>
> 1. It would educate individuals (generalists) to provide assistance and counsel to improve family life.
> 2. It would provide more specialized education for specialists who direct, advise, and assist the generalist in his work with families. This recognizes that there would be levels of competences and specialization needed.
> 3. It would involve interdisciplinary research to improve the process of family service, to determine the appropriate interrelationships of needs, of values, and of processes as they are involved both in family life and in curricular decisions.
>
> Such a college would have an instructional core involving the analysis of family structure and functioning. It would be concerned with knowledge, with the identification, planning, and utilization of research findings, with

[15] Ibid., pp. 8–9.

communications, and it would emphasize the development of processes for assisting families which are consistent with the essential values and which provide solutions consistent with these values.

... The structure of the college itself ... should be derived out of commitments as to the nature of the job to be done and the best ways of approaching it. Study and improvement of the family require agreements on essential needs, essential values, and essential agents or processes. Under essential needs, five require consideration: *food, clothing, shelter, affection,* and *socialization.* The case for each of these as essential to the happiness of an adult and especially to the development of a child is well documented by research. There might, of course, be four or six essential needs rather than five. Generally we err by listing too many concepts and dissipate our energies arguing about them rather than recognizing that a limited number of carefully chosen fundamental concepts will, if pursued with energy and endurance, usually draw in all significant ones. Five essential values require attention: *aesthetics, ethics, hygienics, coherence* (or order or meaning), and *happiness.* Again the number or the particulars are debatable. Essentially, these five state that beauty, morality, friendliness, health, a sense of meaning, and a sense of well-being are the values to be developed by family life. The five essential needs, then, are contributing factors to the attainment of the five values, but certain essential processes must be involved to effect this coalescence of needs and values. First, there must be *allocation of available resources.* Second, and in some senses comprehending the first, is a pattern of *decision-making* or family *governance.* The third essential process in the family, *education,* recognizes that some of the most significant development of the child takes place in the early years prior to school attendance. The educational deficiencies of many home environments provide a handicap from which individuals seldom, if ever, recover completely. The fourth essential is *production.* It comprehends not only the work done by individuals in the family outside of the home which provides the financial resources but also the responsibilities and the work in the home itself. A fifth essential process agent, *recreation,* asserts that families must learn to play together as well as work and live together. The focus on the family involves developing a program which will permit analysis of the operations of a family and the development of suggestions to improve living conditions. It proceeds by considering how the essential agents or processes are utilized in attaining essential values while meeting essential needs ...[16]

Understanding the structure of a field provides one basic element for making decisions about what to teach. You will also need to understand the social relevance of home economics if you are to plan an effective program.

[16] Dressel, Paul L. "Organization in Higher Education, with Special Relevance to Home Economics." Paper delivered at meeting of National Association of State Universities and Land-Grant Colleges, Chicago, Ill., May, 1968, pp. 6–8.

OUR SOCIETY—ITS VALUES AND NEEDS

Education is obligated to help the members of a society learn the ways of living within that society. Individuals must learn what is expected of them in the multiplicity of roles they will play as they complete their life cycle. Along with learning what is expected of them, they must also learn what they must do in order to meet this expectation and, equally important, in what manner they can operate acceptably to achieve it. This is known as the socialization process; it is the shaping of an individual so that he can function in a particular society.

You live—and will teach, most likely—in a society dedicated to the democratic way of life; hence, you are obligated to perpetuate and exemplify democratic values. A democratic society places value on (1) the dignity and worth of individuals; (2) concern for the general well-being of others, and the exerting of cooperative group effort toward solving problems of common concern; and (3) rational thinking as a tool for decision making.

Worth of Individuals

Home economics programs reflect an acceptance of these values when they are planned to reach all individuals regardless of color, socio-economic status, or intellectual capacity. Respect for the individual is evidenced in recognizing that individuals have the right and obligation to pursue their own private sets of values, standards, and goals, so long as they assume the responsibility for the consequences of their actions. You can implement this belief in such ways as gearing your home furnishings learnings to various socio-economic levels or providing students with books geared to their reading level.

Our changing society places ever-increasing stresses on family stability. As you help to clarify individual and family values, don't forget the contributions home economics can make to the lives of single persons. First of all, each person is an *individual* whom you can help to live more effectively. He needs to clarify his values in relation to contemporary social issues. He can improve the quality of his home and community environment. He can become a more competent consumer. Some individuals who are single should receive help in interpreting their goals and planning for family life. But don't neglect those young people who will remain single throughout life and perhaps live alone many years. Also, remember the needs of the single person who may be the head of a household—one which may include elderly relatives or young children. Then, too, there are large numbers of widowed persons who face years of intense loneliness, and home economics can assist them in adjusting to the "single life." Your teaching can help these individuals maintain a sense of dignity, while enabling all of your students to develop greater understanding of the needs of single persons in a society that emphasizes the family.

General Welfare

The broad purposes of home economics are concerned with the general welfare of all families. Through helping individuals in families realize their potential, home economics helps them to raise their level of living.

In a democracy the edict of one person does not usually carry sufficient force to bring about a change; rather, group changes are brought about because of cooperative group action. The family is the first laboratory in which the individual learns that through group action common goals can be achieved. Working as a class or in smaller groups within a class, home economics classes can provide practice in using cooperative effort to arrive at solutions to group problems. This experience is provided when young people work in groups to prepare and serve meals, or when four or five students are encouraged to experiment with alternative methods for solving a common problem, such as creating safe play space for children or examining different sources for financing the purchase of furniture. Such activities as seeing that students assume responsibility for the care of the equipment in the classroom, listen attentively to the ideas expressed by their classmates, and "pitch in" to help a family acquire appropriate legal aid—all of these are avenues you can utilize to give practice in cooperative action to solve a problem of common concern.

Sound Decision Making

A democratic society depends upon intelligent decision making as the means for achieving answers to problems. Western culture places value on the process of rational decision making; hence, education in the American culture is obligated to become education for choice making. Margaret Mead has said:

> . . . we must turn all of our educational efforts to training our children for the choices that will confront them. Education . . . instead of being a special pleading for one regime, a desperate attempt to form one particular habit of mind which will withstand all outside influences, must be a preparation for those very influences . . . The children must be taught how to think, not what to think . . . They must be taught that many ways are open to them, no one sanctioned above its alternative, and that upon them and upon them alone lies the burden of choice.[17]

[17] Margaret Mead, "Coming of Age in Samoa," From *The South Seas,* p. 246. Copyright 1928, 1930, 1935, and 1939 by Margaret Mead. By permission of William Morrow and Co., New York, N.Y.

If the home economics classroom is to help boys and girls learn to think rationally—to make intelligent choices—opportunities for making choices must be a part of the daily classroom routine. You will need to take the time to help your students become aware of the processes of decision making. Much of the time spent in the classroom will be devoted to some phase of the decision making process. Yours will be the task of helping your students become aware of the decisions that normally need to be made in family living, of helping them think through alternative means for arriving at a decision, of finding information and knowledge essential to the intelligent choice of an alternative, of developing some skill in selecting an alternative or mediating among alternatives and carrying the alternative to the point of action, and of helping them see the necessity of assuming responsibility for the consequence of their choice. Most teachers recognize that a greater part of their teaching is geared toward choice making; they need to be equally concerned that they are helping students become aware of that choice making and of the processes they use in arriving at a decision. Students need to be familiar with the kinds of decisions families make and the processes they use for making these choices. Paolucci has categorized family decisions into three groups: social (integrative), economic (allocating), and technical (implementing). She says:

> The process of arriving at a choice in these categories is conceptualized differently . . . Social decision-making occurs in those situations in the family where there is conflict in values or goals. Social decision-making aims to bring the values and goals of the family unit to some level of integration. Here the choice does not consist of selecting one particular alternative because it best maximizes a given goal, but rather the decision process is geared toward creating a new alternative out of an indefinite number of possibilities present in the decision situation. The choice is a result of *mediation* rather than *selection*. In mediation a melding of courses of action rather than a selection or rejection occurs. In a value or goal conflict situation a pre-determined goal is not possible to determine; the goals emerge as change takes place. In this kind of situation, typical when a family decision has consequences that impinge on more than one family member, the choice becomes one of changing some of the values and goals involved and adjusting other psychocultural factors to arrive at some level of resolution. The process of decision-making in social decisions is one of order and direction of change, creating new alternatives out of the milieu possible in the field of choice, rather than selecting one alternative and rejecting all others.
>
> Economic decision-making requires ordering, evaluating and selecting ends. It occurs when ends are competitive. These ends are evaluated by *comparing* the returns possible for each in a given situation, and the end selected is the one that promises to yield greatest return from available resources. A single end may be chosen, or several ends in a given rank order are determined.

(The achievement of one end implies the sacrificing of another end to some degree.) Economic decision-making requires that goals be stated in such a manner that they can be compared and that available resources be known and in some degree measurable so they can be objectively allocated.

Technical decision-making requires that a goal be clearly stated; resources needed for implementing the goal determined and allocated. A technical decision is a procedural decision—the process is one of selecting the most efficient means of implementing or taking action. Few conditions exist within a family setting that do not require social, economic and/or technical decision processes. A model for family decision-making must, therefore, allow for a mediation of goals and values as well as for the selection and ordering of goals and the determination of the most efficient procedure for implementing when a goal is predetermined.[18]

Teaching these decision making processes is feasible in any number of classroom experiences. A home economics teacher can help students become aware of some of the many decisions homemakers make daily and at the same time help them to recognize the processes used for making a decision.

The following illustrates a decision making situation with which one teacher and her class were faced and the process they used for arriving at this technical choice.

Situation: Planning session for meal preparation laboratory
Decision to be made: Kind of pie for dessert
Alternatives considered:

1. Make the pie "from scratch."
2. Purchase a frozen pie.
3. Purchase a bakery pie.
4. Purchase a premixed pastry and filling.

Choice: Purchased bakery pie.

Resources considered: Class time was limited; therefore, it would not be possible to prepare the pie and the other foods that were planned for the meal. Students had little or no skill in making pie, so possibilities for making a satisfactory product in limited time were slim. Added cost for bakery product was not a limiting factor; the quality of a ready-baked product was acceptable to the group.

Consequences of action taken:

1. Girls did not learn to bake a pie—one of the outcomes they had earlier expressed an interest in achieving.

[18] Paolucci, Beatrice, "Decision-making in the Family." Paper delivered at the joint meeting of Child Development–Family Relations and Home Management–Family Economics Section, Annual Meeting of American Home Economics Association, Dallas, Texas, June, 1967, pp. 4–5.

2. Spending the extra money for the ready-prepared pie meant they had less money to spend in the next meal.
3. Meal was completed in allotted class time; in general, it was nutritious, attractive, and satisfactory.

This teacher might have encouraged the class to try out each alternative as a means of providing them with knowledge, information, and skill for making a similar decision in another situation. She did, however, help them to recognize the kind of decision they were making, the alternatives that were available, and the consequences of their decision. Can you see how you might use this same procedure for developing understanding and use of other decision making processes?

Effects of Social and Technological Changes

Western society is oriented to science and technology and to the changes they produce. Technological developments have brought about and will continue to bring about drastic changes in the socioeconomic setting of the family. Because of increased industrialization during the past few decades, families have become consuming units to a greater extent. Mechanization has made it necessary for families to find new jobs. Ease of transportation has made families mobile. Increased knowledge has changed the population picture—people live longer, marry earlier, and need more education in order to fulfill new employment roles. Roles of family members are changing—women work outside the home, children earn spending money at an earlier age yet, paradoxically, remain economically dependent for a longer period of time, and men share in homemaking activities. Advances in mass media and communication have raised the levels of aspiration of all people—seeing, hearing, and knowing what others have and what is available has increased wants. Increased technology and mass production have created changes in the economic structure that have resulted in rising income levels, more ample and varied consumption, increased leisure, and the use of material gains to promote better living conditions.

The rapid social and technological changes have created new functions for the family and consequently new concerns and problems. When family members are disadvantaged by inferior education that limits employability and by inadequate food and housing that impair health, the fruits of an advanced science and technology become liabilities rather than assets. Expectations are roused, but opportunities for meeting these aspirations are curtailed. Families, especially those families in the urban ghetto, have been in part victims of too rapid change. A major social need is that of narrowing the gap that exists between "advantaged, affluent" families and "disadvantaged, poverty-stricken" families in the United States. This is particularly true of the black family in the urban ghetto, which, because of race, has been particularly disadvantaged. Ghetto families have special problems because they often have low incomes, large numbers of dependent children, and mothers who are absent from the home while working to maintain the one-parent household. From the standpoint of health, this deprivation means deficient diets, inadequate shelter and clothing, lack of medical care, which leads to low energy levels and high infant mortality, and low levels of sanitation due to inappropriate facilities.

Change is inevitable. One of the primary obligations you will have as a home economics teacher is that of helping your students learn to adapt to and cope with the changes that affect family life. This means helping *all* students find satisfactory ways of raising the level of living in *their* family and in addition helping each student develop those attitudes and skills that will make him employable.

Scientific innovations, especially those based on biological breakthroughs, have precipitated a so-called sexual revolution. This, in concert with social and technological change, has resulted in a new emphasis and demand for family life and sex education.

Home economics teachers have a key role in family life education. Yours will be the opportunity to help transmit to young people knowledge that will enhance their chances for success in marriage and family life. In preparation for this role, you will need the competencies and knowledge outlined by the Governor's Task Force in Michigan:

1. Physical, emotional, intellectual, and social development of persons through the life cycle.
2. Human sexuality, including, but not limited to, sexual identity and behavior, family planning and reproduction, emotionality, intimacy and values.
3. Management of practical realities of everyday living, such as feeding, housing, clothing, financing, and child rearing.
4. Psychosocial dynamics of family relationships.
5. Family interaction with such aspects of society as government and law, religion and education, economy and employment, recreation and civic participation.
6. Cultural and sub-cultural family patternings, such as variations according to ethnicity, religion, socio-economic class, et al.[19]

[19] "Recommendations for Preparation of Family Life Education." Second Report of the Governor's Task Force on University and Family Life, 1968.

Social, scientific and technological changes have made individuals, families, communities, and worlds increasingly interrelated and interdependent. It is no longer possible to exist completely independent as a family or, for that matter, as a nation. What happens to one family has ramifications for other families; scientific innovations developed in the United States have direct implications for the way of life of family members all over the world. Increased mobility has increased the possibility that an individual will live some part of his life with or among people whose way of life is considerably different from the pattern of living into which he was born. Educators are obligated to help boys and girls understand the culture of other peoples—the way they live and why their ways of meeting basic needs are satisfactory for them. You, as an educator in home economics, can help students acquire this understanding through many aspects of home economics. For example, when studying child development, your students may do comparative studies of child-rearing practices of various families within their own community or those of families of other nations. Food units can be built around meals eaten in other countries. Understanding meal patterns of other cultures aids in broadening the horizon of understanding. Through food habits, your students can better understand the tempo and ways of living in other lands.

Curriculum guides developed by leaders in home economics education reflect an understanding of and a desire to meet what are believed to be the important needs of a particular society at a designated time in history. The way you interpret these needs and implement them in the learning experiences you plan for your students determines whether they will be met.

UNDERSTANDING HUMAN GROWTH AND DEVELOPMENT

Basic to setting the stage for learning is a keen understanding of how human beings grow and develop. Through the combined efforts of many disciplines, but primarily those of psychology, sociology, physiology, and human development, there is now available a reliable body of knowledge that has facilitated this understanding. Continuous research in human behavior will add to this important area of knowledge. Many of the changes in educational procedure during the past few decades have come as a result of implementing human behavior research findings.

Currently there are many basic guides that we can use to attain a better understanding of human growth and development. Basically, they evolve from the theoretical construct that every individual is unique—he grows at his own rate, has his own pattern and ultimate level, and develops as a whole person through simultaneous and interrelated physical, mental, emotional, and social growth.

Psychosocial and Cultural Factors

A group of psychiatrists listed some "universal tasks of adolescents that transcend cultural differences and thus apply to all individuals." These include:

1. All adolescents must learn. What they learn differs from one culture to another.

2. The adolescent must move from his family of origin to a different (his own) family of procreation. To do this, he must sever close ties with the nuclear family and establish them with blood strangers.

3. He must change from being nurtured to providing nurture.

4. Each adolescent is expected to learn how to work and how to love. Both of these abilities are necessary to his functioning as an adult.[20]

Developmental Tasks

A theoretical framework commonly used by home economists as a basis for program planning relative to human growth and development is the developmental task construct. Havighurst defined a developmental task as:

> . . . a task which arises at or about a certain period in the life of the individual, successful achievement of which leads to his happiness and to success with later tasks, while failure leads to unhappiness in the individual, disapproval by society, and difficulty with later tasks.[21]

The developmental task approach has as its framework research and knowledge concerning the physical maturation of humans, identification of those cultural processes peculiar to a particular social setting that demand certain kinds of behavior from individuals at particular times in their lives, and insight into the interaction of those organic and environmental forces which, for each individual, cause him to emerge as a unique personality or self. The concept of developmental tasks is a usable guide for home economics educators because it helps them to identify and state the purposes of home economics as they relate to individuals. At the same time it makes possible placing a specific learning at a time in an individual's life when he is ready to achieve that particular learning.

[20] Group for the Advancement of Psychiatry, *Normal Adolescence: Its Dynamics and Impact*. New York: Charles Scribner's Sons, 1968, p. 34.

[21] Robert J. Havighurst, *Human Development and Education*. New York: Longmans, Green, 1953, p. 2.

Even though a large part of home economics teaching takes place when the individual is an adolescent, you will need to be familiar with the developmental tasks that precede this level and those that would normally follow it. Sometimes the problems you observe in an adolescent result from that individual's failure to make satisfactory adjustment in childhood. Likewise, some of the conflicts an adolescent faces at home may stem from the fact that a parent or grandparent is having difficulty adjusting to the changes required in middle age or later maturity. Chart 2 summarizes the developmental tasks as identified by Havighurst from infancy through later maturity.

The home economics class can help an adolescent work toward the achievement of a number of his developmental tasks. Its primary purposes, however, can best be realized through contributing toward achievement of two tasks, namely (1) achieving the masculine or feminine role; and (2) preparing for marriage and family life. In a society in which the lines of demarcation between masculine and feminine roles are becoming less distinct, the first task becomes more difficult to achieve. This is less true, perhaps, for boys than for girls. The normal social expectation for girls is that of assuming the wife-mother role. In today's world, where women also assume the career role, there are evidences that women are somewhat reluctant to place value on the homemaker role—a point in fact is the manner in which a number of women proclaim that they are "just a housewife." There are indications that, although most teenage girls want and expect to be married, a very few want to be homemakers. Real efforts need to be made in classes of home economics to help girls recognize and clarify their feminine role. In units on "Understanding Self," some time can be devoted to study and discussion of accepting a feminine role; chapter meetings of Future Homemakers of America or other home economics-oriented clubs might well have meetings devoted to this subject. Women in the community who have been successful in the accepting of their feminine roles could serve as excellent resource persons in both instances.

Preparation for marriage and family life requires youth to develop positive attitudes toward family living; it also requires that both men and women be willing and able to assume and perform the many routines essential to successful home management and human relationships. Home economics is basically oriented toward helping individuals in the achievement of these tasks. Class activities relative to clothing, feeding, and housing the family can be geared toward the achievement of this task. Home-management units that deal with establishment of particular family values and goals, the creating of a cooperative and mutually support-

CHART 2 Developmental Tasks From Infancy Through Later Maturity *

Infancy and Early Childhood (Birth to 6 Years)	Middle Childhood (6–12 Years)	Adolescence (12–18 Years)	Early Adulthood (18–30 Years)	Middle Age (30–55 Years)	Later Maturity (55 plus)
Learning to walk Learning to take solid foods Learning to talk Learning to control the elimination of body wastes Learning sex differences and sexual modesty Achieving physiological stability Forming simple concepts of social and physical reality	Learning physical skills necessary for ordinary games Building wholesome attitudes toward oneself as a growing organism Learning to get along with age-mates Learning an appropriate masculine or feminine social role Developing	Achieving new and more mature relations with age-mates of both sexes Achieving a masculine or feminine social role Accepting one's physique and using the body effectively Achieving emotional independence of parents and other adults Achieving assurance	Selecting a mate Learning to live with a marriage partner Starting a family Rearing children Managing a home Getting started in an occupation Taking on civic responsibility Finding a congenial social group	Achieving adult civic and social responsibility Establishing and maintaining an economic standard of living Assisting teen-age children to become responsible and happy adults Developing adult leisure-time activities Relating oneself to	Adjusting to decreasing physical strength and health Adjusting to retirement and reduced income Adjusting to death of spouse Establishing an explicit affiliation with one's age group Meeting social and civic obligations

Learning to relate oneself emotionally to parents, siblings, and other people Learning to distinguish right and wrong and developing a conscience	fundamental skills in reading, writing, and calculating Developing concepts necessary for everyday living Developing conscience, morality, and a scale of values Achieving personal independence Developing attitudes toward social groups and institutions	of economic independence Selecting and preparing for an occupation Preparing for marriage and family life Developing intellectual skills and concepts necessary for civic competence Desiring and achieving socially responsible behavior Acquiring a set of values and an ethical system as a guide to behavior		one's spouse as a person Accepting and adjusting to the physiological changes of middle age Adjusting to aging parents	Establishing satisfactory physical living arrangements

* Robert J. Havighurst, *Human Development and Education*. New York: Longmans, Green, 1953, pp. 9–283.

TABLE 5 Developmental Characteristics of Youth Significant to the Homemaking Education Program *

Early Adolescence	Middle Adolescence	Late Adolescence
More rapid development of motor functions in girls than in boys	More stable physical growth	Physical growth and development to or near the adult stage
Earlier maturity in girls than in boys	Boys' growth equal to that of girls	Sensitivity on the part of some over increased size
Unevenness of physical growth, leading to fears and worries	Great craving for food; appearance of peculiar ideas about food	Continuation of large appetites, but increased interest in diet and exercise
Social relationships change from "the gang" to one or two "best friends"	Less consciousness of body changes; better acceptance of these changes	Physical coordination and dexterity equal to or exceeding that of most adults
Sensitivity over characteristics not accepted by the group	Embarrassment over skin disorders	Disappearance of most differences in maturity between boys and girls
Craving for food, leading to digestive disturbances from overeating	Tendency (in girls) to worry about certain physical conditions	Continued sensitivity over skin disorders
Increase in concern over skin disorders	Improved body coordination and posture	Maintaining attractive appearance now an accepted routine
Short interest span	Strong desire (in both sexes) to be attractive, and to conform to group standards	Increase in close friendships
More social interest on the part of girls than of boys	Increased assumption of responsibility for maintaining good health habits; resentment over parental advice about health	Dating and "going steady" now common practices
Little interest in neatness and cleanliness	Greater interest in sports	More attention given to ways of earning a living

Strong desire for security, for friends whom they like and who like them, for approval from adults	Growing preoccupation with the social value of attractiveness	Eagerness to become self-sufficient and self-supporting
Increased desire for strong bodies, in order to excel in sports	Resistance to parental control; growing assertion of independence	Increased desire for status in the adult world, outside the family group
Interest in independence, but not to the point of giving up the security of dependence	Impatience—in girls, with lack of skill in social situations—in boys, with mechanical failure in material things	Prestige seeking by both boys and girls
Tendency to associate with members of the same sex, to form attachments for friends or for older persons	Occasional dating; girls tend to date older boys	Interest in being different, rather than being "just like" each other
Importance of family status and security	Increased desire to work at jobs that pay wages	More discrimination in choosing friends
Importance of being like others	Beginning of concern over adult problems	Serious thought given to the qualities desired in a prospective life partner
Interest in doing things with the hands	More social maturity in girls than in boys	
Interest in earning money by doing odd jobs	Group feeling remains strong	
Strong desire to prove they are growing up	Satisfaction taken in individual accomplishments that receive recognition of the group	

* *Working Guide for Developing Homemaking Education Curriculum in Local Communities.* Austin: Texas Education Agency, Vocational Education, Home and Family Education, 1957, pp. 5–6.

ing environment for self-expression of family members, and the effective use of resources—both human and material—provide knowledge necessary for competence in this task. Child development and family relationships can make major, direct contributions toward the development of a positive attitude toward family living and child rearing.

Not all of the developmental tasks of youth are equally pertinent to home economics programs. Some progress toward the achievement of all the tasks identified could be realized through your classes; however, your concerted efforts might best be aimed toward those tasks that are uniquely relevant to your area of educational endeavor.

A considerable number of research findings relative to the needs, concerns, and interests of human beings at different age levels are available. Home economics educators usually become familiar with the findings of a number of studies in human behavior when they plan or re-evaluate a home economics program. Through a state-wide study, the leaders of one state identified areas of developmental tasks; behavior of human beings; and needs, concerns, and interest of youth. They formulated a table of developmental characteristics of youth that was used as one basis for developing a home economics curriculum guide for their state. The characteristics that they considered significant for home economics education are shown in Table 5.

A study of the developmental characteristics cited will give you many cues for effective teaching. For example, knowing that the interest span of the early adolescent is short and that he is interested in doing things with his hands, you can plan some classroom learnings that involve use of the hands but that, at the same time, can be achieved in a short period of time.

The developmental characteristics chart also gives you important cues for sequence of home economics learnings. While most middle adolescents are dating, few are seriously considering the selection of a prospective life partner; hence, preparation-for-marriage units are more effective if taught at the later-adolescent level, rather than during the middle- or early-adolescent period. You may want to check the proposed home economics plan for your school against a developmental chart to see if you are reaching students at the most teachable moment.

Because developmental needs differ somewhat depending upon the socio-economic setting as well as the age, you will want to be familiar with those tasks that are especially pertinent to the group you are teaching. Understanding the developmental needs of people will help you to determine the scope and sequence of your home economics program; that is, it will help you determine what to teach when.

UNDERSTANDING HOW PEOPLE LEARN

Learning is changing behavior; when an individual learns he changes his way of behaving. Learning results in acting or thinking in a different way than was done previously; this implies change in relation to certain specific goals. Motivation is the key to behavior change. One of your tasks as the teacher is to motivate others to want to learn. This will be possible if the learners share the same goal toward which you are teaching. Each learner seeks certain goals and their resultant satisfactions; you will seek to help him learn what he wants to learn, but at the same time you are also obligated to help him learn what your training and experience have indicated is significant and pertinent for him to learn. Pupil-teacher planning and pupil-teacher problem solving are based upon the principle that in order to learn the individual must want to learn. The learning should be directed toward his goal; achieving the goal will give him greater satisfaction than not achieving it. Learning is not something that is done to students; rather, it is something that students do to themselves—they change. This necessitates involvement of the learner—he needs to be involved in setting the goals and in selecting the learning experiences geared to the attainment of these goals. This is why you elicit information from your students as to what their concerns and interests are and why you want them to participate in a particular learning experience.

The Process of Changing Behavior

An understanding of the factors that are important in the explanation of human behavior is essential to the understanding of learning. This necessitates seeing how perception and cognition fit into a theory of human behavior and discovering those factors that seem to arouse motives and establish the goals that persist in a specific situation. In particular, it is important to see how certain behavior that is consciously directed toward a goal is chosen and geared toward action that results in attainment of the goal. Baldwin explained this model of behavior change in this way:

> There are three main sections in the model: cognition, goal selection, and goal directed behavior. The first section . . . is concerned with the process of knowing . . . what the situation is like. Cognition includes perception of the immediately perceptible aspects of the environment and also processes of making judgments or inferences about remote parts of the situation.
>
> The second section . . . is concerned with the process of goal selection. An individual does not constantly have the same goals. . . . In any specific situa-

tion one or several motives may be aroused. We must therefore discover what situational factors tend to arouse what kind of motives. Not all motives are realized in overt behavior. Some are inhibited; are ignored because they are unimportant; others are too difficult even to try to satisfy. Some motives, however, do establish a goal that the individual tries to attain.

The third section . . . is concerned with goal attainment or goal-directed behavior. Once a goal is set, there are often alternative ways of trying to achieve it. The selection of the means to a goal, the carrying out of this means, and the guidance of the ongoing behavior toward the goal are all involved in goal-directed behavior.[22]

Hindrances to Learning

Decisions are made in relation to an immediate or ultimate goal that the individual wants to achieve. The selection of one goal is related to the particular motive or motives that are evoked. However, all motives do not result in action toward goals. When two or more motives are aroused at the same time, action does not result. If the motives are in conflict, satisfying one will mean frustrating the others. This is exemplified in the decision the teacher of home economics makes relative to the acceptance of workmanship standards. Often the standards of work she is willing to accept are quite different from those that are acceptable to her students. She is torn between forcing the individual to accept her standard, based on the belief that her training in home economics has given her a yardstick for measuring workmanship standards, and allowing the learner to evolve his own standard, based on the belief that the individual has the right to choose his own standard because he is the one who must bear the consequences of the choice. When motives are in conflict, the individual may choose one and disregard the other, try to satisfy each in turn, or come to no decision and take no action.

Inaction may also result because motives are inhibited. Inhibition may take place because the individual is able to foresee the consequences of satisfying a particular motive. The teacher of home economics may be able to see, for example, that forcing her students to accept her workmanship standard may result in a breakdown of student morale; she may, therefore, choose to take no action in forcing what she believes are acceptable standards of workmanship.

Inhibition may also occur when an individual respects a rule that condemns a specific behavior. The school policy that prohibits youngsters from talking with one another during study hall is usually upheld by teachers, even though in some cases they are certain that allowing some

[22] Alfred L. Baldwin, *Behavior and Development in Childhood*. New York: Holt, Rinehart, and Winston, 1955, p. 115.

persons to talk to one another would result in more efficient use of time and facilitate learning. In this case the decision is made in favor of following the rule rather than an action which would result in what the teacher might feel to be better learning for the students involved.

At times, wished-for goals are impossible to attain or may be attained without action. The desire to be able to help each student individually or to gear the curriculum toward meeting individual differences is very important to many teachers. Yet the impact of large classes crowded into too-little space for limited periods of time make this wished-for goal too often impossible to achieve. On the other hand, the ability to apply principles learned in class to his own individual needs is sometimes attained by the learner through no particular action of the teacher.

The weighing of several motives and the decision to act on one motive in particular is characteristic of goal-directed behavior. It requires a measure of maturity. Whether a motive will result in action is determined by the factors of strength of motive, possibility of success, self-confidence of the individual, and the ability to make a choice and disregard other motives.

> One cue from the cognitive map is self-concept, a picture of the person himself as he sees himself. . . . The decision to act or not to act frequently reveals a great deal about how a person perceives himself. . . . Each step in the behavior process . . . depends upon certain characteristics of the external situation, as perceived or cognized by the individual.[23]

Individuals learn if they want to learn; this is the moral of the adage, "You can lead a horse to water but you can't make him drink." So it is with your students; you can guide them in learning, but you cannot make them learn. They themselves must want to change their present ways of behaving or thinking. Unless a student has some discomfort with his present situation, he will probably not be motivated to change. Learning is dependent upon the intent of the learners to learn. This intent is related to the preconceived ideas the learner has about the learning situation, which are partly the result of his past experiences; to how he accepts the new message (information in the sense that it is the structured experience provided in a school setting); and to what the learner does with the message. A teacher has the task of attempting to know to some degree what ideas a learner has in relation to a particular home economics learning, and of planning learning experiences so that the information gained will actually change his preconceived notions, thus changing his behavior.

[23] Ibid., p. 123.

Factors Contributing to Learning

What can you, as a teacher, do to set the stage for your students to learn? Among the factors that contribute to learning are are following:

1. DETERMINING WHAT IS REASONABLE TO EXPECT STUDENTS TO LEARN. In order to learn, it is essential that what is being determined as an educational outcome is possible as a learning product. For example, learning what kinds and colors of clothing to select in order to be clothed attractively and appropriately is a possible learning product for home economics teaching; on the other hand, changing body structure or facial features in order to be more attractive is not a possible educational outcome. Understanding how people learn can help us determine what is possible for them to learn.

2. PROVIDING OPPORTUNITIES FOR THE STUDENTS TO PRACTICE WHAT THEY ARE LEARNING. Understanding how people learn is essential, too, for knowing what conditions are most conducive to effective learning. For instance, studies indicate that if an individual has the opportunity to put into actual practice that which he is learning, he is less likely to forget what he has already learned while he is increasing his amount of knowledge. You apply this learning principle when you reinforce what the student has done at home in the classroom experiences and when you encourage him to practice at home what he has learned at school. In reality, the home-experience program in home economics is built upon this premise. If the learner has the opportunity to put into practice in daily living what he has learned at school, and is encouraged to do so, the possibilities that his behavior will change—that he will learn—are greatly enhanced.

3. PLANNING EXPERIENCES THAT ARE SATISFYING AND CONSISTENT WITH PREVIOUS LEARNING. Learning is more apt to take place if what is being taught is consistent with other learning experiences the learner has had. Similar learnings tend to reinforce one another, and inconsistent learnings tend to frustrate or cancel out one another. Understanding this learning principle is basic to the effective teaching of home economics. Nearly all students have had some experience in family living—all have had experiences in feeding, clothing, and housing themselves; all are the products of some child-rearing practices; all have shared in human interaction in a group setting. You can make learning for an individual more possible if you know and understand some of the homemaking experiences he has had. This gives you the basis for starting where the student is and some cues for where and how far you can take him through classroom learning experiences. Implementing this learning principle is what is meant by the advice: "Make the learning realistic and func-

tional." This principle of learning implies that home economics subject matter can be learned readily because, for most people, it is not a completely new and unfamiliar kind of learning. On the other hand, to change behavior in relation to family life is not simple, for often it requires that the learner unlearn as well as learn. The new learning will need to be considerably more satisfying than the old if this is to happen.

You can set the stage for more effective learning in your classroom when *you know from what kind of home a student comes and adapt your program to what you know.* At the same time, you have an obligation to add to the experiences he has had at home, to point out alternative ways for solving homemaking problems, to acquaint him with some possible outcomes or consequences of the alternatives considered, and to help him accept and adapt to change. Acceptance of change is more likely to take place if it is built upon previous learning—that is, past experiences in which the learner has participated and which have resulted in either satisfying or dissatisfying results for him. A student must feel secure in a situation before he can look at ideas or feelings which are threatening.

4. CAPITALIZING ON THE MULTIPLE OUTCOMES OF A LEARNING EXPERIENCE. A single learning experience results in multiple outcomes. You will want to capitalize on this learning principle as you plan learning experiences for your classes. For example, the desired outcome for your students, toward which you are directing your teaching in a particular lesson, may be the preparation by the student of a simple breakfast for two in a limited time period. While the student is preparing this breakfast in the allotted time, it is possible for many other learnings to be taking place. He may be learning to prepare the breakfast; he may be learning how to use special time-saving equipment. At the same time he may be learning to be inefficient in the use of energy, to waste food, or to accept a product that is less than standard in quality. It is also possible for him to be learning either good or poor ways of working with others toward the solving of a common problem. There are a number of outcomes that are possible in just this single learning experience. As teachers we need to be more aware of the possibilities for learning inherent in a particular learning experience; and, most important, we need to use that learning experience to its greatest potential. If teachers took the time to have students look at a single learning experience and recognize what is possible for them to learn from it, to have them evaluate that same experience in terms of what they actually did learn, and draw some generalizations from the experience that would be applicable in another situation, *learning would be greatly facilitated and would be more efficient and effective.*

5. HELPING STUDENTS APPLY THEIR LEARNINGS TO NEW SITUATIONS. Meaningful learning results in the development of cognitive structure that facilitates fitting new information in the structure. Transfer of learning, that is, the ability to apply what you learn today to a future time and a different situation, requires that one be capable of seeing relationships and making generalizations. This necessitates that he be aware of the similarities in situations and that he is able to take a number of specifics and reduce them to a general mode for attacking problems. *One of the major jobs in teaching is helping students acquire this competency.* Every learning experience ought to result in the learner becoming aware of the kind of generalization he is using to guide his particular action or actions. A generalization might be described as a principle, a general attitude or value judgment applicable to a number of situations, or a method of operating that is usable in a number of situations. Fig. 2 schematically defines a generalization.

When careful examination of a number of related but different specific situations reveals a common concept of "truth," that inference, if mutually applicable in all cases, is called a *generalization.* This relationship is shown in the diagram in Fig. 2. The solid lines indicate reciprocity between individual cases and fundamental inferences. This generalization has been identified as a result of the inductive process of reasoning. In turn, after its acceptance as a basic concept, the generalization can be applied to and used in understanding other related but different specific situations. The dotted lines above indicate the reciprocal relationships between the generalizations and their uses in interpreting and understanding particular cases. This action is a result of deductive reasoning.

One teacher helped her class draw generalizations and see relationships from a particular learning situation through this student analysis of a classroom experience:

What we did and learned today:

We talked about the observations we made of six-year-olds—our brothers and sisters, the children in the neighborhood, the first grade here in school, and a Sunday school class. We noticed that not all the children were the same size; some acted more grown up than others; some could read and write better than others.

We read in our textbooks about the way children grow. In the reports that were given in class, all the books seemed to say the same things about child growth.

We brought our baby books and compared what we were like when we were a certain age. Some of us walked when we were eight months old; some of us did not walk until after 18 months, but we all walk O.K. now—it didn't make any difference

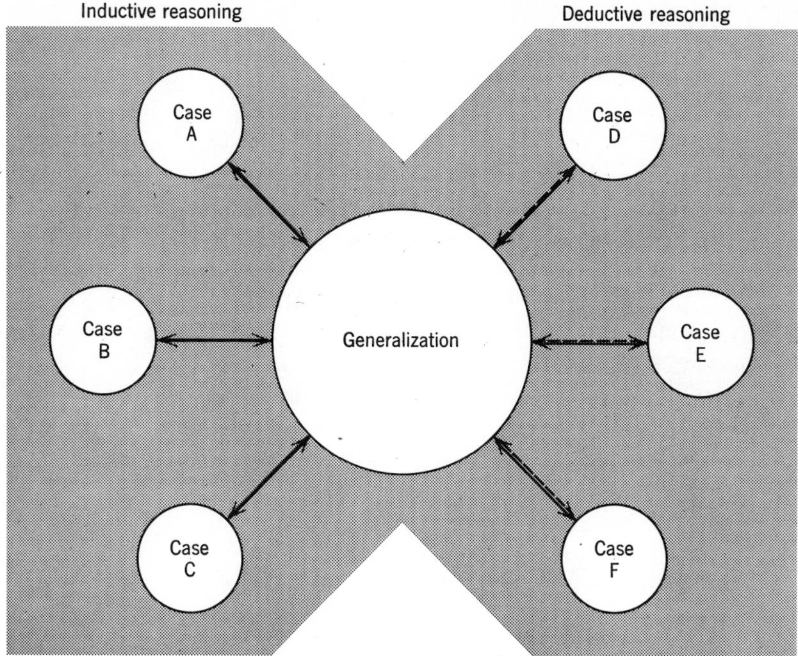

Figure 2. Schematic definition of a generalization. Contributed by Dr. Louise Gentry, Assistant Dean, College of Human Development, Pennsylvania State University, State College, Pennsylvania.

What it means to me:

People don't all grow up in the same way. Some grow faster than others. Every person has his own pattern of growing.

Where I can use it again:

I can remember this when I worry because I'm taller than most of the kids in our room.

When I'm baby-sitting, I won't expect all of the kids to want to do the same things my six-year-old sister does, just because they're six, too.

When I'm a mother, I won't expect all my children to do the same things at a certain age. If the second one doesn't learn to walk as soon as the first one did, I won't think he's not going to be as smart.

By no means is the foregoing discussion exhaustive—it has merely highlighted some of the accepted ideas about how people learn.

As a teacher your task is that of determining the best ways for your students to learn. This means you will need precise information about your students: What is *their* situation? What have been *their* previous learnings and experiences? What are *their* attitudes and needs?

The kind of society in which we live and its needs, changes, and trends in environmental setting; information and knowledge about how people grow and learn; and the structure of the field, give to all home economics programs a commonness of purpose and procedure. It is in the implementation of that program to meet the specific needs of particular groups of people in selected settings that variation exists and is essential. Leaders in home economics education at city and state levels have considered these factors and have developed curriculum guides for home economics education that suggest emphases appropriate for different age levels, learning experiences that are geared to these emphases, resources to which a teacher might turn for help in carrying through these learning experiences, and some ways for securing evidence for evaluation purposes. The state or city curriculum guide should be your first source as you begin to develop a local program of home economics. Yours will be the task of adapting the basic state or city program of home economics for your particular students.

Selected References

Bruner, Jerome, *On Knowing*. Cambridge, Mass.: Harvard University Press, 1962.

Bruner, Jerome, *The Process of Education*. Cambridge, Mass.: Harvard University Press, 1961.

Contemporary Issues in Home Economics. Washington, D.C.: National Education Association, Department of Home Economics, 1965.

Fleck, Henrietta, *Toward Better Teaching of Home Economics*. New York: Macmillan, 1968.

Hatcher, Hazel M., and Mildred E. Andrews, *The Teaching of Homemaking* (2nd ed.). Boston: Houghton Mifflin, 1963.

Havighurst, Robert J., *Human Development and Education*. New York: Longmans, Green, 1953.

Kelley, Earl C., *In Defense of Youth*. Englewood Cliffs, New Jersey: Prentice-Hall, 1962.

McGrath, Earl, and Jack T. Johnson, *The Changing Mission of Home Economics*. New York: Teachers College, Columbia University, 1968.

Raths, Louis E.; Merrill Harmin; Sidney Simon, *Values and Teaching*. Columbus, Ohio: C. E. Merrill Books, 1966.

Spitze, Hazel T., "The Structure of Home Economics as a Basis for Curriculum Decisions." *Illinois Teacher of Home Economics*, **9**: 62–96; 1965–66.

Unruh, Gladys G., *New Curriculum Developments.* Washington, D.C.: Association for Supervision and Curriculum Development, National Education Association, 1965.

Vincent, Clark, "Familia Spongis: The Adaptive Function." *Journal of Marriage and the Family,* **28**: 29–36, February 1966.

Williams, Robin, *American Society: A Sociological Interpretation.* New York: Alfred Knopf, 1960.

Young, Louise A. (editor), *Educating the Teen Ager in Human Relations and Management of Resources.* Washington, D.C.: American Home Economics Association, 1966.

7

Planning Your Home Economics Program

Home economics education is meaningful to people, as it promotes their personal growth, changes their ways of behaving in the family setting, and contributes to their success on the job. If your program of home economics is to be of value to the people whom it purports to serve, it will need to be focused on individuals in a particular family and community setting and will need to be cooperatively planned, executed, and evaluated.

COOPERATIVE PROGRAM PLANNING AT THE LOCAL LEVEL

The home economics teacher who is concerned with making her program realistic and functional for the individuals and families in her community will use some techniques for stimulating interest and involvement in the planning and implementing of that program by those concerned, specifically, her students, and in some instances, their parents and resource persons in the community. Cooperative planning may begin with an advisory committee to give general direction to the program. Ultimately, cooperative planning involves the students and teacher working together to plan and carry out effective learning experiences.

Advisory Committee

An advisory committee can be helpful in planning any type of home economics program, but it is especially important when making plans to train students for gainful employment. The advisory committee serves in a consultant capacity to the local school personnel. Members of the committee should be selected to represent every element of the particular job for which an occupational training program is to be offered.

The purposes of an advisory committee can include assistance in identifying the occupational training needs of the area, planning a realistic and practical curriculum based upon the competences required on the job, providing resource people for special areas of instruction, setting up standards for instruction and equipment, suggesting standards for the selection of trainees, interpreting the program to the general public, strengthening relationships with potential employers, evaluating the training program and success of the trainees on the job, conducting follow-up studies of trained employees, and gaining active support for the program.

Planning for Vocational Education

Although planning a program to prepare students for gainful employment provides an opportunity for a teacher to apply many of the principles discussed throughout this book, cooperative planning is probably the key to success in most occupational education programs. The Vocational Education Act of 1963 focused attention on the need to train persons for jobs related to home economics. In some instances, the training is directed toward *home-focused* occupations, such as homemakers' assistants or companions to elderly persons. Other training is toward *community-focused* occupations such as workers in child day-care centers, supervised food service workers, or hotel or motel housekeeping aides.

Public Law 90–576, which was passed by Congress in 1968, amended the Vocational Education Act of 1963. The Act provides for the appointment of State Advisory Councils, representing the general public and the diverse interests in vocational education. Part F requires approved state plans to allot funds solely for home economics programs that give consideration to social and cultural needs, particularly in economically depressed areas. These programs are designed to prepare youth and adults for the role of homemaker and to contribute to their employability in the dual role of homemakers and wage earners. At least one third of the Federal funds must be used in areas that are economically depressed or that have high rates of unemployment. Emphasis in these programs is on assisting consumers and helping to improve home environments and family life.

In Chapter 3 some suggestions were given to help you become acquainted with the needs of your community. Before you make plans to offer training for gainful employment, you should survey the needs of your community. For example, you might look into the need for homemakers' assistants. If there seems to be a need, your survey would include asking a sample of homemakers with what tasks they would like to have help. What hourly wages would they be willing to pay trained helpers? On the other hand, your program might be directed toward community occupations. In this case, you should identify the employment requirements in wage-earning occupations that use home economics knowledge and skills. Perhaps your survey of the community needs will reveal that many persons are "hard-core unemployed." You would want to find out what programs are in existence to help them, who is conducting these programs, how they are funded, and what each program is doing. Then you are in a position to decide whether your school should establish occupational education and, if so, what service you can render to your community without overlapping the work of other agencies.

Once the direction of your program is determined, be sure to enlist the cooperation of counselors who can help develop understanding of the program and select trainees who can benefit from it. You will probably establish a minimum age so the students will have reached the legal age for employment by the end of the school year. Preparing a guide or booklet to explain the course of study would be helpful in orienting the students and their parents to occupational education.

The teacher or coordinator of the program must have had work experience in the occupational field for which training is set up. His planning will include outlining the various processes to be learned and preparing a schedule that shows approximately when these skills will be taught. Remember that other subjects which are taught in your school may be related to your proposed program. You should seek the cooperation of teachers in these areas in order to provide meaningful experiences for the students.

Your school may find it possible to establish a *work-experience program* that enables a student to hold a job for perhaps 15 hours a week while earning school credit for each class period assigned to work experience. The employer pays minimum wage rates and cooperates with the school in supervision and evaluation. When you select possible employers, try to choose those who are likely to offer jobs that will last through the school semester. Also, look for employers who will cooperate with the school in providing supervision and evaluation of the students. You will use a variety of evaluation techniques, some of which should be designed to encourage the student to describe what he is doing on his job and to evaluate his personal development. Confidential reports from the employer can guide you in working with an individual student as well as provide a basis for you to plan ways of overcoming problems experienced by several of the students and/or employers. As a part of work-experience programs, students have been fry cooks, kitchen helpers, sales clerks, day-care helpers, and waitresses. An advisory committee could help plan and set up other worthwhile experiences in such areas as dry cleaning, child care, garment manufacturing, food preparation, or nursing care.

Teacher-Student Planning

Use of cooperative procedures helps to assure that a home economics program will turn out to be uniquely designed for a particular group. It results in more productive learning, since the intent of the learner is both identified and utilized. Important techniques for family living are being realized at the same time that new learnings are taking place, for much of living together in a family consists of group action to meet common goals or satisfy common needs. Hence, the home economics teacher is obligated to help her students understand the cooperative procedures she is using so that they can become familiar with the method and utilize it in attacking real family problems. Allowing students to participate in the decisions to be made relative to their home economics learning gives them actual practice in the decision-making processes. If these processes are understood and analyzed by the learners, and if intelligence is used to arrive at choices, the total experience will be characteristic of democratic practice. It will provide opportunity for practice in self-direction, cooperation, and creative thinking—all very important learnings. If cooperative procedures are used, students are more apt to be interested in what they are doing, more willing to assume responsibility for the action that is essential to carrying out the learning experience, and more likely to assume responsibility for the outcome of their choices, for they will understand what they are learning and why.

Planning with the students what and why they are learning is essential in program planning. This in no way implies that the teacher's role is that of asking, "What do you want to do in this class this year?" and then proceeding to follow through on the students' suggestions. In the first place, this kind of question is usually not productive for group action—the students just *might* reply that they do not want to do anything! Secondly, this kind of question places the teacher, who has more experience, knowledge, and information concerning her subject-matter area as well as an understanding of needs, concerns, and interests of individuals, in a position where she cannot utilize her background of training to its best potential for her class. The teacher does have a keen responsibility in involving her students in the planning and implementing of their learning experiences if she expects her program to be uniquely designed and geared to her particular class group; at the same time, she must remember she is the *crucial* person in planning. How can she best carry out cooperative procedures to accomplish this end? Are there guidelines she might follow? Are there cautions of which she needs to be aware?

Pupil-teacher planning for a particular class consists of at least three consecutive steps: planning on the part of the teacher prior to meeting her class; planning with students in the particular situation; and reshaping plans made by the teacher in light of student suggestions. Each of these steps is important; none can be omitted if effective learning is the objective.

Before meeting your classes for the first time each year, you should make certain decisions and plans; for that matter, you need to do this every day that you teach. One of the most important decisions to be made prior to meeting a class is whether you want your students to participate in making decisions about what and how they will learn or whether you wish to make all these decisions for them. If you have decided that they will have a part in the planning of their learning experiences, your next step is to decide when and how much they will participate. In other words, you need to outline for yourself the boundaries for decision making. Limitations as well as proposals for choice need to be thought through clearly by you. Prior to meeting a class, your planning includes a number of decisions such as how long to spend on planning, what materials you will need to motivate your students, how the rooms will be arranged, and what methods you will use to elicit student responses.

If you are sincere in your effort to allow the students to participate in the planning of their learnings, you will allow them to make decisions only in those areas in which you are willing and ready for them to make choices. This point is essential if you expect students to trust you, to have confidence in the democratic process, and to gain experience in shared decision making. Too often the teacher believes she is carrying out cooperative planning procedures when, in reality, she is manipulating a class in such a manner that they "come out" with the teacher's predetermined choice. The teacher may have, in her previous planning, already settled on what the group was to learn and how it was to achieve these learnings. Pupil-teacher planning then becomes merely a ritual—and one that leads to distrust of the teacher and lack of confidence in shared decision making as a means of solving problems. Very few teachers will deliberately manipulate students; more often they will do so thinking they are fulfilling accepted cooperative planning procedures. Take the case of Miss Jones, a student teacher in home economics. She illustrated this point when she wrote:

> I had been assigned to work with a freshman group who were in the midst of a hospitality unit. The supervising teacher told me that the girls were to begin working on a special tea that they were going to give for their mothers as a part of Education Week activities. She suggested that I do some planning around a short tea unit. I would have the responsibility of planning, implementing, and evaluating the unit with the girls. Prior to meeting my class for

the first time I made detailed plans: a list of desired outcomes I wanted my students to achieve, plans for table appointments, what the refreshments were to be, and a listing of students on special committees.

When I met with the class I asked them, "What kind of tea would you like to have for your mothers?" I really worked hard trying to get the class to suggest the kind of tea I had already planned. After much maneuvering, supporting and building on suggestions similar to my preconceived plan, and overlooking and ignoring suggestions that were in conflict to them, the class "decided" to have the tea in the home economics room, write formal invitations to each mother, use the lace table cloth, and have a centerpiece of fresh flowers—all ideas which I had neatly jotted down in my lesson plan.

It was in the planning of what the refreshments were to be that the pupil-teacher planning broke down to the point that it was obvious to both the students and me. I had visualized attractive tea cookies and punch as refreshments. When I asked the class what they would like to serve they suggested "Cokes and bologna sandwiches." I tried, but I could get no one in the group to make any other suggestions. In desperation I finally told them that they had to make hot spiced tea and tiny icebox cookies. With this one girl retorted, "If that's what you wanted all the time, why didn't you just say so to begin with instead of asking us to make suggestions that you weren't going to listen to anyway?"

In the follow-up discussion of my lesson with the supervising teacher I asked her what I might have done differently. Together we decided that in reality I was neither willing nor in a position to allow the class the amount of free choice I had implied as I worked with them. The only choices I was both willing and in a position to allow them to make were: (1) choice of kind of icebox cookie; (2) choice of hot tea punch; and (3) choice of work committee. The cooperative planning session would have been more fruitful and certainly more honest had I been aware of the limits and areas of actual decision making. I truly learned the difference between cooperative planning and teacher manipulation that day!

Because of your knowledge, experience, and specialized training in home economics, you are in a position to help your students, during the pupil-teacher planning session, to recognize "where they are" in knowledge about home and family living, and give direction to where it is essential and possible for them "to go" in a particular class or during a particular day. You will want to go to the planning session with many ideas for class goals and activities.

Some teachers utilize check lists for eliciting the ideas of students. Other teachers find that an appealing three-dimensional bulletin board can serve as the springboard for a planning session. A junior-high home economics teacher prepared a bulletin board that depicted a house with a boy and a girl standing outside. Conversation captions around the boy asked: "What do we do or what can we do to help

Figure 3. Bulletin board for cooperative planning.

at home?"; around the girl: "What goes on in there?" (See Fig. 3.)

On the board, the teacher listed possible home and family activities that the students identified. She felt free to add important ones they might have overlooked. Next, both teacher and students listed those activities for which the students currently assumed some measure of responsibility. Discussion led to making judgments concerning whether new knowledge or skills were important to acquire. Problems needing special attention were recorded. With the help of the teacher, students decided upon some areas of new responsibilities that were needed. This class discussion proved to be a fruitful and exciting pupil-teacher planning session.

Success in cooperative planning can be assured if the teacher assumes the responsibility for playing the major decision-making role by defining the limits of choice and making students aware of learning possibilities; recognizes and respects each student's ideas and suggestions; and involves each person in the clarification and identification of classroom objectives. Some cooperative planning is essential at the beginning of the year or prior to attacking a new problem. Also, new situations arising each day will necessitate a measure of cooperative planning.

After your pupil-teacher planning session, you will need to make the final decision as to exactly what objectives your class will pursue, how these will be accomplished, and what means you will use for determining whether the objectives have been achieved.

SOURCES OF HOME ECONOMICS OBJECTIVES

Where does the teacher of home economics go to find appropriate objectives for her home economics classes? Are there some sources upon which she can rely for help?

To suggest that a teacher ought to locate and use already-specified sets of objectives for the teaching of home economics would be more than foolhardy; even if it were possible to cite such a resource (and some may be in existence!), it would be most improbable that these would be appropriate, pertinent, and relevant to a particular class in home economics. There are several sources to which you might appropriately turn for *specific guidance* in determining the objectives for *your* classes in home economics. These are: (1) information about *your* students and *their* families (discussed in Chapters 4, 5, and 11); (2) professional literature containing authoritative judgments and research findings in the contributions home economics can make to solution of socially relevant problems, and (3) the philosophy of education and the experiential backgrounds of others in your school as well as yourself.

Research and Development in Home Economics Education

Home economics programs are organized to facilitate the achievement of the broad purposes of home economics. In varying degrees each individual who is a part of these programs expects to achieve these purposes. If this expectation is to be fulfilled, it becomes necessary to so focus and control the learning setting that these purposes are pin-pointed and described so that they can be identified by all concerned.

A review of research studies pertaining to secondary education in general, and specifically to home economics education, indicates trends that are taking place in curriculum planning. First, there is a trend toward the assurance of *quality programs* for students of *all* levels of ability and all cultural groups. Toward this end, there is an increase in the emphasis being given to programs for exceptional children, particularly for the gifted and for the slow learners. Concerted effort is being directed toward the needs of culturally disadvantaged students too. In many instances, special effort is being made to integrate these students into the regular school program. We discuss particular ways of reaching these students in Chapter 11.

A second trend is an emphasis on learning that assists students in becoming more employable. This trend has been especially emphasized since the passage of the Vocational Education Act of 1963 and the Vocational Education Amendments of 1968. Home economics content can be especially focused to prepare persons for gainful employment in a number of service areas that are essential to the functioning of present day society. Reinwald[1] has summarized these thus: (1) child care services—child care aides in private or public nursery schools, day care centers, playground or recreation centers; assistants in children's homes or hospitals, and in nurseries in department stores, industrial plants and transportation terminals; (2) clothing services—clothing maintenance specialists for department stores, dry cleaning establishments or private individuals; (3) institutional services—laundry services or housekeeping aides in hospitals, hotels, motels, and nursing homes; (4) food services—supervised food service workers in schools, restaurants, and hospitals; assistants to food demonstrators; waitresses; family dinner service specialists; (5) housing and home furnishing services—assistants in flower and gift shops and drapery and slipcover departments; and (6) specialized family services—companions to elderly persons; shopping service operators; homemakers' assistants.

Preparing individuals for the professions in home economics requires concentration in a particular area of home economics. This may begin in classes at the secondary level beamed particularly at the college-bound youngster who plans to continue his education. Nevertheless, college-

[1] Clio Reinwald, "Education for Employment." *National Association of Secondary-School Principals Bulletin*, **48**: 32, December 1964.

bound students must devote the major part of their attention to satisfying college admission requirements and being introduced to the possible areas of home economics which they could study in depth at the college level.

The third trend is the emphasis on *fundamental learning*. In an effort to prepare individuals for effective living in the family, schools are developing interdisciplinary programs for *all* students, kindergarten through adult education, in family life and sex education. Chart 3 gives an overview of some of the differences you should consider in planning programs directed toward family living, gainful employment, and professional home economics positions.

Among the research findings that have implications for planning the home economics curriculum are those relating to the changing roles of family members, especially women. As Moore has pointed out: "It has been estimated that some 98 percent of the women in the nation will within the next decade have worked in paid employment at some period in their lives."[2]

She stated further:

> Today one fourth of all 18-year-old girls are married and one sixth of the 17-year-old girls. One out of each 16 girls in their 16th year is married. These are high school ages. These are young persons who are entering marriage, parenthood, and homemaking in teen years. They face the very real task of maturing *in* marriage, and they need every assistance continuing education can give them.[3]

Also, she pointed out:

> To add emphasis to the need for preparation for home living and family life, it is estimated that by 1963 approximately 600,000 new homes will be established each year with the new households being, in the main, those with modest incomes. Where income is modest, knowledge, information, and skill in home living may make the difference between satisfying and happy relationships and discontent and discouragement.
>
> . . . by 1970 the number of young persons between 15 and 19 years of age will have increased over 63 per cent! Teen-age spending will reach over 10 billion dollars per year, with most of this going into nondurable goods. Such spending requires intelligent guidance.[4]

[2] Bernice M. Moore, "A Sociologist Looks at Homemaking Education." *Practical Home Economics,* 5:13, April 1960.

[3] Ibid., p. 41.

[4] Ibid., pp. 43–44.

CHART 3 The Threefold Programs of Home Economics for Today's Needs *

	Family Living	Gainful Employment	Professional Preparation
Purpose	Preparation for home life and the responsibilities of a family.	Training for employability in a specific job for which opportunities exist.	Preparation for a career as a professional home economist.
Students	All secondary school students (boys and girls). Elementary pupils and adults may be included in the program.	Secondary school students, out-of-school youth, and adults who are screened for certain characteristics required in a particular job.	High school graduates who have interest in and aptitude for college work at a professional level.
Curriculum	All areas of home economics are included in sequential yearly plans.	Development of limited and concentrated skills to meet the standards for immediate employment. Length of time is determined by the job requirements.	A four- or five-year college curriculum resulting in a bachelor's degree with a major in a specific field of home economics.
Facilities	Preferably an approximation of home environment.	Should simulate as nearly as possible the working conditions for the particular job.	Laboratories and classrooms suited to professional education (lectures, discussions, experimentation, individual study, research).

* Adapted from *What is Home Economics?* (a brochure prepared by the Vocational Education Committee, California Home Economics Association).

In spite of the needs of these young people for an understanding of the variety of responsibilities they face in home management and parenthood, a survey of 4800 secondary schools throughout the United States indicated that one-half or more of the time in home economics was devoted to clothing construction and food preparation and serving. Coon[5] questioned why so little time was being allocated to the items dealing with management, family emphasis, nutrition and maintenance of health, consumer education, and community problems that affect the family.

Since the publication of this study a concerted effort has been made by leaders in home economics to help teachers refocus the secondary curriculum, placing more emphasis on human development, relationships and management of resources.

Interviews with 104 young homemakers in Wisconsin revealed areas in which the preparation of young homemakers could be strengthened:

> Meal planning was recognized as the area of greatest need in foods. It is significant that preparing the meals was suggested only one-third as often as was planning the meals. The second most frequently mentioned category was home management. Homemakers felt that more emphasis should be placed on planning family budgets, time-saving short cuts, planning time and work schedules, household hints, and new techniques. In clothing and textiles, clothing construction was reported most frequently. However, a need was also recognized for basic knowledge in mending, remodeling and care and recognition of new fabrics. Other aspects of homemaking suggested for high school home economics were numerous phases of housing and home furnishings, child care and development, personal and social development, family relations, health, and home safety.[6]

Trump,[7] in discussing home economics in the future, assumes that students of all ages are currently family members and hence some home economics education is essential at all levels. His curriculum model (Table 6) offers suggestions for the scope and sequence of a relevant home economics program.

Philosophy of Home Economics

Even though you are well equipped with the opinions of authorities in the field of home economics, you need to develop the ability to draw upon your own resources as you attempt to define the objectives of your

[5] Beulah I. Coon, *Home Economics in the Public Secondary Schools.* U.S. Department of Health, Education and Welfare, Office of Education, OE–83010, (Circular 661), Washington: U.S. Government Printing Office, 1962.

[6] Genevieve W. Schubert and Julia I. Dalrymple, "Problems and Needs of Young Homemakers: Implication for High School Home Economics." *Journal of Home Economics,* **51**:366–367, May 1959.

[7] J. Lloyd Trump, "Home Economics: A Look into the Future." *The Bulletin of the National Association of Secondary-School Principals,* **48**: 83, December 1964.

program. First, and of utmost importance, is your ability to express what you think the goals of home economics should be, who should take home economics, and what indications would reveal that students were making progress toward desirable goals. Once you have clarified your ideas as to the direction in which you want to move, you can apply learnings from your own experience and that of others.

Before you can determine where to begin in stating the objectives of your program, you need to start crystallizing your own philosophy of home economics and its place in secondary education. Of course, your philosophy is not static—your ideas should change continually, particularly as a result of the discussions and readings you carry on in your teacher-education courses. At the beginning of such a course, one student organized her ideas as follows:

> Home economics education is the studying and learning about any or all the elements of family living—individual development and interpersonal relations. The list of included areas is almost endless and yet unique in that you may start your students wherever they are in family living and move forward. I believe that everyone is at some point along the way and has some place to go.
>
> The purpose of home economics education in the secondary school is for the students to learn those skills that will help them to fill their roles as family members in the most satisfying manner for themselves, their families, and their communities. These skills include not only manual, routine operations but also alert functioning of their minds to plan, to execute, to evaluate, and to adjust the daily jobs in home maintenance and family relations. I hope that during this process these students will also study the various attitudes, values, goals, and standards that people possess in different situations and circumstances; as a concluding objective of this process I hope they will formulate their own aims and beliefs and make flexibility and adaptability the keys to their individual organization. These are my objectives for teaching home economics.
>
> At this time I feel that a family-centered approach is the most important aspect of home economics education. The purpose of this kind of education becomes one that is met when this approach is used. Therefore, I feel that home economics is to educate or to train everyone who is a family member. This does not mean that everyone must take home economics; but it does mean that home economics can meet the needs of anyone interested in family living and clarify the role that he, as well as other members, plays. This means that every member of the family can take home economics, but, more specifically, the student in a secondary home economics course can integrate his learning process within his family. In other words, the teacher, as a secondary teacher, may teach the high school boys and girls as well as other family members. She may teach students with a variety of backgrounds and must endeavor to meet their individual needs as well as their class needs. . . .

TABLE 6 Home Economics Curriculum Model [8]

Present Grade Equivalent	Age	Basic Education for All	Depth Education for Some		
K 1 2 3	5 6 7 8	Planned study, informal in treatment of such topics as: relations with family and other persons, care of clothing, respect for others, consequences of acts, problem solving, group planning, personal responsibility for beauty in home and school, etc.	Very little at this point		
4	9	Personal and family health Food habits and practices	From time to time, some students make special, but limited, studies of selected phases of these subjects—to explore their personal talents and interest, and to motivate other students		
5	10	Care and selection of clothing Care of home and surroundings Safety and sanitation,			
6	11	Table manners—service, Duties of family members			
7	12	Personal and family finances The arts in the home, clothing, etc.			
8	13	Food and nutrition Clothing and textiles			
9	14	Home management Child study and family relations			
10 11 12 Adult Education	15 16 17	Review, reinforcement, and updating: special presentations, discussions, and independent study	*Level 1* Student spends 25-50 hours on some topic: *e.g.*, Survey of housing or Food habits in India	*Level 2* Individual or group works for a semester: *e.g.*, Planning and furnishing a new home, or Health and home nursing	*Level 3* Rigorous courses: *e.g.*, Foods, Clothing, Child Study, Principles of Design, or Consumer Economics
		ESSENTIAL KNOWLEDGE | DESIRABLE KNOWLEDGE | ENRICHING KNOWLEDGE			

Although your philosophy undoubtedly will have much in common with the views of other students and home economics teachers, each statement of beliefs about home economics education is highly individualistic. You cannot simply adopt a philosophy that was written by someone else and expect it to function for you. If a philosophy is intended to provide the focus around which a program can be developed, it must be an expression of what you believe in strongly enough that you will be willing to work hard and make the necessary sacrifices to accomplish. As an example of how similar, and yet how individual, two philosophies can be, the following statement represents another student's views of home economics education:

> Home economics is unique in that it draws upon all the other courses in a high school curriculum and applies them to the family. It is an art, as it involves skills that are based on certain traditions and qualities that are intangible and undefinable, such as beauty, taste, and values. It is also a science, because it involves the application of knowledge and truths that have been arrived at through scientific processes. Home economics does not try to teach philosophy, math, physics, art, music, religion, or chemistry, but it attempts to integrate them all and apply them in the daily process of making a home.
>
> The responsibilities of making and keeping a home, upholding family ideals, and of becoming a worthy home and community member are not unique to any one sex, age group, educational or economic level. It is true that one can learn these things without a formal course in home economics, just as one can become an artist without a formal course in art. However, with our more specialized civilization in which no parent could know everything about all subjects, and with many of the arts of homemaking now becoming sciences, there is less formal training of children in homemaking in the immediate family. So home economics is brought to people through the school, radio, television, and magazines, and through the reports of industries concerned with homes and families. . . .
>
> Home economics exists for families. The home economist must help individual families to achieve their goals, but not to the point of insisting that *all* families realize *all* the goals of home economics. If, for good reasons, sewing is not done by families in a certain community, the home economist should

---

Table 6 (*continued*)

Note: During K-3 (primary period), "home base" teachers do most of the teaching with home economics teachers assisting and making some presentations—in a team teaching relationship. Grade 4 and above programs are taught by home economics teachers in teaching teams, using *large-group instruction* for presentations, films, television, and the like, and *small group discussion* for personal interaction, problem-solving, and communication, and *independent study* in home economics laboratories.

[8] Ibid., p. 82.

not force sewing on these families. But she should draw upon her knowledge and training to help families where they need help, whether it be in financial planning or in family relationships.

The study of home economics helps the person to develop as an individual. Through its ever-changing developments, an interest in home economics gives a person an appetite for learning. It makes use of and always requires a mastery of basic skills. It promotes good mental and physical health and also an appreciation of art and beauty. Through its concern for the family it helps one to develop values which give guidance and direction to life. Most of all, the home economist realizes her value to the community by her ability to help families lead happier lives.

Experiential Background of Self and Others

Because you have been and are a part of some pattern of family life, you have had experiences that have colored your thinking and inculcated some values concerning what is important in developing family well-being. This personal background has given you one point of reference from which you derive, consciously or unconsciously, objectives for your teaching. Your professional training has been geared toward exposing you to a variety of sources and experiences that should have enlarged your sphere of understanding of problems of families different from your own.

Just as your own personal and professional experiences provided a point of reference and a source for determining objectives, so will the experiences of others closely allied with you in teaching. Other teachers and parents can point out pitfalls and inconsistencies in the objectives you propose, simply because they are not as involved in the teaching for the achievement of these objectives as you are. Because they have known patterns of family life and professional education experiences different from your own, they can point up some needs, ideals, or characteristics which they consider important to pursue in classes that are concerned with improving the well-being of families.

One very important and available source of objectives for every teacher of home economics is the verbal and nonverbal expression of needs, interests, and concerns of the students in her classes. Youth express their *concerns and interests* in such ways as:

> I'd like to be thinner. What can I eat that will be good for me but still let me be skinny?
>
> My junior high school sister makes me so mad. Sometimes I wish she weren't around. I want to like her. I wonder why she does the things she does? Do other people feel this way about kid sisters too?
>
> We want to understand ourselves better—*our* attitudes and *our* sexuality. We want answers about sex, dating, feelings . . .

I like to buy my own clothes, but I like other people to like what I buy.

When I get out of high school I want to get married and have a family. I just love little children. I want to know the right things to do so I'll be a good mother.

Such statements reveal purposes students have relative to various aspects of their day-to-day living. Implied in the statements are student objectives. For example, the student who expressed the desire to be thinner and to know what to eat in order to achieve this end had in mind a rather specific goal and some idea of a plan of action for achieving it.

Goal: To be thinner.
Possible plan of action: Find out what foods to eat to achieve this.

Can you identify the goal and possible plan of action inherent in each of the other statements the students made? An analysis of such verbal expressions can be helpful in determining classroom objectives toward which your students might be willing and eager to work.

The foregoing statements are typical of currents of thought concerning the needs for home economics content. They are indicative of the fundamental reasons why home economics as a field of study exists and of the ends to which it aspires.

DEFINING HOME ECONOMICS OBJECTIVES

The crucial decision you will make as a teacher is that of determining what is suitable for presentation to the students assigned to you. Screening is a gigantic task. You must determine, from the vast amount of knowledge that is available for exploration in home economics, the specific knowledge that is relevant, pertinent, and essential for a particular group of people in a particular community at a particular time in history. How do you determine precisely what will be taught? Why is it essential to be able to define and state exactly what it is you want to accomplish in your classes?

The teaching of home economics involves three basic and consecutive steps. These are (1) determining and stating objectives encompassing home economics content and a specific behavior change desired in the learner; (2) providing the kinds of experiences that make possible the attainment of these objectives; and (3) seeking pertinent and reliable evidence for deciding whether these objectives have been achieved. The crux of this process is the determination and formulation of objectives. A definitive set of objectives will tell you what you should teach and how you should teach it, and will help you find out what you have taught.

With your basic philosophy plus your knowledge of literature and research as guides, you are ready to take the next step—that of translating these guides into the *general objectives* toward which the work of your department will be directed. The purposes of one high school home economics department were stated as follows:

To appreciate the importance of good family living to the family, to the community, to the nation, and to the world

To understand that family goals and patterns vary; to respect the differences in traditions, in customs and in family patterns

To realize that each person has a special role to play in the family and community; that his contribution is important to successful living

To understand the job of homemaking and acquire appropriate homemaking skills such as planning, preparing and serving wholesome meals; making and caring for clothing; planning suitable and attractive home furnishings; and managing family finances, time and energy

To assume a fair share of the responsibility of maintaining good home and family life

To show appreciation for one's home and family in love, gratitude, loyalty, pride, respect and co-operation

To realize the importance of good relations among family members; to recognize the worth of each member of the family; and to cultivate personal qualities which help in achieving good family living

To accept the family's decisions concerning the use of its resources including income, time and energy, services of family members and material things such as the car, television, and rooms for entertaining

To recognize that all families have difficulties and problems to solve; that the ability to face them and make good adjustments to them strengthens family relationships

To identify the important moral and spiritual values which characterize successful living; to realize their importance to satisfying personal, family, and community living

To create a comfortable, convenient, and attractive physical environment which is suited to the resources and the needs of the particular family that it serves.

These statements are general and do not spell out the specific objectives upon which a home economics class will focus. Neither do they delineate home economics learnings that are appropriate for various age, grade, or maturity levels. As stated, these broad purposes could lead anywhere—or nowhere, but they are requisite to an overall, Gestalt point of view concerning the major problems in family living.

Ideally, the general objective and the group of specifics under it are two ways of saying the same thing; placed in relation, they "clarify" each other.

> Without specifics under it, the general objective is apt to be a "meaningless abstraction." Without a general objective over them, the specifics are apt to lack the kind of meaning which comes when they are seen in relation to the whole of which they are a part, and through it, in relation to even larger wholes.[9]

To be usable for bringing about desired changes in individuals and, ultimately, within families, objectives must be clarified and described in specific, clear-cut, obtainable-action statements. These may then serve as links between the general problem to be solved and the specific decision to be made or question to be answered. They provide a dual vision—forward to learning experiences and backward to purposes.

Stating Objectives for Instruction

An objective is no more than a guide that one uses to determine a course of action, the objective being the ultimate outcome of the directed action. If learning is changed behavior, then the primary purpose of teaching becomes motivating and guiding learners to change their behavior. Home economics education objectives, then, in order to give a sense of direction to teaching, need to be defined so that they identify precisely the kind of behavior change that is being developed. Concurrently, this behavior change needs to be discernible in a prescribed realm of operation. It is circumscribed by the subject matter content area and the situation in which it is expected to function. Tyler said: "One can define an objective with sufficient clarity if he can describe or illustrate the kind of behavior the student is expected to acquire so that one could recognize such behavior if he saw it." [10]

Tyler continued:

> . . . a satisfactory formulation of objectives which indicates both the behavioral aspects and the content aspects provides clear specifications to indicate just what the educational job is. By defining these desired educational results as clearly as possible the curriculum-maker has the most useful set of criteria for selecting content, for suggesting learning activities, for deciding on the kind of teaching procedures to follow.[11]

Mager has stated that:

> A statement of an objective is useful to the extent that it specifies what the learner must be able to DO or PERFORM when he is demonstrating his mastery of the objective. Since no one can see into another's mind to deter-

[9] George E. Barton, Jr., "The Derivation and Clarification of Objectives." *Journal of Educational Research,* **41**:635, April 1948.

[10] Ralph W. Tyler, *Basic Principles of Curriculum and Instruction.* Chicago: University of Chicago Press, 1950, p. 38.

[11] Ibid., p. 40.

mine what he knows, you can only determine the state of the learner's intellect or skill by observing some aspects of his behavior or performance [the term "behavior," as used here, means overt action]. Now, the behavior or the performance of the learner may be verbal or nonverbal. He may be asked to respond to questions verbally or in writing, to demonstrate his ability to perform a certain skill, or to solve certain kinds of problems. But whatever method is used, you . . . can only infer the state or condition of his intellect through observation of his performance.

Thus, the most important characteristic of a useful objective is that it *identifies the kind of performance* that will be accepted as evidence that the learner has achieved the objective.[12]

The definitions of objectives set forth by Tyler and Mager are based on the premise that learning is a change in capability that can be determined from a difference in an individual's performance from one point in time to another.

A fundamental task of the home economics teacher is that of stating instructional objectives clearly and precisely. Instructional objectives are no more than your descriptions of the behavior change that you desire in your students.

Recent work in developing a taxonomy of educational objectives has facilitated the teacher's task of stating objectives in such a manner that they convey to others precisely what intended changes in behavior she is aiming toward in her students. The taxonomy orders phenomena (educational objectives) "in ways which will reveal some of their essential properties as well as the interrelationships among them." [13]

Educational objectives have been classified into three major categories: (1) cognitive—those dealing with knowledge and intellectual skills and abilities; (2) affective—those dealing with interests, attitudes and values, and (3) psychomotor—those dealing with manipulative skills and abilities

1. *Cognitive Objectives.* The cognitive domain contains six major classes: knowledge, comprehension, application, analysis, synthesis, evaluation. The authors state: "Although it is possible to conceive of these major classes in several different arrangements, the present one appears to us to represent something of the hierarchical order of the different classes of objectives." [14]

[12] Robert F. Mager, *Preparing Instructional Objectives.* Palo Alto, California: Fearon Publishers, 1962.

[13] Benjamin S. Bloom et al., *Taxonomy of Educational Objectives.* New York: Longmans, Green, 1956, p. 17.

[14] Ibid., p. 18.

[Condensed version of the Taxonomy of Educational Objectives [15]]

Cognitive Domain KNOWLEDGE

1.00 Knowledge

Knowledge, as defined here, involves the recall of specifics and universals, the recall of methods and processes, or the recall of a pattern, structure, or setting. For measurement purposes, the recall situation involves little more than bringing to mind the appropriate material. Although some alteration of the material may be required, this is a relatively minor part of the task. The knowledge objectives emphasize most the psychological processes of remembering. The process of relating is also involved in that a knowledge test situation requires the organization and reorganization of a problem such that it will furnish the appropriate signals and cues for the information and knowledge the individual possesses. To use an analogy, if one thinks of the mind as a file, the problem in a knowledge test situation is that of finding in the problem or task the appropriate signals, cues, and clues which will most effectively bring out whatever knowledge is filed or stored.

1.10 Knowledge of Specifics

The recall of specific and isolable bits of information. The emphasis is on symbols with concrete referents. This material, which is at a very low level of abstraction, may be thought of as the elements from which more complex and abstract forms of knowledge are built.

1.11 Knowledge of Terminology

Knowledge of the referents for specific symbols (verbal and nonverbal). This may include knowledge of the most generally accepted symbol referent, knowledge of the variety of symbols which may be used for a single referent, or knowledge of the referent most appropriate to a given use of a symbol.

[15] A direct quotation from *Taxonomy of Educational Objectives, The Classification of Educational Goals.* Handbook I: Cognitive Domain. Prepared by a committee of college and university examiners, and edited by Benjamin S. Bloom. New York: Longmans, Green, 1956, pp. 201–207.

° To define technical terms by giving their attributes, properties or relations.

° Familiarity with a large number of words in their common range of meanings.

1.12 Knowledge of Specific Facts

Knowledge of dates, events, persons, places, etc. This may include very precise and specific information such as the specific date or exact magnitude of a phenomenon. It may also include approximate or relative information such as an approximate time period or the general order of magnitude of a phenomenon.

° The recall of major facts about particular cultures.

° The possession of a minimum knowledge about the organisms studied in the laboratory.

1.20 Knowledge of Ways and Means of Dealing With Specifics

Knowledge of the ways of organizing, studying, judging, and criticizing. This includes the methods of inquiry, the chronological sequences, and the standards of judgment within a field as well as the patterns of organization through which the areas of the fields themselves are determined and internally organized. This knowledge is at an intermediate level of abstraction between specific knowledge on the one hand and knowledge of universals on the other It does not so much demand the activity of the student in using the materials as it does a more passive awareness of their nature.

1.21 Knowledge of Conventions

Knowledge of characteristic ways of treating and presenting ideas and phenomena. For purposes of communication and consistency, workers in a field employ usages, styles, practices, and forms which best suit their purposes and/or which appear to suit best the phenomena with which they deal. It should be recognized that although these forms and conventions are likely to be set up on arbitrary, accidental, or authoritative bases, they are retained because of the general agreement or concurrence of individuals concerned with the subject, phenomena, or problem.

° Familiarity with the forms and conventions of the major types of works, e.g., verse, plays, scientific papers, etc.

° To make pupils conscious of correct form and usage in speech and writing.

1.22 Knowledge of Trends and Sequences

Knowledge of the processes, directions, and movements of phenomena with respect to time.

° Illustrative educational objectives selected from the literature.

° Understanding of the continuity and development of American culture as exemplified in American Life.

° Knowledge of the basic trends underlying the development of public assistance programs.

1.23 Knowledge of Classifications and Categories

Knowledge of the classes, sets, divisions, and arrangements which are regarded as fundamental for a given subject field, purpose, argument, or problem.

° To recognize the area encompassed by various kinds of problems or materials.

° Becoming familiar with a range of types of literature.

1.24 Knowledge of Criteria

Knowledge of the criteria by which facts, principles, opinions, and conduct are tested or judged.

° Familiarity with criteria for judgment appropriate to the type of work and the purpose for which it is read.

° Knowledge of criteria for the evaluation of recreational activities.

1.25 Knowledge of Methodology

Knowledge of the methods of inquiry, techniques, and procedures employed in a particular subject field as well as those employed in investigating particular problems and phenomena. The emphasis here is on the individual's knowledge of the method rather than his ability to use the method.

° Knowledge of scientific methods for evaluating health concepts.

° The student shall know the methods of attack relevant to the kinds of problems of concern to the social sciences.

1.30 Knowledge of the Universals and Abstractions in a Field

Knowledge of the major schemes and patterns by which phenomena and ideas are organized. These are the large structures, theories, and generalizations which dominate a subject field or which are quite generally used in studying phenomena or solving problems. These are at the highest levels of abstraction and complexity.

1.31 Knowledge of Principles and Generalizations

Knowledge of particular abstractions which summarize observations of phenomena. These are the abstractions which are of value in explaining, describing, predicting, or determining the most appropriate and relevant action or direction to be taken.

° Knowledge of the important principles by which our experience with biological phenomena is summarized.

° The recall of major generalizations about particular cultures.

1.32 Knowledge of Theories and Structures

Knowledge of the *body* of principles and generalizations together with their interrelations which present a clear, rounded, and systematic view of a complex phenomenon, problem, or field. These are the most abstract formulations, and they can be used to show the interrelation and organization of a great range of specifics.

° The recall of major theories about particular cultures.

° Knowledge of a relatively complete formulation of the theory of evolution.

Intellectual Abilities and Skills

Abilities and skills refer to organized modes of operation and generalized techniques for dealing with materials and problems. The materials and problems may be of such a nature that little or no specialized and technical information is required. Such information as is required can be assumed to be part of the individual's general fund of knowledge. Other problems may require specialized and technical information at a rather high level such that specific knowledge and skill in dealing with the problem and the materials are required. The abilities and skills objectives emphasize the mental processes of organizing and reorganizing material to achieve a particular purpose. The materials may be given or remembered.

2.00 Comprehension

This represents the lowest level of understanding. It refers to a type of understanding or apprehension such that the individual knows what is being communicated and can make use of the material or idea being communicated without necessarily relating it to other material or seeing its fullest implications.

2.10 Translation

Comprehension as evidenced by the care and accuracy with which the communication is paraphrased or rendered from one language or form of communication to another. Translation is judged on the basis of faithfulness and accuracy, that is, on the extent to which the material in the original communication is preserved although the form of the communication has been altered.

° The ability to understand non-literal statements (metaphor, symbolism, irony, exaggeration).

° Skill in translating mathematical verbal material into symbolic statements and vice versa.

2.20 Interpretation

The explanation or summarization of a communication. Whereas translation involves an objective part-for-part rendering of a communication, interpretation involves a reordering, rearrangement, or a new view of the material.

° The ability to grasp the thought of the work as a whole at any desired level of generality.

° The ability to interpret various types of social data.

2.30 Extrapolation

The extension of trends or tendencies beyond the given data to determine implications, consequences, corollaries, effects, etc., which are in accordance with the conditions described in the original communication.

° The ability to deal with the conclusions of a work in terms of the immediate inference made from the explicit statements.

° Skill in predicting continuation of trends.

3.00 Application

The use of abstractions in particular and concrete situations. The abstractions may be in the form of general ideas, rules of procedures, or generalized methods. The abstractions may also be technical principles, ideas, and theories which must be remembered and applied.

° Application to the phenomena discussed in one paper of the scientific terms or concepts used in other papers.

° The ability to predict the probable effect of a change in a factor on a biological situation previously at equilibrium.

4.00 Analysis

The breakdown of a communication into its constituent elements or parts such that the relative hierarchy of ideas is made clear and/or the relations between the ideas expressed are made explicit. Such analyses are intended to clarify the communication, to indicate how the communication is organized, and the way in which it manages to convey its effects, as well as its basis and arrangement.

4.10 Analysis of Elements

Identification of the elements included in a communication.

° The ability to recognize unstated assumptions.

° Skill in distinguishing facts from hypotheses.

4.20 Analysis of Relationships

The connections and interactions between elements and parts of a communication.

° Ability to check the consistency of hypotheses with given information and assumptions.

° Skill in comprehending the interrelationships among the ideas in a passage.

4.30 Analysis of Organizational Principles

The organization, systematic arrangement, and structure which hold the communication together. This includes the "explicit" as well as "implicit" structure. It includes the bases, necessary arrangement, and the mechanics which make the communication a unit.

° The ability to recognize form and pattern in literary or artistic works as a means of understanding their meaning.

° Ability to recognize the general techniques used in persuasive materials, such as advertising, propaganda, etc.

5.00 Synthesis

The putting together of elements and parts so as to form a whole. This involves the process of working with pieces, parts, elements, etc., and combining them in such a way as to constitute a pattern or structure not clearly there before.

5.10 Production of a Unique Communication

The development of a communication in which the writer or speaker attempts to convey ideas, feelings, and/or experiences to others.

° Skill in writing, using an excellent organization of ideas and statements.

° Ability to tell a personal experience effectively.

5.20 Production of a Plan, or Proposed Set of Operations

The development of a plan of work or the proposal of a plan of operations. The plan should satisfy requirements of the task which may be given to the student or which he may develop for himself.

° Ability to propose ways of testing hypotheses.

° Ability to plan a unit of instruction for a particular teaching situation.

5.30 Derivation of a Set of Abstract Relations

The development of a set of abstract relations either to classify or explain particular data or phenomena, or the deduction of propositions and relations from a set of basic propositions or symbolic representations.

° Ability to formulate appropriate hypotheses based upon an analysis of factors involved, and to modify such hypotheses in the light of new factors and considerations.

° Ability to make mathematical discoveries and generalizations.

6.00 Evaluation

Judgments about the value of material and methods for given purposes. Quantitative and qualitative judgments about the extent to which material and methods satisfy criteria. Use of a standard of appraisal. The criteria may be those determined by the student or those which are given to him.

6.10 Judgments in Terms of Internal Evidence

Evaluation of the accuracy of a communication from such evidence as logical accuracy, consistency, and other internal criteria.

° Judging by internal standards, the ability to assess general probability of accuracy in reporting facts from the care given to exactness of statement, documentation, proof, etc.

° The ability to indicate logical fallacies in argument.

6.20 Judgments in Terms of External Criteria

Evaluation of material with reference to selected or remembered criteria

° The comparison of major theories, generalizations, and facts about particular cultures.

° Judging by external standards, the ability to compare a work with the highest known standards in its field—especially with other works of recognized excellence.

2. *Affective Objectives.* The affective domain contains five major classes: receiving (attending), responding, valuing, organization, and characterization by a value or value complex. The authors state,

> The ordering of objectives . . . is of prime importance in the affective domain. . . . The entire domain proceeds from categories which are relatively simple, requiring very little from the student, to categories of objectives which require a fairly complete internalization of a set of attitudes, values, and behaviors. We imagine that the learning of the more highly internalized objectives must start with the more simple and perhaps superficial behaviors specified in the first few categories of this domain. It is entirely possible that the learning of the more difficult and internalized objectives must be in the form of a "loop" which begins with the simple and more overt behaviors, gradually moves to the more complex and more internalized behaviors, and repeats the entire procedure in new areas of content and behavior until a highly internalized, consistent, and complex set of affective behaviors is finally developed.[16]

[16] David R. Krathwohl, Benjamin S. Bloom, and Bertram B. Masia. *A Taxonomy of Educational Objectives, The Classification of Educational Goals.* Handbook II: Affective Domain. New York: David McKay Company, Inc., 1964, pp. 79–80.

[Condensed version of the Taxonomy of Educational Objectives[17]] Affective Domain

1.0 Receiving (Attending)

At this level we are concerned that the learner be sensitized to the existence of certain phenomena and stimuli; that is, that he be willing to receive or to attend to them. This is clearly the first and crucial step if the learner is to be properly oriented to learn what the teacher intends that he will. To indicate that this is the bottom rung of the ladder, however, is not at all to imply that the teacher is starting *de novo*. Because of previous experience (formal or informal), the student brings to each situation a point of view or set which may facilitate or hinder his recognition of the phenomena to which the teacher is trying to sensitize him.

The category of *Receiving* has been divided into three subcategories to indicate three different levels of attending to phenomena. While the division points between the subcategories are arbitrary, the subcategories do represent a continuum. From an extremely passive position or role on the part of the learner, where the sole responsibility for the evocation of the behavior rests with the teacher—that is, the responsibility rests with him for "capturing" the student's attention—the continuum extends to a point at which the learner directs his attention, at least at a semiconscious level, toward the preferred stimuli.

1.1 *Awareness*

Awareness is almost a cognitive behavior. But unlike *Knowledge,* the lowest level of the cognitive domain, we are not so much concerned with a memory of, or ability to recall, an item or fact as we are that, given appropriate opportunity, the learner will merely be conscious of something—that he take into account a situation, phenomenon, object, or stage of affairs. Like *Knowledge* it does not imply an assessment of the qualities or nature of the stimulus, but unlike *Knowledge* it does not necessarily imply attention. There can be simple awareness without specific discrimination or recognition of the objective characteristics of the object, even though these characteristics must be deemed to have an effect. The individual may not be able to verbalize the aspects of the stimulus which cause the awareness.

[17] Ibid., pp. 176–185.

Develops awareness of aesthetic factors in dress, furnishings, architecture, city design, good art, and the like.

Develops some consciousness of color, form, arrangement, and design in the objects and structures around him and in descriptive or symbolic representations of people, things, and situations.*

1.2 *Willingness to Receive*

In this category we have come a step up the ladder but are still dealing with what appears to be cognitive behavior. At a minimum level, we are here describing the behavior of being willing to tolerate a given stimulus, not to avoid it. Like *Awareness,* it involves a neutrality or suspended judgment toward the stimulus. At this level of the continuum the teacher is not concerned that the student seek it out, nor even, perhaps, that in an environment crowded with many other stimuli the learner will necessarily attend to the stimulus. Rather, at worst, given the opportunity to attend in a field with relatively few competing stimuli, the learner is not actively seeking to avoid it. At best, he is willing to take notice of the phenomenon and give it his attention.

Attends (carefully) when others speak—in direct conversation, on the telephone, in audiences.

Appreciation (tolerance) of cultural patterns exhibited by individuals from other groups—religious, social, political, economic, national, etc.

Increase in sensitivity to human need and pressing social problems.

1.3 *Controlled or Selected Attention*

At a somewhat higher level we are concerned with a new phenomenon, the differentiation of a given stimulus into figure and ground at a conscious or perhaps semiconscious level—the differentiation of aspects of a stimulus which is perceived as clearly marked off from adjacent impressions. The perception is still without tension or assessment, and the student may not know the technical terms or symbols with which to describe it correctly or precisely to others. In some instances it may refer not so much to the selectivity of attention as to the control of attention, so that when certain stimuli are present they will be attended to. There is an element of the learner's controlling the attention here, so that the favored stimulus is selected and attended to despite competing and distracting stimuli.

Listens to music with some discrimination as to its mood and meaning and with some recognition of the contributions of various musical elements and instruments to the total effect.

* Illustrative objectives selected from the literature follow the description of each subcategory.

Alertness toward human values and judgments on life as they are recorded in literature.

2.0 Responding

At this level we are concerned with responses which go beyond merely attending to the phenomenon. The student is sufficiently motivated that he is not just 1.2 *Willing to attend,* but perhaps it is correct to say that he is actively attending. As a first stage in a "learning by doing" process the student is committing himself in some small measure to the phenomena involved. This is a very low level of commitment, and we would not say at this level that this was "a value of his" or that he had "such and such an attitude." These terms belong to the next higher level that we describe. But we could say that he is doing something with or about the phenomenon besides merely perceiving it, as would be true at the next level below this of 1.3 *Controlled or selected attention.*

This is the category that many teachers will find best describes their "interest" objectives. Most commonly we use the term to indicate the desire that a child become sufficiently involved in or committed to a subject, phenomenon, or activity that he will seek it out and gain satisfaction from working with it or engaging in it.

2.1 *Acquiescence in Responding*

We might use the word "obedience" or "compliance" to describe this behavior. As both of these terms indicate, there is a passiveness so far as the initiation of the behavior is concerned, and the stimulus calling for this behavior is not subtle. Compliance is perhaps a better term than obedience, since there is more of the element of reaction to a suggestion and less of the implication of resistance or yielding unwillingly. The student makes response, but he has not fully accepted the necessity for doing so.

Willingness to comply with health regulations.
Obeys the playground regulations.

2.2 *Willingness to Respond*

The key to this level is in the term "willingness," with its implication of capacity for voluntary activity. There is the implication that the learner is sufficiently committed to exhibiting the behavior that he does so not just because of a fear of punishment, but "on his own" or voluntarily. It may help to note that the element of resistance or of yielding unwillingly, which is possibly present at the previous level, is here replaced with consent or proceeding from one's own choice.

Acquaints himself with significant current issues in international, political, social, and economic affairs through voluntary reading and discussion.

Acceptance of responsibility for his own health and for the protection of the health of others.

2.3 *Satisfaction in Response*

The additional element in the step beyond the *Willingness to respond* level, the consent, the assent to responding, or the voluntary response, is that the behavior is accompanied by a feeling of satisfaction, an emotional response, generally of pleasure, zest, or enjoyment. The location of this category in the hierarchy has given us a great deal of difficulty. Just where in the process of internalization the attachment of an emotional response, kick, or thrill to a behavior occurs has been hard to determine. For that matter there is some uncertainty as to whether the level of internalization at which it occurs may not depend on the particular behavior. We have even questioned whether it should be a category. If our structure is to be a hierarchy, then each category should include the behavior in the next level below it. The emotional component appears gradually through the range of internalization categories. The attempt to specify a given position in the hierarchy as *the* one at which the emotional component is added is doomed to failure.

The category is arbitrarily placed at this point in the hierarchy where it seems to appear most frequently and where it is cited as or appears to be an important component of the objectives at this level on the continuum. The category's inclusion at this point serves the pragmatic purpose of reminding us of the presence of the emotional component and its value in the building of affective behaviors. But it should not be thought of as appearing and occurring at this one point in the continuum and thus destroying the hierarchy which we are attempting to build.

Enjoyment of self-expression in music and in arts and crafts as another means of personal enrichment.

Finds pleasure in reading for recreation.

Takes pleasure in conversing with many different kinds of people.

3.0 Valuing

This is the only category headed by a term which is in common use in the expression of objectives by teachers. Further, it is employed in its usual sense: that a thing, phenomenon, or behavior has worth. This abstract concept of worth is in part a result of the individual's own valuing or assessment, but it is much more a social product that has been slowly internalized or accepted and has come to be used by the student as his own criterion of worth.

Behavior categorized at this level is sufficiently consistent and stable to have taken on the characteristics of a belief or an attitude. The learner displays this behavior with sufficient consistency in appropriate situations that he comes to be perceived as holding a value. At this level, we are not concerned with the relationships among values but rather with the internalization of a set of specified, ideal, values. Viewed from another standpoint, the objectives classified here are the prime stuff from which the conscience of the individual is developed into active control of behavior.

This category will be found appropriate for many objectives that use the term "attitude" (as well as, of course, "value").

An important element of behavior characterized by *Valuing* is that it is motivated, not by the desire to comply or obey, but by the individual's commitment to the underlying value guiding the behavior.

3.1 *Acceptance of a Value*

At this level we are concerned with the ascribing of worth to a phenomenon, behavior, object, etc. The term "belief," which is defined as "the emotional acceptance of a proposition or doctrine upon what one implicitly considers adequate ground" (English and English, 1958, p. 64), describes quite well what may be thought of as the dominant characteristic here. Beliefs have varying degrees of certitude. At this lowest level of *Valuing* we are concerned with the lowest levels of certainty; that is, there is more of a readiness to re-evaluate one's position than at the higher levels. It is a position that is somewhat tentative.

One of the distinguishing characteristics of this behavior is consistency of response to the class of objects, phenomena, etc. with which the belief or attitude is identified. It is consistent enough so that the person is perceived by others as holding the belief or value. At the level we are describing here, he is both sufficiently consistent that others can identify the value, and sufficiently committed that he is willing to be so identified.

Continuing desire to develop the ability to speak and write effectively.
Grows in his sense of kinship with human beings of all nations.

3.2 *Preference for a Value*

The provision for this subdivision arose out of a feeling that there were objectives that expressed a level of internalization between the mere acceptance of a value and commitment or conviction in the usual connotation of deep involvement in an area. Behavior at this level implies not just the acceptance of a value to the point of being willing to be identified with it, but the individual is sufficiently committed to the value to pursue it, to seek it out, to want it.

Assumes responsibility for drawing reticent members of a group into conversation.

Deliberately examines a variety of viewpoints on controversial issues with a view to forming opinions about them.

Actively participates in arranging for the showing of contemporary artistic efforts.

3.3 *Commitment*

Belief at this level involves a high degree of certainty. The ideas of "conviction" and "certainty beyond a shadow of a doubt" help to convey further the level of behavior intended. In some instances this may border on faith, in the sense of it being a firm emotional acceptance of a belief upon admittedly nonrational grounds. Loyalty to a position, group, or cause would also be classified here.

The person who displays behavior at this level is clearly perceived as holding the value. He acts to further the thing valued in some way, to extend the possibility of his developing it, to deepen his involvement with it and with the things representing it. He tries to convince others and seeks converts to his cause. There is a tension here which needs to be satisfied; action is the result of an aroused need or drive. There is a real motivation to act out the behavior.

Devoting to those ideas and ideals which are the foundations of democracy.

Faith in the power of reason and in methods of experiment and discussion.

4.0 Organization

As the learner successively internalizes values, he encounters situations for which more than one value is relevant. Thus necessity arises for (*a*) the organization of the values into a system, (*b*) the determination of the interrelationships among them, and (*c*) the establishment of the dominant and pervasive ones. Such a system is built gradually, subject to change as new values are incorporated. This category is intended as the proper classification for objectives which describe the beginnings of the building of a value system. It is subdivided into two levels, since a prerequisite to interrelating is the conceptualization of the value in a form which permits organization. *Conceptualization* forms the first subdivision in the organization process. *Organization of a value system* the second.

While the order of the two subcategories seems appropriate enough with reference to one another, it is not so certain that 4.1 *Conceptualization of a value* is properly placed as the next level above 3.3. *Commitment.* Conceptualization undoubtedly begins at an earlier level for some objectives. Like 2.3 *Satisfaction in response,* it is doubtful that a single completely satisfactory location for this category can be found. Positioning it before 4.2 *Organization of a value system* appropriately indicates a prerequisite of such a system. It also calls attention to a component of affective growth that occurs at least by this point on the continuum but may begin earlier.

4.1 *Conceptualization of a Value*

In the previous category, 3.0 *Valuing,* we noted that consistency and stability are integral characteristics of the particular value or belief. At this level (4.1) the quality of abstraction or conceptualization is added. This permits the individual to see how the value relates to those that he already holds or to new ones that he is coming to hold.

Conceptualization will be abstract, and in this sense it will be symbolic. But the symbols need not be verbal symbols. Whether conceptualization first appears at this point on the affective continuum is a moot point, as noted above.

Attempts to identify the characteristics of an art object which he admires.

Forms judgments as to the responsibility of society for conserving human and material resources.

4.2 *Organization of a Value System*

Objectives properly classified here are those which require the learner to bring together a complex of values, possibly disparate values, and to bring these into an ordered relationship with one another. Ideally, the ordered relationship will be one which is harmonious and internally consistent. This is, of course, the goal of such objectives, which seek to have the student formulate a philosophy of life. In actuality, the integration may be something less than entirely harmonious. More likely the relationship is better described as a kind of dynamic equilibrium which is, in part, dependent upon those portions of the environment which are salient at any point in time. In many instances the organization of values may result in their synthesis into a new value or value complex of a higher order.

Weighs alternative social policies and practices against the standards of the public welfare rather than the advantage of specialized and narrow interest groups.

Develops a plan for regulating his rest in accordance with the demands of his activities.

5.0 Characterization by a Value or Value Complex

At this level of internalization the values already have a place in the individual's value hierarchy, are organized into some kind of internally consistent system, have controlled the behavior of the individual for a sufficient time that he has adapted to behaving this way; and an evocation of the behavior no longer arouses emotion or affect except when the individual is threatened or challenged.

The individual acts consistently in accordance with the values he has internalized at this level, and our concern is to indicate two things: (*a*) the generalization of this control to so much of the individual's behavior that he is described and characterized as a person by these pervasive controlling tendencies, and (*b*) the integration of these beliefs, ideas, and attitudes into a total philosophy or world view. These two aspects constitute the subcategories.

5.1 *Generalized Set*

The generalized set is that which gives an internal consistency to the system of attitudes and values at any particular moment. It is selective responding at a very high level. It is sometimes spoken of as a determining tendency, an orientation toward phenomena, or a predisposition to act in a certain way. The generalized set is a response to highly generalized phenomena. It is a persistent and consistent response to a family of related situations or objects. It may often be an unconscious set which guides action without conscious forethought. The generalized set may be thought of as closely related to the idea of an attitude cluster, where the commonality is based on behavioral characteristics rather than the subject or object of the attitude. A generalized set is a basic orientation which enables the individual to reduce and order the complex world about him and to act consistently and effectively in it.

Readiness to revise judgments and to change behavior in the light of evidence.

Judges problems and issues in terms of situations, issues, purposes, and consequences involved rather than in terms of fixed, dogmatic precepts or emotionally wishful thinking.

5.2 *Characterization*

This, the peak of the internalization process, includes those objectives which are broadest with respect both to the phenomena covered and to the range of behavior which they comprise. Thus, here are found those objectives which concern one's view of the universe, one's philosophy of life, one's *Weltanschauung*—a value system having as its object the whole of what is known or knowable.

Objectives categorized here are more than generalized sets in the sense that they involve a greater inclusiveness and, within the group of attitudes, behaviors, beliefs, or ideas, an emphasis on internal consistency. Though this internal consistency may not always be exhibited behaviorally by the students toward whom the objective is directed, since we are categorizing teachers' objectives, this consistency feature will always be a component of *Characterization* objectives.

As the title of the category implies, these objectives are so encompassing that they tend to characterize the individual almost completely.

> Develops for regulation of one's personal and civic life a code of behavior based on ethical principles consistent with democratic ideals.
>
> Develops a consistent philosophy of life.

3. *Psychomotor Objectives.* The psychomotor domain, as currently developed, contains five classes: perception, set, guided response, mechanism, and complex overt response. Simpson states:

> Preliminary investigations with respect to the development of a classification system for educational objectives in the psychomotor domain led to the conclusion that there is a hierarchy among the three domains. The cognitive domain, though certainly very complex, is, in a sense, somewhat "purer" than the other two domains. That is, cognition can take place with a minimum of motor activity. Also, feeling may not be greatly involved—although it would be reasonable to assume some degree of affect. The affective domain necessarily involved considerable cognition as well as feeling. And, the psychomotor domain, as implied in the very name, involves cognition and motor activity, as well as affective components involved in the willingness to act.[18]

[18] Elizabeth J. Simpson, "The Classification of Educational Objectives, Psychomotor Domain." *Illinois Teacher of Home Economics,* Vol. X, No. 4, Winter 1966–67, pp. 117–118.

[Condensed version of the Taxonomy of Educational Objectives[19]]

Psychomotor Domain

The following schema for classification of educational objectives in the psychomotor domain is presented with the full knowledge that it is still in a tentative form.

The major organizational principle operative is that of complexity with attention to the sequence involved in the performance of a motor act.

1.0 ***Perception.*** This is an essential first step in performing a motor act. It is the process of becoming aware of objects, qualities, or relations by way of the sense organs. It is the central portion of the situation—interpretation—action chain leading to purposeful motor activity.

The category of perception has been divided into three subcategories indicating three different levels with respect to the perception process. It seems to the investigator that this level is a parallel of the first category, receiving or attending, in the affective domain.

1.1 ***Sensory stimulation.*** Impingement of a stimulus (i) upon one or more of the sense organs.

1.11 ***Auditory.*** Hearing or the sense or organs of hearing.

1.12 ***Visual.*** Concerned with the mental pictures or images obtained through the eyes

1.13 ***Tactile.*** Pertaining to the sense of touch

1.14 ***Taste.*** Ascertain the relish or flavor of by taking a portion into the mouth

1.15 ***Smell.*** To perceive by excitation of the olfactory nerves

1.16 ***Kinesthetic.*** The muscle sense; pertaining to sensitivity from activation of receptors in muscles, tendons, and joints

The preceding categories are not presented in any special order of importance, although, in Western cultures, the visual cues are said to have dominance, whereas in some cultures, the auditory and tactile cues may pre-empt the high position we give the visual. Probably no sensible

[19] Ibid., pp. 135–140.

ordering of these is possible. It should also be pointed out that "the cues that guide action may change for a particular motor activity as learning progresses (e.g., kinesthetic cues replacing visual cues)."

1.1 ***Sensory stimulation.*** Illustrative educational objectives.

Sensitivity to auditory cues in playing a musical instrument as a member of a group.

Awareness of difference in "hand" of various fabrics.

Sensitivity to flavors in seasoning food.

1.2 ***Cue selection.*** Deciding to what cues one must respond in order to satisfy the particular requirements of task performance.

This involves identification of the cue or cues and associating them with the task to be performed. It may involve grouping of cues in terms of past experience and knowledge. Cues relevant to the situation are selected as a guide to action; irrelevant cues are ignored or discarded.

1.2 ***Cue selection.*** Illustrative educational objectives.

Recognition of operating difficulties with machinery through the sound of the machine in operation.

Sensing where the needle should be set in beginning machine stitching.

Recognizing factors to take into account in batting in a softball game.

1.3 ***Translation.*** Relating of perception to action in performing a motor act. This is the mental process of determining the meaning of the cues received for action. It involves symbolic translation, that is, having an image or being reminded of something, "having an idea," as a result of cues received. It may involve insight which is essential in solving a problem through perceiving the relationships essential to solution. Sensory translation is an aspect of this level. It involves "feedback," that is, knowledge of the effects of the process; translation is a continuous part of the motor act being performed.

1.3 ***Translation.*** Illustrative educational objectives.

Ability to relate music to dance form.

Ability to follow a recipe in preparing food.

Knowledge of the "feel" of operating a sewing machine successfully and use of this knowledge as a guide in stitching.

2.0 ***Set.*** Set is a preparatory adjustment or readiness for a particular kind of action or experience.

Three aspects of set have been identified: mental, physical, and emotional.

2.1 ***Mental set.*** Readiness, in the mental sense, to perform a certain motor act. This involves, as prerequisite, the level of perception and its subcategories which have already been identified. Discrimination, that is, using judgment in making distinctions is an aspect.

2.1 ***Mental set.*** Illustrative educational objectives.

Knowledge of steps in setting the table.

Knowledge of tools appropriate to performance of various sewing operations.

2.2 ***Physical set.*** Readiness in the sense of having made the anatomical adjustments necessary for a motor act to be formed. Readiness, in the physical sense, involves receptor set, that is, sensory attending, or focusing the attention of the needed sensory organs and postural set, or positioning of the body.

2.2 ***Physical set.*** Illustrative educational objectives.

Achievement of bodily stance preparatory to bowling.

Positioning of hands preparatory to typing.

2.3 ***Emotional set.*** Readiness in terms of attitudes favorable to the motor act's taking place. Willingness to respond is implied.

2.3 ***Emotional set.*** Illustrative educational objectives.

Disposition to perform sewing machine operation to best of ability.

Desire to operate a production drill press with skill.

3.0 ***Guided response.*** This is an early step in the development of skill. Emphasis here is upon the abilities which are components of the more complex skill. Guided response is the overt behavioral act of an individual under the guidance of the instructor. Prerequisite to performance of the act are readiness to respond, in terms of set to produce the overt behavioral act and selection of the appropriate response. Selection of response may be defined as deciding what response must be made in order to satisfy the particular requirements of task performance. There appear to be two major subcategories, imitation and trial and error.

3.1 ***Imitation.*** Imitation is the execution of an act as a direct response to the perception of another person performing the act.

3.1 ***Imitation.*** Illustrative educational objectives.

Imitation of the process of stay-stitching the curved neck edge of a bodice.

Performing a dance step as demonstrated.

Debeaking a chick in the manner demonstrated.

3.2 ***Trial and error.*** Trying various responses, usually with some rationale for each response, until an appropriate response is achieved. The appropriate response is one which meets the requirements of task performance, that is, "gets the job done" or does it more efficiently. This level may be defined as multiple-response learning in which the proper response is selected out of varied behavior, possibly through the influence of reward and punishment.

3.2 ***Tial and error.*** Illustrative educational objectives.

Discovering the most efficient method of ironing a blouse through trial of various procedures.

Ascertaining the sequence for cleaning a room through trial of several patterns.

4.0 ***Mechanism.*** Learned response has become habitual. At this level, the learner has achieved a certain confidence and degree of skill in the performance of the act. The act is a part of his repertoire of possible responses to stimuli and the demands of situations where the response is an appropriate one. The response may be more complex than at the preceding level; it may involve some patterning of response in carrying out the task. That is, abilities are combined in action of a skill nature.

4.0 ***Mechanism.*** Illustrative educational objectives.

Ability to perform a hand-hemming operation.

Ability to mix ingredients for a butter cake.

Ability to pollinate an oat flower.

5.0 ***Complex overt response.*** At this level, the individual can perform a motor act that is considered complex because of the movement pattern required. At this level, a high degree of skill has been attained. The act can be carried out smoothly and efficiently, that is, with minimum expenditure of time and energy. There are two subcategories: resolution of uncertainty and automatic performance.

5.1 ***Resolution of uncertainty.*** The act is performed without hesitation of the individual to get a mental picture of task sequence. That is, he knows the sequence required and so proceeds with confidence. The act is here defined as complex in nature.

5.1 ***Resolution of uncertainty.*** Illustrative educational objectives.

Skill in operating a milling machine.

Skill in setting up and operating a production band saw.

Skill in laying a pattern on fabric and cutting out a garment.

5.2 *Automatic performance.* At this level, the individual can perform a finely coordinated motor skill with a great deal of ease and muscle control.

5.2 *Automatic performance.* Illustrative educational objectives.

Skill in performing basic steps of national folk dances.

Skill in tailoring a suit.

Skill in performing on the violin.

Another question that needs further investigation is: Is there perhaps a sixth major category which might be designated as *adapting* and *originating*? Possibly such a level is needed. At this level, the individual might be so skilled that he can adapt the action in terms of the specific requirements of the individual performer and the situation. He might originate new patterns of action in solving a specific problem. Or do these activities take place at all levels? Must the individual have attained a high degree of skill in order to adapt and originate?

The taxonomies of educational objectives are especially useful in helping you state objectives clearly and precisely. You have probably noted that the authors of each domain have hypothesized the hierarchical nature of educational objectives. According to Gagne,[20] learning can be facilitated if one understands the "pyramid" nature of capability development. He views, for example, a given capability as terminal behavior, which he places at the top of what eventually becomes a complex pyramid. To be able to reach the terminal capability one must first be able to perform lower level tasks—so a pyramid is formed. Learning is believed to develop in a somewhat sequential fashion. Understanding the hierarchical nature of each domain of educational objectives and their relationship one to another can be of assistance to you in sequencing learnings.

As you study and compare the behaviors in these three domains, can you see any relationships between the cognitive, affective, and psychomotor objectives at the various levels? Chart 4 might help you to clarify the hierarchical nature of these behaviors.

[20] Robert M. Gagne, *The Conditions of Learning*. New York: Holt, Rinehart and Winston, 1965, pp. 87–112.

CHART 4 Behaviors in the Cognitive, Affective, and Psychomotor Domain

Level of Behavior	Cognitive	Affective	Psychomotor
5 Integration and control	Evaluation	Characterization by a value complex	Complex overt response
4 Relationship of parts; a system	Analysis, synthesis	Organization	Mechanism
3 Action	Application	Valuing	Guided response
2 Readiness to react	Comprehension	Responding	Set
1 Awareness	Knowledge	Receiving	Perception

Cognitive, affective and psychomotor learnings all have their place in home economics. A taxonomy is useful in clarifying what behavior to expect from students—an absolute essential if we are to guide learning efficiently through school learning experiences and if we are to measure changes in behavior. Being able to state objectives precisely should assist you in sharpening your yearly, unit, and daily plans. You will need to think through the appropriate sequence of learning both from a day-to-day level and a year-to-year one. Stating objectives precisely can be helpful. This can be accomplished only when teachers set objectives that have continuity. Enough time must be allowed to bring about long-range changes in behavior. Teachers need to take a *longer* look at problems and they need to allow students more choice relative to their areas of unknowns.

As a means of stating objectives in a form that will be helpful in selecting learning experiences and guiding teaching, Tyler has emphasized that:

> The most useful form for stating objectives is to express them in terms which identify both the kind of behavior to be developed in the student and the content or areas of life in which this behavior is to operate. . . . The objective, "Familiarity with Dependable Sources of Information on Questions Relating to Nutrition," includes both an indication of the sort of behavior, namely familiarity with dependable sources, and the content, namely, those sources that deal with problems of nutrition.[21]

Tyler suggests the use of a two-dimensional chart (Table 7) in which the behavioral aspects of objectives might form headings across the top and the content aspects might be listed at the side. In such a chart, not every behavioral aspect would apply to each content objective, but a

[21] Ralph W. Tyler, *Basic Principles of Curriculum and Instruction.* Chicago: The University of Chicago Press, Syllabus Division, 1950, p. 30.

TABLE 7 Illustration of the Use of a Two-Dimensional Chart in Stating Objectives for a Course in Clothing and Textiles

		Behavioral Aspects of Objectives		
	Objectives	Cognitive Domain	Affective Domain	Psychomotor Domain
Content Aspect of Objectives	A. To be able to use resources	A. To be able to compare the difference in cost of a ready-made dress and a handmade dress		
	B. To become aware of aesthetic factors in dress	B. To be able to identify basic art principles	B. To be willing to purchase a dress on the basis of art principles	
	C. To develop skill in caring for clothing	C. To identify specific procedures for ironing a blouse	C. To assume responsibility for keeping one's clothing ironed	C. To discover the most efficient method of ironing a blouse by trying several methods

teacher could see readily what types of behavior change could be brought about through the various topics that are studied by her students. Among the behavioral aspects that might apply to a study of nutrition are:

1. Understanding of important facts and principles.
2. Familiarity with dependable sources of information.
3. Ability to interpret data.
4. Ability to apply principles.
5. Ability to study and report results of study.
6. Broad and mature interests.
7. Social attitudes.[22]

Planning for the Year

You will want to put some of your plans into writing so that they can serve as your road map throughout the year. Many schools require that the teacher turn in her yearly objectives and a more detailed weekly plan for each school year. Special forms peculiar to the school setting

[22] Ibid., p. 32.

are usually provided; in essence, they usually request a noting of specific goal, method of teaching to be used or classroom experience to be provided, and references or resources to be used.

The amount of detail included in a problem or in a daily lesson plan will be dependent upon your knowledge about the special area and your experience. Even though you are confident of your knowledge and have had experience in working with young people, a measure of written planning is essential to good teaching, for it forces you to clarify both goal and means for achieving it prior to meeting the class. It is much more efficient to define the alternatives and to predetermine the consequences by calculated consideration, rather than to pursue the matter by costly trial and error!

Before you can make specific plans for any one grade or course, you need to have a clear picture of the scope and sequence of all the courses available in your school. As suggested in the previous chapter, leaders in your state undoubtedly have developed a general guide which you will need to adapt to your own program. Your plan for any particular course or grade may include units from several areas of home economics (as illustrated in Chart 5). On the other hand, you may be planning a sequence of units for an occupational field or for an advanced course, in which students develop depth in a specialized area.

Although your yearly plan will be quite general, it should outline all of the main topics you expect to cover. Chart 5 shows the units represented in plans for one grade. For illustrative purposes we are including here the specific outlines for only two of the areas (Unit III, Part II, sections G and H.)

CHART 5 Home Economics Grade 8 Unit Outlines *

Unit I. *Understanding Personal Development*
- I. Concepts of femininity.
- II. Feminine responsibilities.

Unit II. *Understanding Others*
- I. Concept of friendship and bases of friendship.
- II. Understanding other girls.
- III. Understanding boys.
- IV. Understanding parents and other adults.
- V. Understanding older persons.

Unit III. *Occupations Related to Home Economics Requiring Varying Levels of Preparation*
- I. Guidelines for making a vocational decision.

* "Curriculum Guides for a Coordinated Program of Home Economics," *Illinois Teacher of Home Economics,* XI:344–350, Spring 1967–68.

CHART 5 *(continued)*

- II. Relation of home economics to employment of women.
  - A. Characteristics of women in labor force.
  - B. Family adjustments necessitated by employment of homemaker.
  - C. Motivations for women working.
  - D. Factors which influence a girl's vocational plans.
  - E. Changes affecting employment of women.
  - F. Changes in status of women.
  - G. Roles of women.
    1. Assume multiple roles.
    2. Increased emphasis on role as wage earner.
    3. Less differentiation between roles of men and women.
  - H. Contribution of home economics in preparing women for varied roles.
    1. Educates for establishing a satisfying personal and family life.
    2. Provides knowledge and skill for wage earning.
    3. Offers training at all levels of aspiration.
    4. Helps in managing work at home and on the job.
    5. Provides for creative and leisure time activities.
  - I. Occupations requiring home economics knowledges and skills.

Unit IV. *Selecting and Caring for Personal Clothing*

- I. Value considerations with respect to clothing.
- II. Relationship between dress and behavior.
- III. Other considerations in selecting clothing.
- IV. Quality factors in selecting.
- V. Care of personal clothing.

Unit V. *Use of Personal Leisure*

- I. Definition of leisure
- II. Ways in which leisure is used and examples of each, in terms of activities carried out alone, with friends, or with family.
- III. Constructive and destructive use of leisure.
- IV. Use of entertainment media.

Unit VI. *Communication in Social Situations*

- I. The social occasion as an opportunity for communication of friendly, gracious feelings.
- II. Entertaining at home.

Unit Planning

The yearly plan provides an outline of topics to be covered, but you will need to be more specific as you plan to teach each of the units. Exactly how specific you need to be is something you will learn from experience. At first you should probably be quite thorough in stating objectives, content, learning experiences, teaching aids, and evaluation. You may wish to indicate which objectives from the three Taxonomies

CHART 6 Part of a Unit Plan on Occupations *

Objectives

Knows that any one woman may assume different roles as she progresses from stage to stage in the life cycle. (C-1.22 Knowledge of trends and sequences †)

Can visualize assuming many different roles. (A-4.1 Conceptualization of a value)

Content

One's role concept is influenced by the expectations and approval of others.

An individual functions in a variety of roles and may assume more than one role at a time.

Most women today assume multiple roles.

When homemakers work outside the home, they assume an additional role as wage earner.

The employment of women has resulted in less difference between roles of men and women in the family.

Teaching Aids

Books

Barclay, *Teen Guide to Homemaking,* Chapter 17, "Your Share in the Family," Chapter 18, "Your Relations in the Family."

Learning Experiences

1. Discuss the meaning of a person's "roles." (C-1.11 Knowledge of terminology)
   Give examples of present roles as eighth graders: student, baby-sitter, family member, FHA member.
2. Look at pictures of a little girl, teenager, mother of young children, mother of teenagers, middle-age woman and an elderly woman. Write brief descriptions of selves at stages portrayed by each picture. (A-4.1)
3. List the variety of responsibilities which women have. Relate these to women's various roles. (C-1.12 Knowledge of specific facts)
4. Select and display on bulletin board pictures which illustrate the variety of roles assumed by women: wage earner, wife, mother, cook, nurse. (C-1.12 Knowledge of specific facts)
5. Brainstorm on predictions for "The Woman of 1980." (C-1.22)
6. Divide into groups and pretend to be: brothers, sisters, mothers, fathers. Each group lists roles on board and then compare roles. Identify similarities among roles. (A-4.1)

Evaluation: Appraise students' view of their roles by reading their descriptions of themselves as a person at various stages of life. Rate students on their ability to perceive themselves. Observe the students' ability to project the future roles of women. Note their perceptions of roles of different family members.

* "Curriculum Guides for a Coordinated Program of Home Economics." *Illinois Teacher of Home Economics,* XI:367–378, Spring 1967–1968.

† Parenthetical statements in this chart are references to the appropriately numbered sections of the taxonomies of objectives quoted earlier in this chapter.

are involved in the various experiences you plan. An example of a unit plan for carrying out one part of the Grade 8 yearly plan is shown in Chart. 6.

Daily Lesson Planning

In your daily lesson plan you will be quite specific about such items as your objectives, what activities and procedures you will use to accomplish these objectives, questions for discussion, and means of evaluation. Chart 7 is an example of a lesson plan that uses a structured set of questions to guide in developing generalizations with students. As you study this lesson plan, keep in mind the following kinds of questions to which Simpson refers as "guides to developing conclusions in the form of principles and generalizations." [23]

1. Questions for which the answer will be found in the situation.
2. Questions calling for an examination of similar ideas in other situations.
3. Questions asking the students to draw inferences, to begin to see cause and effect relationships, to begin to express their own opinions or ideas in regard to situations.
4. Questions that ask students to formulate a generalization of their own, based on an examination of data from the film, case situation, or drama. . . .
5. Questions that ask students to examine these ideas as they apply to their present day life; questions that ask what authorities say about certain problems.
6. Questions that ask students to illustrate the meaning of their generalizations. . . .

CHART 7 Lesson Plan Using Structured Set of Questions as Guide in Developing Generalizations *

Lesson: Exploring Values That Influence Choices in the Area of Home Furnishings
Unit: The Home and Its Furnishings

Objectives:

1. Understanding of certain values that affect choices in the area of home furnishings.
2. Some understanding of the sources of these values.

[23] Elizabeth J. Simpson, "Teaching for the Development of Concepts and Generalizations." *Illinois Teacher of Home Economics,* Vol. IX, No. 5, p. 246.

* Elizabeth J. Simpson, "Teaching for the Development of Concepts and Generalizations." *Illinois Teacher of Home Economics,* Vol. IX, No. 5, p. 246.

CHART 7 *(continued)*

3. Increased understanding of and respect for other peoples' values and ways of expressing them.
4. Increased understanding of own values.

Activities and Procedures:

1. Introduction: "Previously we discussed some of the factors to be considered in planning home furnishings. We mentioned the makeup of the family with respect to (1) number in family, (2) ages, (3) sex of family members, (4) interests, and (5) activities. We discussed the income of the family as a factor to be considered. The art principles and their application have also been discussed as considerations in making home furnishing decisions."
"Now, there is another very important consideration that we haven't even mentioned. All of us prize certain things or ideas in life. What we prize enters into our choices in all areas of living—whether we are selecting a dress, or a house, or deciding how to discipline a child."
"Let's look at a typical family situation and see what the mother prizes that will enter into her decisions about home furnishings."
2. Students present Minute Drama I.
Scene: Mother is in living room cleaning while the daughter cleans a bedroom.
DAUGHTER (as she runs into the living room): Mom, let us throw this old perfume bottle away. There isn't a thing in it. It's just a dust collector. I'm tired of cleaning it every week. I could see some purpose in keeping it if it were pretty. But, in my opinion, the shape is awful and it hasn't any purpose!
MOTHER: I wouldn't begin to let you throw that bottle out. Why, your father gave me perfume in it before we were married. It is quite dear to me. I always thought it was rather beautiful. (With a dreamy look in her eye) I guess you'll just have to put up with my sentimentality.
(Value: Sentiment)
3. Discussion:

	Discussion guide	*Content*
(Guide, A. pt. 1)	"What did the mother prize?"	sentiment her relationship with her husband
(Guide, B. pt. 2)	"These things that we prize are also called our values. Have you known people who held values similar to those of the mother? Tell us about them."	
(Guide, C. pt. 3)	"Why do you think that the perfume bottle seemed so important to the mother? Let's speculate about this a little."	Perhaps the husband gave it to her for some special occasion—and, therefore, it has a sentimental attachment for her. The perfume bottle itself is not a value, but it is an expression of a value.

CHART 7 *(continued)*

D. "Let's explore this matter of values in relation to home furnishing a bit more. Suppose we act out some other situations in which values are involved."

4. Students present several other Minute Dramas.
5. Discussion questions for each:
   (Guide, pt. 1) A. "What is the value presented here?" (list on board)
   (Guide, pt. 2) B. "Do people you know hold similar values?"
6. Discuss: "Have we omitted from our minute dramas or discussion any values that influence choices in the area of home furnishings?"
   (Guide, pt. 2) Aesthetics-Beauty
   Relationships
7. "Where do these values come from? How do we get to be people who value beauty, or privacy, or comfort so much that our choices are influenced by these things that we prize?"
   (Guide, pt. 3) Our experiences in the family and elsewhere.
   Values held by those who are models for us—parents, teachers, peers.
8. "Let's now take a more personal view of values related to the home. Let's suppose that you are out of high school and are going to a strange town to work or to go to school. What do you think that you would look for first of all in a room or apartment for yourself?" Discuss:
   (Guide, pt. 3) A. "What values would serve to guide you?"
   B. "How would these values influence your choices?"
   C. "What are the possible sources of these values?"
   Discuss—The same value may have a different degree of importance for another class member. Why? How does this affect decisions made in home furnishings?
9. "Suppose we summarize what we have learned up to this point about values in relation to home furnishings." (Write conclusions on board.)
   (Guide, pt. 4) A. What we prize (value) in life enters into our choices of home furnishings.
   B. Many people hold the same values, but differences may be found in the relative importance they place on the values and the ways in which they express them.
   C. People differ with respect to values because they have different backgrounds of experience; have had different people to imitate and with whom to identify; and have different needs and interests.
   D. We gain increased understanding of other people as we gain an appreciation of what they prize (value).

CHART 7 *(continued)*

10. "Now, let us look at what authorities in the area of home furnishings say about this matter of values."
(Guide, pt. 5) Read Craig and Rush, *Homes with Character,* p. 3 (for example)
11. "Do the conclusions that we drew still seem to be sound?" (Discuss.)
12. "How may we apply these conclusions to our own lives?" (Discuss each.)
(Guide, pt. 6)

Means of Evaluation:

Pencil-and-paper test on values that influence choices in area of home furnishings—perhaps, using case situations and having students identify values held by different persons and discuss the possible influence of these values on choices.

Students' comments regarding their own and others' values and the influence of these on choices in area of home furnishings.

RELATING OBJECTIVES TO LEARNING EXPERIENCES AND EVALUATION

Statements or objectives are useful only to the extent that they can be applied in the actual learning experiences of a class. Once a teacher has defined the specific behavior and content toward which her daily, weekly, or unit planning is to be directed, her next step is to formulate a series of possible experiences through which her students might reach the desired objective. In discussing the meaning of a "learning experience," Tyler pointed out:

> The term "learning experience" refers to the interaction between the learner and the external conditions in the environment to which he can react. Learning takes place through the active behavior of the student; it is what *he* does that he learns, not what the teacher does. It is possible for two students to be in the same class and for them to be having two different experiences.[24]

Underlying Principles

Although a teacher cannot *do* the learning for her students, she can set up an environment and structure a situation to bring about the desired type of reaction. In a sense, she manipulates the environment in an effort to change a student's behavior. To do this successfully, she must determine the kind of situation that will bring about the desired ends and then she must decide how she can set the stage for this kind of environment. Among the principles that guide her are her understandings of what a student must have if he is to learn effectively. These are (1) an opportunity to practice the implied behavior; (2) an

[24] Ibid., p. 41.

opportunity to deal with the implied content; (3) satisfaction in carrying out the implied kind of behavior; and (4) a coherent picture of what he is trying to accomplish.[25]

Each activity or learning experience that is chosen should measure up to the following criteria:

1. CONTINUITY. Whenever a subject area is included at more than one grade level, learning experiences should provide for a *vertical* reiteration of major elements. This means that some review of previous work must precede new learning, so that there is a sound foundation for developing new understanding. Students in advanced classes will need continued opportunity to develop the competences that are fundamental to their new experiences.

2. SEQUENCE. Each successive experience builds upon previous experiences with a *minimum* of duplication and with a different approach that goes more deeply and broadly into the area under study.

3. INTEGRATION. A *horizontal* integration, or coordination, of the various experiences a student is currently having will help him to learn more rapidly, and to unify his behavior. The central theme of the home economics course, or problem, should be recognized by the students; they should be able to see the coherence and unity of their activities. In addition, it is frequently possible to relate home economics units to those of other courses in which the students are enrolled concurrently. Such coordination brings new and deeper meanings to their learning situations.

4. SIGNIFICANCE. Students find challenge in problems that are real and significant to them. Each experience that is selected as a means of solving the basic problem should be worthwhile and justifiable in terms of the time required to carry it out.

Application of Principles in Home Economics

Each day's lesson should be planned around a very specific objective that is clear both to the teacher and the students. Daily planning on the part of the teacher includes (1) stating each of the general objectives toward which the class will direct its attention; (2) determining the specific kinds of knowledge, understandings, skills, attitudes, and values that will contribute to the general objective; (3) selecting appropriate learning experiences that will help the class to fulfill these objectives; and (4) indicating what measurements she will use in order to tell whether or not a student's behavior has changed in the direction of the class goals.

Sometimes an objective requires several class periods in which to

[25] Ibid., pp. 42–43.

develop adequate learning experiences; the teacher still needs to formulate carefully her plans for certain accomplishments each day so that her students will go home knowing what they have learned and how it fits into their long-range goals. Indications of changed behavior may show up immediately; on the other hand, a teacher should not be discouraged if the expected indications have not appeared by the end of a particular unit of study, or if a student who once gave evidence of a desirable change in behavior seems to revert to some earlier habit. Changing behavior is not easy, but it is most rewarding both to you and your students when a student finds satisfaction from a change in the direction of a desirable class objective.

You will want to experiment with different ways of planning your program. We have included an illustration of plans for the year, a unit, and a day. These are illustrative of *one* way of planning; you will need to develop an approach that is unique for you and your situation.

Objectives are the specifications for changing behavior. They tell you what kind of behavior change you want to evoke, but they do not indicate how you can effect this change. Chapters 9 and 10 will guide you in selecting activities and materials that will assist you to bring about the desired outcomes in an interesting and economical manner.

Selected References

Bloom, Benjamin, S., et al., *Taxonomy of Educational Objectives.* New York: Longmans, Green, 1956.

"Conceptual Teaching-Learning," *Tips and Topics in Home Economics* vol. 3, no. 2, December 1967, Lubbock, Texas: Texas Technological Institute.

French, Will, *Behavioral Goals of General Education in High School.* New York: Russell Sage Foundation, 1957.

Garrett, Pauline G., *Post-Secondary Education in Home Economics.* Washington, D.C.: American Vocational Association, 1967.

Home Economics, New Directions: A Statement of Philosophy and Objectives. Washington, D.C.: American Home Economics Association, 1959.

Krathwohl, David R., Benjamin S. Bloom, and Bertram B. Masia, *A Taxonomy of Educational Objectives,* Handbook II, Affective Domain. New York: David McKay, 1964.

Lawson, Dorothy, "Education for Improved Family Living," *Bulletin of the National Association of Secondary-School Principals,* 48: 15–27, December 1964.

Learning and the Teacher, Yearbook 1959. Washington, D.C.: Association for Supervision and Curriculum Development, 1959, pp. 29–60.

Mager, Robert, *Preparing Instructional Objectives.* San Francisco: Fearon Company, 1962.

Mallory, Berenice, "Curriculum Developments," *Bulletin of the National Association of Secondary-School Principals,* **48**: 51–65, December 1964.

Moore, Bernice M., "Families of America, Variations on a Theme," *Bulletin of the National Association of Secondary-School Principals,* **48**: 3–14, December 1964.

National Committee of Home Economics Educators, "Home Economics in the Secondary School," *Bulletin of the National Association of Secondary-School Principals,* **48**: 89–97, December 1964.

Otto, Arleen C., *New Designs in Homemaking Programs in Junior High Schools.* New York: Teachers College, Columbia University, 1958.

Simpson, Elizabeth J., "Planning for the Year, The Unit, The Daily Lesson." *Illinois Teacher of Home Economics* IX: 226–288, 1965–1966.

Spitze, Hazel T. "The Structure of Home Economics as a Basis for Curriculum Decisions." *Illinois Teacher of Home Economics* IX: 62–96, 1965–66.

Travers, Robert M. W., *Essentials of Learning.* (2nd ed.) New York: Macmillan, 1967.

Tyler, Ralph W., *Basic Principles of Curriculum and Instruction.* Chicago: University of Chicago Press, Syllabus Division, 1950.

United States Department of Health, Education and Welfare, Office of Education, *Curriculum Resources Material, Conceptual Framework and Generalizations in Home Economics.* Washington, D.C.: Division of Vocational and Technical Education, Professional Resources Unit, Auxiliary Service Branch, 1966, p. 2.

Woodruff, Asahel D., *Basic Concepts of Teaching.* San Francisco: Chandler Publishers, 1961.

Model Curriculum Guides

Curriculum Guide in Child Development. Phoenix, Arizona: State Department of Vocational Education, 1967.

(A detailed *teaching-learning* unit that clearly *states* and *orders* objectives for teaching. The content is selected, stated in some detail, and ordered for effective learning. Learning and evaluation experiences are sequentially developed so that students can *develop concepts* over time and and try them out in everyday situations. An excellent example of a teaching plan.)

Home Economics Education Syllabus. Albany, New York: The University of the State of New York, the State Education Department, Bureau of Home Economics Education, 1965.

(This syllabus presents a comprehensive plan for a home economics program, grades 7–12, with suggestions for elementary school and adult groups. Essential concepts and subconcepts are identified for each area, behavioral outcomes are defined so that teaching effectiveness can be measured, generalizations are presented, essential learnings are suggested, and references for both teacher and students are identified.)

8

Developing Critical and Creative Thinking

Education may be conceived as a system of learning experiences that bring about desirable changes in students. Among other changes in your students, you will be concerned with their intellectual growth. Guilford has analyzed the "Structure of Intellect" into several primary categories. Among these are:

1. *Cognitive memory*—simple reproduction of facts or other items. Cognitive abilities involve the discovery, recognition, or comprehension of information in various forms. An example in which a home economics teacher is stressing cognitive memory is this:

> T: What were some of the main points covered in our discussion about credit?
>
> MARY: One of the things we learned was that there was an attempt to make persons who offer credit reveal its true cost.

2. *Convergent thinking*—analysis and integration of data, leading to one expected answer because of the tightly structured framework through which the individual must respond. This type of thinking may be involved in solving a problem, summarizing material, or establishing a logical sequence of ideas.

> T: Can you sum up in one sentence the main idea of Vance Packard's book, *The Waste Makers*?
>
> JOHN: Business firms keep trying to get us to consume more and wastefulness is becoming part of the American way of life.

3. *Divergent thinking*—ability to generate one's own ideas or take a new direction. The individual can take off from established facts, see further implications, or make unique associations.

T: Suppose birth control pills were available to single college girls through the Student Health Center—what could we expect to happen?

PEG: Girls might experience psychological tensions from engaging in behavior for which they are not ready.

4. *Evaluative thinking*—ability to construct his own value dimension, make an assessment, offer a modification of a prior judgment, or declare opposition to the position of another person.

T: What do you think of Murray as a "father figure" in the play, "A Thousand Clowns?"

BOB: Well, he was a lot of fun to be around and he spent time with his nephew, but he had a crazy notion about not letting work interfere with his life.[1]

CRITICAL THINKING

Critical thinking is the ability to solve problems by using logical methods. Generalized problem solving involves identifying the problem, planning alternative behaviors that may resolve the problem, activating the most promising of these behaviors, evaluating the consequences, and generalizing the process to new problems as they arise. The real question is: "How do I solve problems like this one?" rather than "How do I solve this problem?"

Thinking and learning are not identical processes. A student may quickly forget a large portion of what he has learned, but the ability to think has lasting value that should help a person adjust to new situations in his daily living. Although factors that affect one's ability to think clearly need further experimental study, there is some evidence that a person's attitudes and emotional state may affect adversely his ability to think logically.

Process of Critical Thinking

The steps involved in critical thinking might be listed as follows:

1. IDENTIFYING AND DEFINING THE CENTRAL ISSUES. Crucial words and phrases need to be defined according to the ways in which they will be used in discussing the immediate problem. Schuster has said that there are two kinds of definitions: (1) *report* or *dictionary definitions* are statements of common usage which may need further clarification of

[1] Adapted from John C. Gowan et al., *Creativity: Its Educational Implications.* New York: John Wiley and Sons, pp. 262–265.

any particular meanings that have been adopted by certain groups or at certain times; and (2) *stipulative definitions* declare the intention of a person to use a word in a given meaning during a given discussion.[2]

The difference between these two types of definitions might be illustrated with the word "cooperate." The dictionary says it means "to act or operate jointly with another or others; to concur in action, effort, or effect." This becomes a stipulative definition when the students describe specific kinds of action that indicate how a person behaves when he cooperates in a home economics class—for example, he is considerate of the other class members, and he does his part cheerfully for the good of the group.

One type of fallacious reasoning results from failure to define the meaning of a term, or from defining it in one sense and then shifting to another meaning in drawing one's conclusions.

2. RECOGNIZING THE UNDERLYING ASSUMPTIONS AND FORMING HYPOTHESES. The *Illinois Teacher* defined an assumption as "a proposition treated as true without examination. Assumptions may be generally accepted, they may not be accepted, or there may be some doubt as to their truth. Sometimes we are aware of the assumptions upon which we act, and at other times we are completely unaware of the underlying assumptions—we take things for granted." An illustration that might be used to show how assumptions serve as short-cuts was given: [3]

> Suppose you call a co-worker and arrange for a Future Homemakers of America committee meeting for 8:00 P.M. next Wednesday. You agree to meet her at Jane's home at that time. In making this arrangement, and later acting upon it, what are the assumptions?
>
> 1. It is assumed 8:00 P.M. means the same thing to both parties.
> 2. You are both thinking about the same Jane.
> 3. It is assumed you both consider this agreement binding.

Once the students decide which things they can reasonably take for granted, they choose their premises. Then they think about various possible solutions and formulate a plan of action centered around their hypotheses. A hypothesis is an informed guess that has a reasonable chance of being correct. Students might state the hypothesis that teenagers in their class eat adequate and nutritious meals. Or, they might hypothesize that there is a difference in the nutritional adequacy of meals they eat on school days and those eaten over the weekend. A

[2] Cynthia A. Schuster, "Can We Teach the High-School Student To Think?" *Educational Research Bulletin*, 37: 97, April 9, 1958.

[3] "Thinking—A Major Outcome of Education." *Illinois Teacher*, Vol. II, No. 3, p. 31.

hypothesis may be stated in the form of a question—such as, what part of the day's nutrients do our class members obtain from snacks?

3. SELECTING AND ORGANIZING RELEVANT FACTS AND EVALUATING THE EVIDENCE. Students need guidance in discriminating between facts that are relevant and those that are irrelevant to a problem. As they read, they should learn to evaluate how the evidence was obtained and whether the conclusions need to be revised in the light of more recent data. They should learn to recognize the need for further data to confirm, qualify, or negate the evidence that is available. In addition, they should be able to differentiate between factual evidence and opinion.

4. DRAWING WARRANTED CONCLUSIONS. The process of logical thinking is not complete until a student learns to come to a conclusion. Among the abilities that are involved in drawing warranted conclusions are the following.

Ability to see the point. The ability to recognize the point in question and to stick to it until it has been dealt with is the first essential in reaching a sound conclusion.

Ability to restrict generalizations. Schuster pointed out that hasty generalizations or leaping to a general conclusion from too few instances is very common. People fail to distinguish between an illustration and a proof. Or, they assume that two things that occur simultaneously or in sequence have a causal connection.[4]

Ability to base conclusions on sound facts. As mentioned above, facts must be separated from opinions. Precautions must be taken against errors of observation, memory, or personal bias.

Can you see ways you can apply these ideas as you work with your students?

Teaching Critical Thinking

As a teacher, you can help students improve their ability to think clearly. Students will not learn to think merely by reading or studying the thinking of others. Very likely the students will benefit more from actual experience in problem-solving than from learning the rules of logic. Thinking is a basic tool skill that must be developed through constant emphasis and use.

If you are to be effective in teaching your students to think, your own training must be adequate. You will need infinite patience in pointing out examples of fallacious thinking and clear thinking as they occur in your classes. Encourage your students to do this too. Schuster suggested ways of teaching students to avoid fallacious reasoning and to cause them to desire to think straight:

[4] Schuster, op. cit., p. 93.

[An effective teacher] will judge when to mete out praise, when to offer gentle correction, and when to indulge in banter or sarcasm. In one tone and another he will have to repeat hour by hour, day by day, and year by year, such comments as: "How do you like that! From two examples he jumps to the conclusion that it is always so"; "I ask for a proof that *all* combustion requires oxygen, and you give me a report of one experiment in which oxygen was used up during combustion. How would you like it if I proved that weenies are always served with sauerkraut by showing you one meal of weenies and sauerkraut?"; "We asked you for reasons why you disapprove of ________, and all you have told us is how much you hate it!"

The "you might as well say" technique is sometimes effective. . . . You might as well say that since

All Americans approve of eating, and
The King of England approves of eating,
Therefore, the King of England is an American.[5]

A teacher should be very careful to explain why students' answers are inadequate. She may stimulate them to think further by asking such questions as: "How do you know?" and "Why is it so?"

Discussions are good means of demonstrating how to think through a problem. In our increasingly pluralistic society, there are competing values and attitudes. Like many teachers, you may be tempted to avoid controversial issues and follow a bland, passive approach. The superior teacher recognizes that the classroom is a place where students learn to understand and assess the forces making for conflict and tension in society. He brings broad knowledge of society and scholarly objectivity to help students identify facts and consider varied interpretations.

Debate is another effective technique for teaching students to think critically. They learn to admit when their evidence is only a probability. They learn to expose the fallacies in the thinking of members on the opposing team. You will need to help them evaluate between "successful persuasion" and "sound evidence."

As you choose learning experiences, your objective should be not to teach students *what* to think but rather *how* to think. By your own attitude and example, you can communicate to them a desire to think clearly. Bacmeister suggested a number of ways to encourage straight thinking:

1. Set an example. Work out a problem together. Let the pupils see how you go about it.

2. Provide stimulating situations. Keep pupils richly supplied with materials and experiences that provoke thought.

[5] Schuster, op. cit., pp. 94–95.

3. Supply useful information.
4. Cultivate imagination. If new facts are raw materials, imagination is the bonding agent which combines them into useful forms. . . . It is the power of the mind to construct or picture things.

Dramatic play or "pretending" of one sort or another . . . is fine exercise in logic, imagination, and memory.

5. Emphasize varied relationship thinking. Seeing relationships between things is the real essence of thinking, and we can help our children to do so flexibly if we keep emphasizing the many types of possible relationships.
6. Beware of personal bias.
7. Correct bad habits of thinking.
8. Think in broader terms.[6]

Examinations afford excellent opportunity to test the students' ability to solve problems. Questions dealing with the understanding of definitions are easy to state in objective form but often they measure memory rather than the ability to apply facts. Chapter 12 presents types of questions that may be used to evaluate student progress in critical thinking.

CREATIVE THINKING

Creative thinking refers to originality in any type of activity. Torrance described in a vivid manner the tragedy of rewarding certain kinds of behavior while overlooking equally valuable talents. He recounted the story of a monkey who could fly but couldn't climb a tree. No one gave him credit for his unique ability; everyone laughed and ridiculed him for not being able to climb a tree. Finally, the monkey found relief when he was frightened out of his ability to fly and people stopped calling him names. Then there was the lion who couldn't roar; he could only purr. Although he could do many clever tricks, he was regarded as a complete failure. Torrance's analogy of "flying monkeys and silent lions" highlights the failure of many teachers and parents to recognize the creative talent a child has and the attempts of many teachers to channel growth into a rigid pattern that may not permit the development of an individual's unique abilities.[7]

Identifying Creative Individuals

Although a minimum amount of intelligence is necessary before a person can have creative ideas, there seems to be little or no correlation between creativity and intelligence beyond an I.Q. of about 120. It is easier for most teachers to identify individuals who are highly intelligent

[6] Rhoda W. Bacmeister, *Growing Together*. New York: Appleton-Century-Crofts, 1947, pp. 104–113.

[7] Gowan, op. cit., p. 138.

than those who are highly creative. Those individuals who are both highly intelligent and highly creative are recognized as having unusual but sound ideas and to be good at planning.

There are many kinds of giftedness. *Verbal fluency* characterizes persons who are successful in such careers as writing, teaching, politics, and religion. *Motor fluency,* or the ability to manipulate lines, shapes, colors, and sounds, is found in artisans, designers, artists, and musicians. Ability to manipulate and interpret *symbols* is important to persons who would be designers, architects, mathematicians, and scientists. *Unusual sensitivity* and ability to interact with others is a talent possessed by leaders, politicians, social scientists, teachers, and salesmen. *Originality of ideas* and their expression can be recognized in writers, researchers, actors, artists, designers, and humorists. A talent that we sometimes fail to recognize as potential for creativity is that of ability to *organize and synthesize,* such as we find among researchers, scientists, trouble shooters, textbook writers, lawyers, and salesmen.

Divergent thinking can be recognized in situations in which an individual is free to generate his own ideas or to take a new direction. He can take off from established facts, see further implications, or make unique associations. One form of divergent thinking is represented by ideational fluency. For example, when a person is asked to list all the uses he can think of for a common brick, he might say: "build a house" and "build a school." These would be counted as two responses. On the other hand, a person who changes the categories of his response is showing flexibility. He might suggest: "make a paper weight," "drive a nail," "throw at a cat," and "grind up for red powder." Elaboration refers to the ability to take the bare outline of a plan and to produce the detailed steps necessary to make the plan work.

Other characteristics of the creative include a high level of energy, perseverance to stick with a problem until a creative solution is reached, curiosity, ability to manipulate and restructure ideas, tolerance for ambiguity, openness to experience, independence of judgment, self-confidence, humor, and diversity of interests.

Highly gifted students are often disliked by their teachers and fellow students because of their independent ideas, preference for new and difficult problems, energy, alertness, and high achievement. Your problem as a teacher is to help creative individuals maintain the characteristics essential to the development of their creative talent and, at the same time, to avoid alienating their peers. Stein offered the following suggestions concerning the social role of the teacher: help the gifted student to maintain his assertiveness without being hostile and aggressive; to work alone, but not be isolated, withdrawn, or uncommunicative; to be aware of his superiors and peers as persons; to "know his place" without being timid, submissive, or acquiescent; to "speak his mind" without being domineering; to be subtle at times, but not cunning or manipulative; to be sincere, honest, purposeful, diplomatic, and unwilling to accept "short cuts"; and to learn to be broad without spreading himself too thin, deep without being too "bookish" or "scientific," and "sharp" without being overcritical.[8]

Principles in Teaching Creativeness

Although we still have much to learn about the nature of creative thinking and the kinds of programs that stimulate creative thinking, a few basic principles seem to be clear. First, we can assume that every individual has some measure of creativity that is capable of being developed by practice. Individuals differ in their ability to think creatively, just as they differ in other abilities. Training, knowledge, and ability are factors that may contribute to differences in capacity for creative thinking. Teachers and parents must learn to value a variety of kinds of achievement, since people tend to develop along the lines they find rewarding.

Another assumption about creative thinking is that it can be taught. The process of creative thinking involves complex behavior that is not automatically an outcome of the educational program. All subject areas provide opportunities for teaching creative thinking, although certain areas may lend themselves more readily than others do.

Home economics offers many possibilities. Finding ways to mediate important family values as ways of living change, creating an emotionally and spiritually satisfying home environment for every family member, resolving conflicts, and performing mundane tasks in ways that lead toward self-actualization should each tap the creative thinking ability of your students.

A third basic principle is that a social setting that favors individualism encourages students to develop their ideas. Overemphasis on conformity and cooperation may stifle originality. In home economics education we need to guard against giving an impression that there is *one right* answer to a problem, as this stifles creative thinking. Home economics teachers should encourage students to think independently, test their ideas, and communicate them to others.

Perceptual blocks may interfere with the development of creativity. Failure to use all the senses in observing, difficulty in isolating problems, and narrowing a problem too much can limit a person. Also, an individual who holds tightly to his categories of perception and over-

[8] Ibid., p. 238.

generalizes from past experience may tend to emit the same response when he perceives a new stimulus somewhat similar to a previous one. He has difficulty judging new persons or events independently of their similarities to his past encounters.

Cultural and emotional factors may be relegated to the development of creative thinking. A desire for security, a negative outlook, fear of making a mistake, perfectionism, and self-satisfaction may inhibit a person from applying creative thinking. Overemphasis on conformity, cooperation, competition, logic, or reliance on authority, can stifle creativity in problem solving. To be conducive to creative thinking, a problem must have sufficient difficulty so that it cannot be solved from previous experience or knowledge. Problems that can be reasoned out quickly fail to encourage creative thinking.

Program to Improve Creative Thinking

In selecting learning experiences that emphasize creative thinking, you will need to consider the habits you will try to teach, the personal qualities that students should develop, the functions of the teacher in encouraging creativity, and teaching techniques that might have merit for accomplishing this.

1. WHAT ARE THE STEPS IN THE CREATIVE PROCESS? Essentially, creative thinking includes about four stages:

Preparation—a time during which one acquires the skills, techniques, and experience that make it possible to pose a problem for oneself. This period involves learning about the problem environment, the structure of the problem, and things that might be relevant to the problem.

Incubation—a period of withdrawal, quiescence, or relaxation as far as awareness of the problem is concerned. As a teacher, you might encourage a student who has worked on a problem without seeing a solution to let it incubate and see if a new idea will hatch.

Illumination—a stage in which an individual suddenly sees where the solution lies and may even see the details of the solution. This is often described as the "ah-ha" or "I've found it" experience. Insight almost miraculously breaks through unexpectedly.

Consolidation—a process of clearing up the details of the problem solution and working out its implications. This may involve verification, evaluation, revision, and elaboration of the insight one has experienced. A creative mind is continually reaching toward new designs and insight.

2. WHAT ARE YOUR FUNCTIONS AS A TEACHER IN PROMOTING CREATIVE THINKING? Creativity is discouraged by teachers who stress convergent

thinking—the analysis and integration of data leading to one expected answer because of the tightly structured framework through which an individual must respond. This type of thinking may be involved in solving a problem, summarizing material, or establishing a logical sequence of ideas. Creativity is discouraged also by emphasizing memory work, by maintaining a high authoritarian level in the classroom, and by overprotecting the students.

The role of the teacher, then, is to be less directive and more responsive to the students. A list of creative ways of teaching might include the following: [9]

Recognize the unused potential of a student.
Respect a student's need to work alone.
Withhold judgment long enough to allow for a creative response to occur.
Provide for periods of nonevaluated practice.
Encourage a student to achieve success in an area and in a way possible to him.
Permit the curriculum to be different for different students.
Give a student a chance to make a contribution to the group.
Encourage self-initiated projects.
Reduce pressure; provide a relatively nonpunitive environment.
Respect the potential of slow learners.
Give support against pressures to conform.
Place an unproductive student in contact with a productive, creative one.
Capitalize upon hobbies, special interests, and enthusiasms.
Tolerate complexity and disorder, at least for a time.
Emphasize doing something with the knowledge that is acquired, rather than just acquiring knowledge.
Be concerned over the students' mental health.
Be respectful of unusual questions.
Respect imaginative or unusual ideas.
Show students that their ideas have value.
Point out the consequences of various actions and let students evaluate the goodness or badness of the various results.
Assist students to be more sensitive to environmental stimuli.
Encourage manipulation of objects and ideas.
Lead students to test systematically each new idea.
Create "thorns in the flesh" to help students develop sensitivity to defects and to recognize the disturbing element.

[9] Ibid., p. 183 (adapted).

Create necessities for creative thinking.
Provide for both active and quiet times for the production of ideas.
Make available resources for working out ideas.
Encourage the habit of working out the full implication of ideas.
Become adventurous.
Give students approbation for digging into things and questioning what the book says.
Let students resist premature closure in solving problems and reaching conclusions.
Treat students as thinkers, not simply as information receivers and retrievers.

If your classroom provides for uniqueness of response and open-ended activities, your students will probably say: [10]

I've gone as far as I need to at this time.	*rather than*	I've finished.
I had to change some of my plans.		I did exactly what you said.
I hope it's going to work.		I hope it is right.
I'm not quite satisfied.		I hope you like it.

One approach that may encourage creative thinking is to have students use their imaginations in "Charades." Since no words can be spoken, they must use many different ideas to present in a dramatic manner brief pictures of home and family life.

Another approach is to emphasize the asking of questions. Students can be encouraged to ask questions that are related to what they study. One class decided that, rather than discuss their readings in class, they would each write down three pertinent questions that the reading raised for them. These questions then became the focal point of the class discussion. Students can be guided in seeking answers to their own questions. Still another technique is to encourage creative thinking through the use of problem-solving test questions. (See Chapter 12).

Selected References

Barron, F., *Creativity and Psychological Health*. Princeton, New Jersey: D. Van Nostrand Co., 1963.

Baughman, M. Dale, *Teaching Early Adolescents to Think*. Danville, Illinois: The Interstate Printers and Publishers (no date given).

[10] Ronald C. Doll (editor), *Individualizing Instruction*. Washington, D.C.: Association for Supervision and Curriculum Development, 1964 Yearbook, pp. 86–87.

Berlyne, D. E., *Structure and Direction in Thinking*. New York: John Wiley and Sons, 1965.

Bruner, Jerome S., *On Knowing*. Cambridge, Mass.: Belknap Press, 1962.

Getzels, J. W., and P. W. Jackson, *Creativity and Intelligence*. New York: John Wiley and Sons, 1962.

Gowan, John C.; George D. Demos; and E. Paul Torrance, *Creativity: Its Educational Implications*. New York: John Wiley and Sons, 1967.

Simpson, Elizabeth, and Louise Lemmon, *Teaching Processes of Thinking in Homemaking Education*. Department of Home Economics Topics 11. Washington, D.C.: National Education Association, Department of Home Economics, 1959.

Torrance, E. Paul, *Guiding Creative Talent*. Englewood Cliffs, New Jersey: Prentice-Hall, 1962.

Williams, Frank E., "Intellectual Creativity and the Teacher." *The Journal of Creative Behavior* 1: 173–180, Spring 1967.

9

Determining Learning Experiences

Learning objectives are best fulfilled when appropriate methods and materials are used. Although methodology and instructional aids are closely related, and although they work together in influencing the quality of learning experiences, these aspects are treated in separate chapters because they are so extensive and important. This chapter presents guides for using effective group methods, laboratory experiences, home and community experiences, and independent study. Chapter 10 discusses the use of educational media to help students learn. You will notice that many learning experiences actually combine one or more teaching methods with one or more types of media.

Among the principles to guide you in the selection of learning experiences are the following:

1. THE METHOD IS SUITABLE FOR THE FULFILLMENT OF A SPECIFIC PURPOSE OR PURPOSES. Whatever methods are used should focus attention on a central purpose. Instruction should then proceed in an orderly manner toward the attainment of the specific objectives that contribute to the overall purpose. Techniques may differ in their efficiency for reaching a variety of goals such as the development of knowledge, understandings, attitudes, appreciations, habits, or skills. Furthermore, a single learning experience may contribute toward several outcomes. For example, while a student is learning to solve a problem, he also acquires information and develops attitudes. While a student develops skills related to the serving of meals, he also has experience with interpersonal relationships.

2. A VARIETY OF METHODS MAY BE USED TO ATTAIN THE SAME LEARNING OBJECTIVE. Students can learn individually and in groups; they can learn from ideas, real objects, and other audio-visual media; they can learn from reading and listening; and they can learn from projects and activities. Variety in the methods used by a class helps to maintain students' interest in their work, permit flexibility in planning, and provide for individual differences among students, classes, and teachers.

That a variety of approaches may be used to reach one objective was illustrated in a study of "Children in the Family," suggested as part of the ninth-grade home economics course in Cincinnati. One of the objectives was "planning happy, safe, and satisfying experiences for children which help them learn about their world." Among the suggested learning experiences were:

a. Plan children's play so that they can follow their impulses and express their feelings in constructive activity, can enjoy well-chosen play equipment, suitable stories, and games.

b. Observe infants and young children to determine what kind of toys, play equipment, and games have greatest appeal for each age level.

c. Exhibit household articles that are safe and sanitary and that provide satisfying play experience.

d. Compare the cost of a variety of toys suited to different ages: commercial and made at home.

e. List some of the skills pre-school children develop through play and through self help; describe how they learn by helping mother around the house and yard.

f. Discuss the importance of answering children's questions.

g. Work with adults in planning and making trips with children to learn what is beyond their home environment; to meet other people; to enjoy nature; and to learn about the community.

h. Use posters to illustrate the rules for keeping children safe in the home, at play, on the street.[1]

Probably no class would have the time or interest necessary to carry out all of the suggested activities. Since many different techniques might be used in teaching each area of home economics, the teacher and students are challenged to consider what their needs are and what procedures will best fulfill their purposes. The teacher sets certain limits in accordance with the state and local curriculum guides, but there is much opportunity for flexibility in determining specific learning experiences.

3. LEARNING EXPERIENCES ARE ADAPTED TO THE INDIVIDUAL NEEDS OF THE STUDENTS. Students differ in their speed of learning, energy output, depth of interest, level of maturity, family background experiences, and social class status. Activities that are meaningful for the individual students and for particular classes should be selected. Students should be capable of carrying out the necessary behavior and they should find satisfaction in doing so. They may gain status with their families by using effectively at home some of the information and skill they learn at school.

[1] *Home Economics Education,* Junior High School, Grades 7–8–9. Curriculum Bulletin 40. Cincinnati Public Schools, 1960, p. 153.

4. THE TEACHING METHOD PROVIDES FOR THE COORDINATION OF LEARNINGS. Students who learn to coordinate their learnings will be able to recall and apply what they have learned in one situation to another one. Students learn to integrate their feelings, thoughts, and actions. Coordination is made possible as a rich environment is provided and available resources of the school and community are used. Fleming suggested: "Each problem or activity undertaken by a class can include consideration of the interrelationships of that activity with all homemaking activities and its possible effect on various family members." [2]

Can you see how a teacher could guide her students in meal planning to help them learn specific types of information about planning a nutritious meal, particular skills needed by the father or mother in serving the meal, and a willingness on the part of all the family members to cooperate in making the family meal a pleasant time? Do you realize how important it would be for a home economics teacher to have some understanding of the social and food practices of homes in her community so she could key her teaching to agree with the home practices with which her students were familiar? Unfamiliar foods and strange manners of serving meals can be accepted more readily by students who regard them with a spirit of experimentation rather than as a criticism of their style of living.

5. LEARNING EXPERIENCES PROVIDE FOR GROWTH IN COOPERATIVE GROUP PROCESSES. Informal, friendly relationships may be as effective in changing attitudes or practices as are more formal methods. As students learn to work in small groups or as an entire class, they learn to show respect for the rights of individuals and to appreciate democratic processes.

6. STUDENTS GROW IN THE ABILITY TO PLAN THEIR OWN LEARNING ACTIVITIES. Effective learning experiences are developed cooperatively. The teacher must be well-prepared to guide the students in their planning and the students must be well-oriented for their activities. The teacher's role in guiding the students includes protecting them from situations with which they are not prepared to cope, providing for success in learning, and challenging students to grow by going beyond the immediate situation. The home economics classroom provides an appropriate setting for the teacher and students to experiment with new appliances, supplies, and techniques and to use their results in making decisions about the use of work capacity, materials and money in the home. Cooperative work experiences in which a teacher and employer cooperate in planning suitable opportunities to learn and practice new skills can also help

[2] Mary O. Fleming, "Report of One School System in Action." *California Journal of Secondary Education,* 31:244, April 1956.

students develop the maturity required to perform satisfactorily on a job.

7. THE STUDENTS ARE INVOLVED ACTIVELY IN THE LEARNING SITUATION. Rote learning is ineffective. Students learn best when they have opportunities to explore, construct, do, react, and question. They develop initiative, creativity, self-confidence, and leadership as they find themselves in situations that demand these qualities. Although the external conditions are the same for an entire class, learning experiences differ for each individual, depending upon how the student interacts with his environment.

EFFECTIVE GROUP WORK

One of our newer sciences, group dynamics, is concerned with the principles of group behavior and growth. Some growth experiences are available to individuals in groups which might be missed in relationships between a teacher and an individual student. Group work has a dual purpose: to contribute to the personal-social growth of the participants, and to aid in the achievement of desirable goals. We have learned that a group of able persons does not necessarily make an able committee. Also, we know that there are ways of helping groups to become more mature and productive. This section presents some of the principles of cooperative teacher-pupil planning, methods of guiding the work of small groups and committees, variations of the discussion method, and the use of dramatization. Group work is important in home economics, as the family is a small group. Ways of working together effectively in small groups at school can transfer directly into working together effectively as family members.

Cooperative Planning

People differ in the ways they plan, but careful planning will usually contribute much to the success of a project. Teenagers may not be convinced of the importance of planning, since their own lives go along from day to day with very little long-range direction or planning. They probably are not aware of the planning that is done by their parents, who may have had enough experience to be able to do much of their planning mentally without writing down their ideas. Home economics classes offer excellent opportunities for students to have shared experiences in cooperative planning and problem solving. As they carry through their plans, even those that are imperfect, teenagers grow in the ability to think independently.

Outcomes of Cooperative Planning

Hatcher demonstrated the outcomes of teacher-pupil cooperation in planning when she conducted an experiment on the teaching of foods and consumer buying at the high school level. Her results were overwhelmingly in favor of the teacher-pupil planning method—students in this group showed more improvement in interest, attitude, initiative, independence, and judgment than did the students in the teacher-planned classes. They were superior also on paper and pencil tests, ratings based on meal preparation, scores on their food products, and dietary rating. One of her most striking findings was that the least capable teacher in the teacher-pupil planning group was able to change the food practices of her students somewhat more than did the best teachers using the teacher-planning method.[3]

Other studies have indicated similar results. When students share in planning and discussing food habits, they are more likely to change their food habits than are students who listen to lectures in which they are urged to eat certain foods. Teacher-pupil planning helps students to increase their initiative, to develop leadership ability, to experiment with other ways of doing something, to be more critical of each other's work, and yet at the same time to learn to cooperate with each other.

Why is teacher-pupil planning such a valuable procedure? The experience places the students in a realistic situation designed to meet their needs. Class activities are based upon concrete problems. Students gain understanding of their environment and learn how to use resources in solving their problems. The teacher-pupil relationship is likely to create an atmosphere of friendliness and respect. As students share in making decisions, they grow in satisfaction and group cohesiveness.

Guiding Principles

Although cooperative planning has proven to be highly successful for approaching problems in all areas of home economics, its use will not insure success. The teacher must be acquainted with appropriate procedures for using this method effectively and she must feel at ease in using it. Her advance preparation includes setting up tentative objectives, or boundaries, within which the class may proceed with its planning. She may need to help students state their goals and eliminate those that are not workable or are not appropriate for their particular class and to consider ideas that the students may not have thought

[3] Hazel M. Hatcher, "An Experiment to Determine the Relative Effectiveness at the Secondary Level of Two Methods of Instruction." *Journal of Experimental Education,* **10**:41–47, September 1941.

about. She has a responsibility in helping them recognize needs beyond their present interests and concerns; she raises their level of learning expectations.

A helpful list of guiding principles in cooperative planning has been developed by the State Department of Vocational Education in Arizona:

1. The leaders in a cooperative effort should understand and believe in cooperative procedures.
2. Careful pre-planning by the leader or leaders should precede cooperative planning.
3. All people who are affected by a plan or policy should share in making it.
4. The group members should look at their progress from time to time and try to improve their work by means of systematic evaluation.
5. All people who are affected by a plan or policy should be kept informed of progress or changes being made in plans or procedures.
6. Plans, including purposes and job assignments, should be definite and clear to each individual who is to live by the plans.
7. Procedures used in cooperative planning should be such that conclusions will be reached and decisions made on the basis of pertinent evidence and desirable objectives.
8. An atmosphere of freedom and congeniality should prevail in the group, encouraging honesty and frankness, and encouraging individual and group growth.
9. The group should progress in an orderly manner, with members sharing the important feeling of a "job to be done."
10. There should be a functional division of labor. (Responsibilities should be divided in terms of interests, abilities, time, etc. and should be clearly defined among participants.)
11. Members of the group should know the possible choices before a decision is made.
12. Limitations should be set before, rather than after, decisions are made.
13. Once freedom of choice has been given a group, the leader should not exercise veto power, even if he is not sure of the outcome.
14. Some records should be kept for the purpose of maintaining continuity of planning. (Records should indicate the persons who took part in the planning, state clearly the problems discussed, indicate major trends of the discussion, decisions reached and plans for the future.)
15. Group members should be guided in their work by their belief in the importance of the individual and democratic values.
16. Shared decisions should be made, utilizing the consensus method when possible.
17. Something definite should be accomplished at each group meeting.
18. Plans should be made for follow-up (putting the plans into action).[4]

[4] "Guiding Principles in Cooperative Planning." Mimeographed. Phoenix: Home Economics Division of the State Department of Vocational Education.

Small Groups and Committees

The size of a group should be determined by the defined purpose of the group and the need for interaction with other group members. Security in a group is dependent upon the ability of its members to communicate and to receive a sense of acceptance.

In order to carry out their functions, members of a group need to know what their purposes are and how to proceed in an orderly manner. The purposes of group thinking may include identifying and solving common problems, bringing about individual growth, and developing attitudes and understanding. When used properly, group work can result in close matching of assignments to abilities, full participation by the individual, increased feelings of security, practice in democratic processes, and a change of pace from regular classroom procedures.

Types of Groups

The number and kinds of groups that might be used in home economics classes depend upon many factors such as the length of the class period, size of the classroom, size of the class, age of the students, materials available, and the movability of equipment. Group work can facilitate some kinds of learnings in home economics. Because home economics focuses on the family—a group of two or more individuals working toward a common goal—group work in home economics classrooms can provide practice for acquiring competence in interpersonal relations. Students learn by observing how their ways of working, thinking, and feeling affect others in the group. These observations provide cues for operating effectively in real family settings.

In general, three types of groups might be used:

1. CONVENIENCE GROUPS. When introducing the idea of group work, you might start with a very simple problem that can be discussed by informal groups. These groups might be formed in any convenient manner, such as having the students count off from 1 through 4 around the class, with all of the "number 1" students forming a group, etc. A random method, such as this, may be the basis for assigning students to "family" groups in the foods laboratory at the beginning of a semester. As the students gain experience in group work and as you become familiar with their interests and abilities, you might try methods of grouping that take individual differences into consideration.

2. ABILITY GROUPS. Students of similar intellectual ability enter home economics classes with widely different background experiences, interests, and aptitudes. As the semester proceeds, the varying rate at

which students learn may cause these differences to become more pronounced or to be lessened. Since students differ in their knowledge about various aspects of home economics, experience or ability in one area does not necessarily reflect an equal level of ability for all of the topics that will be covered during a semester. Homogeneous grouping, then, is a flexible arrangement that brings together students of similar interests and abilities for specific projects or portions of a project. An example of flexible ability grouping may be seen in a clothing construction class in which the teacher demonstrates a process to a group of students who are ready to work on that step. Slower students receive similar instruction at a later time, when they are about to begin the process.

A variation of ability grouping occurs when a fast learner is paired with a slower or less-experienced learner. The rapid learner can help the slower student to understand the principles involved in the learning process. At the same time, the slower student may be able to demonstrate skill in a given homemaking process. The rapid learner benefits from the opportunity of clarifying her own thinking and helping in the solution of real problems.

3. INTEREST GROUPS. A class may be given an opportunity to plan several related projects. Students may be allowed to choose with which topic or group they would like to work. A sociometric technique, such as that described in Chapter 5, may be the basis for assigning a student to a group. Groups composed of friends and people who feel secure with each other are likely to have more energy to spend participating in the task.

Productive Groups

Among the criteria for productive group work are the following:

1. THE GROUP MEMBERS UNDERSTAND THE PROBLEM AND ARE READY TO WORK ON IT. Fernandez pointed out that groups should not be used just for variety. They may be organized for specific purposes such as helping students to master a skill that has already been achieved by others in the class. Groups may carry out special projects in which they are interested. Reports or demonstrations may be planned and presented by small groups.[5]

[5] Louise Fernandez, *Grouping for Effective Teaching in Home Economics.* Bulletin 1958. Washington, D.C.: National Education Association, Department of Home Economics, p. 7.

2. THE TEACHER FULFILLS HER ROLE. The teacher is responsible for utilizing her knowledge of the students' abilities and needs in planning groups in which the members share a common goal and have the necessary resources to solve their problems. She helps each group to define its problem and decide on the steps necessary for its solution. She stimulates the students to think by raising questions and suggesting alternatives. She suggests ways in which they might secure information. She observes how the members of the group work, helping them to develop good habits of responsibility for their share of the work. She coordinates the activities and outcomes of the various groups.

Perhaps the most difficult part of her role is to let the group make its own mistakes. Students have a right to try, yet fail in their attempt. The teacher's goal is to support them in facing reality, not to protect them from reality.

3. THE STUDENTS CONTRIBUTE TOWARD GETTING THE WORK COMPLETED. Sometimes individuals try to meet their own needs at the expense of group well-being. Anti-group roles are illustrated by students who deflate others, call attention to themselves, seek sympathy, display lack of involvement in the group's work, assert authority, and plead for a special-interest group as a cloak for their own prejudice.

In an article written for members of the Future Homemakers of America, Lemmon pointed out the various kinds of behavior that assist groups in getting a job done with a feeling of group cohesiveness. In *getting the job done,* a person might take the following roles: [6]

Originator

Originator: One who breaks the ice and makes suggestions.

Opinion seeker: One who asks another what she thinks about an idea.

Fact seeker: One who suggests checking the facts before going deeper into a problem.

Fact finder: One who has checked facts before coming to the meeting.

Opinion giver: All opinions must be aired before a *group* decision can be made.

[6] Louise Lemmon, "You in a Group." *Teen Times,* **13**:4–5, March 1958.

Coordinator: One who stops to tie up the loose ends.

Detail girl: One who takes time to look at a suggestion, develop its details, and see how it looks.

Reality tester: One who tests suggestions for their workability.

Coordinator

Summarizer

Summarizer: One who can condense everything that has been said and help the group see the light at the end of the meeting.

In helping the group *run smoothly,* a person might take the following roles:

Encourager: One who helps a shy or hesitant person, perhaps through a smile.

Procedure setter: One who helps the group plan ways of working and reminds them of the plan when a group gets caught in conflict.

Follower: Each one is a member of the audience at times.

Mediator: One who helps members resolve conflict, perhaps through compromises that she suggests.

Encourager

Clown

Clown: One who comes in with a few laughs, making everyone feel better, when tension is high.

Gatekeeper: One who tries to see that everyone has a chance to talk.

Census taker: One who finds out how near agreement the group is on a problem.

Drakeford studied the characteristics that were common among groups effective in helping people change. Commitment to an association with others, and yet willingness to accept personal responsibility, were principles underlying each of the self-help groups. Other principles included setting high standards, making heavy demands, developing slogans or catchy statements, and having a leader "model the role" he wants the other group members to follow.[7]

4. RESOURCE MATERIALS ARE AVAILABLE FOR THE GROUPS TO USE AS NEEDED. Students must have access to sources from which they can obtain reliable information pertaining to their problems. The teacher may need to encourage them to seek facts, rather than to depend upon their own opinions or past experiences. She may need to help them develop the skills necessary for using available resources in solving their problems.

5. THE GROUP EVALUATES ITS PROCESSES AS WELL AS ITS IDEAS. A mature group is one in which the members have developed skill in solving its problems and in adjusting to the group processes. Evidences of maturity in the group process are seen when the members outline the group objectives, when all of the members are involved in working toward common goals, when the group sticks to its topic, when the members feel that their work will be useful, and when they take time to look at their accomplishments.

The use of group work techniques can facilitate learning. In making the crucial decision as to how you can provide the best learning experience for your students, keep in mind that your *primary concern is achieving a particular learning objective*. Placing students in small

[7] John W. Drakeford, "The Common Denominators in Groups that Help People Change." *The Dis-Coverer* 4, 1–6, October 1967.

group situations may provide some alternative methods for achieving your desired result.

Discussion Methods

Group discussion methods involve an interchange of questions and ideas among the participants. The purpose of a discussion may be simply to encourage the exchange of ideas, without attempting to reach a decision. On the other hand, the discussion-decision method goes a step further and determines definite goals for action.

Various research studies have compared the effectiveness of discussion procedures and lectures. Discussions have been found to be approximately as effective as lectures when the acquisition of information was measured immediately after the experimental periods. Measurements at a later time indicate that discussion methods may be superior to lectures or reading for the retention of information. Discussion methods have been found to be superior also in contributing to the application of the material learned and in building attitudes that are important in shaping behavior patterns.

Although research has indicated possible advantages of using discussion methods, not all research studies are in agreement as to what these are or how to attain them. The effectiveness of a group discussion may be related to the age levels and abilities of the students, the class size, the subject matter to be covered, and the experience and skill of the teacher. The following sections point out some of your functions as a teacher, ways in which students can help to make a discussion a significant learning experience, and various types of discussion techniques.

Functions of the Teacher

As a group leader, the teacher must be responsive to the goals of the group, even those not yet articulated. She defines limits, provides support, and guides in the selection of a suitable problem—one that is real to the students and one that needs an early solution. The teacher should orient the students to the discussion technique and to the particular topic that will be discussed. The points to be discussed should be worked out cooperatively with the students. Materials to provide background information should be made available. A time schedule needs to be planned. Tables and chairs should be arranged in a manner that creates the proper climate for free interchange of ideas.

During the discussion, either the teacher or a student may serve as leader. The leader is responsible for guiding the discussion but not dominating it. She listens, conveys empathy, and sets a friendly tone that accepts and gives consideration to all contributions. The leader must have thorough knowledge of the topic being discussed but should avoid having a preconceived notion as to the directions or outcomes of the discussion. Opportunity and encouragement should be provided for each member to make a contribution. Periodic summaries are helpful. A final summary should highlight the conclusions that have been reached. It is at this point that generalizations, applicable to other situations, can be formulated.

Whether or not the teacher serves as leader, she has responsibility to see that the discussion is worthwhile. She might contribute in a variety of ways: clarify the problem, suggest other aspects to be considered, define the meaning of terms, emphasize important ideas, correct mistakes or misinterpretations, bring quiet students into the discussion, redirect a discussion that is being monopolized by a few students, help students to organize or express their ideas, stimulate students to reason out problems and develop good judgment in evaluating what they hear, maintain interest in group participation, or suggest possible class activities as outgrowths of the discussion.

Warters classifies leadership functions into two broad categories—task functions and social-emotional functions. "The basic functions of the leader are to help the group set and define goals, progress toward achievement of these goals, and maintain itself as a group." [8]

Student Participation

One definition of leadership is that the individual who is chosen as leader meets the needs of the group. Group members gain security by identifying with the leader. Serving as leader for the discussion may be the most important contribution that a student can make. A well-informed student with leadership ability can guide the group in asking appropriate questions, see that various viewpoints are presented, interpret ideas that are not expressed very well, and summarize the progress that has been made.

Each member of the discussion group should be aware of the importance of his contribution in making the discussion a success. Each student should strive to understand the purposes of the discussion, show interest in the group, and try to bring in helpful information from his own experiences, reading, or talks with an informed person. Discussions imply that the student has prepared himself for making intelligent contributions. He will have searched for knowledge prior to the class discussion. Thus the class period becomes productive for all; it results in pooling ideas based on knowledge rather than on pooled ignorance, fallacy, or inexperience.

[8] Jane Warters, *Group Guidance: Principles and Practices*. New York: McGraw-Hill, 1960, p. 32.

A silent person may feel inferior to the others. Sometimes he fears that no one will listen to his ideas. He may not want to reveal his feelings or expose his ideas. Group members desire feedback and they like to have everyone equally vulnerable. The leader should help the quiet ones to feel wanted and secure. At the same time, the leader must recognize that good thinking and talking are not likely to go on at the same time. Silence may indicate that the group needs time to digest ideas.

Each student should be willing to abide by the suggestions for effective procedures so that no one tries to monopolize the discussion and all have opportunity to make contributions. Students may need help in expressing themselves; attention should be given in advance to the verbal skills possessed by the students.

Since the extent of student learning is related to the interaction of the pupil with the situation, each student should be encouraged to weigh the ideas that are presented and to decide whether they are sound. He should try to apply to his own needs various ideas or experiences that are brought out by the discussion members.

With the emphasis on encouraging students to think for themselves, the leader becomes another group member rather than a source of final solutions. An atmosphere of friendly cooperation helps students learn to give and take and to respect honest differences of opinion. Groups tend to accept suggestions that deviate from their norms if offered by well-liked individuals, while discarding such ideas from persons whom they reject.

Students should have the opportunity to share with the teacher in evaluating their discussions. They might think about such questions as the following: Did every member contribute to the discussion? Did the members have adequate information? Did the group receive aid from the leader in solving its problems without becoming dependent on the leader? Were the members cooperative and friendly even when their ideas were in conflict? Did the group progress toward common goals? Was the group realistic in choosing its problem and setting its goals? Were the students stimulated to think? Do the students feel that they have gained ideas or attitudes that will help them solve their individual problems? Did the group reach a decision, if one was sought? Are they willing to take action toward their decision? Will they assume the consequences of this action?

Variations of Discussion Techniques

An informal discussion is usually most effective when no more than twelve persons are in the group. However, various means have been developed for applying discussion techniques in larger groups and for stimulating interest in spontaneous discussions. Fleck suggested the following *warm-up techniques:* [9]

1. MATCHING PARTNERS. Problems, quotations, pictures, newspaper clippings, or other means of presenting subject matter related to home economics may be prepared in advance. Each picture or card is cut into two pieces. The students find their partners and each group of two students discusses the implications of a particular problem. Fleck recommended this procedure especially for teaching in the areas of family life, child development, and consumer education.

2. REACTIONS TO SPECIFIC WORDS. A discussion on eating between meals was introduced by having the students in a nutrition class write their reactions to the word "nibble." Their answers, which were tallied and read to the class, included: "Makes me think of calories," "That's what I do when I watch TV," and "I nibble when I am lonesome."

3. INCOMPLETE SENTENCES. An incomplete sentence that is written on the board may stimulate discussion. One example suggested by Fleck is: "I think a father should________."

4. EMOTIONALLY TONED PICTURES. A newspaper or magazine picture that is related to the subject matter might be shown with an opaque projector. Child care and family relations topics can be introduced in this manner through such pictures as a young couple on a date or a child who is leaving for camp.

5. CHALLENGING QUESTION. A question like, "What does Thanksgiving mean to you?" might start a discussion. Each student could present her idea and then "pass it on" with a request for the next student to tell what she thinks.

The above approaches can serve as motivators for particular kinds of home economics objectives. You may find them useful as techniques for discovering problems your students have relative to a particular subject matter area; as culminators for a particular concept—to help you really "clinch" a point; or as a focal point for evaluating a unit. Again, *whatever teaching methods or techniques you employ* are secondary to *what you aim to teach.*

The various *types of discussion techniques* include:

a. "DISCUSSION 66." A technique that is applicable for large groups, for starting a discussion, or for injecting life into a lagging discussion is known as "Discussion 66" or "Buzz" groups. The number 66 was originally chosen because six persons were to talk about a problem for 6 minutes. Actually, the number of persons and the length of

[9] Henrietta Fleck, "Add New Dimensions to the Discussion Method." *Forecast for Home Economists,* 74:7, November 1958.

time can be varied according to the needs and size of the group. When there are 25 or more persons in a group, some members tend to be primarily listeners. Dividing into small groups gives such members an opportunity to participate more actively. Each group may attack the same problem and pool their thinking following the "buzz" sessions, or each group may work on a different aspect of the problem. The subgroup organizes by selecting a chairman and perhaps a secretary-spokesman. Ideas are discussed freely and summarized for presentation to the larger group.

A seventh grade teacher had her class break up into "buzz" groups with a few reference books available for each group. Each "family" developed "Ten Commandments for Good Dishwashing for Our Family." These were reported to the rest of the class and a revised version was mimeographed for each student.[10] This technique makes it possible to acquire the ideas of many in a short time.

b. FISHBOWL. The Fishbowl design has an "inner group" discuss a topic while an "outer group" observes how the discussion is going. For example, a few students might be assigned to count how many students participate in the discussion, who looks as though he wants to say something but doesn't, who gets interrupted and by whom. Following 8–10 minutes of discussion, the observers report on what they heard and the groups reverse their roles. An evaluation should follow the role reversal.

c. PANEL DISCUSSION. A few of the students, or a panel of guests, may be used to discuss certain topics. Each member of the group comes well-prepared. The moderator introduces the subject and calls on one of the members to lead off. Other members are free to react to the ideas presented. The moderator guides the direction of the discussion, keeping it within predetermined bounds, and summarizes the principal ideas on various sides of the issue. Whenever possible, the class should be given the opportunity to ask questions, once the participants have made their presentations. At any rate, some opportunity should be given students for reacting to ideas presented to them in a panel. This could be done during another class session.

Connauton suggested using an equal number of teenagers and parents in panel discussions on problems that arise between teenagers and their parents, such as smoking and drinking, girls going to visit boys at college, and early marriage.[11]

[10] "Co-operative Planning Pays Dividends." *Illinois Teacher*. Vol. II, No. 1, p. 11.

[11] Marie F. Connauton, "A 4-Part Family Living Course." *Practical Home Economics,* 4:15–16, December 1958.

d. SYMPOSIUM. In a symposium, there is usually one problem under consideration, and each participant is held responsible for presenting the particular aspect that he is especially qualified to discuss. Each is given a certain number of minutes for his presentation, and, when all aspects have been presented, the participants exchange ideas or raise questions with each other. When time permits, the audience, too, should be given a chance to ask questions of the participants.

e. DEBATE. Topics that lend themselves to "pro" and "con" positions may be debated by teams of students. One member of the "pro" side begins by pointing out reasons for favoring the issue in question, and then a member of the opposing team gives reasons for being against the issue. The other members of each team have opportunities to present new evidence or to answer the arguments presented by their opponents. In a formalized debate, the class or a committee might serve as judges to decide which team presented the most convincing arguments and evidence.

Brainstorming

Brainstorming is a technique that has been used by a number of business firms to encourage creative ideas. Basically, brainstorming consists of placing a group of about twelve people in a climate that encourages creativity with the suggestion that they produce a "storm" of ideas to help solve a specific problem.

Selection of a Problem

Best results are obtained when the problem is simple rather than complex, and particular rather than general. The problem must be one that can be talked about, the subject should be familiar to the students, and the problem must have a number of possible solutions. A teacher must be cautious in the selection of a problem, in order to avoid encouraging "top-of-head" thinking about problems that involve human relationships. Perhaps brainstorming should be limited for the most part to "how-to-do-it" techniques, such as ways to set the table, prepare food, or do a step in clothing construction.

One type of problem for which brainstorming might be used is the selection of a project. If the Future Homemakers of America chapter were planning to have a community-improvement project, a storm of ideas might help the group members to select an interesting and profitable one. Ideas for home experiences or money-raising projects might be suitable topics for brainstorming.

In our society where teenage marriages are prevalent and families are so mobile, students could do creative thinking about such problems as: how to select a particular piece of furniture that will serve various functions, what other uses might be made of a given piece of equipment, and how to improvise necessary equipment for the comfort of sick persons.

Procedures

The four basic rules for making a brainstorming session fruitful were listed by Osborn as:

> 1. *Criticism is ruled out.* Adverse judgment of ideas must be withheld until later.
> 2. *"Free-wheeling"* is welcomed. The wilder the idea, the better; it is easier to tame down than to think up.
> 3. *Quantity is wanted.* The greater the number of ideas, the more the likelihood of winners.
> 4. *Combination and improvement are sought.* In addition to contributing ideas of their own, participants should suggest how ideas of others can be turned into *better* ideas; or how two or more ideas can be joined into still another idea.[12]

Role of the Teacher

The teacher should be very familiar with the principles underlying the development of creative thinking and the brainstorming approach. She might orient the participants by conducting a "warm-up" or practice session on a very simple problem. Usually a *general* problem should be stated in advance so the participants may do some background reading and come prepared with ideas. Advance information about the *specific* problem may not be desirable because individuals may discard some of their ideas before presenting them to the group or they may determine ahead of time which is the best idea and then attempt to push that one. Spontaneity and the elimination of judgment are two factors that contribute to the effectiveness of brainstorming.

As the leader of the group, the teacher should set an atmosphere of encouragement so that individuals will feel free to express their own ideas and to carry on the chain-reaction with ideas started by others. The leader may need to see that a participant presents only one idea at a time so as to give the others a chance to present their ideas. If ideas are slow in coming, the teacher might suggest certain categories as leads. Occasionally, the teacher has to go still further and suggest possible solutions from a list that she has developed in advance. The discussion should be kept within the boundaries of the topic. One or two students should be appointed as secretaries to take down the ideas as they are

[12] Alex Osborn, *Applied Imagination* (rev. ed.). New York: Scribner's, 1957, p. 84.

presented. Ideas, rather than the names of the contributors, should be of primary importance.

Among the questions that the teacher or participants might ask to stimulate the flow of further ideas are the following:

1. What can be eliminated?
2. What could this be made to look like?
3. What else is like this?
4. In what other ways could this be used?
5. What can be substituted for this?
6. What if this were larger? or smaller?
7. Can the shape be changed?
8. What change can be made to speed up the process? or to slow it down?

Follow-up

The brainstorming process itself has value in stimulating creative thinking. Since it is especially useful in solving a real problem, the follow-up procedures are important. The ideas should be edited, classified, and screened. The most promising ones should be selected and developed further; otherwise, there is no real purpose to the brainstorming process.

Dramatization

Several forms of dramatic methods may be used to advantage in home economics classes. Students may assume various roles spontaneously, they may read prepared scripts, or they may project their ideas through inanimate objects such as puppets.

Role Playing

Psychodrama, sociodrama, and role playing are techniques in which the self is viewed as a totality of roles that an individual plays in his interpersonal contacts. To achieve good human relations, he must be able to understand his own roles and those of others and to respond appropriately to counterroles. Role playing enables students to explore their behavior problems through interaction with others. It is directed toward self-integration, reduction of conflict, and the development of insight about self and others.

When used in the classroom, "role playing" refers to a spontaneous drama in which students assume certain roles and play them as they perceive them. Role playing has many possibilities, among which are the following: (1) presenting emotional subject matter in an impersonal manner; (2) helping students see that other people have problems similar to theirs; (3) providing a realistic and interesting way of handling problem situations; (4) enabling the students, especially those who play roles, to identify themselves with real people; (5) giving an outlet for emotional feelings or tensions; (6) helping students to check the reality of their self-perceptions and to gain insight into their own behavior; (7) helping students discover new ways of behaving or perceive the need for new skills in relating to others; (8) developing understanding of human relations and group behavior; (9) providing experience in acquiring empathy and thus developing interpersonal competence; (10) providing an enjoyable learning experience in which students can solve problems creatively; and (11) offering an opportunity to rehearse new ideas or skills in a protective setting.

The basis for a role-playing situation should be a specific problem that is suitable for acting, real to the group, and geared to the appropriate age level. The problem should be explored through discussion until it is defined well and understood clearly by the students. Wood suggested several situations in teaching family relations where role playing might be used: "The Prompt Family, Setting the Curfew, Taking Younger Children with You, and How to Keep Peace in the Family." [13]

Spitze reported the use of role-playing with disadvantaged adults. Two teachers portrayed homemakers who had just returned from the grocery store. They compared the contents of their grocery bags, for which each had spent ten dollars. Then the group discussed their own food buying experiences.[14]

One of the possible ways of creating role-playing situations is to read a short story, stopping it at a crucial point. Members of the class could assume roles of the characters and act out the rest of the story as they see fit. Another possible way is to select a picture, from a book of family pictures such as *The Family of Man*,[15] and have the students enact the situation. These approaches enable the students to view a situation more objectively than they might if they were given the freedom of evolving their own situation and to accomplish this within the limits of a class period. Actually, the greatest learning for the *whole class*, not the players, is probably from the follow-up discussion; ample time should be given to this.

[13] Mildred W. Wood, "Use of Role Playing in Teaching Family Relationships." Practical Home Economics, **31**: 12–13, November 1952.

[14] Hazel T. Spitze, "Consumer Education for Disadvantaged Adults: a Guide for Teachers." *Illinois Teacher of Home Economics*, Vol. XI, No. 1, Fall 1967–68, p. 9.

[15] Edward Steichen, *The Family of Man*. New York: Simon and Schuster, 1955.

Preferably players should volunteer for their roles but, in certain instances, they may need encouragement to accept roles for which they have interest, need and/or understanding. An unfavorable role may be played by the teacher or by a mature, secure student. Both the players and the audience need to have a clear understanding of the situation and the roles to be played as well as a knowledge of what to look for during the experience. The players may be given a short time to "set the stage" or decide how they want to begin. However, no further planning should be done, in order that the scene may be kept spontaneous.

While the role playing proceeds, students in the audience may watch certain players, study the interaction between players, watch for good and bad moves, decide whether something different should be tried, and suggest ways in which they think the situation might be improved. The audience should avoid laughter or other means of conveying approval or disapproval to various roles. The teacher should stop the acting when the problem has been defined clearly or resolved and before tensions begin to mount.

Following the role-playing, the class might discuss such points as what the players and the audience felt they learned, strong and weak aspects of the ways the roles were played, how various conflicts were resolved, and what other ways might be used to solve the problem. Among the techniques that may be used to make the evaluation profitable are the following:

1. SOLILOQUY. The actors in a role-playing situation usually find this to be a dynamic experience. If the actors have an opportunity between scenes to step out of their roles and tell the audience about their real feelings, the audience can share a moving part of the role-playing experience.

2. ROLE REVERSALS. In the first part of a role-playing scene, a player might benefit from taking the role of a person different from himself, to help him understand how that person might feel. For example, a child might take a parent's role. Later, during that scene or in another scene, the roles could be reversed so the child would be playing his own part. For a young child, this provides an opportunity to practice what he might say when the real problem situation arises.

Teenagers might gain insight into the feelings of others by starting in opposite roles, where a girl plays the part of a boy, and a boy takes the part of a girl. Once they feel at ease in these roles, they might go naturally into the reverse situation in which each plays his own sex role.

3. RE-ENACTMENT. Following the discussion of the various roles and how the situation might have been handled differently, another scene

might be enacted in which the same players or a different set of actors would try to carry out the suggestions for improvement. They would have a basis for determining whether or not the new ideas were suitable.

The teacher's responsibility in the use of role playing is to insure that it is a learning experience and not just an enjoyable or relaxing time. Through proper selection and orientation of the players, she can help the students to put themselves into the roles they are expected to play and to express their feelings well. She must guard against letting the discussion become merely a debate of opinions. If the students lack a factual basis for arriving at conclusions about a situation, the teacher should make resource materials available and encourage their use.

Pantomime

Some situations in home economics lend themselves to expression without the use of words. Fleck suggested that pantomime might be used to demonstrate school-bus etiquette, efficient ways of doing homework, steps in baking a cake or in putting a hem in a skirt, and proper utilization of the attachments of a vacuum cleaner.[16]

Reading Scripts

Published plays, written by an individual or by an association interested in promoting good family relationships, may be used in the study of child development or personal and family relationships. A student who is to take a certain part should have an opportunity to read the play in advance and decide what kind of character his part depicts. Excerpts from the play, or an entire brief play, might be read to the class. Preparation of the audience in advance and a discussion of the play following its reading are important, just as they are in role-playing.

Puppets and Marionettes

Fleck pointed out that "Students enjoy making their own puppets from socks, paper bags, scraps of cloth, buttons, yarn, balls for heads, and the like. They may be operated as simple hand puppets or can be made into the more complicated marionettes operated with strings."[17]

The time spent in preparing the puppets should be considered in relation to the value of the learning experience. Simple puppets that are suitable for classroom use can be prepared rather quickly and spontaneously. More elaborate ones might be necessary for performances

[16] Henrietta Fleck, "Dramatic Methods Add Spark to Teaching." *Forecast for Home Economists,* 75:39, February 1959.

[17] Ibid., p. 39.

in which guests are included, such as assembly programs or open-house occasions for the parents.

Role playing, dramatizations, and using puppets and marionettes are all techniques of teaching rooted in social psychology; they are illustrative of projective techniques.

Group Interaction in Student Clubs

Working with groups in the ways described up to this point can be effective in extracurricular activities as well as in home economics classes. Many high school teachers serve as advisers for the Future Homemakers of America, and college faculty members have advisory responsibilities for home economics clubs. You may be asked to sponsor a service organization, honor society, group of future teachers, or some other club. In your role as group adviser, you will profit from an understanding of why people join groups, how to develop leadership within the group members, and what kinds of behavior might disrupt group activities.

Bloland described the adviser's role under three general categories:

1. MAINTENANCE FUNCTIONS. In fulfilling this role, the faculty adviser is meeting minimal requirements and using the least initiative. With some groups, all that is required is to help maintain the existence of the student organization in such ways as providing continuity with the traditions of past years, heading off situations that might reflect unfavorably on the organization, arbitrating intra-group disputes, and providing advice when called upon.

2. GROUP GROWTH FUNCTIONS. Skilled advising assists a student organization in improving its effectiveness and progressing toward its goals. A faculty adviser might teach group members the techniques and responsibilities of good leadership, guide them in following good organizational practices, help them to develop self-discipline and responsibility, and keep the group's focus on its goals.

3. PROGRAM CONTENT FUNCTIONS. The adviser can help to bring about an integration of curricular and extracurricular experiences and can stimulate intellectual development of the student participants. The adviser's activities might include introducing program ideas with an intellectual flavor, providing opportunities to practice skills acquired in the classroom, helping the group apply principles and concepts learned in the classroom, pointing new directions to the group, and providing knowledge and experience.[18]

[18] Paul A. Bloland, *Student Group Advising in Higher Education*. The American College Personnel Association Student Personnel Series No. 8. Washington, D.C.: The American Personnel and Guidance Association, 1967, pp. 12–13.

Bloland summarized general responsibilities of advisers, pointing out that these vary according to the school's traditions and policies. Most advisers of home economics clubs would have responsibilities for:

1. Teaching or coaching functions.
2. Consultation on programs and projects.
3. Providing continuity, orienting new officers, and helping to develop long-term plans.
4. Counseling individual students.
5. Interpretation of policy.
6. Supervision.
7. Meeting emergencies, such as an accident while on a field trip, an emotional outburst, or a personal crisis.
8. Financial supervision—accounts receivable, current balance, and prompt payment of bills.
9. Social activities, perhaps as a chaperone.
10. Attending organization meetings.
11. Protecting organizational records and having them available in an accessible area.[19]

EXPERIENCES IN THE LABORATORY

A worthwhile laboratory problem is a "well-rounded learning or work unit which . . . includes manipulation, construction and experimentation, planning and problem solving, together with the necessary demonstrations and related cultural knowledges and understandings." [20]

Demonstrations

Lecture-demonstrations are used to present material to an audience so that its members can both see and hear it. They may be used to introduce something new that will be practiced later by the students in their laboratory work or they may substitute for laboratory work, especially when a limited budget does not permit the purchase of materials for laboratory use. Since meat cookery is likely to be quite expensive, a demonstration of a roast might be substituted for direct laboratory experience.

Effective Uses of Demonstrations

The purposes of demonstrations have been summarized very well in the *Illinois Teacher:*

Sets a standard for a product.

Establishes a pattern of procedure for preparation of a given product.

[19] Ibid., pp. 15–17.

[20] Roy G. Fales and Roy V. Orendorf, "Projects—or What" *American Vocational Journal,* 35:14, March 1960.

Helps students to judge the amount of time needed for preparation and cooking of the food.
Sets a standard for work habits.
Illustrates hard-to-describe terms and processes.
Gives pupils a chance for critical analysis.
Motivates the desire to try the product.[21]

Demonstrations are used commonly to teach skills, such as those in food preparation, home care, and clothing construction. Nevertheless, they can be used effectively to convey personal mannerisms, relationships between people, and other aspects that might be difficult to explain with words alone. They can be used as part of the regular classroom experiences for any age level in a home economics class. Their use need not be restricted to classrooms, however. An open house for parents affords an excellent opportunity for demonstrations to illustrate to parents what home economics education includes.

To increase the interest and learning potential of a demonstration, a teacher should be creative in thinking of ways to involve the students in the demonstration. One way to keep their interest alive is for the teacher to call on students to help her do something or to time a procedure. Another approach is to appoint in advance a student assistant who will work with the teacher on the time schedule, division of responsibilities, and actual presentation of the demonstration. Still another method is to have students give demonstrations by themselves. Of course, the teacher must give them adequate guidance to be sure that the rest of the class will profit from seeing the demonstrations. Students can learn a great deal from giving demonstrations; they may gain a sense of timing, knowledge about the subject covered, and ability to organize and think ahead.

Student demonstrations sparked interest in a nutrition class when the students paired off into teams, each student choosing her partner; one member of each team reported on a vitamin or mineral, while the other member demonstrated the preparation of a particular food that was rich in that nutrient.[22]

Evaluation of Demonstrations

The principles underlying the effective use of demonstrations might be classified as follows:

1. THE DEMONSTRATOR HAS THE PERSONAL QUALITIES NECESSARY TO PUT THE MATERIAL ACROSS TO THE STUDENTS. One of the most obvious personal qualities of the demonstrator is her appearance. A pleasing appearance

[21] "Teaching Foods and Nutrition in the Space Age." *Illinois Teacher*. Vol. II, No. 5, p. 32.

[22] Ibid., p. 33.

and good posture are important. Clean and becoming clothing contributes to a pleasing appearance. Clean hair, hands, and fingernails are important in setting sanitary standards.

The demonstrator's personality can "sell" what is being demonstrated. Enthusiasm, vivacity, poise, and a sense of humor help the audience to receive her ideas. The demonstrator's appearance of being at ease, her adaptability to the changing interests of the members of the audience, and her flexibility in meeting interruptions or emergencies help the audience to have confidence in her. Open-mindedness and willingness to listen to ideas that differ from her own help to make the audience receptive.

A natural and sincere voice is a real asset. Pleasing pitch, clear enunciation, varied emphasis, and a well-modulated voice should be among the demonstrator's goals. She should endeavor to be heard comfortably by everyone in the group.

2. THE DEMONSTRATOR HAS PREPARED THOROUGHLY. Advance preparation includes thinking through the main points that are to be stressed and having thorough knowledge of the principles underlying the demonstration. In addition, the demonstrator plans carefully for each step that is necessary to put across the main points. Each demonstration is rehearsed before being given in front of an audience.

Preliminary preparation includes a time and work plan. The time schedule is worked out in detail. Market orders are planned to provide the necessary supplies and to allow for a little extra in case of an emergency, such as might arise from the mixing of a little egg yolk with a white that is to be beaten for a meringue.

Routine or time-consuming tasks should be done in advance so that the demonstration time can be used for new learnings. Routine measurements, opening of cans and packages, and some chopping can be done prior to the demonstration.

The demonstrator should check in advance to be sure that the right equipment is on hand and that all equipment is in good working order. Modern equipment is usually desirable. However, equipment similar to that used in homes of the community might be used to make the transfer of learning easy.

3. THE DEMONSTRATION SHOWS GOOD ORGANIZATION OF TIME. Simple skills require less time to demonstrate than do more complicated ones. The demonstrator should follow the plan for presentation that was worked out carefully in advance, making sure that various steps are done in their proper sequence. Illustrative materials are often effective.

The demonstrator should strive to make movements constructive. This can be done by working quickly and with ease of manipulation.

Although a demonstration should move along quickly, the demonstrator should not rush through it. Wastefulness in time, motion, and use of supplies should be avoided.

4. MATERIALS FOR THE DEMONSTRATION ARE WELL ORGANIZED. The introduction to a demonstration should give the audience a clear picture of the purpose and sequence to be followed. Explanation throughout the demonstration should be adequate to present the principles. Coordination of talk and motion is an art that contributes to an effective presentation.

The demonstrator can help the audience by outlining the steps and striving to make the demonstration simple and clear. A summary should be given and definite conclusions should be drawn before the lecture-demonstration is complete.

5. THE WORK AREA IS WELL ORGANIZED THROUGHOUT THE DEMONSTRATION. An attractive setting for the demonstration should be selected. A colorful plant placed near the demonstration area can help to add interest.

The work area should be orderly at all times. Waste products should be discarded so they do not distract from the attractiveness of the setting.

At all times, processes being demonstrated should be visible to the audience. Equipment should be placed so as not to block the view of members of the audience. An overhead mirror may be helpful to enable all students to obtain a closeup view of something that would be concealed on a flat table. The demonstrator should face the audience and take pains to show how the product looks at various stages.

6. THE RESULTS OF A DEMONSTRATION INDICATE THAT IT WAS EFFECTIVE. Since a demonstration is used to help students learn, one way of evaluating the results is to note the reactions of students. Do they seem to be interested? Have they been challenged to think? How do they apply what they have learned?

Another way of judging a demonstration is through the product or products that were prepared. Were they done on time? Did they set a satisfactory standard? Were they displayed effectively?

The demonstration method is usually used to a greater extent as class size increases. Visibility becomes a major problem because the students must be able to see the details if they are to profit from a demonstration. Audio-visual materials, the use of which is discussed in Chapter 10, may be used effectively to present demonstrations. Among the advantages of a filmstrip or movie demonstration are these: (1) the demonstration is given by an expert; (2) actual time necessary for preparation is reduced; and (3) materials that might be too costly or difficult to bring into the classroom can be shown effectively.

Laboratory Experiences

Often lectures or readings are less effective in bringing about changed behavior than is actual experience in doing the desired activity. Laboratory experiences have been one of the unique features of home economics classes since their introduction into the school curriculum. Nevertheless, firsthand experiences do not necessarily bring about the desired learning results. The fact that home economics education has used laboratory activities successfully through the years does not mean that laboratory experiences should be the only or even the major type of teaching procedure. If laboratory activities are planned nearly every day because the students enjoy them and the teacher can get by with little preparation, the students probably are learning very little in spite of their opportunity to be active in a "learning" experience.

One of the newer emphases in teaching is to limit the amount of time devoted to laboratory experiences and to place increased emphasis upon intellectualizing from the laboratory experiences. The learner must see the relation between skills learned in the laboratory and his own needs and goals.

Learning Potentials of Laboratory Experiences

Laboratory experiences motivate students because they provide opportunities for direct participation in planning and doing activities related to the facts and principles that are being studied. Students who have difficulty with verbal comprehension may find laboratory experiences interesting and helpful in clarifying concepts.

Laboratory work may also allow the students to have experience with a concrete task rather than just an abstract idea. Through this activity, they may have direct experience with people, things, or processes. Opportunity for each individual to practice the desired behavior is afforded through laboratory experiences.

Laboratory experiences can stimulate students to be creative or to express themselves. For example, a foods laboratory affords opportunities for students to prepare foods in different ways and to react to changes in flavor or texture. Students can learn to generalize and to apply generalizations in new situations.

Laboratory work may provide a student with a meaningful group experience. Students' concepts of people with different backgrounds are broadened as they work side-by-side. Furthermore, a democratic laboratory situation is conducive to bringing about changes in attitudes. Inconsistency or invalidity of one's beliefs may be revealed in a friendly setting.

Steps in Laboratory Work

A laboratory experience consists of much more than the actual doing. Its three stages are planning, executing the plans, and evaluating. When an experience is relatively simple, all three steps may be included within a single class period. However, many times planning takes place during a preliminary period or periods and the evaluating is done in a period following the activity.

1. PLANNING. Prior to the planning period, the teacher introduces the students to the nature of the project. A demonstration is often effective in introducing skills. The teacher and students determine together what are the goals of the activity. Students should think about and compare various means of attaining their goals. Freedom of expression should be encouraged so that an experience can be adapted to the individual interests, needs, and abilities of the students.

2. EXECUTING THE PLANS. While the plans are being carried out, the teacher has opportunity to observe managerial practices, social relations, and other factors that are not necessarily parts of the techniques that are being executed. An activity period for the students is very demanding of the teacher, who must be constantly alert to see that safety precautions are observed, to guide students in the correct use of supplies and equipment, to make simple repairs or assist students in adapting their plans in case equipment breaks down, to help students think through ways in which they might improve their use of resources, and to be sensitive to the social relations that are developing within the teams or groups of students. Personal tensions or insecurities may be observable before they become great enough to cause antisocial behavior. Attention should be given to the cleanliness and orderliness of the work area throughout the laboratory period and particularly before the end of the period.

3. EVALUATING. Evaluation of the success of a laboratory experience should be in terms of the specific goals of the class. The students, under the guidance of the teacher, should consider the effectiveness of their own activities. Among the questions that might guide them in their evaluation are the following:

1. Did we have a definite and attainable goal?
2. Was the activity focused upon a basic understanding, not just "busy work"?
3. Was the activity natural and lifelike?
4. Was the problem of personal significance and interest to us?
5. Did we exert wholehearted effort to achieve our goal?

6. Did we grow in the ability to plan and direct our own activities?

7. Did we use the basic steps of problem solving in designing and proceeding with our laboratory experiences?

8. Were we able to relate previously learned facts and principles to this activity?

9. Did this experience help us to grow in our understanding and ability to generalize?

10. To what other situations can we apply the understandings we have gained from this activity?

11. Was the activity completed in the time allotted for it?

12. Was the amount of time required for preparation justified by the results we obtained?

13. Did the cooperation of the group strengthen our individual ambitions to make the desired behavior changes?

14. Were our concepts, values, and feelings modified through this experience?

Activity in the laboratory is not an end in itself but is an integral part of a total learning experience. As examples of how laboratory work can be integrated into the study of home economics, the following suggestions might guide a class in planning experiences pertaining to meal preparation for five consecutive class periods. Of course, each class has different needs and abilities that must be taken into consideration; this pattern is merely suggestive and it should be adapted to the goals, time schedule, maturity, and interests of a group.

First day: Plan a specific meal for a family group.

Decide on a specific menu to follow the suggested pattern. Plan the other two meals to make a well-balanced day's menu. Study recipes, consider buying problems, check supplies, and prepare a market order.

Second day: Study the nutritive value of a menu pattern.

Read magazines, bulletins, or books for information on the special problems for the week. Discuss the nutritive values, principles of cooking, buying suggestions, and ways to prepare and serve the foods.

Third day: Prepare a work schedule.

Analyze the jobs to be done. Assess resources available—equipment, abilities of students, time, and money. Determine the sequence of activities. Divide the responsibilities among the members of the family group. Preliminary preparation of the meal may be started.

Fourth day: Prepare and serve the meal.

Degree of efficiency in carrying out the plans, order and cleanliness, and attitudes should be observed.

Fifth day: Evaluate the planning, preparation, and serving.

Each family group should consider its objectives, how well they were accomplished, and what improvement might be made another time. Each group might present a report that would be helpful to the entire class. The class might discuss how to get the greatest possible benefit from its laboratory work. Students may be given the opportunity to search for answers to questions that are related to their laboratory experiences.

HOME AND COMMUNITY EXPERIENCES

If a home economics program is to achieve its objectives, it must assist students to apply what they learn at school to the daily living at home and in the community. A teacher should give guidance and special emphasis to ways that home economics education applies to family living in her community by the effective use of home and community experiences, resource persons in the classroom, and field trips.

Extraclassroom Experiences

A real measure of the effectiveness of your teaching is the extent to which your students are able to illuminate and alleviate home and family living problems. What is learned in school does not automatically transfer to what the students do at home—but you can help to create conditions that will interest the students in applying the things they learn at school to their home living. You can help them plan experiences that will reinforce their classroom learnings and make a contribution to their personal and family development.

The term *home experiences* refers to "learning activities related to family problems which are planned, carried out, and evaluated by the pupils in their homes, under the guidance of the teacher and parents, for the purpose of personal development and improvement of home life.[23] Home experiences may be of two types, according to the needs of the students and their families:

> *Home practice:* the practical application of specific school learning to home activities for the purpose of developing skill in and appreciation of sound homemaking procedures.
>
> *Home project:* the application of principles and techniques of homemaking to the solution of a particular personal or family living problem. The project is planned, carried out, and evaluated by the pupil in the home with the guidance of the teacher and parents.[24]

[23] *Definitions of Terms in Vocational and Practical Arts Education.* Washington, D.C.: American Vocational Association, 1954, p. 15.

[24] Ibid., p. 15.

An example of a home practice would be a student's preparation of a food product at home after the student has seen the procedure demonstrated by the teacher or in a film at school. A home project is more comprehensive, and problem-oriented rather than skill-oriented. A student might decide to plan, prepare, and serve the evening meal for the family for a week. He might choose to place particular resource limits on his experience, so as to enhance learning. For instance, he might place a limit on money expenditure or time.

One teacher encouraged her students to share their home practice experiences with other class members, and at the same time she motivated the class to try at home what they learned at school through a "participating bulletin board." Schematically, it looked like Table 8.

TABLE 8 What Have You Done? *

I. What We've Done at School

Discussed alternative ways of getting protein in the diet. Examined diet patterns of cultures where meat was limited.

II. Ideas to Try at Home

Find out how your family meets its protein requirement. Read about eating habits of other countries. Visit with an "old timer," a person from another country, etc., to get ideas of how others fulfill protein needs.

III. My Try-out or Testimonials

Lois Young: We had enchiladas and refried beans last night. I liked them much better than I had expected to.

(Other students fill in their accomplishments.)

* The title was written with yarn. This idea was in the form of a printed cardboard or tear sheet that could be replaced weekly. Plenty of space was provided for students to fill in ideas to try and their testimonials.

This section will help you to understand some of the principles underlying the effective use of home and community experiences. You will find also suggestions to help a teacher guide her students in the selection, development, and evaluation of their experiences.

Principles

The fundamental principle to keep in mind as you introduce the idea of home and community experiences to your students is that these are a natural and integral part of home economics education. As the plans for a course are being developed cooperatively, students should be encouraged to think in terms of what can be done best in the school and also what needs to be done outside of the school.

Lippeatt experimented with two methods of directing home experiences. (1) The experimental method consisted of using home experiences as part of the total home economics experience to enrich the program according to the abilities and interests of the students; and (2) the control method involved simply adding home projects to the regular classroom activities. She found that the students under the integrated method recorded four times as many projects during the school year as the students in the control group. Interviews with the students revealed slightly more acquisition of new and improved skills by the students in the experimental group than by those in the control group. In parent interviews, reports of considerable change in the girls' behavior at home came more frequently from parents of students in the experimental group, than from those whose daughters were in the control group.[25]

A second principle is that students learn by doing. Home experiences provide opportunity for students to obtain additional practice and develop greater skill than would be possible within the limitations of classroom time. More of the class hours may be spent with the demonstration of new techniques, the clarification of principles, and increasing available knowledge, when opportunity for practice outside of school is used. The learning takes on added significance because it takes place in a real life situation. School learnings are reinforced and more likely to "take" if what is learned at school makes sense and has meaning at home.

In the third place, home experiences help to meet the varying needs of students who differ in their abilities, interests, needs and home backgrounds. Some students need a great deal more drill than others do to achieve the same level of accomplishment. Home practice provides an opportunity for such students to develop a comfortable feeling with various techniques. They perform at their own rate without the pressure of competition with respect to time and other students' abilities and skills. For those students who are capable of going beyond the classroom activities to the place when they can carry responsibilities and learn to manage their own activities, home and community experiences provide problem-solving situations.

Bemis studied the kinds and qualities of home experiences achieved by students of low, average, and superior intelligence. She found that slow-learning and retarded students had a tendency to choose home

[25] Selma F. Lippeatt, "An Experimental Study to Determine the Relative Effectiveness at the Secondary Level of a Home Experience Program Planned as an Integral Part of the Homemaking Curriculum and a Home Experience Program Used as a Supplement to Classroom Activities." Unpublished doctoral dissertation, *Pennsylvania State University Abstracts of Doctoral Dissertations*, **16**:404–405, 1953.

experiences that were not realistic in terms of their abilities; they had difficulty in using printed materials to help them solve their problems, in managing their resources, in achieving their goals, in bringing their projects to a successful conclusion, and in applying generalizations. She recommended that slow students might benefit from home practice of skills. On the other hand, superior students should receive greater challenge to develop their "creative, managerial, and leadership abilities." They were able to use resources in solving their problems and to achieve success with experiences requiring the "application of generalizations, abstract reasoning, and weighing of values." [26]

A fourth principle is that home experiences provide opportunities for home and school cooperation to promote learning. One key to the success of a home experience program is making sure the parents of the students understand the purposes and nature of the projects. In order to make home experiences seem interesting and worthwhile to the students and their families, the home economics teacher herself must realize their possibilities and be convinced of their values. Then she will probably be interested in informing other members of the community about some of the worthwhile, successful experiences of her students. Completed projects and reports of what the students have learned through their home experiences provide excellent materials for exhibits, window displays, newspaper articles, and letters to parents of students in other classes in which home experiences are being introduced.

Home experiences can help to promote healthy relationships between the student and her family as the student learns to appreciate the functions of the home and to contribute toward its operation. Likewise, the other members of the family can grow in their appreciation of the home and their understanding of and respect for the home economics department as they see evidences of careful planning and execution of ideas. Not to be neglected is the satisfaction a home economics teacher gains from working with the students and their families in helping them solve real problems. Through conferences and home visits, the home economics teacher gains insight into the needs of her community. Opportunities abound for involvement of teacher and students in community projects. Assisting at day care centers on weekends, organizing neighborhood play groups for children, preparing special birthday celebrations in homes for the aged, and working with Project Head Start are all avenues that enrich a student's understanding of community needs and provide him the opportunity to help in alleviating these needs.

[26] Jane S. Bemis, "Home Experiences of Michigan Ninth and Tenth Grade Pupils of Varying Abilities." Unpublished doctoral dissertation, Pennsylvania State University. (As abstracted in *Journal of Home Economics*, **52**:208–209, March 1960.)

The entire home economics program can become more relevant as a result of using home and community experiences effectively.

Guiding Experiences

The teacher's role in guiding home and community experiences might be divided into four aspects: selecting, planning, developing, and evaluating the experiences.

When and how experiences are introduced, especially to beginning classes, can influence student receptivity of the idea. Many teachers introduce them during the first few weeks when the year's work is being planned. Others prefer to wait until they can visit homes or explain home experiences at an open house. A bulletin board or display may be an effective device to show the kinds of projects students might choose. A former student who can share her home experiences with the students might also spark enthusiasm and interest.

Among the characteristics of a good home or community project are the following:

1. It contributes toward the goals of the home economics education program.
2. The student is interested in it.
3. It is within the capabilities of the student.
4. It provides a new and challenging experience for the student.
5. The family or community agency is willing to cooperate with the student.
6. The student and/or the family have the necessary resources to carry out the project.
7. The values of the project will be worth the time, effort, and money that the student must spend on it.
8. Necessary information to help carry out the project is available.
9. It includes opportunity for personal growth and growth in family or community relationships.

In guiding some students toward selecting a suitable experience, the teacher may need to direct their thinking to their responsibilities to their family, even though employment or other activities take considerable time outside of the home. Other students may be carrying very heavy home responsibilities; the teacher may guide these students to work on ways of simplifying some of the tasks that are time-consuming or fatiguing. A home or community experience is not merely a requirement that the student fulfills. Rather, it is an opportunity for him to receive special help in solving a real life problem that is crucial to him.

Home experiences may be developed in any area of the home economics program. The following suggestions for home experiences have been adapted from some that were developed in the state of Washington:

Clothing: construction of clothing for a younger child, making over or renovating a garment, keeping clothing accounts and planning a clothing budget, mending, care of their clothing, selecting clothing for a special occasion.

Foods and Nutrition: planning and preparing family meals, food preservation, improving storage space for foods, preparing family meals at different price ranges, purchasing groceries.

Family and Community Relations: planning family recreation and a reading hour, taking responsibilities in hospitality, doing community work, home nursing, home safety, caring for children at church nursery, visiting and writing letters for people confined in a home for the aged, learning from grandmother how to prepare dishes from another land.

Child Care: caring for a small child, doing something with and for a child, teaching a younger child, helping a kindergarten or nursery school teacher, organizing a play group.

Home Furnishings and Housing: improving the inside of the house, window treatment, storage space, improving the outside of the home, assisting parents with a move into a new home.

Home Care: assisting with home responsibilities, taking complete responsibility for a specific task in the home.

Home Management: planning and directing the preparation of dessert for a church supper, arranging for the family laundry to be picked up, planning and carrying out a family cook-out.[27]

An entire class, or a small working committee, might decide to work on a school or community experience. Community surveys, family practices, home activities, or food availability could provide valuable information for home economics classes. Service projects, such as planning an exhibit for a store window or providing food or service for families, could benefit people in the community while providing valuable learning experiences for the students. Adolescents are keenly interested in working for worthwhile causes; community experiences can provide constructive outlets for them.

In selecting a community project, the students should consider the local problems and ways in which they might help to improve com-

[27] Adapted from Laura E. McAdams, *A Guide for Directing Home Experiences.* Mimeographed, University of Washington, pp. 16–23; and from *Homemaking Education: Home Experiences.* Home Economics Bulletin 21. Olympia, Wash.: State Board for Vocational Education, pp. 6–8.

munity living. The purposes of the project must be stated clearly. Permission from the school principal should be obtained before undertaking a school or community project. Cooperation of community group leaders is advantageous. If students will need to leave the school, parental approval should be obtained.

The steps in problem solving are the basic procedures involved in planning home and community experiences. Briefly, these consist of:

1. Stating what one plans to do for the project.
2. Analyzing the time, work, and money that will be necessary to solve the problem, and assessing how much of these resources are or can be made available for use.
3. Obtaining the necessary information to solve the problem.
4. Weighing alternative methods for solving problems.
5. Making choices as to how one will proceed.
6. Proceeding to carry out the plan.
7. Evaluating the results continually.
8. Revising the plan if necessary and trying other approaches until the project is completed successfully.

In thinking through his plans, a student must try to be specific about *what* he hopes to achieve, *how* he can accomplish each part of his plan, *when* he can do each step, *how much* it will cost, and *where* he can receive help.

The teacher may be able to guide students by assisting them in finding references to help them solve their own problems. The wise teacher guides students only insofar as they need help, and does not do too much of the thinking for the students. On the other hand, the teacher may need to suggest ways of overcoming problems that might be keeping students from making progress and thereby discouraging them.

If a student is engaged in a home experience and the teacher can arrange to visit the home while the project is being developed, she can gain firsthand knowledge of the factors that affect the planning and carrying out of the project. She learns much more about the student by seeing him in the home setting, and the student also understands the teacher better by seeing her outside the classroom. Suggestions regarding preparation for home visits were given in Chapter 4.

Planning and carrying out a community service project can involve the entire class in determining the goals of the project, what equipment and supplies are necessary, and how each subcommittee's work can contribute to the project. Committee members may shift around to obtain varied experiences during a project. Each committee should keep written records of its activities, accomplishments, and problems. Publicity in local newspapers and exhibits showing the improvements resulting from projects can inform the community members of the valuable contributions home economics education makes to the community.

Community projects need not be large or "glamorous." One chapter of Future Homemakers of America rendered a great service to its community by volunteering to assist a nearby hospital by rolling bandages or doing any other kind of work that was needed. Through such a project, the students learned many ways that volunteers could render helpful services to their community.

Many of the techniques of evaluation, as will be described in Chapter 12, can be used by the students and teacher to evaluate home and community experiences. Effective devices include score cards, rating scales, tests, diary records, and written statements by the parents, community members, and/or students.

To extend the benefits of a home experience beyond those received by the student and his family, the student may share results of certain projects with other class members. Through occasional brief reports or through a final oral report, a student could explain specifically what his goals were and how he went about accomplishing them. He might be able to bring in illustrative material to show "before" and "after" contrasts. He should keep records of time and money used and evaluate what he learned from the experience. Evaluation should be a continuous part of the project, not just its conclusion. It functions as a student checks his progress, weighs alternatives, and searches for knowledge. It should also help him formulate new goals and procedures.

As an illustration of the kind of report that might be written, one student gave the following account of her home project on "Caring for My Sister":

> I was certainly glad when we started to study Child Development, since I was having plenty of trouble caring for my little sister. Mother went to work when Susie was 2½ years old, and it wasn't long before Susie had very bad habits. I did not want to take care of her in the first place, and each day I dreaded my task more. When our home economics teacher suggested that some of us might like to do a project at home, I decided to turn this into one.
>
> I told my home economics teacher about my difficulties, and she said she would help me. From some of the reading we had done at school, and from our classroom discussions, I thought I knew why Susie was such a problem, but I wasn't sure. To begin with, I knew that Susie did not have suitable toys. I had been planning to make her some like those we made at school, but I hadn't had time. Another thing I knew was that she didn't have a place to keep her things. She had to sleep in my room and hang her clothes in my clothes closet. I wouldn't let her keep her toys in my room because I didn't want it in a mess all the time.

After discussing the project with my teacher I decided to do the following:

1. Give Susie one corner of the bedroom and fix it up for her things.
2. Make some toys for her.
3. Try to find out why she had some of her bad habits and learn what to do to change them.

First, I got some orange crates and made a cute little wardrobe. I covered the crates with wall paper and made a rack from an old broom handle. Now Susie had a place to hang up her clothes. I got some small hangers for her coats and dresses. She could put shoes, underclothing, socks, and other things on the shelves inside the orange crates. I fixed some more orange crates for her to put her toys in. I gave her one corner of my room and placed the wardrobe and toy boxes out to make a partition. It made a little room for her. She was so proud and has put her clothes and toys away without a fuss lately.

I also made Susie some toys. I read about toys for a three-year-old first. Father had some old scraps of lumber so he cut out some blocks for me to sand and paint. Besides the blocks I made a peg board, and a puzzle. These toys will help Susie to develop muscle coordination. I also made a doll out of an old stocking. This she needs for imitative play. Later I plan to make more things for her.

Susie will be a good cook when she grows up because now I am letting her help in the kitchen when I get dinner. She loves it and shows Father what she makes. It is certainly much better than trying to find things that are new and different to keep her out of mischief while I get dinner on the table.

Susie used to have temper tantrums but doesn't seem to have them any more. I think she was upset by Mother being gone most of the time. Also, having a place of her very own and something to do helps.

I read several good library books about children. I also sent for some bulletins showing how to make toys. I didn't realize there were so many books and bulletins nor had I known where to get them. Mother is interested in reading them, too.

I have learned to keep my feelings in check during this project. I have counted to 10 many times when I was going to scold Susie for something, and the difference in her behavior is all of the compensation I need for all my effort. I don't think I will ever get as much satisfaction from doing anything again. I will soon be able to use what I have learned working with Susie, as I am to be married this summer.[28]

Use of Community Resources

Community resources are those persons, places, or objects in a community (apart from the school) that have educational value. Most communities have rich sources of people who are willing to be called upon

[28] Adapted from *Home Projects in the Homemaking Program*. Sacramento: California State Department of Education, Bureau of Homemaking Education, 1949, pp. 28–29.

but are waiting to be discovered. A home economics teacher who is alert to the types of personal experiences and abilities that might enrich her classes may discover talents among members of her social groups or their friends. Students have wide contacts and can sometimes make very helpful suggestions of places to visit or persons who could make outstanding contributions by coming to the school.

Resource Persons in the Community

Resource persons are people who can provide educational experiences based upon their own personal or professional experiences. They may be professional members of the community, skilled workers in occupational fields related to home economics, homemakers, or persons who have found satisfying ways of using their creative abilities. They may be used in many different ways, according to their educational backgrounds and the nature of their contributions.

People who believe in the educational benefits of their public-school system want to be helpful to the teachers and students. They may feel very inadequate when asked to demonstrate or participate in a class discussion, but they are usually willing to help if they are given the necessary encouragement and guidance. In fact, they will be flattered that you think they have something worthwhile to offer.

In addition to the feeling of pride and enjoyment they experience from sharing their talents, resource persons become personally involved in the home economics education program. Perhaps they have never known much about it. They may never have been aware of its breadth or the ways in which it prepares students for their home and family living. You have an opportunity to interpret the program to your guests and to stimulate them to learn more about home economics so they can make an effective contribution to your program.

The students benefit greatly from the personal contacts they have with members of the community. Persons who are actively involved with the phases of home or community life that the students are studying can make the study come alive and highlight practical applications. Each resource person has his own individual ideas, which supplement anything that the students may be able to read. Resource persons can stimulate students to obtain further information about certain aspects of a problem, and can help to clarify points in answer to questions that the students might raise. New sources of help in the community can be opened, especially to disadvantaged students.

Variety can be stimulating and helpful. In a field of study that is as broad as home economics, only an exceptional teacher can have equal mastery and up-to-the-minute information in all phases of home economics. The use of resource persons can provide an opportunity for the students to have accurate and recent materials from a person who is an authority on a particular topic.

Before a guest speaker is invited to come into the classroom, the teacher and students should plan together what they are trying to accomplish during the study of a particular unit. Once their goals are clearly in mind, they may realize that certain objectives could be covered best by bringing in a resource person. The teacher may initiate the idea of inviting someone with personal experience to help answer specific questions, or the students may know someone who has had an experience that might be shared with the class.

Either the teacher or a student may extend the invitation for a resource person to visit the class. The invitation should state clearly what the class is interested in knowing, perhaps giving a list of questions that the speaker might answer. Also, the method of the guest's participation should be clear to him.

Barkley pointed out that resource persons can contribute in a variety of ways in the classroom. They can participate in symposia, panel discussions, and informal class discussions. They can give demonstrations or talks. They might be interviewed by students who are members of a team or working committee. She suggested the types of persons who could be used effectively for various topics in home economics. Many of her suggestions have been included in the following list: [29]

Persons	Topics
A. *Community Members:*	
Doctors	Nutrition; mental or physical health; adjustment to marriage; pre-natal care.
Clergy	Selecting a marriage partner; family values mediated by a particular religious group.
Public health nurse	Physical care of a child or sick person; mental health; improvising health equipment in emergencies.
Florist (or person whose hobby is raising flowers)	Flower arrangement.
Lighting expert	Functional home lighting.
Successful hostess	Time and energy management; new ideas for food combinations; table settings; entertainment.
Man whose hobby is cooking	Food preparation.
Young mother	Child care and development; techniques for dovetailing child care and housework.

[29] Adapted from Margaret V. Barkley, *Look to Human Resources in the Teaching of Homemaking*. Washington, D.C.: National Education Association, Department of Home Economics, Bulletin, 1957, pp. 3–6.

Persons	Topics
Child psychologist	Behavior of children.
Graduates who took home economics in high school	How home economics has helped them; how high school courses can be more beneficial.
Husband and wife	Family financial management; how family made crucial decisions.
Banker	Consumer credit.
Parents with special ethnic background	Foreign foods; special family rituals such as Christmas celebrations, weddings, etc.
Parents with different size families	Buying foods; changing managerial pattern as family size increased.
Homeowners	Solving storage problems; remodeling a home; purchasing a home.
Representatives of agencies (such as Red Cross, Salvation Army, health center, visiting nurse association, child welfare association, community planning board, recreation department)	Helps and services available to families in the community; ways students can cooperate with community agencies.
B. *Teachers and Students of:*	
Industrial arts	Furniture construction and refinishing; improving and improvising storage areas; making toys.
Science	Simple electrical repairs; equipment operation; textile and food chemistry; physics principles involved in lighting.
Art	Basic art principles in home decoration; selection of decorative objects for the home; planning a coordinated wardrobe; color psychology in food, clothes, and home decoration.
Physical education	Planned physical activity for weight control; application of body dynamics principles in performing housework.
Kindergarten	Development of children; children's interests in art, music, literature.
Music	Records suitable for family recreation.
Agriculture	Flower cultivation and landscaping.
Business law	Laws that protect consumers; wills; legal problems of the family; marriage and divorce laws.

A student hostess might greet the visitor upon his arrival at the school and show him where the department is located. A student might also take responsibility for introducing the guest to the class. With the consent of the guest or guests, a talk or panel discussion might be tape-recorded so that future classes could benefit from the experience without having to take the time of the resource person to visit the class again. Of course, a tape recorder may not convey the enthusiasm and personality of the speaker quite as well as his actual presence could, but recordings can be used very effectively to present information from a "voice of authority."

The real value of any learning activity comes from evaluating the experience in light of the original, clearly defined objectives. We cannot afford to leave to chance the drawing of conclusions and generalizations. Both the students and the teacher need to be cognizant of what was being taught and how much they learned. After the visit of a resource person, the class should examine what was learned from the experience by discussing such questions as the following:

1. Did the presentation fulfill the purposes set up for the experience?
2. What new knowledge, skill, understanding, or appreciation was gained? Can this new learning be applied to the problems under consideration?
3. What principles were defined that are applicable to other situations?
4. Is the activity worth repeating? If so, what improvements can be made in the planning and carrying out of the experience? [30]

A resource file aids the teacher in planning future use of guest speakers. In addition to containing such information as the name and address of the guest, a card might indicate the topic or topics that this person could present, a summary of the principles that were covered when this person spoke to the class, and an evaluation of how well this experience met the needs of the class.

Each time a resource person visits a home economics class, a "thank-you" note should be sent promptly to express the appreciation of the teacher and students. The teacher may write her own note of appreciation. In addition, notes from the students give the guest insight into ways in which the experience was of benefit to them. Students also learn the courtesy of expressing appreciation when someone renders a helpful service.

[30] Ibid., p. 10.

Field Trips

Study trips into the community can provide rich sources for instruction in many phases of home economics. Field trips are known by a variety of names, such as instructional trips, study trips, school journeys, and school excursions. All of these terms refer to an educational procedure in which students go to observe and study materials in their functional settings or to observe workers in their occupational environments.

Perhaps the most obvious benefit of field trips is the interest they hold for the students. Opportunities to break away from classroom routines and tensions are always welcome. Students are motivated to learn as they have opportunities to examine materials and obtain new ideas. Field trips can be used to arouse interest in a new unit of study, to promote interest during a unit, or to review what has been covered.

Field trips furnish students with information that may not be available as effectively in any other way. First-hand experiences with materials in their natural settings may increase the validity of the students' understandings of a subject. Knowledge can be clarified and applied to concrete, real-life experiences. Furthermore, various subjects of the school curriculum can be integrated into a meaningful whole.

Field trips can help students to grow toward many of the objectives of home economics. For example, students can develop their powers of observation, learn where to go for facts or to seek help with family problems, modify their attitudes, see how people live, develop appreciations, become interested in profitable uses of their leisure time, develop initiative, and receive background to enrich their study of a subject.

In addition to the many ways in which field trips can enrich the educational experiences of the students, they have public relations value also. The blending of school work with actual life not only enriches the students' understanding of the community, but it also contributes to the community's understanding of the school. In the process of planning with the teacher and students to make their visit worthwhile, the community hosts learn about the objectives and scope of the home economics program.

Meshke studied the use of community resources in ninth and tenth grade home economics classes. The ninth grade classes were studying "Food Selection and Purchase" and the tenth grade classes were studying "Selection and Care of Electrical Equipment." Experimental classes visited food stores (ninth grade) and stores in which they could investigate electrical equipment (tenth grade). Other classes, known as the "classroom" groups, used as many contacts with stores as possible in their classroom experiences—descriptive and pictorial materials, and newspaper advertisements. "Control" groups received no information or special help; the teachers taught the units any way they desired. Students who had actual store experience showed superior achievement on written tests. The findings suggested also that students with store contacts were more self-reliant, more likely to exercise judgment in meeting problem situations, and more likely to practice at home what they had learned.[31]

In spite of the many advantages of field trips, there are certain limitations or possible difficulties that may cause administrator reluctance or teacher inertia toward the inclusion of field trips. A field trip can be justified only to the extent that it contributes to the objectives of a course. The trip is not an end in itself; it may not be an educational experience unless it is carefully planned and utilized. Considerable time is required to make the plans that are necessary for an effective experience. When more than one class period is necessary, a trip may be difficult to fit into the school schedule.

In determining the usefulness of a given experience, a teacher and her students need to think in terms of the criteria by which to select a field trip. They might ask such questions as the following about how well the proposed experience can be used:

1. Will the field trip experience be the best means for reaching the goal?
2. Is the experience suited to the maturity and interests of the students?
3. Is it part of a planned learning sequence?
4. What can the students learn through the use of this community resource?
5. Is the trip feasible from the standpoint of time, cost, and scheduling?
6. Will the field trip be likely to lead into other related and valuable activities?
7. Is the material to be covered known well enough by the teacher to insure adequate planning?
8. Can the experience be utilized effectively within the time that can be devoted to it?
9. Does the location permit suitable travel arrangements to be made?
10. Will the information that is presented be authentic, accurate, and up-to-date?
11. Will the experience encourage critical and constructive thinking?

[31] Edna D. Meshke, "The Effects of Utilizing Selected Community Resources in Ninth-Grade and Tenth-Grade Homemaking Classes." *Journal of Experimental Education,* **12**:1–9, September 1943.

A great variety of community resources lend themselves to worthwhile field trips for home economics classes. Among the places that might contribute to home economics objectives are the following:

Clothing and Textiles: clothing factory; store; cleaning, dyeing, pressing, or laundry establishment; museum.

Family Economics: bank; broker's office; stock exchange; credit union; small loan company; credit bureau; social welfare agency.

Family Living: settlement house; community center; family service agency; family court; nursery school; youth recreation center; home for senior citizens; nursing home.

Food and Nutrition: packing, pickling, bottling, canning, or condensing plant; stockyard; elevator; warehouse; storage plant; bakery; dairy; grocery store; wholesale food market; restaurant or school cafeteria.

Health and Safety: well-baby clinic; sanitarium; hospital; first-aid station; home; office; factory.

Housing and Home Furnishing: slum, middle-class, and exclusive residential districts; mobile home park; public housing development; house under construction; exterior and interior of a building; landscaping; furniture, equipment, or appliance manufacturer; distributor; retail store; interior decorating shop; picture gallery; museum; home of a class member to study storage and organization, characteristics that make cleaning easy, and low-cost decorative objects.

To guide yourself or other teachers in future years, you will find a file of possible field trips very helpful. Such information as the following might be contained on each file card:

1. Name, address, and phone number of the place to visit.
2. Visiting days and convenient hours.
3. Suggested transportation.
4. Time required.
5. Admission fee, if any.
6. Nature of the guide service.
7. Eating facilities (if needed).
8. Name of person to be contacted.
9. Specific details about where to meet the person in charge.
10. Age or grade level for which the experience is most suitable.
11. Nature of printed material available from the company.
12. Evaluation of the trip for its intended purpose.

Four basic steps are necessary in organizing and following through with field trips as successful learning experiences: the trip must be planned with the community host, the students must be prepared to profit from the experience, the field trip itself should be worthwhile, and suitable follow-up activities should result.

A teacher who has a file such as the one just described has some idea of where to start. If no such list is available, she might follow some of the suggestions given in Chapter 3 about getting acquainted with the resources of her community. The students may share with the teacher in determining their goals and in deciding if a field trip would help, and what type would provide the most effective learning experience.

If possible, the teacher should visit the place in advance and talk with the host about the purposes of the trip. Together they can plan a tour that is suited to the purposes of the group within the time that can be allocated. Sometimes a list of questions that the students would like to have answered can be given to the host.

Each school district has its own particular recommendations about the arrangements that should be made prior to a field trip. Generally, permission for the trip should be secured from the parents and the school administration. Arrangements for transportation need to be made. If students will be away for more than one class period, permission should be obtained from their other teachers. Provisions for financing the trip may need to be worked out—school bus or public transportation with students paying their own fare, bag lunch or eating in a restaurant, and other expenses such as admission fees. A complete list of the students taking the trip, the destination, route, and time schedule should be left in the principal's office.

The students should be informed about such details as the place to be visited, expenses, schedule, and provision for meals. In addition, they should share in planning the proper clothing and equipment, such as notebooks, pencils, and cameras if permitted. They should know what behavior is expected of them on the trip and what safety precautions they should practice.

More important than the plans for the physical arrangements, is the clear understanding by the students of the purposes of the trip—why they are going, where they are going, and what they should expect to find there. Their interest can be aroused through the use of background materials or discussions. They may formulate specific questions to which they will seek answers on the trip. They may develop a framework to guide their observations and note-taking.

The teacher is in the difficult position of having to provide necessary background to make the experience profitable to the students, and also guard against giving them too much information. Students may feel that they have already learned enough about the subject, and they may lose interest in the field trip if too much advance preparation is given. Instruction the day before the visit may be sufficient to spark student interest.

Plans for an entire class to leave the school may be highly complicated and unnecessary. Committees representing the class might arrange a visit after school hours; often they acquire better information by doing this than could be obtained by a large group. Following committee reports to the class, discussions might be held. Advance preparation is just as important for a committee as for an entire class. Students may need guidance on how to conduct an interview as well as on the types of information to seek. The teacher may, but need not always, accompany a committee. Nevertheless, she should be sure that the persons being visited know how much background the students have and what information they are seeking.

Another opportunity for a student or a committee to go into the community to seek information about a certain class objective might arise if it is not feasible to have a resource person come to your class. A student might interview a resource person with information on a particular subject and report to the class. One class, whose members wanted to gain special insight into child-rearing practices of the past, interviewed, with a portable tape recorder, fifteen grandmothers who were over 70 years of age. Prior to the interviews, the class had developed an interview schedule so that their interviews would have a similar focus and their queries would elicit responses to particular kinds of data. In this way, a few class members were able to bring to the whole class the real life experiences of a number of resource persons in a provocative and interesting manner.

Instruction can take place en route to the destination if students are alerted to things of interest along the way. Once the group reaches the place to be visited, the teacher should be sure to introduce the hosts clearly and loudly enough so that the students can hear their names and titles or positions. A large group may be divided into several smaller groups to permit students to see and hear better, but each group should follow one plan.

Students should be given opportunity to talk with the guide and to have their questions answered. A class journalist should be chosen in advance. His responsibility is to prepare a complete and accurate record of the trip. In the event that time for questions must be restricted, the journalist might be presented to the guide and his list of questions might be given priority, as representing those of the entire class. Unless a journalist is used, emphasis should be given to questions of concern to the group rather than just to individual students or the teacher.

Nevertheless, provision should be made for fulfilling the special interests of an individual.

If the plan for time and sequence has been followed, the group will be ready to leave at the scheduled time. The teacher and students should express their appreciation for the opportunity of observing and receiving information about the subject they were studying.

The teacher and/or students should write "thank-you" letters within a few days after the field trip. Letters should be sent to all who shared in making the trip possible—hosts, guides, speakers, parents, and drivers. The class should discuss the trip itself—in what ways they found it profitable, what experiences interested them the most, what they learned or failed to learn from the trip, and how it could have been improved.

Learning activities following the trip might include reports by individuals or groups, discussion of reports, and finding answers to questions that were stimulated by the field trip. Information gathered in follow-up activities should be related to the original problem or unit that inspired the field trip.

One type of follow-up activity might be to share learnings with other classes or members of the community. Students might write an interesting account of the trip for the school paper or local newspaper. They might assemble materials for a school display, including such things as samples gathered from the place visited, objects, posters, or pictures. A record might be prepared to give future home economics classes a picture of the trip.

Students with initiative may be stimulated to plan and carry out a project to incorporate the suggestions that grow out of a field trip. If plans for a school or community project are an outgrowth of a field trip, they may be correlated with another phase of the school program, thereby helping students to integrate their learnings.

One of the most worthwhile kinds of involvement in the community takes place when the home economics students volunteer their services wherever needed. They could learn much about disadvantaged families by taking the children on weekend outings or by tutoring children who lack basic skills for learning. They could befriend a person who is living in a rest home or one who is confined to bed. Arrangements for such continuing kinds of services could be made through community social welfare agencies.

INDEPENDENT STUDY

Of major importance in strengthening home economics education is the ability to individualize instruction. A number of approaches might be used to encourage independent study in the classroom and beyond classroom experiences. For example, individual research projects can be very stimulating for the more able students. All students should be encouraged to do special reading. Some of the newer programmed or packaged materials are designed to allow an individual to pursue independent study. Single-concept films, filmstrips, and tape recordings can also be used by individuals who have need for or interest in pursuing a certain topic. Further discussion on the selection and use of such materials is presented in Chapter 10.

In this chapter a number of alternatives have been discussed which you will want to consider as you determine how you will teach. Keep in mind that the most effective method is determined largely by the kind of home economics objective you have defined. A possible learning experience needs to be screened through several sieves before it is utilized. Some of these are:

1. Will this experience result in achieving the objective we have defined?
2. Is the method appropriate for my students, in my school setting?
3. Will this experience express an efficient use of resources available to me—my skills and abilities, time, space, energy, and materials?
4. Do I feel confident in guiding this kind of an experience?

Rarely is a learning experience an end in itself. Its function is to facilitate reaching a particular goal to modify the behavior of the student.

Selected References

Berne, Eric, *The Structure and Dynamics of Organizations and Groups*. Philadelphia: J. B. Lippincott, 1963.

Brown, Marjorie (editor), *Home Learning Experiences in the Home Economics Program*. Minneapolis: Burgess Publishing Company, 1963.

Byrd, Flossie M., and Minne H. Woodall, *An Approach to the Study of Human Development and the Family through Literature in the Secondary Schools*. No. 1. Prairie View, Texas: Prairie View Agricultural and Mechanical College, December 1966.

Flanders, N., *Interaction Analysis in the Classroom—A Manual for Observers*. Ann Arbor, Michigan: The University of Michigan Press, 1966.

Future Homemakers of America, Office of Education, United States Department of Health, Education, and Welfare: *A Guide to Help You Grow as a Future Homemaker of America,* 1964; *An Advisor's Guide to Help Future Homemakers of America Evaluate Their Own Growth,* 1967; and *Chapter Handbook,* 1966.

Horn, Fern, "Using Independent Study in Home Economics." *Illinois Teacher for Contemporary Roles,* Vol. XII, No. 5, Spring 1968–69.

Lifton, Walter M., *Working With Groups* (2nd ed.). New York: John Wiley and Sons, 1966.

Shaftel, Fannie R., and George Shaftel, *Role-Playing for Social Values: Decision-making in the Social Studies.* Englewood Cliffs, New Jersey: Prentice-Hall, 1967.

Smith, G. Kerry (editor), *In Search of Leaders.* Washington, D.C.: American Association for Higher Education, National Education Association, 1967.

Somerville, Rose M., *Family Insights through the Short Story.* New York: Teachers College, Columbia University, 1964.

Warters, Jane, *Group Guidance: Principles and Practices.* New York: McGraw-Hill, 1960.

10

Educational Media

As you have learned from previous chapters, an effective learning situation is one in which students are motivated to learn and they can see clearly what they are trying to learn and how they can apply it.

By selecting and using audiovisual materials properly, you can motivate and sustain the interest of your students, clarify information, present new ideas, stimulate discussion, challenge independent thinking, influence attitudes, summarize what has been learned, and provide experiences that encourage transfer of knowledge and skills to new tasks. In order to have materials available to you when they are needed, you will have to plan carefully. You will be using your time and energy more efficiently as you employ the best means of getting points across to your students and of clearing up misconceptions. Be receptive to information or ideas that can help you to present material in a new light. By all means use your creative ability in producing your own supplementary teaching aids.

The use of audiovisual materials does not necessarily insure that students will learn more quickly or thoroughly than they would through traditional methods. You will need to learn how to select materials carefully, preview them, and use them effectively. Materials must be used when and where feasible. When they are presented to a class, they should be accompanied by a clear explanation or suggested study guide. Careful planning is necessary to provide adequate care and storage for the materials. Equipment for proper use of projected materials requires a budget adequate to cover the initial investment and upkeep. Audiovisual materials can never substitute for good teaching, but they can be a very effective tool in the hands of a well-prepared teacher.

In selecting instructional materials, a teacher might answer the following questions about their usefulness for a specific situation:

1. Is it the best means available to realize the goal?
2. Will this material make the learning situation more realistic and concrete?

3. Is it appropriate for the age, intelligence, interests, and experience of the students?
4. Will it make learning easier and quicker?
5. Does it present information in an interesting manner?
6. Does it supply a concrete basis for conceptual thinking?
7. Does it stimulate the students to think critically?
8. Does it encourage the integration of subject matter?
9. Does it help the students to develop and improve skills?
10. Will it stimulate the development of responsibility and cooperation among the students?
11. Does it present an up-to-date picture of ideas and information?
12. Is it worth the time, expense, and effort involved in its use?
13. Are its physical qualities satisfactory?
14. Does it stimulate emotional as well as intellectual experience?
15. Does it challenge students to engage in self-expressive, constructive activities?
16. Will it be available at the proper time to fulfill the class objectives?

For ease in classifying the various educational media, they are discussed under the following headings: *reading* materials, materials for *viewing,* materials for *listening,* and *programmed* instruction. Actually, a number of instructional aids fit into more than one category—for example, a sound motion picture is both seen and heard.

READING MATERIALS

Reading is an important area that tends to be neglected in home economics classes. Students, particularly those of average or less than average intelligence, usually profit from visual presentations and from actual experience in the laboratory. Although these methods contribute significantly to students' information and interest, they can never replace the benefits that could be derived from reading. In like manner, reading can never substitute for or replace good teaching. A home economics teacher who introduces a variety of teaching aids and uses them effectively will enrich the learning experiences of her students.

How can you, as a teacher, help teenagers to like reading? Basically, two principles might guide you: (1) if students are to learn to like reading, they must read; and (2) when students read, they should find it an enjoyable experience and one that they would like to continue. The first principle is easy to carry out with students of high intelligence who have the background and ability to learn readily from a printed page. Nevertheless, students at all levels of ability should have reading experiences that are on their level. Words are merely symbols; the reader must bring meaning to these symbols.

If the second principle is to be fulfilled, students need guidance in understanding reasons for reading. Reading can be enjoyable and informative. It can give students information about the background of events in today's world. It can substitute for a vast variety of personal experiences that would be necessary otherwise in understanding the business and social world in which they live. It can offer new ideas to stretch the students' imaginations. And, through reading a variety of materials, students may learn to find answers to their own questions and to draw satisfactory conclusions. It can make learning continuous for them long after they have "finished school."

This discussion of reading materials is divided into three sections—the first part presents information about text and reference books, the second part discusses magazines and newspapers, while the third part deals with small, supplementary materials.

Text and Reference Books

Textbooks provide a carefully organized, common core of experience for a class. Today's text and reference books are reasonably accurate, informative, interesting, and even glamorous. Although they should not be used as a crutch to be followed rigorously from day to day, they can be helpful as a basis for specific problems and projects. As students are guided in using books as a source of information for decision making, they must be assisted in evaluating the authenticity of the information presented.

The selection of text or reference book should be made very carefully. The author's qualifications for writing the book should be examined. The point of view of the author should be considered in light of the school's philosophy and the objectives of the class. Particular values mediated by the book should be identified. Factors that contribute to the appearance of a book include suitable format, clear print, well-designed illustrations, and durable binding. Information contained in a book should be organized to facilitate learning and it should be research-based, up-to-date, accurate, and sufficient to cover the fundamental areas under consideration. Usefulness of a book is enhanced by such features as an index, table of contents, clear explanations, interesting style, suitable vocabulary, provisions for individual differences in interests and abilities, reviews or summaries, and suggestions for self-evaluation. Cost of a book should be considered in light of the overall departmental budget and the contributions the book might be expected to make.

Mather recommended evaluating the text as a means of communication, using the following criteria: [1]

Does the text fit as closely as possible the readiness of the students for whom it is intended, and does it develop new readiness not now present?

Does the text assist the student in understanding why certain responses are superior for given aims, rather than presenting them as prescriptions?

Does the text make provisions for sufficient realistic experience, through narration, proposal of supplementary experiences, and laboratory work, that students will be able to abstract generalizations from reality, i.e., actual experience?

Does the text formulate explicit and transferable generalizations?

Does the text provide for problems either by suggesting real activities or by posing problems in symbolic form? Do these problems call for use of generalizations under realistic conditions, and require the student to determine what principles to use as well as how to use them?

Does the text provide an opportunity to use concepts from many fields of study in examining the same problems?

Does the text help the learner recognize all the important outcomes of his work? Does it provide him with means of evaluating his progress along these lines?

Illustrations become less necessary as students gain experiences and develop imaginative ability. When they are used, they should contribute to, rather than detract from, the intellectual content of the book. Mather suggested questions to guide in evaluating illustrations: [2]

1. In what way do pictures and other graphic material really contribute to the content of the book; or are they primarily "window-dressing" to make the book attractive?
2. Are illustrations located adjacent to the related idea discussed in the text?
3. Are captions interesting, meaningful, and stimulating as well as useful?
4. Is the number of illustrations
   (a) adequate for this subject and your students?
   (b) so many that text material is skimpy?
   (c) so few that much supplementary material will be needed?
5. Are the charts, tables or diagrams used appropriately and easy to understand?

[1] Mary E. Mather, "A Look at Resources for Teaching Home Economics." *Illinois Teacher of Home Economics,* Vol. VI, No. 9, 1963, p. 399.

[2] Ibid., pp. 396–397.

6. Are illustrations suitable for students in your classes? Will there be problems in identifying with situations pictured in relation to:

(a) Sex of student? Is the book primarily for girls, or will boys find it satisfactory if also enrolled in your classes?

(b) Age of student? Are ages of people and situations shown consistent with age level to which text is addressed and for level at which you wish to use book?

(c) Racial or national original of students? Is only one type of family or person pictured?

(d) Socioeconomic level? What ideas in housing, home furnishing, table services, recreation and use of leisure time are shown?

(e) Rural, urban or suburban orientation? Does one dominate or is more than one type represented?

Among the suggestions that might help you to use books effectively in your classes are following:

1. Guide students in examining the essential features of a book—point out the significance of its title and the utility of the table of contents, index, illustrations, and aids to learning (such as exercises or supplementary references).

2. Demonstrate how to read a book. To show the students that studying is more than reading, a teacher might read aloud a complete section that is to be studied. Then she might go back and read a small portion of it, comment on it, interrupt with questions, paraphrase it, or refer to previous sections. Finally, when the section has been completed, she could guide the students in summarizing and discussing what was read.

3. Teach students what the technical words mean rather than assume that they know. New words should be defined and explained.

4. Correct any errors or counteract biased viewpoints that might be presented in a book.

5. Use a book to lead into other projects or to further reading rather than letting a book define the limits of a unit of study .

6. Encourage the students to read on a level that they are capable of understanding, but one that requires some effort to understand.

7. Provide a rich assortment of books and pamphlets and encourage students to browse when they have free time. It is discouraging for a student to volunteer to investigate a certain topic and then discover that information is not available.

Magazines and Newspapers

Basic textbooks and a variety of useful reference books are indispensable supplies in a home economics department, but they do need to be supplemented with other reading matter. One means of obtaining recent information is through the use of current periodicals and newspapers. Since the departmental budget may not stretch far enough to include all of the subscriptions that might be desired, the *Illinois Teacher's* suggestions for extending it may be helpful: (1) encourage the students to use the magazines and newspapers that are available in the school and public libraries; (2) permit students to bring a magazine from home for the class to discuss, but be sure that the magazine returns home promptly and in good condition; and (3) practice *selective buying* of single issues that have valuable information rather than taking yearly subscriptions of magazines that may have little application to your classwork.[3]

In evaluating one's choice of magazines, the *Illinois Teacher* suggested answering the following questions: [4]

> Is the present collection of magazines well-balanced in terms of the importance of the topic in the curriculum and the helps already available in school files?
>
> Are the magazines in your own major field of interest unduly represented in the total collection?
>
> Are certain aspects of home economics conspicuous by their absence?
>
> Are the contents of the magazines readily adapted to students' lives? Are the technical skills and supplies within the reach of students? Are the economic standards shown at most only a little higher than those students may realistically expect?
>
> Are the social practices appropriate to the location and mores of the community?
>
> Is careful economy practiced, not only in selection but also in maximum utilization?
>
> Are the magazines cared for by students with the respect due them? Is every part of every magazine used to the best advantage? Do students share in deciding on those materials of permanent value, and in clipping and filing them for future classes?

Feature articles, news stories, cartoons, and advertisements from daily newspapers can enrich class discussions and stimulate students to search for facts. Sometimes news items are appropriate for posting on the bulletin board. Ideas for captions may be gleaned from newspaper articles. Sometimes lettering for these captions can be cut from large newspaper headlines.

[3] "A Look to the Year Ahead." *Illinois Teacher,* Vol. II, No. 9, p. 32.

[4] Ibid., p. 33.

Supplementary Reading Materials

Government bulletins are helpful to home economics classes, particularly because of the variety and accuracy of information they contain. Federal bulletins may be obtained from the Superintendent of Documents, United States Government Printing Office, Washington, D.C. 20402.

Another source is the Cooperative Agricultural Extension Service in each state. Information about the bulletins available may be obtained directly from the county Cooperative Extension Service office or Agricultural Experiment Station in your state. Since their programs are designed to assist families in improving their level of living, Cooperative Extension personnel prepare bulletins on all aspects of family and community life. Materials from this agency are especially pertinent to the home economics teacher because they are (1) based on local needs; (2) prepared by experts in the particular field; and (3) undergirded by empirical research data.

Home economists who work for business firms develop a variety of educational materials for teachers and students. Business firms are able to combine the services of research workers, expert writers, photographers, and advertising specialists with those of home economists in producing factual and interesting teaching aids. Business firms help to meet educational needs and, at the same time, they increase understanding of and demand for their products or services.

Business-sponsored educational materials consist of posters, charts, exhibits, pamphlets, booklets, leaflets, filmstrips, movies, and recordings. Other sections of this chapter discuss points to consider in selecting and using several of these types of materials. Emphasis here is on reading materials such as bulletins, booklets, and leaflets.

Small materials, such as bulletins and leaflets, can be written and published more quickly than books. Consequently, they serve an important function in supplementing text and reference books. Teachers and students can receive up-to-date, accurate, individualized information on new products and the latest developments in various aspects of home economics. A variety of reading material adds interest to the classes. Through effective use of supplementary materials, a teacher can help students to think critically and evaluate the kinds of materials that will be available to them after they leave school.

Although the use of pamphlet material has many advantages, it also has certain problems. Teachers sometimes feel that they lack time to look for suitable materials and to order, evaluate, and file them. Even with the coupon sections that are contained in home economics magazines, it does take time to order materials from a number of different places. Perhaps this problem can be overcome by making the selection of teaching materials one of the learning experiences provided for a class. Students who help select, send for, evaluate, and file materials will develop greater appreciation for them. A student librarian can be of real service to her class while she is learning.

Teachers should be cautious in their use of free and inexpensive teaching materials. Educational materials are intended to be supplementary, but not to replace basic reference books or teaching methods. A teacher's job should be creative; she should be careful not to let other people, or teaching materials, do the work that she should do for herself.

Selection

Through cooperative efforts, home economics educators and home economists in business have helped business firms improve the quality of their teaching materials and have assisted teachers in using them effectively. As you select business-sponsored teaching aids, consider the following characteristics:

1. Is it suited to the learning level, experience, and needs of your students?
2. Will it make learning easier and more interesting?
3. Will it help to develop self-direction and resourcefulness?
4. Will it help to develop good judgment and logical thinking?
5. Is any activity described in the aid suited to the age, economic level, and equipment available to your students?
6. Does it supplement information available in reference books?
7. Is the subject matter presented accurately and without bias?
8. Does it present information that is pertinent to your lesson plan and up-to-date?
9. Is it well organized, clear, and easy to read?
10. Is it well designed and illustrated?
11. Does the material challenge you, the teacher, to further learning?

Walsh suggested that a teacher consider also the psychological and sociological aspects when selecting instructional materials. Among the points to look for are the following: [5]

> *Avoidance of unintentional stereotyping or careless wording* which might tend to perpetuate antagonisms now current in our culture.

[5] Letitia Walsh, "Developing Ability to Evaluate Teaching Aids," *Journal of Home Economics,* **49**:423–424, June 1957.

Emphasis placed upon modern economic practices; for example, intelligent use of credit versus condemnation of all borrowing.

Acceptance of different values held by different social classes, as in lower class interest in economy, upper middle class satisfaction in creativeness through clothing construction.

Adjustment of recommended techniques to the limited time and skill of homemakers employed full time or inclined to reject work in the home.

Positive attitude toward family-centeredness expressed consistently in family activities suggested by materials.

Realism as perceived by students so that, for example, they may identify with the mother-daughter team picture because account has been taken of differences in skills and time available.

Advertising may or may not be an objectionable feature of business-sponsored educational materials. If biased information is presented or if one particular brand is promoted to the exclusion of comparable products, materials might need to be rejected. However, some advertising may be permissible, particularly when it is used to help students develop critical thinking.

Responsibilities of the Teacher

While you are still in college preparing to be a teacher, you are taking the first steps toward the proper use of teaching materials. First, you are becoming familiar with a variety of sources of information and facts about various products and the principles that should guide homemakers in their selection and use. While you are teaching, you should continue to grow in your knowledge and understanding of facts so that you can evaluate the accuracy with which they are presented.

Another step that you can take during your preservice training is to start collecting and organizing a file of teaching materials. To be useful, your file might be classified under the principal subject areas of home economics, with appropriate subdivisions. If a regular filing cabinet is not available, firm cardboard boxes may work satisfactorily for the filing and storage of bulletins. As you gather materials, evaluate them carefully so that your file will contain helpful materials. Review it periodically to keep it well organized and up-to-date. Students may assist in developing departmental files that they can use readily and easily. They should be encouraged to refer to the files continuously for information pertaining to their regular classwork, for ideas related to individual or committee reports, or for guidance with their home and community experiences. Students might enjoy taking recipe leaflets and booklets home for their families to use.

Packaged Materials for Independent Study

Unipac is "a self-contained set of teaching-learning materials designed to teach a single concept and structured for individual and independent use in a continuous school program." [6] The Institute for Development of Educational Activities serves as a motivating force to help teachers prepare Unipacs, and it provides a curriculum bank where teachers deposit and withdraw materials. To be eligible to withdraw curriculum materials, a teacher must contribute a Unipac to the curriculum bank.

Each self-contained package or unit of instruction contains:

1. The major idea, skill, or attitude to be learned.
2. Behavioral objectives indicating what performance and achievement levels the student is expected to attain.
3. Multi-dimensional learning materials and activities: suggestions for a variety of *visual* materials such as textbook selections, other reference materials, programmed materials, and films; tapes and other recorded materials for *listening;* and *physical* activities such as model building, experiments, and acting. A student may use whatever type of material is best for his unique learning style or he may use more than one approach.

Pre-evaluation provides a measure of the behavioral objectives the student may have achieved already. Self-evaluation guides the student as he proceeds through the Unipac. Post-evaluation indicates when he has performed at or above the minimum level specified in the Unipac. Suggested projects are designed to encourage the student in developing self-initiative, in defining a problem for "quest study," carrying out his own research, and arriving at some level of resolution with regard to his chosen problem.[7]

MATERIALS FOR VIEWING

A teacher may use visual materials in several ways. Sometimes materials are viewed momentarily as the teacher holds them up for all of the students to see or as they are passed around the group. Since an opportunity for longer viewing of many materials is desirable, exhibits or displays may be arranged. Using a projector gives the entire class a common learning experience.

[6] "What is a Unipac," I/D/E/A UNIPAC Program, 5335 Far Hills Avenue, Dayton, Ohio 45329.

[7] Philip G. Kapfer and Gardner Swenson, "Individualizing Instruction for Self-Paced Learning." *The Clearing House,* **42**: 405–410, March 1968.

Display Materials

When it is not possible to see the real thing in its natural setting, it may be feasible to bring an object into the classroom. Since this is not always possible or desirable, models, specimens, or mock-ups may be used effectively to show what the real object is like. Three-dimensional objects form the basis for interesting and informative exhibits. Two-dimensional, or flat materials, such as pictures and charts, contribute to learning in a variety of ways, such as in bulletin board or flannel board displays. The ever-present *chalkboard* also can be very helpful in promoting learning.

Three-Dimensional Materials

Home economics education is rich in opportunities for using real objects and models. Before deciding on a specific type of instructional aid, the teacher might review the criteria suggested earlier in this chapter for determining its usefulness in helping the students to reach certain goals. A few of the uses, advantages, and limitations of various types or real materials are presented here to aid a teacher in making her final selection:

1. REAL OBJECTS. Tangible objects may be helpful instruments for teaching. Actual articles that are feasible to bring into the home economics classroom for various units of study include:

Area	*Objects*
Child Care	Toys, layettes, children's clothing, books, records, and record player.
Clothing and Textiles	Raw fibers, unfinished textiles, fabrics, thread, tools for clothing construction, completed garments of various styles and qualities.
Foods and Nutrition	Foods in their raw state, processed foods, packages and other containers, cooking utensils, table linens, table ware, table decorations.
Home Furnishing	Wallpaper sample books, tools for refinishing or renovating furniture, materials for flower arrangement.

Among the factors to be considered when deciding whether to use real objects are their expense, size, ease of bringing into the department, whether the students will be able to see their important features, and whether the students can be permitted to handle the objects.

2. SPECIMENS. Specimens are used to represent a complete object or

group of similar objects. For example, one buttonhole may be used to represent a set of buttonholes for a blouse. Specimens may be incomplete, as in the case of buttonholes, to represent the various stages involved in their preparation.

3. MODELS. Models are exact replicas of real objects. Models of large objects are usually smaller than the real thing to permit easy use and storage, whereas small objects are often enlarged to permit students to see them easily. Certain features may be simplified and the model may have moving parts to give the students an idea of how the real object works. A good model is eye-catching, attractive, and informative, with the important features accented.

Models are more effective when they can be taken apart and put together again by the students. The teacher should be careful to leave students with the correct impression of the size of the real object. She might have the real object on hand to compare with the model or she might compare its size with that of a familiar object.

The teacher may obtain commercially prepared models, make her own models, or have the students make the models. Foster reported an extensive cooperative project in which students learned about home furnishings. The shop and home economics departments planned a home for a hypothetical family consisting of father, mother, and two teenage daughters. The boys built a model home while the girls studied color schemes; floor, window, and wall treatments; and furniture selection and arrangement. This project provided opportunity for the students to take a field trip to a furniture store, to work as committees on planning for designated parts of the home, to reach a group decision on a coordinated plan, and to paint and furnish the model home. The completed model was displayed for the spring Open House of the Parent-Teacher Association. After the display, the classes planned to present the house to a kindergarten or an orphanage.[8]

Student-made models give an opportunity for self-expression and for demonstrating what they have learned. On the other hand, students are sometimes able to learn complex or abstract ideas more efficiently from studying a prepared model rather than from taking time to construct their own. The learning value of time spent by students in making a model needs to be assessed; a model is merely a means to an end and not an end in itself.

Simple uses of models may be effective. By using a prepared model of a home, students can examine construction techniques, closet space,

[8] Dorothy Foster, "How We Cooperated with the Shop on a Home Furnishings Project." *Practical Home Economics*, 3:69, September 1957.

traffic flow, and furniture arrangements. They may save time by making paper models of furniture cut to scale. East pointed out that models may be used to reduce or enlarge the size of an object, to explain difficult concepts, to show working parts, to attract interest and attention, to encourage student participation (they might bring models they have made outside of school), to give students a chance to express what they have learned, to review or reorganize, or to show some selected aspect in a simple way. Models can be used to assist students in understanding abstract concepts such as "interrelatedness of resources," or "central-satellite" decisions.[9]

An important, new emphasis in the use of models is in the area of human behavior. Society has come to realize the importance of *role* models with whom students can identify. The teacher must be particularly active in pointing out desirable role models if her students are now following antisocial models.

The use of a model should be integrated with the other class activities. The model should contribute to the immediate learning situation as well as to the students' general background. It should stimulate thinking and discussion. Further learning activities might grow out of a careful analysis and study of a model.

4. MOCK-UPS. A mock-up is a simplified and clarified representation of the real thing. It emphasizes certain important features and eliminates unnecessary details. Sometimes it is a giant enlargement, while other times it is smaller than its prototype. The purpose of a mock-up is to demonstrate how an object works. For example, the principles involved in the operation of a thermostat might be shown through a mock-up in which unnecessary details could be omitted and the parts enlarged. A mock-up could be used to show how fuses and circuits are used in home wiring.

5. EXHIBITS. Any of the three-dimensional materials described above may lend themselves to effective exhibits, whose purpose is to communicate ideas. Home economics teachers are likely to have four types of opportunities to use exhibits. Closest at hand is the exhibit case or table within the home economics classroom. Next, a teacher might branch out to an exhibit case in a prominent part of the school corridor. Opportunities may be available to use window space in one of the community stores. And finally, an exhibit may be contributed to a large community event, such as a county fair.

East summarized concisely three points that make an exhibit success-

[9] Marjorie East, *Display for Learning*. New York: Holt, Rinehart, and Winston, 1952, p. 39.

ful: "(1) people must look at it; (2) people must get interested in it; and (3) people must think about it." [10]

Among the suggestions to guide you in preparing effective exhibits are the following:

Idea: An exhibit should be built upon a single idea or theme. Enough explanation needs to be given to make the purpose clear but not enough to cause the viewer to lose interest.

Viewer Needs: An exhibit should be planned for a specific purpose and for a specific type of viewer. Among the purposes of an exhibit might be to display completed classroom or home projects of the students, to interest students in joining the Future Homemakers of America chapter, or to inform parents and students about the opportunities for careers related to home economics.

Location: An exhibit should be placed in a spot where people are likely to notice it, such as near the bottom of a stairway, opposite a doorway, or below a chalkboard.

Mechanical Aspects: Attention will be attracted to exhibits where color, lighting, motion, and sound are used effectively.

Labels: Short, appropriate, and novelty labels attract attention. Key words may be featured through larger letters, a different style of lettering, color, background material or shape, or striking location.

Exhibits must be viewed if they are to be effective. When students plan and prepare an exhibit, they might evaluate it by observing such things as how many people notice it, how long they look at it, what comments they make about it, and what questions they ask. You may add to the success of an exhibit by providing for participation—buttons to push, levers to pull, recorded narration, or written evaluation forms. In the classroom, an exhibit may be used to introduce a subject, to help with the development of a unit, or to summarize a unit. An exhibit needs to be displayed long enough for the students to satisfy their interests but not so long that they become tired of looking at the same thing.

Flat materials

Two-dimensional materials can make an important contribution to the home economics class. Picture and graphic materials are usually easier to store and less expensive than either the real objects or models would be. Photographs, drawings, cartoons, posters, and other types of flat materials may be prepared by students, teachers, or commercial concerns. They can motivate, instruct, summarize, and lead into further

[10] East, op. cit., p. 279.

study. They cover a wide variety of subject matter. They can emphasize key ideas, clarify abstract concepts, and help to develop correct impressions of real things. Among the types of flat materials that are useful in home economics education are:

1. PHOTOGRAPHS. Pictures can be gleaned from many sources: current magazines, newspapers, text or reference books, post cards, posters, and reproductions of paintings. Students should be encouraged to bring in pictures that will illustrate the principles being taught. The students can be given an opportunity to explain the picture to the class and possibly to display it on the bulletin board or in an exhibit case. Recognition helps to stimulate interest and encourages students to be alert when they see pictures.

Photographs, taken by a teacher or by the students, can provide a record of unusual experiences (such as field trips), illustrate typical aspects of the home economics curriculum, show the various steps in a process, help students evaluate their own laboratory experiences and standards, illustrate the application of principles in situations that are inaccessible for field trips, compare the "before" and "after" pictures of a home or community project, provide a record of memorable recreational and social activities, and serve in a number of other ways.

Pictures should be selected in terms of their contributions to the class goals and their viewers. A good picture is a valid representation of the real thing, whether it is in color or black-and-white. It creates a mood that may be as important to learning as its intellectual content. It has a good composition, effective use of color, and high technical quality. It attracts attention and arouses curiosity.

Pictures that are selected for group use should be mounted to protect them and enhance their appearance. Mounting makes them easier to store, more convenient for passing around, and more satisfactory for displaying on a bulletin board or projecting with an opaque projector. Those to be shown together may be of uniform size. Neutral tones help to direct attention to the picture rather than to the mounting. Construction paper, fabrics, wallpaper, or other materials appropriate for the subject of the picture may be used for mountings.

Be sure that the students are able to see whatever pictures you use. It may be advisable for you to project the picture, to copy it or duplicate it for each student, or to post it on the bulletin board. It is better to use few pictures and discuss them fully than to use many pictures that are not integrated into your lesson.

Dale has pointed out that a picture may be "read" on various levels: enumeration of objects, description of what was seen, and interpretation.

Students need guidance to go beyond the stages of listing things they see and describing the present action. They can learn to interpret a picture and draw inferences about it.[11] East suggested that a teacher might ask questions to lead students beyond the picture: "Why is that man doing that? What had to happen to this object before it could look like this? What may change this in another few years?" [12]

2. CHARTS. Charts combine drawings, words, and pictures in an orderly and logical manner. They may be used to show relationships, to trace the development of something, or to classify and organize material. Among the common types of charts are:

Tree: The base is composed of several roots that lead into a common trunk. An example of the tree chart might be the various college majors in home economics, each leading to the single profession—home economics—with its many branches or specialized career opportunities.

Stream: The reverse of the tree chart is called a stream chart; a variety of aspects combine to form a single element. For example, the price of a ready-made dress is composed of the costs that accrue from services rendered by individuals such as the fiber manufacturer and finisher, the clothing designer and manufacturer, the advertising and sales promotion agents, and the retailer.

Flow: The organization of a club or institution is shown through the use of a chart that indicates each level of responsibility and how information is communicated among the various persons. The organization of a Future Homemakers of America chapter, with its local officers and committees, might be shown in a flow chart along with its relationship to the state and national levels of responsibility.

Tabular: A table may be shown to indicate such information as the sequence in the development of a process or arguments for and against something, such as home ownership.

A "flip chart" consists of a series of charts in which a topic is covered sequentially. As each chart is displayed, usually on an easel, the material can be explained and discussed. Flip charts may be used out of sequence, as a review or as an introduction to new material. The set may be separated and displayed on the bulletin board as a review.

Charts may help the students to understand classroom routines and the organization of a laboratory. A housekeeping chart can list the various tasks with the group or individual who is responsible for each week. A chart may be inserted in each drawer or cupboard to indicate the correct placement of kitchen equipment.

[11] Edgar Dale, *Audio-Visual Methods in Teaching* (rev. ed.). New York: Holt, Rinehart and Winston, 1954, p. 246.

[12] East, op. cit., p. 67.

When students make their own charts, they may learn to organize, develop their artistic abilities, and work with others in making and carrying out their plans. The major disadvantage is the time consumed in the preparation. Commercially prepared charts may offer a suitable variety of material with eye-appeal and a high level of information. They may be used as models for the students or to save the students' time.

3. DIAGRAMS. Diagrams are symbolic, simplified drawings that may be used to present abstract concepts. They are usually more effective when used with other materials such as films or models than when used alone. They may be presented in a variety of forms: on a chalk board, bulletin board, or flannel board, through duplicated copies, or by projection with an opaque, overhead, or slide projector. They may be better for reviewing and summarizing than for introducing complex information. Instruction sheets that are included with commercial patterns are examples of diagrams that can be very effective with students who have adequate background information to understand the symbols and apply the information.

4. GRAPHS. Graphic presentation is used to show relationships and present information interestingly and quickly. Encourage your students to use graphs in illustrating their reports. This will help them to analyze their data carefully and to present facts concisely.

Briefly, the principal types of graphs that are helpful in home economics education include:

Line: For continuous data, such as changes in the weight of rats on an experimental diet, lines may be drawn to connect each point where measurements are indicated. Two or three lines may be plotted on the same graph to give a quick comparison of relationships and trends.

Bar: Discrete data, such as the number or percent of students who included each of the major food groups in their diet over a seven-day period, may be presented in bars. The graph might be arranged in such a way as to compare the length of these bars with the results of some other group or with the same students on a later occasion. To add interest, the bars might be pictorial, showing people, houses, food, or some other symbol related to the subject of the graph. Quantity is indicated by the number of symbols or length of a bar rather than by the size of a symbol.

Circle, or Pie: When the parts add to one hundred percent, each percentage can be translated into a fractional part of a circle. For example, a three-dimensional circle, resembling a dollar, might be used to represent the family's food expenditures. The circle could be divided into pie-shaped pieces to show the percent spent for each of the basic food groups. This is particularly effective when the segments can be placed one at a time in building up the whole picture, as in a flannel board presentation.

5. POSTERS. A poster is used to attract attention just long enough to get a point across at a glance. It may have an emotional appeal aimed at reinforcing an attitude or urging a course of action. It may be used to motivate students at the beginning of a unit of study or to remind them of something that they forget easily, such as the importance of a good diet or safety habits. It may provide atmosphere, as in the case of a luncheon or party built around foreign foods and culture. When students prepare their own posters, the posters become media for creative expression as well as for summarizing ideas.

Posters may be used effectively on bulletin boards within the home economics department or they may contribute to displays in other parts of the school or community. They should be changed frequently if they are to challenge the viewers.

An effective poster has a center of interest, and is attractive and interesting. It has a dynamic quality. It is simple, yet dramatic. It is appropriate for the group that will be viewing it. Good design, clear lettering, and effective colors combine to help a poster capture the interest and attention of passers-by. Lettering may be made easier by using precut letters, rubber stamps, stencils, lettering guides, and felt-tip pens.

6. CARTOONS. Cartoons use pictorial representation, often in exaggerated form, to get a message across quickly and in good humor. They may be prepared by creative students or they may be gathered from newspapers, comic strips, or magazines.

Cartoons are particularly effective in arousing interest and presenting a realistic family or other human relations situation in an impersonal manner. Students could discuss the probable family situation that inspired the cartoon. Cartoons present brief, personalized stories packed with action. They can illustrate good and poor techniques with simple, stick figures.

In using cartoons, a teacher should be careful to adapt them to the maturity of her group. Subtle humor might be lost or might give the wrong impression if a cartoon is used with students who are too immature to grasp its meaning. Dale cautioned that a cartoon is "sharply *for* or *against* something." A cartoon oversimplifies and may appear to represent the attitudes of all members of a group. Students need to develop a critical approach in interpreting the symbolism.[13]

7. BULLETIN BOARD. A tack board, or bulletin board, can serve a variety

[13] Dale, op. cit., pp. 316–317.

of purposes. It attracts attention and may be a good means of creating interest. It is capable of introducing new ideas, presenting information, developing a clearer understanding, and enlarging the students' vocabulary. It can stimulate thought and discussion. Not only does it lend atmosphere to the classroom, but it can help students develop an appreciation of beauty, and provide an opportunity for them to express themselves creatively.

The term "bulletin board" suggests that it is a place for posting announcements of class events or news items. "Tack board" is another name for the bulletin board; it implies a wider range of uses, such as introducing a new unit, developing various phases of the unit, supplementing class instruction and reference materials, summarizing learning experiences, or lending atmosphere for special occasions.

To be effective, bulletin board displays should be changed frequently (every week or two). When a unit is being planned, a schedule can be set up for committees of students to be responsible for the bulletin board. Each committee knows in advance what topic to develop and during which week the display is to be ready. East pointed out that, as students plan and prepare a bulletin board display, they must go through an organizing process. They have to be sure of their facts in order to give the right impressions. They develop emotional attitudes toward themselves (satisfaction from seeing their work displayed) and from working closely with other students. She suggested that a teacher let students watch her develop plans and prepare a bulletin board display, so that, while performing these operations, the teacher could explain to the students her reasons for choosing certain colors, shapes, words, and pictures.[14]

Among the principles for making effective use of bulletin board displays are the following:

1. A bulletin board should convey a particular purpose or goal.
2. A bulletin board should have a center of interest and the display should have effective balance of color, line, and mass.
3. Contrast may be achieved through the use of light and dark colors, bright and neutral colors, varying sizes, or textures.
4. Unity is achieved by having one central theme, and carrying it out with simplicity and repetition of color, shapes, and sizes.
5. Three-dimensional materials may add interest.
6. Lettering should be neat, well-spaced, and large enough to be read clearly.

[14] Marjorie East, "What Students Learn When They Create Bulletin Boards." *Practical Home Economics,* 4:26, April 1959.

7. The size and shape of the bulletin board should be considered when planning margins, balance, and points of emphasis.

8. Interesting captions are composed of surprising word combinations, clever phrases, or questions. They are brief and forceful. Ideas for captions in the various areas of home economics include:

Child Care

Fun with Little Folks	Togs for Tots
Joy with Toys	Treats for Tots
Do You Know Your Baby Sister?	Tips on Toys

Clothing and Textiles

Sew What?	Nine Lives for Your Clothes
It's Not What You Wear; It's How You Wear It	Clothes Talk—What Do Your Clothes Say?
Stitch in Time Saves Nine	On the Spot
This Is the Way We Press	Fresh as a Daisy

Family Economics

Where Will Your $$$$ Take You?	Use Your Sense and Save Your Dollars
How Far Does Your $ Go?	

Family Relations

Telephone Manners	Don't Depend on Daisies!
Which Family Is Yours?	Who's Who in the Family
Families Can Be Fun	Do's and Don'ts on Dates
Shall We Go Steady?	

Foods and Nutrition

Sprinkle Your Diet with Vegetables	Crossroad to Good Health
Time-Saving Cookery	Map Your Meals
Sing a Song of Salads	Pack a Lunch That Packs a Punch!

General

After High School—What?	Your Key to Success
Summer Highlights to Remember	Let Us Give Thanks

Health and Home Nursing

Get Into Shape	Figure-atively Speaking
How Do You Size Up?	How Safe Is Your Cleaning Cabinet?

Home Management

Simplify and Systemize	Time's Money—Don't Steal It
Yours to Choose	Does Money Manage You?
	Easy Does It

Housing and Home Furnishing

Posing Your Posies	This House Is Our Home
Is Your House a Home?	Give Your Room Atmosphere
Framing Your Windows	Color Know-How
Closets with Nothing to Hide	See Your Home in a New Light [15]

8. PEG BOARD. A peg board, which contains small holes at regular intervals, may be used for display, particularly when three-dimensional objects might be too heavy for a bulletin board. Peg boards may be attached to the wall or may stand free and be moved as a room-divider, creating work areas for individuals or small groups, each area having its own display space. Pictures may be placed directly on the board. Brackets and shelves allow the use of such articles as ceramics.

9. FLANNEL BOARD. A flannel board, or felt board, may be made from a lightweight board or other rigid material that is covered with flannel or another fuzzy-surfaced fabric. Materials such as felt, flannel, velvet, suede, sandpaper, blotting paper, garnet paper, colored yarns, pipe cleaners, steel wool, and styrofoam adhere to the surface. Illustrative objects may be cut directly from such materials or a small sensitizing strip may be attached to the back of other materials.

A flannel board can be used effectively with students of any age level, including college students and adults. Its values are: adaptability to the use of pictures or other materials that are cut from magazines or other sources, flexibility in introducing and rearranging items, manipulation or building up piece-by-piece to form the whole picture, and interest-capturing through the element of surprise.

Techniques for using a flannel board effectively include careful planning so that the teacher or student using it knows what is to be presented and in what order. The placement of items should be practiced in advance to insure having sufficient space and a pleasing arrangement. Each item should be clear and large enough to be seen from a distance. The board should be slightly inclined and approximately at the eye level of the observers. A neutral background lends itself to interesting contrasts as the items are presented. Good lighting is important. Usually a lecture, or a recording, accompanies the building up of a flannel board scene.

Home economics teachers might use the flannel board for such purposes as showing new styles in clothing, color contrasts in interior design, furniture arrangement, house planning, essential food groups,

[15] Selected from Emma Cook and Virginia Baxter, "Bulletin Board and Its Use." California Conference for Vocational Homemaking Teachers, Mimeographed report, 1955; and "Visual Aids, Our Silent Teachers." *Illinois Teacher,* Vol. II, No. 8, pp. 18–19.

foods composing a menu, table setting, cost comparisons, operation of equipment, and organizational charts. It can be a useful tool in teaching abstract concepts that can be developed gradually.

Students can learn from preparing items to use on a flannel board effectively in presenting a committee report. They might evaluate their experience by thinking through such questions as the following:

1. Did the presentation accomplish a specific purpose?
2. Did it meet the needs and interests of those using it?
3. Were the materials appropriate?
4. Were the materials displayed attractively with contrasting colors and uncluttered space?
5. Were the peculiar merits of the felt board being used to greatest advantage?
6. Did each display present a single, clear-cut idea? [16]

10. MAGNETIC BOARD. A magnetic board may be used for demonstrations in ways similar to a flannel board. Small magnets may be mounted behind pictures, graphics, or objects so they can be displayed on a steel board.

11. CHALKBOARD. A device that is available in most classrooms with very little expense is the chalkboard. Although it was traditionally black, it now comes in various colors to blend with the room. Chalk of a contrasting color is used for best results.

The purpose of a chalkboard is to present material of immediate concern in an impromptu manner. This purpose is fulfilled when the chalkboard is used for such purposes as to help students understand the meaning of new words, spell them correctly, make comparisons, understand an assignment, plan their class work, develop an outline, summarize relationships, gain insight into a particular problem, or see the process as well as the finished diagram. By using the chalkboard, a teacher can help students to concentrate, or she may recall their attention if she notices that they seem to be thinking about something else. Students can benefit from the opportunity of contributing to the group or receiving constructive criticism from their class members.

Effective use of a chalkboard involves careful attention to the space available, size of letters, and legibility. The chalkboard should be kept clean and clear of unrelated material. Complicated illustrations may be reproduced prior to class time by the use of a grid, opaque projector, or template. Simple figures can be used to illustrate a point. With practice, a teacher can learn to talk to the class while she writes on the

[16] Charles H. Dent and Ernest F. Tiemann, *Felt Boards for Teaching*. University of Texas, Visual Instruction Bureau, Division of Extension, 1955, p. 23.

chalkboard and to stay clear of what she has written. Adequate light, without glare, is essential.

If chalkboard space is inadequate, large sheets of newsprint tacked to an easel or on the wall make a satisfactory substitute. They have the advantage of providing a record that may be kept for future use. These sheets are often called "tear sheets." When accuracy and finish are important, the extra effort of preparing a chart, or tear sheets, may be worthwhile.

12. DUPLICATED SHEETS. A chalkboard should not be used as a substitute for materials that need to be copied in detail by the students. Duplicators, or dry copying machines, can provide accurate copies and save the time of students. You might try duplicating such materials as: [17]

- Outlines of subjects, with suggested activities
- Guide sheets and study guides
- Examinations and objective tests
- Pictures, graphic materials, or articles from magazines or newspapers
- Assignments
- Bibliographies
- Organization of units of work
- Maps, charts, graphs, and signs
- Score cards
- Guidance questionnaires
- Checklists
- Statistical information
- Summaries and criticisms
- Programs
- Inventories and surveys
- Reports by individual students or committees
- F.H.A. program booklets and other forms
- Home project outlines.

Projected Materials

Most school systems are equipped with a variety of projection equipment. Besides the necessary projectors, equipment should include a screen sufficiently large for classroom use and a means of darkening the classroom. Materials to be projected are often on film—either in the form of slides, a filmstrip, or a sound motion picture. However, flat materials or small three-dimensional objects may be used in an opaque projector. Handmade transparencies are convenient to use with an overhead projector.

One advantage of projected materials is that they tend to focus attention on the screen. A wide variety of materials can be filmed, sketched for use with an overhead projector, or shown directly with an opaque projector. Students of all ages from elementary through adult levels are interested in projected materials and learn from them. Materials that can be projected onto a large screen permit all of the students to see the

[17] "Visual Aids, Our Silent Teachers," op. cit., p. 7.

same object at one time without having to wait their turn to have something passed to them. Little storage space is necessary for most types of films.

Effective use of a projector involves the same three steps that were described in the previous chapter: *advance planning,* including previewing the items to be projected and preparing the class to know what to look for; *skillful administration,* including the smooth operation of equipment and presentation of necessary information; and *evaluation,* including determining how well the teaching material fulfilled its functions and how much the students gained from the experience. As a result of what they see or hear, students can learn to associate a spoken word with a set of visually perceived attributes, to deduce the defining attributes of a class of events, to identify sequences of events, to see functional relationships between phenomena, to avoid danger, and to engage in aesthetic experiences.

Slides

Slides and filmstrips are used to show things that can be understood without motion. They may be in color or black-and-white. Filmstrips are made up of a series of slides that are shown in a fixed sequence. Both slides and filmstrips may be used to show people, activities, charts, cartoons, graphs, or a variety of other materials. They may be more effective in conveying information and stimulating discussions than in influencing attitudes. They are convenient to use and relatively low in cost. A single projector, with separate attachments, can be used for both slides and filmstrips.

Photographs of real people or scenery, animated pictures, or graphic slides can enrich the study of home economics in several ways. Color transparencies can be invaluable for showing various standards of living and family customs among different cultures in the United States as well as in other countries. They can be used to teach vocational skills—demonstrating the skill itself, providing opportunity for the students to stop at any point and study a particular step, and showing the kinds of settings in which this skill might be practiced.

A major advantage in using slides is their flexibility. A teacher or student can select certain slides that fit in with what a class is studying and arrange them in any order that seems most appropriate for the interests and needs of a class. Slides are adaptable to situations other than classroom teaching—they may be used effectively with an automatic changer at an Open House exhibit for parents, to show a variety of home economics education experiences.

Another advantage of slides is the ease of making them. The following list indicates types of teacher- or student-made slides that could contribute to home economics education:

Line Drawings: Compare good and bad design in furniture, show suitable hair styles for various face shapes, illustrate typical posture problems.

Typed and Written Material. Present detailed information, such as a list of foods rich in calcium.

Photographs: Compare good and poor flower arrangements, compare good and bad examples of local architecture, show the sequence of steps in doing something, show the growth and development of children, compare the effects of experimental diets on rats, bring home the sights you have seen on your trips, record events of your group for their pleasure and for use in public relations, keep a record of excellent work done by students, keep a record of your own successful displays.[18]

Hand-made slides using etched or clear glass may be washed off and used over again. They provide creative experiences for the students and lend themselves to meeting the immediate interests and needs of a class.

The slide projector is rather small, lightweight, and easy to operate. Several models provide some type of tray or stack arrangement that permits slides to be prearranged without having to handle each slide as it is projected. Be sure to preview all slides before showing them to your class so you can check the technical qualities of the slides and projector as well as decide what to teach about each slide. Some projectors can be operated by remote control, permitting a teacher to remain in front of the class. Individual slides or trays may be labeled for easy reference and stored in convenient files.

Independent study or review of material presented in a lecture enables a student to absorb what he can at his own pace. Using a carrel, projector, and tape recorder, he can view selected slides while listening to a commentary taped by the teacher. Some students would benefit from regular review; others would use the materials just before an exam. Some students would find small group seminars helpful in providing for a detailed examination of material and exchange of ideas.

Slides do have a few possible limitations. Transparencies mounted in cardboard may be damaged by handling or by too-long exposure in a projector that lacks an adequate cooling system. Glass mounting of slides overcomes these disadvantages but adds the possibility that the glass might be broken with careless handling. Extra time and cost are involved

[18] Marjorie East, *Display for Learning*. New York: Holt, Rinehart and Winston, 1952, pp. 216–217.

in mounting slides in glass. Slides occupy more storage space than would be required for the equivalent number of pictures in a filmstrip. Duplicates of original slides may lose some of the clarity of their colors.

Filmstrips

Many of the features and advantages of slides are true of filmstrips as well. A filmstrip is a sequence of transparent slides that run continuously on a film instead of being cut apart and mounted individually. One of its major advantages is compactness—an entire series of pictures may be rolled and stored in a very small can.

A picture can be left on the screen as long as necessary for a class, while the teacher or students explain and discuss its content. Sometimes a disk or tape recording accompanies a filmstrip. When this is used, the pictures have to be turned at proper intervals to keep up with the sound. A prepared manuscript may come with a commercially prepared filmstrip. You may use it in its entirety, adapt parts of it to the needs of your students, or even use your own imagination in commenting on the various pictures. In any event, a filmstrip can convey a complete story in its proper sequence.

Single-concept film loops are available, illustrating each step in clothing construction from buying a pattern to completing a tailored garment. These film loops require only a few minutes of viewing time. They are accompanied by self-help student guides, which are adaptable for independent study.[19]

Among the limitations of a filmstrip are the lack of motion and the fixed order of scenes. Since the pictures usually are selected and their sequence determined by someone other than the classroom teacher, a filmstrip may not present the material needed by her students at the level which they are capable of understanding. Furthermore, the film may tear along the sprocket holes if the projector is threaded improperly.

Filmstrips may be used effectively in a variety of ways such as teaching skills, providing information, stimulating aesthetic appreciation, arousing interest in further activities, and reviewing learnings. When determining whether to select a filmstrip rather than another type of teaching device, you might consider the following questions:

1. Is motion essential for student understanding?
2. Is a suitable filmstrip available for the particular objectives of my class?
3. Is the content of the filmstrip accurate and up-to-date?

[19] Edwin Grieser, "Clothing Construction Film Loops." Manchester, Mo.: Webster Division, McGraw-Hill Book Company.

4. Is the film technically well-produced?
5. Will the filmstrip provide information and suggest new ideas?
6. Will the filmstrip be likely to clear up misconceptions the students have?
7. Does the filmstrip deal with problem situations that might be faced in real life?
8. Will the organization of the filmstrip help students to see the developments clearly?
9. Does the filmstrip encourage student participation and critical thinking?
10. Will the use of the filmstrip lead to other activities such as an interest in experimenting?

Before showing the filmstrip, make clear to your students how it relates to what they are studying. You might list major points or questions to which they should pay particular attention. A study guide is sometimes helpful. It might list new words, key concepts, or questions. Another approach is to tell the students that, when you finish showing the filmstrip, they will be asked to list its main points.

A filmstrip usually should be shown in its entirety the first time so the students will see the unity in its presentation. Ordinarily the captions should be read aloud by the teacher or a student. The filmstrip may be shown later with interruptions for discussion, or small sections of it may be repeated for further emphasis. Captions may not need to be read aloud during the reshowing or review of a filmstrip. A follow-up discussion or test after the filmstrip is shown helps to reinforce learnings.

Opaque Projector

An opaque projector, or Delineascope, is a means of projecting nontransparent, flat materials directly onto a screen. It is inexpensive to use because it makes a wide variety of materials readily available without the necessity of photographing them. It is versatile, permitting the use of pictures, charts, graphs, and small three-dimensional objects. It is so easy to operate that students can learn to do it readily. Little time is required to prepare materials for use in an opaque projector, since books, photographs, samples of students' work, and objects can be used as they are or with simple mounting.

Home economics teachers can enrich their teaching by using an opaque projector to display illustrations or objects such as:

Clothing and Textiles: posture pictures, dress designs, patterns, pattern layouts, fabrics, labels.

Family Relations and Child Development: pictures of children or families, children's literature, games for the family, cultural patterns or customs of families.

Foods and Nutrition: pictures of food, food combinations, table setting, labels, nutritional facts.

Home Management: students' work plans, checking devices, record books, models of decision processes.

Housing and Home Furnishing: interior design, landscaping, woods, plastics, household fabrics, floor plans, labels.

An opaque projector might be used for such purposes as the following: projecting outlines for posters or murals onto large sheets of wrapping paper or the chalk board; illustrating visually the schedule or plans for the class period; clarifying or giving emphasis to certain parts of a textbook; encouraging students to read interesting reference books by showing some of the pages they contain; illustrating or analyzing a point; developing a series of illustrations covering an entire topic; giving meaning to current events; encouraging students to think creatively and present illustrated reports to the class; helping students gain self-confidence when presenting an oral report to the class; introducing a new unit or type of assignment; analyzing errors or showing student work that is well done; expanding students' technical vocabulary; developing an appreciation of art principles; providing opportunities for students who can draw to receive recognition for their work; and permitting an entire class to interpret and discuss a cartoon.

As is true of using other types of visual aids, effective use of an opaque projector requires advance preparation. Materials may be mounted separately or in the form of a continuous strip. If materials are to be used directly from books or magazines, they should be arranged in the proper sequence. A rehearsal is necessary to be sure that all the materials will fit into the projector and will show necessary details clearly enough for the students to see them. Since the materials used in an opaque projector were not developed specifically for classroom use, they may lack clarity when projected. Earlier models of the opaque projector required that the room be darkened much more than is true of today's models. Newer models are rather lightweight in spite of their bulk. A teacher should plan to set up the projector in advance and preview her materials to be sure they will give a clear image.

To increase the effectiveness of the actual showing of materials in an opaque projector, the teacher should help the students know what to look for. The pictures should not only be carefully selected, but also be presented at the right time to be a natural part of the learning experiences. Attention should be given to the number of pictures that can be used at one time and to their sequence. A brief, pointed discussion might accompany each picture, but the discussion should not drag out.

Following a presentation, the students may have opportunity to apply what they have learned. In reviewing the work, certain key pictures may be reshown. A written or oral test may be used to evaluate what the students have learned. The opaque projector lends itself to a variety of evaluation devices. Pictures may be presented as the basis for students to answer objective or brief essay questions. Objective test questions may be projected. One limitation of the technique of projecting test questions that require written responses is that all of the students are forced to work at a similar speed, when actually certain ones are slower readers and may need more time to think about their answers.

Overhead Projector

An overhead projector, which consists of an open glass plate with a mirror above it, permits a teacher to face her class while explaining or illustrating a point. The projection area ranges in size, depending upon the type of projector; some provide a space about 10 inches square on which a transparency is placed. Since the projector can be used with little darkening of the room, it is a very handy device.

A home economics teacher might use the overhead projector in several ways: to draw her own sketches or diagrams as illustrations, to point with a pencil or stylus to significant details, to write outlines, to develop the steps in a procedure, or to make additions or corrections to a prepared transparency. Students can prepare transparencies in advance or use the overhead projector as they report to the class. Color can be used. Water-soluble marks can be removed easily, if desired, and the ozalid transparencies reused, making this an inexpensive teaching aid. Permanent transparencies may be made with special types of ink or a wax-coated plastic on which material may be typewritten.

A teacher may construct a diagram as she presents her material by placing overlays, or one piece of plastic over another. An overlay could consist of several sheets, each containing part of the diagram, perhaps with a different color on each part. Commercially-prepared transparencies are available. Visu-Book uses a set of 34 color transparencies with overlays on the teaching of clothing construction.[20] Transparencies are available also for teaching home management, sexuality, and nutrition.

[20] Martha Golding and Judy Stam, *Principles of Creating Clothing: A Visual Approach* (featuring the Visu-Book). New York: John Wiley and Sons, 1967.

Motion Pictures

Sound motion pictures offer an immense variety both in subject matter and quality. They make unique contributions in fields where movement and action are important. They are effective particularly in situations that would be difficult or impossible to present as well in any other way, such as in showing a historical situation or development, bringing a distant scene to the classroom, presenting a demonstration given by an unusually capable person or one that deals with expensive materials, enlarging something that would be difficult or impossible for a group to see in an ordinary demonstration, reducing the size of something that is too extensive to be examined thoroughly in a short period of time or too large to be brought into the classroom, speeding up a process that normally takes quite a long time, or showing (through animated drawings) a process that would be impossible for a person to see even with a microscope or telescope.

Motion pictures have a number of advantages when they are used properly. They can focus students' attention in a darkened room on a screen that contains highly interesting material. They can reach a large group at relatively low cost. They can provide a common experience for both the slow and rapid learners, one from which individuals can profit according to their ability—whether they merely see, in a descriptive sense, or can gain deep insights. Motion pictures are also efficient in communicating ideas to persons whose reading skills are weak.

Possibly because of their wide availability and high interest factor, certain misconceptions have developed about their merits and use. Motion pictures can and should supplement other types of teaching materials—they should not be regarded as self-sufficient. They can help a teacher improve her teaching, but they are not intended to substitute for good teaching. A filmstrip, demonstration, or field trip may be less expensive and just as effective as a motion picture. They can be both interesting and informative—an educational film should do more than provide entertainment.

Certain limitations of motion pictures should be kept in mind when a teacher decides whether to select a motion picture or some other instructional aid. A motion picture is most valuable when it is shown the first time without interruption, thereby retaining the logical sequence of ideas. Consequently, discussion that might be helpful during a showing must be postponed until the conclusion of the movie. The speed of a motion picture is constant for all of the viewers, yet students differ in the ease with which they can learn and in their ability to retain what has been presented. A motion picture may not be available at the time when it fits best into the class schedule. A film may not arrive early enough to permit the teacher to preview it. It may not be feasible for the movie to be repeated as a review for a class.

Effective use of a motion picture depends first upon careful selection. Among the factors to consider are:

1. EDUCATIONAL CONTRIBUTIONS. A good motion picture is appropriate for the age level and socioeconomic background of the group. It fulfills specific purposes such as providing accurate information, helping to develop a skill, stimulating interest, presenting a problem, or building desirable attitudes and values.

Motion pictures may be classified into three types:

Documentary: shows real events in their natural setting with a factual treatment. A good documentary film usually is educational. It shows how people live, think, and act. It is especially helpful in giving students a realistic understanding of human relations, social problems, and historical settings.

Expository: shows how something is done, made, or managed. For example, a film might show how to administer first aid, construct a simple skirt, or freeze foods at home. Many films have been produced by manufacturers or distributors to describe the development, manufacture, and use of their products.

Entertainment: provides pleasure, excitement, or temporary escape from reality.

2. SUBJECT MATTER CONTENT. The content of a motion picture should fit in with the overall plans for the course as well as the specific unit being studied. It should be of interest and value to the class. Information should be authentic, up-to-date, and adequate. Presentation of the material should be well organized, clear, and stimulating. Important concepts may be repeated in a variety of ways. A commercially sponsored film should be examined for conspicuous advertising, exaggerated claims, and biased presentation of information.

3. TECHNICAL QUALITIES. Good photography is basic in the production of attractive, clear, sharp pictures. True, natural colors may increase understanding. Sound effects and voices should be clear and pleasing. Dramatic presentations should be satisfactory and interesting. The length of time should be suitable for the subject being presented, the interest span of the class, and the length of the class period.

When preparing a class to view a motion picture, a teacher should tell them briefly what the film is about, why they are going to see it, and how long it will take. She should guide the students in knowing what to watch for by explaining the types of new information it contains, defining difficult words or phrases, and suggesting a list of questions that the film can help them answer. Note-taking during the showing of a motion picture may interfere with students' attention and not contribute to greater learning.

The use of a motion picture demands careful planning on the part of a teacher. Whenever possible, she should preview a film as a basis for preparing a list of questions to guide the class discussion. If it is not possible to preview a film, she should be familiar with the teaching manual or other information that is designed to help teachers use the film effectively. She should check to be sure that the motion picture projector has been ordered and is in good working condition. The loudspeaker should be placed where it will give good reproduction of sound. Students should be seated where they can see the film in a direct line without distortion. The room should be darkened sufficiently for contrast and clear colors. Proper ventilation should be maintained throughout the showing.

You may develop class readiness by discussing what the students already know about the subject of the film and what they should expect from its showing. Key words might be listed on the chalk board and discussed. Specific questions might be presented as a guide to viewing.

After viewing a motion picture, a class might profit from various activities that would help the students review, clarify, or pursue further interests. One means of helping them remember what they have seen is to discuss the questions that were suggested in advance and to clear up other questions that the students raise. The main points of the film can be outlined or summarized. The need for additional facts may be revealed and the students can refer to books or other references for further information. The film can be repeated as a means of review or clarification of a complex technique. Students may practice the skills taught in the film. A panel discussion can be held on a controversial topic that is an outgrowth of the film presentation. The students may dramatize a related episode, write themes on their interpretation of the meaning of a concept, develop a bulletin-board display related to the film, take a field trip for further information about the subject, or invite a member of the community to talk on personal experiences or to enlarge upon ideas presented in the film.

The teacher's follow-up activities should include an evaluation of the film itself, the students' reactions to the film, and suggestions for increasing its effectiveness if it merits use on another occasion. A file of motion pictures, classified by the various subject areas of home economics education, will assist in making future selections of films. A card should contain such information as the following about each motion picture that is used:

Subject area	Brief statement of contents
Title of film	Appropriate grade level(s)
Running time	Reasons for using the film
Black-and-white or color	Merits of film for class purposes
Source or distributor	Suggestions for effective use
Rental fee	

MATERIALS FOR LISTENING

Much of the information you will communicate to your students will be by spoken and audiovisual means, yet even well-motivated students remember little more than half of what they hear when tested for immediate recall.

Students may differ in their ability to profit from listening. Hampleman summarized conclusions from research studies indicating that (1) easy materials may be understood better by listening than by reading, but reading is superior to listening when the materials are difficult; (2) students of low mental ability comprehend better by listening than by reading; reading was superior to listening for students of high ability; both methods were similar in effectiveness for students of average ability; and (3) listening and reading comprehension were about equal on tests of delayed recall.[21]

Duker identified six tasks essential to the process of listening. The good listener should: [22]

1. Prepare himself for the act of listening, approaching the activity with an attitude of inquiry and focusing his previous knowledge on the subject at hand.
2. Know what was said, separating this from what he expected to hear or would have liked to hear.
3. Retain selectively what he hears, selecting important points worth remembering.
4. Analyze what he hears—as he hears it and later as he reviews what he heard.
5. Evaluate what he hears—as to its objectivity, bias, authority, or logic.
6. React to what he hears.

As a teacher, you can help students develop the ability to listen proficiently. If you are to be effective in helping them learn to listen, you

[21] Richard S. Hampleman, "Listening!!!" *Educational Screen and Audio-Visual Guide,* 37:175, April 1958.

[22] Sam Duker, "Listening: A Communicative Skill." *Educational Screen and Audio-Visual Guide,* 42: 136–137, March 1963.

must set an example by listening to them. Another way to help students develop good listening habits is by removing distractions. When a class is listening to a radio program or a recording, the students should concentrate on what they hear and not try to divide their attention by reading at the same time. A teacher who repeats instructions several times may be encouraging bad listening habits. If directions are given simply and clearly once, students should be trained to listen and not to expect to have them repeated. When a controversial subject is being presented, students might be encouraged to plan questions that will help them to be sure they understood what their opponents said.

As you evaluate listening comprehension, you will look for the students' ability to recall details you have presented orally, to follow the sequence of oral directions, to identify the central idea of an oral presentation, and to distinguish between relevant and irrelevant materials.

The major types of instructional materials for listening, which will be discussed in this section include television, radio, recordings, and telelectures. Opportunities for your students to practice listening may be presented when you make assignments, give directions for them to follow, and ask them to summarize main points in broadcasts or films.

Television

Since television actually combines listening and seeing, its advantages and limitations may be similar in many respects to those of motion pictures. In view of the rapid growth of television and its promising future development, television may be used in at least two ways by home economics teachers: (1) classes may view commercially or educationally prepared programs; and (2) teachers or classes may share in the preparation of a program or course.

A home economics teacher may find that a number of television programs that have been prepared for the general public can enrich her classes. One of the teacher's responsibilities is to find out in advance what programs are scheduled for viewing in her area and which of them seem to relate to the content of her courses. The local newspaper, television guides, and advance network releases help a teacher to know what is scheduled.

One limitation in using television is that previewing is not possible. However, you can estimate the probable value of a program from your previous experiences with the program, the reputation of the sponsor or producer, or the caliber of the expert or demonstrator being featured. You should select programs that are suited to the level of your students and that will help them to understand a particular unit of work.

Assignments for home viewing of television programs may be made, just as reading assignments have become an accepted part of the school's program. In this way, a teacher may even help to raise the level of programs that are viewed by families in her community. Critical viewing of television advertisements could be related to a study of consumer buying.

Essential Qualities

Whether a teacher uses a commercially prepared program or participates in the preparation of an educational television program, she should understand the essential qualities of a good television program. These include: [23]

1. The program is educational, not just entertaining.
2. The program helps the students to develop their own abilities, solve their problems, understand themselves and others, and/or increase their skills.
3. The viewer is involved in the program itself or in an activity that may follow the program.
4. The program shows something in a simple manner with a clear explanation of *why* it is so.
5. The use of local community experts or familiar people attracts an audience.
6. The program is presented in an objective manner, without distorting facts for showmanship purposes.
7. The program stimulates interest, shows application, raises questions, suggests activities, and challenges students to learn.

Experiments on the effectiveness of teaching by television indicate that college students can learn as much or more from a televised class as from attending a "live" class. Among the reasons for the effectiveness of televised classes might be that students can see and/or hear better as every student acquires a front row seat, attention is focused on the screen, enthusiastic and gifted lecturers are used, and the professors present more stimulating lectures. Although the lack of opportunity for asking questions may be one of the limitations of a televised program, students have found that they are forced to pay closer attention to the lecture. Fears have been expressed that instruction may become stereotyped, that students will lose their initiative, and that standardized ideals and measurable thought patterns will be promoted. Opponents have responded with the question: "Who, in good conscience, can say that our own teaching does not foster impersonality, conformity, and standardization of ideas, ideals, and interests?"

[23] "Television for Teaching Adolescents and Adults." *Illinois Teacher,* Vol. II, No. 4, pp. 8–12.

Effective Use

Television can contribute to many areas of the home economics curriculum:

Child Development. Students could evaluate programs for children to view; demonstrations could show proper care and guidance of young children; panel discussions could consider principles of guiding children.

Clothing and Textiles. A series of programs on clothing construction could include the selection of sewing equipment, operation of a sewing machine, pattern fitting and alterations, cutting and marking, seam construction and pressing, machine-made and bound buttonholes, and many other processes involved in the construction of a skirt and blouse.

Family Finance. Discussions and illustrations could be presented on financial planning, insurance, investments, and buying principles for the family.

Foods and Nutrition. A master chef could present a demonstration of his specialty; a teacher could demonstrate something that would require expensive supplies or equipment; an expert could demonstrate a difficult technique; food selection and suggestions for wise buying could be presented; or interest in nutrition could be developed through experiments or illustrations of nutritional deficiencies. Video tapes and televised lectures have been used in the training of dietitians to record group discussions, role-playing interviews, and staged employee training sessions.

Home Furnishing. Fleck suggested that demonstrations could be used on the making of slip-covers or other articles for the home; a chalk talk could give ideas for storing dishes; or a flannel board could be used for house planning.[24]

Home Management. Murphy used four teams of two high school girls to present the "Tale of a Shirt." While one girl demonstrated various aspects of laundering, the other girl narrated and gave reasons for the things that were being shown. A mistress of ceremonies opened and closed the show. Each team was in front of the camera for a very short time during the thirty-minute program.[25]

Home Nursing. A televised Red Cross Home Nursing course was taught successfully and with less time than by traditional methods.[26]

Personal and Family Relationships. Many of the movies or family programs can be used to illustrate social behavior for various occasions, the

[24] Henrietta Fleck, "Communication by Television." *Forecast for Home Economists,* **74**:7, January 1958.

[25] "Television for Teaching Adolescents and Adults," op. cit., p. 4.

[26] Ibid.

needs and values of various types of families, and ways of solving family problems.

When evaluating the use of a television program in the classroom, a teacher might consider such questions as the following:

1. Did the program provide a learning experience that could not have been provided as effectively by other means?
2. Did the program fit into the unit of study or the general course?
3. Were the purposes of the program made clear to the students?
4. Did the students have guidance in what to watch for?
5. Were various points of view presented that allowed students to form their own conclusions?
6. Could the students see a clear image and hear easily?
7. Were charts, pictures, flannel board, or other illustrative materials used satisfactorily?
8. Did the program encourage students to read, do simple research, or engage in creative activities to reinforce the concepts presented?

The *Illinois Teacher* pointed out the benefits a teacher might receive from appearing on a television program:

> . . . Telecasting will improve your classroom teaching. You will learn to simplify your methods, to work within a time limit, and to repeat and summarize until learning really takes place. A few appearances on television . . . will give status to your department and influence mothers of adolescents to urge enrollment in your classes. . . . If you are able to present several short programs, you might deliberately and effectively interpret your homemaking and family living program to your community through the variety of your aspects.[27]

Among the new developments on the educational scene is the portable video-tape recorder, which can be used in classrooms or carried to field activities. This is particularly valuable to student teachers and students participating in preschool child education so they can have an immediate evaluation of their performance. Students in vocational programs can benefit from seeing how well they perform certain skills.

Radio

Since almost every student has access to a radio at home or a portable set that can be used away from home, a home economics teacher has many opportunities to guide students in listening to selected radio programs. One advantage of radio is the emotional impact that comes

[27] Ibid., p. 41.

through dramatic presentations or panel discussions. Richardson suggested a general guide for use with family living classes so the students would know what to listen for: [28]

1. What was the problem?
2. What family members were involved?
3. How did they solve the problem?
4. Was everyone satisfied with the solution?
5. In what ways was it solved well?
6. How could it have been solved better?

One difficulty in using radio in the classroom is that a program may not be scheduled at a convenient time for live broadcasting. However, when it is possible for a class to listen to a radio program, the teacher can help to make this experience worthwhile by preparing her students. They should know something about the nature of the program, and they might have a list of specific questions that they should try to answer. During the broadcast, the teacher should be sure that reception is suitable for students in all parts of the room. She might take notes on the broadcast to guide in a discussion later and she might list key words or names on the chalkboard. Following the broadcast, students might have a free discussion of what they heard or they might discuss the questions that were listed previously. They might engage in creative activities or they might seek further information related to the broadcast.

A home economics teacher's responsibility for the effective use of radio does not end with guiding students in their classroom or home listening. Fleck indicated four ways in which radio can be used to tell about home economics:

> 1. Press releases can be sent to radio stations as well as to newspapers.
>
> 2. Another way to communicate by radio is to be a guest on a radio program. . . . You might be interviewed by someone, give a talk, or serve as a member of a panel.
>
> 3. A third way of using radio is to have your own program. . . . Mrs. Marguerite Horn, supervisor of home economics in the elementary grades in Poughkeepsie, New York, has a program which she broadcasts on Saturday mornings. She emphasizes such areas of home economics as new trends in nutrition, ways to prepare food to retain its nutritive content, and suggestions for improved family living.
>
> 4. Using spot announcement on radio provides another way to keep the public alert to the importance of home economics.[29]

[28] Marilyn Richardson, "Let's Use Radio and TV." *Practical Home Economics,* 4:93, September 1958.

[29] Henrietta Fleck, "Communication by Radio." *Forecast for Home Economists,* 73:6, December 1957.

Among the topics that have interest and value for use by home economics teachers in planning radio programs, Fleck suggested the following: [30]

Child Development: ideas on child care, characteristics of children at various ages.

Clothing and Grooming: selecting clothing to express your personality.

Family Economics: a simple way to record the family budget, ways to cut the food budget.

Family Relations: understanding one's parents, inexpensive ways to have fun.

Foods and Nutrition: new use for a food, losing weight, preparing meals in a hurry, refreshments for a club meeting or a children's party, cooking outdoors, food of other countries.

General: interesting class activities, career opportunities in home economics.

Home Management: household hints to reduce work capacity in a specific task.

Home Nursing: home care of the sick.

Tele-Lectures

Modern telephone equipment opens possibilities for bringing experts into the classroom. The telephone company's "Speakerphones" are amplifiers attached to the telephone, enabling users to talk and listen without using the handset. Calls can be taped and played back for other classes.

Plans for a "phone the experts" program can be initiated by a letter from the teacher or a class member, asking permission to telephone the expert at a specified time. The letter should clarify what approach will be used. For an informal classroom presentation, students might study a particular topic and draw up a list of questions to be used by students selected to act as interviewers. A tele-lecture, on the other hand, may consist of a formal presentation by the guest, followed by a time for questions.

To make the presentation more interesting and to give the students a feeling of having personal contact with the guest, the speaker might be asked to provide a photograph for publicity purposes and color slides to illustrate the lecture. If illustrations are used, the lecturer should submit a manuscript indicating which slides should accompany particular comments.

Preparations at the classroom or lecture hall include having someone introduce the speaker prior to placing the telephone call. Usually it is more satisfactory for the guest lecturer to be called at home than at his

[30] Ibid.

office. If the speaker knows what time to expect your call, he can be prepared to answer, thereby making possible a station-to-station call. A telephone company representative will make the first contact with the guest and check the clarity of reception.

If a tele-lecture is given to a large group, ushers can pick up questions around the lecture hall. The questions can be given to a few students who might rotate in asking them. It would be helpful for the guest speaker to repeat each question before answering it so that everyone will hear the questions.

Recordings

Although both radio and television have an important place in home economics education, they do have possible limitations. Disk and tape recordings can help to overcome the scheduling difficulties involved in the use of radio programs. They have many other uses such as the recording of special teacher presentations, speeches or panel discussions in which guests participate, student discussions or dramatizations, comments to be synchronized with filmstrips, and materials for evaluation. Tape recordings may be used in giving directions, such as for the use of equipment, thus freeing the teacher to be with another group. They are of benefit also in evaluation—of the teacher herself, the subject matter she has taught, or a student discussion. Tapes can be made available to a student who was absent during a lecture or who feels a need to hear part of a lecture again. The idea of mailing a "living letter" to a pen pal, a family, or another chapter of Future Homemakers of America might be appealing. "Living books" are invaluable for blind students and students who are partially sighted.

Recordings have the advantage of motivating students through a new approach or a different voice. A teacher can listen to them in advance and evaluate them for class use. They may be played over again, eliminating the need for repetition by the teacher. Tape recorders are simple to operate and recordings can be made at school or in the home. Transcripts may be either permanent or temporary. Although the cost is very low when tapes are re-used, the initial cost of a high quality machine and the cost of replacing it must be considered.

To use recordings effectively, a home economics teacher might take the following steps:

1. Select programs that are appropriate for the maturity of the students.
2. Know how to obtain the best quality presentation from the record-playing equipment.

3. Prepare the students for the listening experience.
4. Guide and encourage worthwhile follow-up activities.

PROGRAMMED INSTRUCTION

Programmed instruction has been described as a

means of instruction with most, if not all, of the following characteristics:

1. Capability of instructing effectively with little or no direct participation by a teacher.
2. Precise definition of objectives, achievement of which can be measured.
3. Logical organization of material to accomplish these purposes.
4. Arrangement of material in relatively small steps, each building on the preceding one, so that students can proceed nearly, if not entirely, independently, generally with a minimum of error.
5. Repeated testing or tryout of the programs with students and consequent revision as an essential procedure in the development of the program, to insure that students can proceed virtually independently and that learning outcomes have been achieved.
6. The requirement in the program of frequent responses, making the student an active participant throughout the learning experience.
7. Immediate confirmation or correction of response.
8. Opportunity for each student to proceed at his own pace.[31]

Programmed learning follows a logical sequence that leads a student through a specified set of behaviors designed to bring about a particular desired behavior. A typical learning program consists of (1) presentation of limited segments of information; (2) questions or problems to which the student responds; (3) immediate reinforcement when his answer is correct; (4) movement by small steps through the ordered sequence of items; and (5) review at appropriate intervals throughout the program.

Types of Programming

Essentially, two types of programming, or a combination of them, are used: linear and branching (or intrinsic). In linear programming, each student proceeds through the entire sequence of items. In a branching program, the student is asked to evaluate the state of his knowledge and to proceed to one of several points.

1. LINEAR PROGRAMMING. Skinner's approach, known as linear programming, is one in which small bits of information are given and the student is questioned immediately. Skinner's first principle is *active responding*. Through a constant exchange between the program and the student,

[31] *Wiley and Programmed Instruction*, New York: John Wiley and Sons, p. 2.

learning activity is sustained. Since a student does not necessarily learn just by having words placed in front of him, this approach requires him to process the information in order to respond to an immediate question.

The second principle is *minimal errors.* Since whatever response the student makes is likely to be reinforced, it is important that the student make the correct response on his first attempt. An orderly development of the subject matter is one way to control students' responses. Hinting, prompting, and suggesting are techniques used to help the student get the right answer. Programmers operate on the principle that, if the student makes an error, it is a fault of the program, not of the student. The program needs to be revised to the extent that almost all of the students can respond correctly to each item. Important as this principle is, it creates a real dilemma for programmers. If a program is geared to the average student, some students would not be able to handle it because of too low intelligence, inadequate reading ability, or lack of previous training. At the other extreme, some students may be bored or at least be capable of moving much more quickly than the program permits.

Questions are being raised about these two principles (active responding and minimal errors). They have a tendency to produce long programs. Likewise, there is increased reaction against the need for "small steps." Rather than to fractionate a concept, it may be preferable to present a more apt example of it.

Another principle of linear programming is that the student's response is confirmed; he receives *immediate knowledge of results.* For students who are inclined to be anxious or unsure of their responses, this confirmation can be helpful. Also, if a student has made an error, he can correct it immediately before continuing the sequence.

Prompts vary in strength and in probability of controlling the correct response. A *copying* frame is one in which the student merely has to copy one or more words. This type of prompt usually represents steps that are too small and insulting to the students. A question, such as the following, can be answered without any real understanding:

> A deficiency of vitamin C leads to scurvy.
> Scurvy is caused by a deficiency of ______________.

A *formal* prompt is one that gives a specific clue to the structure of the desired response, such as the first letter, the number of letters in a word, or the number of words in the desired response:

> Give the word used for a family's financial plan: __ __ __ __ __ __.
> The primary colors are: _________, _________, and _________.

A *thematic* prompt provides information about the meaning rather than the structure of the response (equivalence to some word or phrase, relationships, relevance of a past association to the new situation):

Like a business firm's, the family's material resources include: ______________, ______________, and ______________.

Various approaches are used to arrange items in sequence. One approach, known as RULEG, consists of presenting material sequentially with the rule first, followed by a series of examples. Some proponents of this system, in which the rules are provided as a means of leading the student to solve problems or examples, claim that it produces faster and more error-free results. In contrast, the EGRUL system starts with low-level problems for the student to solve and then leads him to generate the rules. A *spiral* structure introduces many threads early and spirals the student upward into increasingly complex presentations of the subject matter.[32]

Among the errors that are common when writing frames for linear sequences are "failure to select a significant response word, verbosity, overcuing, failure to include sufficient review items, eliciting the same response too frequently in a sequence, and overuse of a particular type of response." [33]

2. BRANCHING OR INTRINSIC PROGRAMMING. The rationale for branching or intrinsic programming was developed by Crowder. This approach consists of presenting information in a paragraph or two, followed by multiple-choice or free-response questions to measure comprehension of the material. The student's choice of answer determines what material he will see next. If he chooses the right answer, he is presented automatically with the next paragraph and question.

The sequence of principal frames leading students forward is linear in nature but the branching introduces remedial or explanatory loops, or review passages, for students who need further information before they can progress in the mainstream. The effectiveness of the extra help provided depends upon the programmer's knowledge of the kinds of mistakes students are likely to make. This results in what is called a "scrambled book," in which the student does not read one page after another but must answer one mainstream question correctly in order to get directions for getting to the next such frame. Branching can serve as a timesaving device as compared with a linear system in which small

[32] Susan M. Markle, *Good Frames and Bad*. New York: John Wiley and Sons, 1964, pp. 92–102.

[33] *A Guide for Wiley Authors in the Preparation of Auto-Instructional Programs*. New York: John Wiley and Sons, 1967, p. 7.

steps may be wasteful and redundant. On the other hand, an individual may miss valuable information contained in the frames he skips.

According to Markle, a standard intrinsic frame contains six parts:

(a) the answer the student chose in the last frame;
(b) feedback, or discussion of why the answer is correct;
(c) new information;
(d) a question testing his comprehension of the new information;
(e) two or more alternative answers to select from;
(f) a page number (or on a machine, a button designation) telling him where to go next for each alternative.[34]

Feedback is particularly important. Even if a student obtains the correct answer, he may have done so merely by chance. Crowder has postulated that learning takes place by reading and exposure, and that active responding is not necessary. Frequent questions check on the student's understanding of what he read. If he lacks certain knowledge or misunderstood what he read, he is directed to different sets of material.

Among Markle's suggestions for writing good frames are these: [35]

1. Prepare your first draft for you alone, writing as rapidly as you can the sequence of what you want to teach.

2. Gear your program to the initial level of the students for whom it is intended by basing it upon their reading level and previous learning and by using appropriate examples.

3. Analyze what you have written for truth, clarity, and facility of expression. Try to spot ambiguities and pomposities before the student sees the program.

4. Ask yourself two judgmental questions: "Is this frame necessary?" "Where is that necessary frame?"

5. A frame should represent as large a step forward in the student's acquisition of the subject matter as he is capable of taking.

6. The frame should elicit the kind of behavior sought from a student. For example, a student could demonstrate his understanding of a term by defining it, giving an example of it, labeling correctly examples of it, or recognizing when something is not an example of it. He could demonstrate his understanding of a rule or principle by stating it, being able to use it, and knowing when not to use it.

In general, a program should be used only as *one means* of teaching a course. It has been found appropriate for remedial courses, for supplementing what can be offered in the regular curriculum, and for self-

[34] Markle, op. cit., p. 130.
[35] Markle, op. cit., pp. 173–178.

study. Probably its major contribution in home economics can be in presenting initially the fundamentals of a unit, such as basic terms, concepts, and principles. The proper construction and sequencing of frames helps the student to *discover* connections, relationships, and patterns as the subject is developed. Creative programming motivates the student to learn and involves him in seeking further knowledge. The teacher is freed to concentrate on the more complex and creative aspects of the subject. No single teaching technique is best for every problem. The teacher should use whatever teaches best.

The hallmarks of good programming have been described as being similar to those of good teaching: creativity, flexibility, and variety. It is difficult to write small bits of information in an interesting style, but a skilled programmer includes appropriate examples, anecdotes, analogies, graphic illustrations, and touches of wit. A conversational style can be effective in this technique, which simulates the tutorial method. The program should be concise and structured so that the student is continually acquiring new insights. The writer of a program should let his personality be reflected in the program.

Research has answered the basic question, "Can students learn from programmed instruction?" Programmed instruction has facilitated learning in a variety of ways:

- with slow learners, mature, and superior students
- in teaching a variety of subject matter
- in bringing about desired behaviors such as rote learning, paired associate learning, application of formulae, construction of deductive logical proofs, formation of concepts, critical thinking and reading
- for teaching all or part of a course
- in the classroom or at home
- when using casually without specific assignments or supervision
- in teaching machines, programmed texts, and films
- when using different styles—with or without branching, different kinds of prompts, varying the amount of repetition, using steps of different sizes, covert and overt responses, and different kinds and amounts of reinforcement.

Further research can help to clarify programming's conditions of effectiveness. Perhaps certain kinds of students can learn most from programs of a particular style used in specific settings. For example, students of higher ability can benefit from branching programs that enable them to skip repetitions and to work at optimum speed. Younger and less intelligent students need more practice in handling materials of relative difficulty.

Teaching machines seem to offer only one advantage over programmed materials in book form—the students are prevented from looking ahead to the correct answers before attempting to answer questions for themselves. For some kinds of material, such as paired associates, a great deal of learning results merely from reading programmed items whose blanks have been filled in previously.

There is little evidence of the necessity to provide for practice and reinforcement at each step of the program. Probably learning is enhanced when the student makes an overt response if it is relevant to what is learned and if the material has difficult or unfamiliar words. Requiring trivial responses disrupts the reading process and may interfere with good learning habits.

In keeping with the cognitive theory of learning, retention can be increased by providing students with "advance organizers" or "ideational scaffolding" for the material. A hierarchical organization of learning stresses the dependence of more complex learning upon the basic fundamentals that have already been taught. Spaced review improves retention.

Computer-Assisted Instruction

Computers make possible the use of sophisticated approaches to individualizing instruction. Instead of programming information in the form of a book, as described in the previous section, the program could be prepared for storage in a computer with instructions as to how the computer should react to various student responses. The student could use a typewriter-like keyboard to answer questions and communicate with the computer. Responses from the computer might be printed on paper or displayed on a screen. Sometimes an audio device supplements the visual display.

The computer has been accused of dehumanizing instruction. This may be true, though it need not be. Because of its greater flexibility and ability to recognize individual needs, the computer can provide more individualization. Certainly it does offer an intense learning environment for those basic learnings that can be programmed well. It can free the teacher to work more creatively and to interact with the student on a higher level, once the basics have been mastered.

Computer-assisted instruction can present a mass of information quickly, can be integrated with other audio-visual materials, and can be adapted to the learners if the program writers know their needs. However, not many programs are available currently, and some of those that have been developed have not been geared sufficiently to the intended audience. The computer has a tendency to restrict the types of learning behaviors possible.

Computer-aided instruction offers a number of advantages. The student moves as rapidly as he can or wishes to. He interacts with a tutor who has endless patience, ability to observe, and ability to diagnose weaknesses that are often overlooked in human evaluation. His prior responses determine the sequence of instruction, providing a remedial loop when necessary. Statistical data are available immediately either for an individual's behavior (his responses, errors, delays, and misinterpretations) or for the group performance.

Oakland Community College in Michigan and Oklahoma Christian College in Tulsa have emphasized the learning center as the focal point for independent study. Students work in carrels with faculty and tutors always available. With access to a large number of recorded programs from many locations on campus, a learning center could serve students on a 24-hour basis. As a supplemental technique, computer-assisted instruction can be used effectively in schools and colleges. Nevertheless, it would probably be a serious mistake to orient one's program completely around this or any other one instructional technique.

At the present time, the cost of computer instructional programs keeps them from being competitive with live teachers. Even if the cost can be reduced enough to warrant their use in a specialized field such as home economics, you would want to evaluate the potential benefits of computer instruction in relation to the cost. The only justification for using computerized instruction should be that it enables a student to learn something important better than he could learn it on his own or under traditional methods of instruction.

Several questions might help you to evaluate the cost-benefit of using a computer: What is the cost of preparing materials in relation to the gain in educational achievement? What is the cost per student hour at a teaching station? Can your school system afford the cost of supporting even a small, effective computer system? Keep in mind that the real cost of a computerized service goes beyond the rental fee and includes such additional items as line toll charges (if based on a rented console plugged into a telephone line), payroll for specialized personnel, and supplemental materials for teachers and teacher aides.

At the present time it is difficult to foresee how important a role computers will have in home economics education. We must not allow ourselves to become so intrigued with computer-based instruction that we start looking for something to teach with the computer. We must be constantly alert to the latest research evidence showing what can be done best by computers. We need to define our objectives carefully and examine whether computer-assisted instruction is appropriate and feasible as part of our total curriculum.

An educational system has been developed in which the computer aids a teacher in providing an individualized program of study tailored to the needs and abilities of each student. Stored in the computer will be detailed information on what the individual knows; how he learns; and what his interests, potentials, and plans are. From a comprehensive file of "teaching-learning units," an individual daily study plan is built for him. His progress is analyzed and reported. This system assigns the student only those objectives which he can achieve at his present stage of development. If you teach in a high school or college, you should be giving serious thought to ways of meeting the needs in future years when children who are now receiving computer-assisted elementary education move to your level.

Laboratories in home economics often prove to be unduly expensive parts of the program. The cost of equipment and supplies could be reduced sharply by simulating laboratory conditions through the use of visual materials and a computer. It may not be necessary for each student to bake a cake in order to see the effects of using too little baking powder or too high an oven temperature. The student could make decisions and immediately receive feedback on the outcome of some variation.

Although programmed instruction via computers probably has limited application in home economics teaching, computers can make a variety of contributions to education. For example, they can aid in measuring achievement of students. A convenient timesaving service includes the machine scoring of objective-type tests, with the results reported to the teacher on alphabetical lists of students with their test scores, mean score, and percentile ranks of all the scores; an item analysis shows how well each item discriminated between good and poor students, the difficulty of each item, and the usefulness of various alternatives in multiple-choice items. This type of item analysis can be used to improve the items for future tests.

Computers will be used increasingly in the counseling of students. Programs are available for maintaining permanent records with instantaneous access to information on an individual's aptitude and achievement test scores, courses completed in high school, and courses taken in college. The computer can give data on the total number of units attempted, units earned, grade points earned, and grade-point balance (deficiency or surplus). A more complex program has been developed that incorporates information on various careers and helps an individual determine how well suited he is to vocational fields he is considering.

Computer services offer assistance to high school or community college students who want to attend a four-year college that is compatible with their personal, academic, and social needs.

As schools move away from highly structured schedules, they will need the aid of a computer in scheduling students for their classes, planning a master schedule that includes each teacher's assignment to certain classes, and arranging appropriate rooms and times for each course. Such a system is essential in schools where the class periods are of varying length, where students are in nongraded courses, and where team teaching is used.

Another potential use of the computer is in obtaining research information at the flick of a dial. Library research programs already are making "dial-access" systems possible so that a student or faculty member can simply dial the library communication system at any hour of the day or night and ask the computer to search out information for him. The "information explosion," which doubles our body of scientific literature every eight to ten years, is placing such a demand on library and information resources that we must look for new ways of storing and retrieving information.

Not only will computers play an increasingly important role in our schools, but they will also affect the content we teach about homes. Many people are seeking the aid of computers in arranging dates. The question still to be answered is how successful are the marriages that result from computer matching. To what extent are you able to help your students prepare for life in a computerized society? How will you change your teaching about credit if our society converts to a system requiring little or no cash, using a master credit plan? How will you change your teaching in food buying and preparation when a homemaker simply sits in her kitchen and presses buttons on a dial to order food supplies or to have a whole meal cooked electronically and delivered through a slot? What are the implications for family life in an age when adolescents are rebelling against the faceless society and saying, "Do not fold, spindle, or mutilate me!"? How different will the management of a home become when the homemaker is freed from routine housekeeping duties? What creative functions should our young people be learning to enrich their lives in a mechanized society? Perhaps you are saying that it is too soon to prepare your students for this kind of tomorrow, but are you thinking about the tomorrow they will face?

Simulation Games

Bushnell discussed the use of simulation and games, pointing out their benefits specifically for disadvantaged students. In a game, the information about a particular situation is presented to a student and he is asked to make decisions that are fed into the system, resulting in a new set of facts based upon the consequences of his decisions and calling for new decisions. Games that are relevant to students' lives can get a great deal of factual knowledge across. They can be based upon any number of problem areas, with content being largely intellectual, mechanical, or interpersonal. Bushnell stated that the "Family Game" might have "a therapeutic effect on students whose family relationships are disturbed to some degree."[36]

A simulation is a model, a physical or symbolic representation of a part of reality, designed to incorporate or reproduce those features of the real object or situation that the researcher or educator believes significant for his problem. The important factor is that the components or variables in the model respond in a manner comparable to that of the behavior of the real system. As employed by social scientists, simulation makes use of models constructed in such a way that they become functioning. These models are representations of behaving systems that attempt to reproduce *processes in action* (that is, decision-making processes); they provide information about changes in the variables and relationships within the system over time. Games are defined as experimental or training techniques that are concerned with studying human behavior or teaching individuals. Games have the characteristic of reciprocal actions and reactions among wholly or partially independent individuals who may hold different goals. As defined for class use, a simulation game is a sequential decision-making exercise structured around a simulated model of a family operation in which the participants assume the role of managing (that is, deciding about) the simulated operation.

In a college course on decision making and management in the family, Paolucci used an adapted simulation game, *Life Careers,* developed by Johns Hopkins University and the Simulations Corporation. The game consisted of a brief description of either a married male or female in a college setting, and decisions that were to be made by teams of four or five in the following areas: (1) use of work or school time (including satellite choices of courses, study, kind of work, and the like); (2) use of discretionary and/or family time; and (3) choices of who works, future career, where to live, number of children, and so on (all possibilities as the game evolves). As the students role-played family members in the decision making role, they had access to certain information. Limits, which were determined statistically, were placed by the game. A predetermined set of cultural values used by the game makers was the basis

[36] Don D. Bushnell and Dwight W. Allen, *The Computer in American Education.* New York: John Wiley and Sons, 1967, pp. 62–63.

for a point scoring system. Each student team played ten rounds, representing ten years. In the process of playing the game, the student *experienced:*

(1) what it feels like and what it takes (inputs) to make a social decision. (One group never got beyond this point.)
(2) being forced to *create* alternatives when the field of alternatives became very limited by the real world (such as job possibilities after flunking out of school.)
(3) the interrelatedness and interdependence of choices. They became aware of the irrevocable nature of some decisions. They discovered that "pay off" in some instances may appear to be great, but over the long haul "immediate gratification" is costly.
(4) making economic and technical choices.[37]

Among the advantages of using games in management teaching are:

(1) Games condense a large amount of decision-making experience into a relatively short period of time.
(2) They demonstrate the interaction between decision-making areas.
(3) They provide the experience of role playing the different roles built into the managerial situation.
(4) They demonstrate vividly the effects of sequential decision making and the interrelationships of decisions.
(5) They facilitate "safe" experimentation by allowing the student to make different sets of decisions for the same problems and comparing outcomes.
(6) They call attention to the importance of determining the significant factors in a situation and relating these properly to long-range planning.
(7) Participants learn to deal effectively with group goals as they take into account the differing viewpoints of fellow players.
(8) Games provide highly objective feedback, which allows participants to evaluate their decisions objectively.
(9) They produce a high degree of involvement of fellow players and have high motivational value.
(10) Games allow the introduction of students to cross-cultural and cross-socioeconomic situations.

On the other hand, games have some limitations and possible disadvantages. For example:

[37] From a tele-lecture presented by Beatrice Paolucci on "Teaching Home Management Through Simulation." Western Regional Home Management Conference, Oregon State University, Corvallis, Oregon, November 1968.

(1) Some characteristics of games make the situation less realistic for some students.

(2) Games are costly in dollars and time to both students and faculty.

(3) It takes time to develop the simulated games, although many are available at varying costs for certain areas of study, especially for elementary and secondary schools.

(4) It takes time to learn to play games.

(5) The use of out-of-class time to play the game is complicated because of the need for controlled information centers.

(6) Time and a number of assistants are required to supervise and score games.

(7) A simulation game may not be highly motivating for some students—who view it as a game.

This would be a good time for you to review some of the previous chapters and make your own generalizations about the relationship between principles of learning, instructional methods, and educational media. Can you see how well these various approaches provide for active participation of the learner, immediate feedback, variety, comprehension, and relevance to real life? Can you state a single objective important in some area of home economics and plan a variety of learning experiences that will enable you to motivate and really teach individual students from disadvantaged homes as well as those from middle-class homes? Can you see which approaches might be effective in working with slow-learning or gifted students? The next chapter will help you to understand and deal with some of the individual problems that demand a resourceful teacher.

Selected References

Adams, Lela, and Ruth M. Dow, "Developing Understandings about Values Through Films." *Illinois Teacher of Home Economics.* Vol. IV, No. 5.

Brown, James W., Richard B. Lewis, and Fred F. Harcleroad, *A-V Instruction Materials and Methods.* (2nd ed.) New York: McGraw-Hill, 1964.

Bushnell, Don D. and Dwight W. Allen, *The Computer in American Education.* New York: John Wiley and Sons, 1967.

Freedman, Florence B., and Esther L. Berg, *Classroom Teacher's Guide to Audio-Visual Material.* Philadelphia: Chilton Books, 1967.

Hilton, A. M., "Cyberculture—The Age of Abundance and Leisure." *Michigan Quarterly Review* 3: 217–229, October 1964.

Lumsdaine, A. A., and Robert Glaser, *Teaching Machines and Programmed Learnings.* Washington, D.C.: National Education Association, Publication Sales, 1960.

Mager, Robert F., *Preparing Objectives for Programmed Instruction.* San Francisco: Fearon Publishers, 1962.

Mather, Mary E. "A Look at Resources for Teaching Home Economics." *Illinois Teacher of Home Economics.* Vol. VI, No. 9, 1963.

Wittich, Walter A., and Charles F. Schuller, *Audio-Visual Materials, Their Nature and Use.* (4th ed.). New York: Harper, 1967.

11

Meeting the Special Needs of Individuals

To be effective as a teacher, you must be familiar with the needs of students and plan appropriate programs and learning experiences for them. Your task is complicated by the fact that every student is exceptional in some way. Try to accentuate the positive in each individual by putting the *person* first and his *exceptional quality* after. Above all, teaching requires you to have appreciation and respect for the individual.

Exceptional characteristics of students are not always easy to identify, and an individual sometimes has multiple handicaps. This chapter should help you to be aware of hidden meanings behind the symptoms or behavior you observe in your classroom. Be careful not to make snap judgments about what is causing problem behavior. Exceptional education is a highly complex and specialized field of study. This chapter is merely an introduction to some of the physical, mental, social, and emotional differences that may be found among your students. Do seek professional help from your home economics supervisor, administrator, school nurse, physician, counselor, psychologist, or qualified specialists in your community when you identify a student with some special need.

Your failure to identify and help these students may cause them to drift along, fail or be disappointed in school, or even drop out of school. Since most students are required to stay in school until they are sixteen, you can help them to profit from their experiences. No matter how great their handicaps, students who are able to be in regular classes want understanding, not pity, from you and from their classmates.

SLOW LEARNERS

In our discussion, we will use the term "slow learners" in a broad sense, referring to any student who is overage by more than a year or who cannot meet the intellectual standards that are average for his grade. Generally schools deal with at least two levels of mentally retarded persons—the slow learners, who are defined as being in the I.Q. range of about 75 to 90, and the educable mentally retarded, who are in the range of 50–75 I.Q. Estimates indicate that as many as 20 percent of a school population may be educable, though subnormal in intelligence.

Identifying the Slow Learner

The most critical area of identification is the intellectual. A slow learner has a reduced rate and capacity for learning, particularly of abstract material. His reasoning power and ability to generalize are very limited. He is likely to read little and to have poor retentive ability. His attention span is short except for what is familiar and interesting to him. Because of his inability to measure up to what is expected of the average student, he experiences great frustration. His past school records show consistently mediocre attainments. He is often found among the school dropouts, juvenile delinquents, and unemployed.

Physical identification is not easy. Sometimes the slow learning child is also slow to mature, physically inferior, clumsy, and lacking in eye-hand coordination. He may have less general stamina and strength, causing him to have a higher incidence of illness and to lose more time from school than is normal.

A slow learner is likely to come from the lower socioeconomic homes. You will need to be very careful to differentiate between the students who are really slow learners and those who are functionally slow, perhaps due to meager or unwholesome background experiences. Like most adolescents, a slow learner desires to be well-liked, though he may be timid. Leadership ability, except in very small groups, is rare. Emotional tendencies and interest in the opposite sex may be strong. He probably lacks common sense and the ability to exercise good judgment. He likes quick results and becomes impatient waiting for deferred returns. When pressure becomes too great, a slow learner may become a bully or he may withdraw and be conforming. Adjustment to junior high school is difficult, as he must learn to cope with many teachers and new subject areas. He is very responsive to commendation.

Role of the Home Economics Teacher

Educators in recent years have given cognizance to the fact that slow learners who are in school are destined to become husbands or wives, fathers or mothers, employees, spenders of income, consumers of mass media of communication, neighbors, and voters. Among the school's primary objectives should be to help these students prepare for worthy home membership and for earning a living. Home economics can make a contribution to these objectives through experiences that help them to live safely, get along with other people, find satisfaction in their use of leisure time, be adequate homemakers, manage their money, appreciate the arts, and communicate their ideas.

How the home economics teacher can help slow learners depends on such factors as the school setting, the number of students in the class, whether slow learners can be taught in special classes or whether they are mixed with students of average and superior ability, and the facilities for grouping students according to their interests and abilities. Probably the most effective teacher is the one who develops a therapeutic environment—who shows respect for the individuality of each child, who creates an atmosphere that is friendly and warm, and who helps each child experience feelings of success and belonging.

Specific suggestions for working with slow learners include:

1. Know the beginning level for each student and begin there, but challenge each to live up to his potential.

2. Use a unit approach, emphasizing short units with immediate goals that suggest situations closely related to life outside of school.

3. Give simple directions orally and repeat them as often as necessary (without showing impatience).

4. Provide a great deal of individual help at a time when he is ready. This may include doing something with him, rather than just showing or telling him how to do it.

5. Show the student what to do and how to do it. Demonstration and verbal discussion are not enough. It might help to have a slow learner assist with various steps in a demonstration. You could begin the step and have the student complete it under your guidance. This direct sensory experience makes it easier for him to carry out his laboratory work later.

6. Demonstrations may need to be given in small groups and repeated as necessary. Try to make provisions for helping slow learners remember the steps and how to do them. One helpful technique is to demonstrate just one step at a time and have the students complete that step immediately.

7. Provide concrete and practical learning experiences. Slow learners learn by *doing*.

8. Work-study programs or occupational programs are important to help slow learners develop skills for wage-earning. They could be trained to assist homemakers, to serve as waitresses, to be nurses' aides, to make alterations or do dressmaking, to be workers in housekeeping departments of institutions, or to work in quantity food service.

9. Field trips can provide important concrete experiences.

10. Films, television, and radio are valuable only if used with proper introduction and careful follow-up. If these are used for entertainment, they cheat the student of his learning time.

11. Knowledge that is not used will not be learned. Be sure your daily plans include opportunities for students to practice what they are expected to learn.

12. Your immediate aim is to help the student function with what he is learning, even though he lacks comprehension of it.

13. Help the student develop a memory for what he learns. One important step is to train him to perceive accurately. Introduce new words one at a time and provide instances for him to recall these.

14. Since slow learners have difficulty with symbols, such as the names and amount of supplies, a "picture sequence" on the bulletin board could be helpful. The student could check to see if his work is being done right.

15. Teacher-made worksheets and booklets are often less costly and more functional than published materials. Retarded students may learn better from someone who knows them than from people who have written textbooks. However, some textbook companies have published materials that are helpful for slow learners.

16. Materials that are developed should be simple, colorful, and perceptually honest. They should use short steps and provide for immediate, meaningful reinforcement. They should make use of several learning receptors—sight, sound, smell, movement, taste.

17. Provide worthwhile busy work to keep students occupied while you work with a particular individual.

18. Praise, awards, and honor rolls motivate slow learners to be interested in learning.

19. Tests should be short. Oral tests, with questions read by the teacher, may be helpful.

20. The teacher's relationship with slow learners can be made or broken by a sense of humor. The teacher needs to be able to see something funny in a situation, to laugh with the students but not at them, and to see the humor even when she is the object of a joke.

21. Help the parents and other students to accept slow learners.

22. Condition the students to learn to be cooperative and well-mannered.

23. Nutrition is vital. When students are hungry and tired, they have difficulty learning. Their families may be uninformed or financially unable to help them develop good nutrition, health habits, and personal grooming.

GIFTED STUDENTS

The term "gifted students" has different meanings and is many times restricted to the highest three to five percent of the students. Actually, the kinds of enrichment proposed for gifted students would benefit a much larger group, perhaps the upper 20–25 percent in a heterogeneous class. A teacher who believes that every student is gifted in some way will be challenged to enable each student to develop his capacities. Although this portion of the chapter will emphasize academic ability, be alert for students who are gifted in other important ways. Your home economics classes can provide opportunities for students who are gifted in leadership, science, art, human relations, and motor ability. In Chapter 8 we discussed ways in which an individual can be creative and/or gifted.

Characteristics of the Able Student

Those who define giftedness in terms of I.Q. do not agree on whether to start with 120, 130, or even a higher level. A newer approach to the identification of able students is to select those with high "functional ability." In other words, the superior student is one who has high intelligence and who has learned to use it so that his performance is correspondingly high. If you have a student with unusually high I.Q. but whose accomplishment is mediocre, be sure to read the next section, which is concerned with the underachieving and failing student.

The best indicators of superior intelligence are mental characteristics. You might look for such functional abilities as doing a high level of abstract thinking, using a superior vocabulary accurately, raising challenging questions and being interested in answering them, expressing ideas with originality, deriving principles and generalizations, showing initiative, reading rapidly and widely, following complex directions, concentrating on a problem, discovering cause-effect relationships, learning rapidly with little repetition, analyzing problems quickly or thoroughly, collecting things, having a mature and imaginary sense of humor, and participating in many extracurricular activities.

Although no person will possess all of the characteristics described, there is a tendency for superior traits to go together. The gifted student may be taller, stronger, or more mature physically than others of his age. He is likely to possess good muscular coordination, enjoy good health, and be physically attractive.

Socially and emotionally he tends to shine also. He is poised, self-confident, persistent, trustworthy, and not easily upset or discouraged by failures. He gets along well with others and is sensitive to their needs.

He is inclined to prefer older persons and look for adult approval rather than approval of his peers. He is critical of himself and others. Routine work bores him easily. The passive attitude of those around him may make a gifted student impatient, rebellious, and "difficult." On the other hand, he may withdraw and seek his satisfaction through outlets apart from the school.

Enriching the Program

It may be possible for you to make special provisions for gifted students, particularly by providing summer session courses in home economics for college-bound students whose regular programs do not allow room for electives. Nevertheless, home economics teachers generally must work with these students by enriching their regular classes. The real challenges you face are to get these students into your classes, to stimulate them to work up to their capacity, and to help them gain a clearer understanding of their roles as homemakers and community members.

Since these students will probably be going to college, you might help them relate the content of your courses to their plans for college. For example, they could plan for living away from home, particularly for making a dormitory room attractive and livable. They could plan a college wardrobe. They could compare the costs involved and the opportunities afforded by attending a state college, a state university, and a private college. Don't forget that careers in home economics should be of interest to college-bound students!

The role of the educated woman in our society is another emphasis that might help to enrich your classes. A student might study trends pertaining to the average age for marriage, the average age of the mother when her youngest child is in school, and the average number of years a mother can expect to be employed. Be sure your able students understand that women who obtain higher education are likely to have fewer children and to devote more years to a profession than the average woman does. Even though her husband's income is adequate, she may enjoy the opportunity of using her professional training while making a contribution to her community through paid or voluntary work. If she is to be able to manage the home and provide the services her husband's position may require, she will need to develop unusual sensitivity and skills.

The key to successful enrichment is to provide varied, interesting, and worthwhile activities that involve complex ideas and the interrelation of ideas. Having a student help you with clerical duties, fix a bulletin board or display, or help slower members of a class cannot be considered enrichment. Giving a student "more of the same" type of work can become repetitious and boring. The student who is a rapid learner, a good organizer, and skillful thinker needs to have individualized projects that provide opportunity for him to select and plan. Less highly structured instructions and assignments stimulate originality. One caution is in order here: in providing enrichment, try not to duplicate what will be covered in the next year's course.

Most of the techniques described previously on learning experiences are applicable to work with gifted students. "Cluster grouping" of a small group of the most able students will enable them to work on difficult projects. Programmed instruction of the branching type permits superior students to bypass needless repetition. Guest speakers can share interesting experiences, or an able student may demonstrate advanced or original work in which he has developed unusual skill. Leadership opportunities may be provided through panel discussions or debates. Individual field trips may be taken by high-ability students, who will report their experiences to the rest of the class. Among the field trips might be visits to college home economics departments, research laboratories, and other places where graduate home economists are employed.

Individualizing regular assignments can be an important way of enriching home economics courses. Able students can be encouraged to find deeper meanings in their work and to look for *reasons* underlying the methods that are used. Scientific principles can be stressed as the students are encouraged to explain certain reactions. They can perform experiments of greater complexity than the average student. They can apply creative touches in their clothing or interior design projects. They should be permitted opportunities to help plan the goals and activities of the course. A wide variety of text, reference, and resource materials should be provided to enable them to branch out beyond the required assignments.

Research indicates that teacher expectation makes a real difference in the performance of students at all levels of ability. The level of motivation is influenced by the framework of expectation. If you do not expect a great deal from your students, you cannot look forward to a lively response on their part. Show your students that you value intellectual achievement and have a genuine respect for excellence. Transmit to them a curiosity, scientific attitude of mind, and spirit of fun in trying to get an answer.

These are students who should be given opportunities for self-evaluation of their work. They should be encouraged to evaluate their own personal growth rather than to make comparisons with other students, particularly with the less able students.

UNDERACHIEVING AND FAILING STUDENTS

One of the major goals of a teacher is to help each student perform to the extent of his abilities. Underachievement poses a real dilemma for teachers. Extensive research has been done in an effort to differentiate the underachiever from a student who is functioning at a level commensurate with his abilities. Although various studies do not agree on the characteristics of underachievers, we can be confident that achievement is dependent upon more than intellectual ability.

In our discussion of underachievement, we are thinking of a discrepancy between a student's intelligence and his grades, or as someone has described it, "ability without ambition." Identifying and helping these students is important from several standpoints. Your community cannot afford the waste that results from a loss of talent when students of ability fail to develop their potential. Such failure can be harmful to the individual's adjustment and increase the likelihood that he will become a dropout. Your ability to differentiate between the student who could achieve and the one who is not amenable to help will enable you to expend your time and effort to best advantage. A word of caution is in order: be careful not to write off any student as being unsalvageable without really giving him a chance.

Differences between Achieving and Nonachieving Students

Students who are achieving at the level of which they are capable tend to be those who possess maturity, seriousness of interests, and willingness to take the consequences of their behavior. They have a conviction that their effort is meaningful. They are capable of working under pressure. In verbal and numerical reasoning, they are superior to the underachiever. Their social relations are characterized by awareness and concern for service to others, a sense of responsibility, dominance, persuasiveness, optimism, and permissiveness. They are less positive of their goals but more realistic about them. They have self-confidence and strong motivation to achieve.

In contrast, underachievers have personal problems that conflict with their having a satisfactory academic experience, but they seldom recognize that they have a problem with their school work or with emotional instability. They tend to have false or distorted perceptions of themselves and of society. They are inclined to set their aspirations too high or too low. When their goals are too high, they are not able to carry through and the result is a low regard for themselves.

A problem that is common to many underachievers is their hostility toward authority figures, particularly parents and teachers. This may be revealed in a dislike of adults, resistance to externally imposed tasks, and inability to perceive the attitudes of others. Studies indicate that the majority of underachievers come from homes of an average or better socioeconomic level. Rebellion resulted from parents' urging, pushing, and nagging.

Underachievers tend toward overactivity, excessive sociability, and extroversion. They show disregard for social responsibility and take little responsibility for themselves. They develop habits of laziness.

Underachievers have been described as easygoing individuals with little tendency to worry and to develop psychic tension, but you should be alert to the possibility that they may be covering up. For example, boasting and aggressiveness may cover up fear. Some investigators have reported higher percentages of health problems among students who are failing. These include poor vision, bad teeth, and excessive overweight. They are inclined to have a high percentage of illness, perhaps caused by anxiety.

Underachievers tend to be superior in spatial and mechanical aptitudes and to be more adept at dealing with things than with people or words. Since they may not be as capable of working with words and numbers, they sometimes lack interest in the usual classroom learning experiences. They may lack efficiency in study habits, be careless in their work, and be unable to concentrate on it. Probably they lack information on the requirements of their chosen vocational fields; they expect to earn high salaries and achieve a degree of fame. Although their plans are likely to be inappropriate, they seem to be quite sure of the vocational choices. They are likely to spend much time on outside jobs and extracurricular activities. Two key words that have been used to describe the goals of underachievers are *fun* and *fame*.

The preceding paragraphs overly simplify the characteristics of underachievers. In reality, research findings are conflicting in the factors they identify, and there are many additional reasons why students develop a persistent pattern of underachievement. For instance, many adults frown on working to capacity. Their peers show disrespect for students, especially girls, who use their brains effectively. Teachers sometimes emphasize getting along with others rather than encouraging an individual to develop his specialized interest and intellect. In our achievement-oriented culture, students may be blocked by their lack of confidence and fear of failure. Flunking out of school or college may represent a way of rebelling against a parent in the struggle for independence.

Guidelines for the Teacher

If one of your students is failing to achieve at his proper level, your first step should be to evaluate the school atmosphere and the value orientation of your classes. Remember that it is easy to stereotype students either as overachievers or underachievers. Many times failure of a student should, in fact, be attributed to failure of the curriculum, the methods of teaching, or the teacher as a person. It is not clear whether a student learns because he likes a teacher or whether he learns because he feels that the teacher likes him.

Our task as home economics teachers is to build on the capabilities a student possesses and to assist him in building new resources, new intellectual skills, new ways of solving problems, and new ways of working. Some suggestions for motivating underachievers include:

1. Be sure that the learning experiences are closely related to the students' needs.
2. Create an atmosphere in which the students are kept busy and interested so they don't want to "goof off."
3. Let students explore their ideas. Someone has said that adults do not underachieve; they merely use their time for the things that interest them.
4. Have stimulating discussions in class, rather than "rehashing" the textbooks.
5. Keep a supply of current books, magazines, and newspapers available and encourage their use.
6. Use programmed materials to provide individualized instruction.
7. Help the students improve their study habits and thinking skills. You may need to refer them to a specialist who can help them develop their reading ability.
8. Use sociometric techniques to help break up cliques of failing students who are associating with other failing students and thereby reinforcing their poor self-image. Provide exemplary role models for them.
9. Treat them as if they were the mature individuals you expect them to be.
10. Show the students warmth of personality and your willingness to work for their good.
11. Assist them with minor problems of personal and social adjustment. Refer them to a counselor for help with more severe problems.
12. Develop a work-study program to help students prepare for satisfying employment.
13. Keep up-to-date information on sources of financial aid for stu-

dents who could not continue in school or college without such assistance.

CULTURALLY DIVERSE STUDENTS

In many communities today our pluralistic society is reflected in the cultural diversity of our classrooms. When we refer to students as being culturally different, we are thinking of those whose racial, nationality, religious, and ethnic characteristics distinguish them from the majority. Their speech, manners, attitudes, and habits may be distinctive. They may have backgrounds and personality structures that differ significantly from others.

Cultural diversity may present a variety of problems to a teacher. The students are exposed to two sets of norms, one set at home and another set at school. Often, these norms pull in opposite directions. Other students may respond to their peculiar behavior with prejudice. Teachers and students may be inclined to treat all members of a particular minority group according to their stereotyped image of that group, failing to recognize that there are diversities within each group as well as between groups. All too often the teacher fails to recognize special problems and potentialities of an individual.

The Culturally Different

The first part of this book gave suggestions to help you become acquainted with your community, the homes and families of your students, and the individual students themselves. As you become acquainted, you will be able to identify which minority groups are present and to what extent. In some areas, for example, you may have quite a few students from Cuban, Chinese, Japanese, Indian, Mexican, Negro, Puerto Rican, or other backgrounds. It will not be possible in this chapter to elaborate on specific characteristics of these or other minority groups. To do so might mislead you into thinking of each individual student as fitting the description of that minority group. You should study some reference material for a better understanding of the culturally different groups in your community. Remember that each group has both rich and poor people, professional and business persons, government officials, and others in almost every walk of life.

A large group deserving of your attention is composed of culturally disadvantaged families. Some culturally different families may be culturally disadvantaged, but these terms are by no means synonymous. Among the disadvantaged are high percentages of American Indians, Negroes, Puerto Ricans, slum dwellers, unskilled workers, members of one-parent households, the aged, and families who moved from rural to urban environments. Major problems confronting disadvantaged families include:

Housing. Shortage of adequate housing for low income families; opposition of community associations and individuals to having culturally different families move into their neighborhoods; relationship between inadequate housing and crime, delinquency, health, and education; overcrowding; poor repair; lack of public concern over their plight; frustration that may turn to in-group hostility and aggression.

Employment. Discrimination in obtaining training commensurate with potential and employment in line with their skills; unemployment or underemployment; high percentage receiving public and private assistance; variable income due to instability of earnings and varying amounts earned.

Education. High rate of absence from school; failure of parents to stress the value of education and high achievement; inability to relate formal educational experiences to a satisfying future; lack of knowledge as to what opportunities might be available to them for schooling and jobs; insufficient motivation; low level of expectancy at home and school, so they never really tax themselves to capacity; lack of confidence that training will pay off; desire for immediate marketability of their learnings; deficiency in skills necessary to gain knowledge.

Health. Affected by inadequacies in housing, employment, and schooling; lower percentages who can afford private medical care and hospitalization; larger percentages who are charity patients at public clinics and hospitals.

Social welfare. Higher percentages receiving public and private welfare assistance; family disorganization; dependency of senior citizens; inadequate child care; high truancy rates; excessive school dropouts; living on the borderline between self-sufficiency and being public charges.

Crime and delinquency. Higher percentage of conventional crimes, delinquent acts, arrests, indictments, convictions, and parolees.

Retarding effect of home background. Absence of stimulating conversation, good books, sharing information, mental activity, encouragement, and positive attitudes toward hard work and study.

American middle-class families tend to place high value on achievement, and they are willing to take risks to win the respect of others. They regard hard work and efficient planning as means toward achievement. In contrast, the lower-class person values security rather than risk-taking. From a succession of failures, he is likely to develop a sense of fatalism or apathy, rejecting the importance of achievement and hard work.

Middle-class students have a style of expression that is more conceptual, idea-oriented, and verbal, while lower-class students are more concrete, thing-oriented, and non-verbal.

Middle-class children have been taught to be "good" and to control anger and aggression. They are willing to postpone gratification in order to obtain a future reward. They value self-denial, rationality, formal education, and self-mastery. Lower-class persons tend to view the future as uncertain, and so they look for immediate rewards and pleasures. Self-control and responsibility are less evident. They have learned to express anger and aggression directly. Early difficulties in school may have caused them to develop negative feelings about school, low self-concepts, and resentment against teachers. One of the greatest contributions you can make to the lower-class students is in the emotional realm, helping them to develop better self-images and insight into their feelings and values. You can also assist them in building self-respect by seeing that they acquire new ways of solving problems and are successful in attaining a new skill, such as ability to work efficiently with children.

The Challenge of Diversity

The challenge confronting you is to help students value their differences and develop skills to promote harmonious living. Education is a means of enhancing and transmitting culture. As a home economics teacher, you should look for and take advantage of opportunities to endorse and support values and behavior patterns that differ from your own. In this way, you will help a student to retain his identity, language, and culture. At the same time, you will want to help individuals to alter their values, sense of personal worth, and patterns of anxiety. You will do this by discovering and liberating their talents, stimulating and adjusting their aspirations, and expressing what they *are* rather than trying to fit the pattern others might expect of them.

If you are to be in a position to understand, appreciate, and participate in another culture, you will need to be familiar with the historical background of that group in the United States. Each group has a unique social, psychological, and educational milieu. In order to know what is happening to an individual, you will need to know about his peer group and the circumstances of his home life. Try to assume the role of that individual and see the teacher and community through his eyes. You will be most effective if you strive for a fusion of cultures, keeping the best of both, rather than for a complete assimilation of the student into the white middle-class culture.

Be aware of community developments that pose problems for minority group members. You should know also about opportunities to help them establish decent housing, desirable jobs, improved nutritional practices, adequate education, better sanitary and medical facilities, personal rights, and unbiased law enforcement. By cooperating closely with community agencies, such as police and welfare, you can help your students and their families to be aware of special opportunities that your community offers to cultural minorities.

Working with the parents of your students may present unusual problems. Parents of minority groups are especially reluctant to come to school. Perhaps you could take advantage of open house or P.T.A. meetings. You might try working with the father in a family in which he makes social contacts and speaks more English than the mother. An older child or an interested adult can be helpful contacts.

Be open and real in your dealings with students and their families. Show them that you recognize, rather than deny, differences. Try to handle real issues and not just talk on the surface. Be helpful rather than judgmental and accepting rather than rejecting.

Do try a variety of techniques for working with groups in which you have minority students. For example, experiment with sociometric groupings as a means of promoting better group relations. Use programmed instruction, with its capability of taking into account wide differences in backgrounds and needs of the students. Bring in a resource person from a minority group to demonstrate or talk with your students about family customs. Take advantage of various group approaches, such as discussions and role playing, to overcome stereotypes and prejudices. Be sure to increase your own understanding by making prearranged home visits and visits to community recreation programs serving minority groups. Provide an environment where books are available and reading is valued. Recognize that existing achievement and intelligence tests are biased toward the white middle-class background.

Gowan and Demos suggested some ways for counselors to work with potential dropouts. Perhaps in your work with disadvantaged students these suggestions would be helpful:

1. Develop an acceptant and understanding attitude toward him.
2. Encourage participation in activities where he can obtain positive recognition.
3. Give him credit for effort even when he doesn't achieve to academic standards.
4. Assist him to relate his school experiences to life situations.
5. Get him involved in remedial experiences (especially reading).
6. Help his parents gain a more realistic understanding of their child.
7. Refer him to school specialists (social workers, speech correctionists) and out-of-school agencies.

8. Help him develop a positive attitude toward school attendance.
9. Emphasize that a high school diploma greatly enhances the possibility of success in our society.[1]

Contributions of the Home Economics Program

Students from culturally diverse backgrounds need an understanding of the broad areas of home economics. They need to see how home economics can help them to achieve greater personal satisfaction and a higher level of living. The following suggestions may stimulate you in thinking of ways in which home economics can promote better understanding of home life:

1. *Child Development*

High school students may have much of the responsibility for the care of their younger siblings, and so they need an understanding of the growth and developmental needs of young children. They can be taught necessary skills in bathing, dressing, feeding, and guiding children's behavior for use in their own homes as well as in baby-sitting for other families. Since many of them will marry at an early age, this training will help their future families.

Project Head Start has taught us the importance of early, planned educational experiences. Interrelated programs for infant care and parental counseling have made an impact in underprivileged areas. Among the outstanding job opportunities for high school and junior college home economics students are those in early childhood education. While these students prepare to be teacher aides, they will learn knowledge and skills that will be valuable with their own families. Furthermore, as students become the "indigenous workers" in community child care projects, new opportunities for parent education will become possible for the home economics teacher.

Interesting class discussion could center around such topics as the effects of parental attitudes and child-rearing practices on children, traditions passed on orally from one generation to another, family ties, and the status of women in various cultures. A home economics class can be a laboratory that introduces students to democratic living. As they interact with the teacher and other students, they acquire patterns of behavior that may persist throughout their lives. Feelings of satisfaction can be gained from sharing ideas and materials, such as treasured family articles (not those of great monetary value). Good personal-social relations might

[1] John C. Gowan and George D. Demos (editors), *The Disadvantaged and Potential Dropout*. Springfield, Illinois: Charles C. Thomas, 1966, p. 135.

stress ways in which cultures differ in etiquette, social graces, role of the hostess, and what is expected of a guest.

2. *Clothing, Textiles, and Related Arts*

Students from disadvantaged families need emphasis on such basic matters as the importance of cleanliness, ways to achieve cleanliness of body and clothing, mending, simple alterations, and spot removal. Color selection should include the colors that look best on various shades of brown skin. Illustrative materials should be developed for this purpose.

Since nearly every student likes to have attractive clothing, your classes could help young people consider their existing wardrobes and how to get the best value for their money when buying or making clothing. The expense will need to be considered in light of the needs and comfort of other members of the family. Students of higher socioeconomic backgrounds might study how people dress in other cultures and what their arts and crafts are. Advanced students might relate some of their findings to influences of other cultures on American ways of life.

Homes of disadvantaged students are often small, run-down shelters in a slum area, occupied by large families. Your efforts may need to be concentrated on how to arrange furnishings attractively and how to make inexpensive improvements, such as new curtains, slip covers, or pillow covers. Effective and time-saving methods of house cleaning may need to be stressed.

Teaching housing and home furnishings can be quite different in a community where the students represent diverse cultures but not disadvantaged families. Field trips may be included for students to study the design and manufacture of high quality furniture, china, silver, or glassware. A model house may offer opportunity for students to see historical accessories and furniture from other countries. Department stores sometimes feature ancient crafts and modern adaptations along with music and special menus from around the world. Planning a room with Scandinavian or Oriental design could be a worthwhile project. Selecting furnishings and accessories to blend with a treasured family article, such as a Persian rug, could make a valuable contribution to the family. Museums, such as those featuring American Indian relics, can give students better understanding of another way of life.

3. *Food and Nutrition*

Food is a pleasurable part of many cultures. In all cultures it has symbolic meaning, signifying religious, social and/or cultural values. If you teach international foods, be sure to include some understanding of the country and customs as well as the actual preparation of food. Other aspects that will add interest will be typical menus, cooking and eating utensils, table settings, and food for feasts and holidays. Rather than limiting your lessons to one foreign food, or even one meal, try to have your students learn about the diet of a particular group and how a nutritious diet could be obtained using foods characteristic of that group.

Menus from restaurants that feature foreign foods can be brought into the classroom for study. Possibly some of the students could afford to visit such restaurants, where they could see the walls lined with scenes from the country, appropriate accessories, waitresses in regional costumes, and varieties of food being prepared and served. Some of the flavor of other countries could be obtained from various sections of a supermarket that carries imported items. The class or Future Homemakers of America Club might sponsor and prepare an international dinner to which guests could be invited.

Students from lower class homes probably have limited opportunity to learn middle class table manners at home. Learning correct methods of food service may be important to them as a means of obtaining jobs or becoming acceptable in middle-class social groups. Students, including those from a higher socioeconomic status, can learn a great deal from preparing meals on a welfare budget—appreciation of the need for knowledge and skill in nutrition, consumer education, and management become apparent.

An important contribution of Negroes to our culture can be pointed out through a study of George Washington Carver's work on various uses of the peanut. Be sure to stress the nutritional applications of this work.

The school lunch can be a valuable learning experience as well as an opportunity to supplement the food eaten at home. When working with students from disadvantaged families, help them to find interesting ways of using plentiful and nutritious foods.

4. Consumer Education

An ever-mounting problem in all families, but especially in low-income families, is debt. Students from all socioeconomic levels should be encouraged to understand their roles as consumers. Guest speakers can be very helpful on such matters as the cost of credit, the consequences of going too heavily into debt, and ways in which young couples have found success with their family financial management.

Comparative shopping may be especially helpful to disadvantaged students, giving them tips on selecting grades of merchandise according to their intended usage, camparing the costs of various products and brands of the same product, and recognizing when something is a "bargain."

A student from a deprived home probably has not had opportunity to learn about setting goals and making plans, since he may never have heard his parents do advance planning for a vacation, new furniture, or their children's education—all difficult when income is limited and sporadic. He knows little about various social services and institutions within the community, such as libraries, legal aid, medical clinics, and recreation programs, many of whose services are available free. Be careful not to impose middle-class values on your students, but expose them to different values so that they will have alternatives for choosing their own values. Exposure to new ways helps one choose from a base of knowledge rather than continue an old way because one is ignorant of the new.

In your work with classes of mixed background, keep in mind that each student can benefit from learning more about a variety of kinds of families. Home economics can be a means of breaking down barriers between various groups. You can help your students examine a number of ways of solving a problem. By doing this, you can help to avoid conflicts that might arise between the students and their families if only one procedure had been stressed.

DISTURBED STUDENTS

Mental and emotional disorders are prevalent in the United States. High school teachers have a substantial share of students who manifest shyness, anxiety, depression, fears or phobias, psychosomatic disorders, deviant sexual behavior, hostility, truancy, or violations of the law. The extent to which you need to be concerned about the problem of mental illness seems evident in the prediction that one out of every twenty persons will sometime be in a mental hospital for emotional or personality disorder.

Concept of Mental Health

Mental health has been defined by Thorpe from the negative point of view as "the absence of symptoms of maladjustment. . . . Such symptoms range along a continuum from feelings of inferiority or guilt, through psychosomatic disorders and the psychoneuroses, to the organic and functional psychoses." Thorpe presented the positive side in this way: ". . . satisfactory adaptation to the requirements of group life and the experiencing by the individual of the greatest success which his abilities make possible, with a maximum sense of well-being on his own part and the highest possible benefit to society. The individual on this level is sufficiently mature emotionally to conduct himself adaptively under practically all circumstances." [2]

A composite of a healthy person as postulated by such leading psychologists as Shoben, Jahoda, Allport, Rogers, and Combs would include the following characteristics: openness to experience; self-acceptance and self-control; personal responsibility; social responsibility and warm and deep relations with others; identification with others and compassionate regard for all; integration, a unifying philosophy of life, values, and standards; autonomy and realistic perceptions; environmental mastery; and creativity and imagination.

Recognizing the Disturbed Student

There is no one cause of emotional disturbance, and usually you should expect to find a combination of several indications. You may see evidences of character difficulties, or social, mental, or emotional disturbance. Watch for behavior that differs from the norm—extreme shyness, inability to make and keep friends, sudden and unexplained drop in school work, bad temper, aggressive acts, apathetic attitudes, docility, crying, habitual lying, persistent tardiness, truancy, and rebellion.

Identifying disturbance is a complex procedure. Emotional disturbance cannot be viewed apart from mental, physical, and social health. A severe impairment of vision or hearing may have an emotional problem related to it. Emotional problems may produce physical illness or obesity. Many problems stem from unsatisfactory parent-child relations, which may be in the past and/or present. Some emotional patterns become relatively fixed early in life, while others are refined as a child grows.

Understanding an emotionally disturbed person requires much more depth in psychology than you can obtain from this book. You may be dealing with someone who takes every step in fear or someone who feels that he cannot depend on anyone else, that no one really cares about him. As life becomes difficult, some people try to build and maintain a wall against the world. Their efforts to protect themselves may sap their emotional and intellectual energy. In an effort to relieve physical tensions, some try to keep in constant motion. For them, a classroom represents confinement. Some try very hard *not* to please the teacher rather than run the risk of being overcome by the demands of an adult.

Perls summarized different views toward the behavior of modern man:

> According to William Glasser, he is *irresponsible* and needs to develop responsibility for himself. According to Eric Berne, he is a *game player*.

[2] Louis P. Thorpe, *The Psychology of Mental Health.* (Second edition.) New York: The Ronald Press Company, 1960, pp. 4–5.

> According to Albert Ellis, he is a *person operating on illogical assumptions.* According to Everett Shostrom, he is first a manipulator who needs to become aware of the manipulative styles of relating to others. Second, he is a person who needs therapeutic goals which are comprehensible and which will motivate and excite him to live his life to its fullest potential.[3]

Shostrom described eight classifications of people who are manipulators. You might recognize yourself or some of your students in his descriptions.

THE DICTATOR—exaggerates his strength, dominates, quotes authorities, and tries to control his victims. Did you ever feel it was your duty to point the right way to your students and keep them under firm control? If so, you might try converting your strength into the capacity for democratic leadership.

THE WEAKLING—is passively silent, extremely sensitive. He doesn't hear; he forgets; or he plays stupid. One way for a student to control a teacher is to say he had difficulty understanding what the assignment was all about. If he got a low grade, it was the teacher's fault for not making the assignment clear. Shostrom pointed out that almost invariably the "Under-Dog" wins out over the "Top-Dog." He has a variety of subtle techniques.

THE CALCULATOR—is a bright person who deceives, lies, or tries to outwit and control other people. To him, life is a battle that he tries to win. Did you ever try a high-pressure technique to control your students by creating guilt in those who did not conform? Did you ever quote the latest research on nutrition or family breakups and not leave any room for variation from what you regard as the "truth"?

THE CLINGING VINE—enjoys dependency, being led and taken care of, having someone do his thinking for him, demanding attention, and asking questions that are not designed to get answers.

THE BULLY—is an aggressive person who uses his temper to control others. He can be hostile, cruel, unkind, and sarcastic.

THE NICE GUY—aims to please. Who can criticize someone who is always nice and sweet? Thus, the "Nice Guy" is hard to cope with and always wins out. Can you think of someone who always tries to do the right thing? someone who "kills with kindness"? someone who influences others in favor of what she wants by tempting them with a delicious cake?

THE JUDGE—is a critical person who distrusts everybody, is resentful and slow to forgive, and takes delight in making judgments as to the

[3] Everett Shostrom, *Man, the Manipulator* (Foreword). Nashville: Abingdon Press, 1967, p. 9.

rightness or wrongness of what someone does. Can you think of anyone who is so convinced as to what is right or wrong that he shuts off any further discussion on a topic?

THE PROTECTOR—is supportive and nonjudgmental, spoils others, is overly sympathetic, and refuses to let those he protects grow up for themselves. Although many teachers and parents have a goal of protecting their children, it would be better for adults to guide them gently to find their own way.[4]

Educating the Disturbed Student

Students bring a variety of problems to the classroom, and they also bring a variety of manipulative techniques. As a teacher, you should seek expert help in understanding a student who has emotional problems. Your school probably has a counselor, nurse, social worker, psychologist, or consulting psychiatrist who could work with you or work directly with the disturbed student. This professional worker might screen students and refer the more disturbed cases to a psychiatrist or community agency for further treatment.

One important point for you to remember is that the attitudes of the teacher are reflected in the attitudes of the students. The way in which you express feelings and emotions can set the tone for the students' expression. If you become upset easily, your mood can disturb the class. If you show that you have worked through your own personal problems so that you can be relaxed and cooperative, you are likely to contribute to the development of mental health in your students.

This is not to say that emotions should be strangled or eliminated from the classroom. Rather, they should be so conditioned that their intensity and duration are justified by the situation that provoked them. Emotions can add beauty and richness to life. They can be a driving force and a check on behavior. For example, love may drive a person to action and fear may restrain him from taking action. Within limits, students should have opportunities to participate in activities that possess emotion-arousing potentialities, such as aesthetic expression available in clothing or home furnishings experiences.

Working with emotionally disturbed students places you in a delicate situation. You can never be quite sure what to expect, and so your plans must be regarded as tentative, always subject to change if the class or an individual is restless. You may help by drawing a student into a casual conversation. You may let an individual work alone. Perhaps you will need to provide tasks in which a student could work off energy and get

[4] Ibid., pp. 35–39.

rid of pent-up emotion (such as polishing furniture, cleaning windows, or cleaning shelves). Your goal would be to improve the student's conduct immediately; then you could work on basic causes later. Many disturbed students need more love and understanding than the ones who receive normal amounts at home.

Tift gave examples of various situations and ways in which such students could be handled. Although the teacher responded differently to each problem, she pointed out that each time the approach included:

1. Stating clearly to the child what his inappropriate behavior consisted of.
2. Identifying your own feelings about this behavior.
3. Providing a supportive structure for a change of behavior.
4. Using, whenever appropriate, the participation of other students in this supportive structure.[5]

PHYSICALLY HANDICAPPED STUDENTS

The presence of a physically handicapped student in your classroom may cause you to have anxiety over your responsibility and the effects on the other students. The handicapped child has been defined by the Committee on Child Health of the American Public Health Association in this way:

> A child is considered to be handicapped if he cannot, within limits, learn, work, or do things other children of his age can do; if he is hindered in achieving his full physical, mental, and social potentialities. The initial disability may be very mild and hardly noticeable, but potentially handicapping, or it may seriously involve several areas of function, with the probability of lifelong impairment.[6]

When a handicapped student is placed in a regular class, he benefits from a feeling of being able to do what his peers do and his classmates gain understanding of the needs of a handicapped person. Although each handicapped person is an individual who has his own personality and needs, certain needs are basic to all individuals:

1. The need for belonging.
2. The need for achievement and recognition.
3. The need for economic security.
4. The need to be relatively free from fear.
5. The need for love and affection.

[5] Katharine F. Tift, "The Disturbed Child in the Classroom." *National Education Association Journal,* 57: 12–14, March 1968.

[6] Irving Ratchick and Frances G. Koenig, *Guidance and the Physically Handicapped Child.* Chicago: Science Research Associates, 1963, p. 5.

6. The need to be relatively free from feelings of guilt.
7. The need for self-respect and a willingness to share experiences with others.
8. The need for guiding purposes to direct one's life.[7]

If these needs are not met, the handicapped person is likely to experience:

1. Greater frustration than the unhandicapped experience.
2. Absence of many usual play and social activities.
3. Slowness in schoolwork owing to concern about the handicap.
4. Insecurity about the vocational future.
5. Withdrawal as an escape for meeting difficult situations.
6. Heightening and exaggeration of the problems of adolescence.[8]

There are too many different kinds of handicaps for us to consider in this book, but the following summary may alert you to some conditions that deserve special attention.

Cerebral Palsy

This orthopedic handicap may be evident in uncontrollable automatic movements, disturbed balance, awkward gait, and slurred speech. The individual may have trouble eating. Physical, occupational, and speech therapy may be required. Try to plan your program to develop his full academic and physical potential.

Diabetes

Symptoms include excessive thirst, frequent urination, loss of weight, and hunger. Diabetes can be controlled through diet, insulin, and drugs. Signs warning of insulin shock include sweating, nervousness, dizziness, and hunger. Sugar, candy, or orange juice may ward off insulin shock. Avoid overprotectiveness.

Epilepsy

A seizure may involve the loss of consciousness for only a few seconds or, in the case of *grand mal,* may involve a generalized convulsion. Epileptics may show moodiness, rigidity, meticulosity, pedantry, perseveration, desire for affectional security, and anger out of proportion to its cause.

Hearing Disorders

A deaf child is handicapped by an inadequate vocabulary and sometimes by defective speech. He may be submissive, introverted, suspicious,

[7] Ibid., p. 17.
[8] Ibid.

and slow learning. He may use lip-reading and he should be encouraged to use what hearing he has. The power to understand written ideas should be developed. All sorts of visual aids can be helpful.

Obesity

Overweight may result from faulty metabolism, hormonal imbalance, or emotional causes. Most obese children overeat. A diet under a physician's supervision is essential. An increased amount of physical exercise may be helpful. Since our society views an obese person as unattractive, psychological counseling may be necessary.

Speech Impairment

Speech handicaps may include *articulation* (sound production, omission, distortion, and substitution), *voice production* (pitch, quality, nasality, harshness), *fluency and rate* (rapid speaking, repetition), *stuttering,* and *aphasia* (difficulty in using various aspects of language). They may be related to cleft palate, impaired hearing, cerebral palsy, viruses, environment, family attitudes, shock, or psychogenic factors.

Visual Handicaps

The partially-sighted may be introverted, self-centered, unable to distinguish colors, and unduly sensitive to light. They may mask their feelings of inferiority. They need security, recognition, and acceptance. A creative teacher will help them use their hearing to the utmost, will provide tangible experiences, and will adapt visual materials in tactual form. Physical adjustments in the classroom, which may be helpful to the seeing students as well, include adjusting the light, preventing glare, and providing proximity of materials on boards or demonstration areas.

Sometimes a student chooses a handicapped person as a "best friend" just because of his disability. You should help your students realize that the physical disability should not be the reason for either accepting or rejecting a person.

Sometimes a person offers to help a disabled person because it makes him feel good. Actually, the hadicapped person may not need or want help. Certainly he does not want pity. His future depends upon his losing the label "different."

What can your students do when there is a handicapped student in the class? They can be sure to give that student the same chance for forming friendships as the other students have. They can try to understand any differences cause by his handicap. They can encourage him to participate in group activities he would enjoy and in which he would not hinder the group. They can assist him in laboratory activities if necessary.

In this chapter you have been exposed to a variety of problems, some of which you may observe among your students. Your classes can, and should, be meaningful to the exceptional student. As a member of a family—today and in the future—he will need to acquire confidence and competence to function in a variety of personal and family roles. Your home economics classes can help him acquire these. One procedure that you can use is to differentiate the assignments you give, according to the needs and abilities of the individual students. Some student will need assignments to parallel the classwork, to enable them to see the same concept from a different point of view. Other students can handle *supplementary* assignments that encourage them to probe a subject more deeply, gaining additional information related to the topic being studied. You will need to challenge other students through *complementary* assignments designed to help the students see this topic in relation to the other parts of which the complete set is composed.

Selected References

Barbe, Walter B., *The Exceptional Child.* Washington, D.C.: The Center for Applied Research in Education, 1963.

Barry, Ruth, and Beverly Wolf, *Motives, Values and Realities.* New York: Teachers College, Columbia University, 1966.

Brown, Ina C., *Understanding Other Cultures.* Englewood Cliffs, N.J.: Prentice-Hall, 1963.

Carter, Catherine, and Doris Manning, "Special Home Economics Offerings for the Academically Talented." *Illinois Teacher of Home Economics,* Vol. IV, No. 8, 1961, pp. 343–390.

Department of Home Economics, National Education Association, *The Slow Learner in Homemaking Education.* Washington, D.C.: National Education Association, DHE Topics 10, March 1959.

Fernandez, Louise, *The Gifted Student in Homemaking Education.* Washington, D.C.: National Education Association, DHE Topics 9, 1958.

Garrison, Karl C., and Dewey G. Force, *The Psychology of Exceptional Children.* New York: The Ronald Press Company, 1959.

Gezi, Kalil I., and James E. Myers, *Teaching in American Culture.* New York: Holt, Rinehart, and Winston, 1968, pp. 172–187.

Glasser, William, *Reality Therapy: A New Approach to Psychiatry.* New York: Harper & Row, 1965.

Glasser, William, *Schools Without Failure.* New York: Harper and Row, 1969.

Gordon, Milton M., *Assimilation in American Life.* New York: Oxford University Press, 1964.

Gottlieb, David, and Charles E. Ramsey, *Understanding Children of Poverty.* Chicago: Science Research Associates, 1967.

Gowan, John C., and George D. Demos (editors), *The Disadvantaged and Potential Dropout.* Springfield, Illinois: Charles C. Thomas, 1966.

Heck, Arch O., *The Education of Exceptional Children* (2nd ed.). New York: McGraw-Hill, 1953.

Holt, John, *How Children Fail.* New York: Pitman Publishing Corporation, 1964.

Illinois Teacher of Home Economics, *The Slow Learner—A Challenge and Responsibility.* Urbana, Illinois: University of Illinois, 1963.

Johnson, George O., *Education for the Slow Learners.* Englewood Cliffs, N.J.: Prentice-Hall, 1963.

Keenan, Dorothy M., "Home Economics and the Superior Student." *Illinois Teacher of Home Economics,* Vol. VII, No. 2, October 1963, pp. 45–86.

Kirk, Samuel A., *Educating Exceptional Children.* Boston: Houghton Mifflin, 1962.

Kolbourne, Luma L., *Effective Education for the Mentally Retarded Child.* New York: Vantage Press, 1965.

Kornrich, Milton (editor), *Underachievement.* Springfield, Illinois: Charles C. Thomas, 1965.

Lee, Dorothy, *Freedom and Culture.* Englewood Cliffs, N.J.: Prentice-Hall, 1959.

Long, Nicholas J., William C. Morse, and Ruth G. Newman (editors), *Conflict in the Classroom: The Education of Emotionally Disturbed Children.* Belmont: Wadsworth Publishing Co., 1965.

Passow, A. Harry (editor), *Education in Depressed Areas.* New York: Bureau of Publications, Teachers College, Columbia University, 1963.

Ratchick, Irving, and Frances G. Koenig, *Guidance and the Physically Handicapped Child.* Chicago: Science Research Associates, 1963.

Reissman, Frank, Jerome Cohen, and Arthur Pearl (editors), *Mental Health of the Poor.* New York: The Free Press, 1964.

Schultheis, Robert A., and Alvin Vaughn (editors), *Changing Undergraduate Business Teacher Education Programs To Prepare Teachers for Culturally Different Youth.* A Report of an Institute Cosponsored by the Department of Business Education of Temple University and the Center for Vocational and Technical Education. Philadelphia: Temple University, June 3–14, 1968.

Shostrom, Everett L., *Man, The Manipulator.* Nashville: Abingdon Press, 1967.

Strom, Robert D., *The Tragic Migration: School Dropouts.* Washington, D.C.: Department of Home Economics, National Education Association, 1964.

Thomas, R. Murray, *Social Differences in the Classroom.* New York: David McKay, 1965, pp. 3–45, 66–80.

Wall, W. D., F. J. Schonell, and Willard C. Olson, *Failure in School.* Hamburg: UNESCO Institute for Education, 1962.

Webster, Staten W. (editor), *The Disadvantaged Learner: Knowing, Understanding, Educating.* San Francisco: Chandler Publishing Company, 1966.

Wellington, G. Burleigh, and Jean Wellington, *The Underachiever: Challenges and Guidelines.* Chicago: Rand McNally, 1965.

PART IV

Evaluation of Progress in Home Economics

12

Evaluating Student Growth

Teaching is more than presenting facts—it is developing new ways of thinking, new skills for meeting life's problems, new habits, and new attitudes.

Evaluation of the progress being made by our students will very likely be one of the most difficult but rewarding experiences you have as a home economics teacher. The challenge of evaluation rests in planning suitable ways for collecting evidence of student learning and in using your findings to promote optimum growth of the students toward all of the objectives of your educational program.

PHILOSOPHY OF EVALUATION

The word "evaluation" implies much more than measurement. It involves gathering evidence about student behavior as a means of determining the extent to which the student is progressing toward potential goals. Evaluation is a process that demands resourcefulness and ingenuity on the part of the teacher; it is not a mechanical or routine means of assigning scores to the students.

Functions of Evaluation

In a school program evaluation serves three major purposes that might be classified as guidance, curricular, and administrative. As a home economics teacher you share responsibility for each of the three functions of evaluation even though your school has a specialist primarily responsible for each.

Guidance

Evaluation helps a teacher to know the individual needs, interests, and abilities of her students. (See Chapters 3, 4, and 5.) Information about a student's interests, reading speed and comprehension, personal and social adjustment, and aptitudes can enable you to work more effectively to meet the needs that are unique to each individual.

Standardized tests of intelligence and achievement are given in many school systems. Knowledge of an individual's ability in relation to his achievement can help you stimulate a student to greater accomplishment or assist a student in setting goals that are more nearly within his capabilities. Remember that a student who seems to be unintelligent may really be timid or lacking in motivation. Realistically, when we say a student is an underachiever, we mean that we have not been able to predict his performance accurately.

Furthermore, evaluation can help students to develop an understanding of their strengths and weaknesses and to learn how to plan for the future. Students need guidance in self-evaluation in order to learn to face themselves objectively and to realize the importance of growth toward independence. A school counselor or psychologist is available in most school systems to guide students with personal, educational, and vocational problems. Nevertheless, each teacher can help students in their adjustment by encouraging them to find out what their abilities are and to plan ways of overcoming weaknesses that might be interfering with their achievement.

Curricular

Home economics teachers look constantly for new ways of motivating students to learn. As a teacher becomes familiar with what students are capable of learning, she is able to differentiate the content that is most suitable for each grade level and for the abilities of each particular class. Artificial motivation decreases in importance as suitable learning experiences are planned. Through pretesting, a teacher can learn what a student already knows and thereby plan where he needs to start in her class.

Through a diagnosis of the degree to which specific objectives are being attained by your students, you can determine which subjects or objectives should receive more emphasis. A study of the factors that cause learning difficulties can help avert these problems in future classes.

Administrative

Home economics teachers are expected to assist with the administrative duties of the school by providing certain records and reports. Student records are the most familiar and probably the most time-consuming type of record for the average teacher. Their importance justifies careful attention. Evaluation techniques help a teacher to determine the extent to which an individual is achieving various educational objectives. With this information, she provides scores or ratings that can be used in the placement of students entering a new school, classification of students according to their ability, promotion to higher grades, selection of honors recipients, and determination of the qualification of graduates for admission to institutions of higher education.

Parents are entitled to information about the progress of their children; evaluation is the basis for improving public relations. Besides the periodic reports on their own children, community citizens (particularly the taxpayers) are concerned about what is being accomplished by the school. Since home economics education is often more expensive than many other phases of the school program, a home economics teacher needs to be prepared with facts to show the values and accomplishments of her program.

Proper evaluation of teaching is very important; therefore, the two following chapters are devoted to the appraisal of the physical and social environment of the classroom, and the self-appraisal of the teacher. A teacher cannot expect her students to grow in the ability to evaluate themselves unless she takes seriously her own responsibility for self-evaluation.

Characteristics of an Effective Evaluation Program

Four guides are suggested to help you determine the effectiveness of your evaluation program:

1. IS IT CONSISTENT WITH AND AN AID TO DEMOCRATIC HUMAN RELATIONSHIPS? America was founded on the recognition of the worth of each individual and his right to freedom of thought. The survival of democracy is dependent upon the extent to which individuals accept the responsibility for being informed and develop the ability to think critically. Democracy recognizes that, although all men have equal privileges, each is responsible for growing according to his ability.

As you plan your evaluation procedures, keep in mind that each of your students is worthy of respect and should experience, to some degree, the success that is in keeping with his ability. Remember that effective evaluation is not an opportunity for you to do something *to* a student, but rather to achieve something *with* him. The threat of evaluation can be removed when students and teachers realize that its true purpose is to help promote growth.

2. IS IT A CONTINUOUS PART OF AN EFFECTIVE LEARNING SITUATION? The psychology of an effective learning situation indicates that a learner needs to have confidence in his ability to learn, readiness to learn, emotional organization and ability to handle the learning situation, successful experi-

ences sufficient to maintain his interest and sense of worth, and knowledge of his progress.

Effective evaluation situations are built upon the same characteristics as is any other type of learning situation. An individual must have a sense of his worth, a readiness to be evaluated, an understanding of the purposes of the evaluation, the ability to maintain his emotional organization during the evaluation process, prompt knowledge of the results, and a willingness to accept and implement the results.

Evaluation is an integral part of the learning process. Very often the kind of evaluation that students expect during a unit of study influences the amount and quality of their learning. Likewise, the nature of the teaching is frequently influenced by the types of evaluation a teacher uses or plans to introduce during a unit.

Evaluation must be continuous in order to reach its maximum effectiveness. A home economics teacher needs to know about the background and achievement of students as they enter her class in order to make a fair estimate of how much they have gained from her class. As mentioned previously, she needs to evaluate continuously to find out how well the students are progressing toward the goals, to help them overcome difficulties or weaknesses in their learning, and to guide them in reshaping and defining new goals.

3. DOES IT INCLUDE AN APPRAISAL OF PROGRESS TOWARD ALL OF THE GOALS OF HOME ECONOMICS EDUCATION? Increased knowledge is probably the easiest goal to measure, but it is by no means the only important goal. The teacher should be concerned not only with the amount of information her students have acquired but also with their ability to locate further information; to know reliable sources from which they can find answers to related problems; to understand how to solve new problems; and to think critically about the information and opinions expressed by others. Unless the teacher helps the students to grow in self-direction, they will be handicapped in continuing to learn after completing their years of formal schooling.

Among the highly intangible goals of home economics education is growth in personal attributes. Evaluation should be planned to measure progress toward the growth of responsibility, cooperation, appreciations, interests, attitudes, values, and other aspects that contribute to effective home and family living.

4. DOES IT HELP BOTH THE TEACHER AND THE STUDENTS TO IDENTIFY THEIR OWN STRENGTHS AND WEAKNESSES AND TO PLAN INTELLIGENTLY FOR THE NEXT STEPS? Unless the results are used effectively, the time and effort demanded for the preparation and administration of evaluation techniques cannot be justified. Not every evaluation instrument needs

to fulfill each of the three functions described above. Nevertheless, each evaluation technique should be selected for a specific purpose; it should be developed and interpreted in terms of that particular function. Student growth in learning and ability should be a primary consideration when planning and using any form of evaluation. The teacher's effectiveness can be judged to a large extent by the growth of her students.

MEASURING STUDENT PROGRESS TOWARD LEARNING OBJECTIVES

In carrying out the functions and characteristics of an effective evaluation program, a teacher may select instruments that someone else has developed or she may choose to prepare her own techniques. Although one of the purposes of this chapter is to introduce you to some of the tests that others have found useful, you need to weigh very carefully how well such tests really meet your needs. Since an effective home economics education program is planned in accordance with the needs of a particular community and individual students, an evaluation instrument that was highly successful in one situation may be most inappropriate and inadequate for another setting. Evaluation must be in terms of what was taught—the objectives of your own program. A good test helps define your objectives for your students. Students tend to do those things they know they are expected to do.

Criteria for Effective Instruments

The following criteria should help you determine the effectiveness of an evaluation instrument, whether prepared by you or someone else:

1. VALIDITY. The most important characteristic of any test is its validity—the extent to which it is capable of achieving your aims. When you are examining a test that has been published, you should read the test manual to find out what the test *claims* to measure. No matter how well a test fulfills its claims, that test will be valid for you only to the extent that you use it with students who have the necessary background and maturity to understand the directions and to respond to the questions. Furthermore, you must provide proper conditions for the administration of the test. A quiet room, physical comfort, and motivation for the students to do their best are among the conditions that increase the validity of a test situation.

Validity may be determined by studying the test content or by comparing assessments with outside criteria. *Content* (or *curricular*) validity means that the test adequately covers the material that textbooks, courses of study, and opinions of experts consider to be important in a particular subject area. When you select or plan a test, be sure that it represents a good sampling of your course content, emphasizing the aptitudes, skills, and knowledge in proportion to their relative importance in the course. A good means of insuring content validity is to determine in advance a "table of specifications" showing that each topic is sampled in proportion to its emphasis in the course and that important behavioral objectives are evaluated. Table 9 shows the specifications that were outlined for an objective test in foods and nutrition.

TABLE 9 Table of Specifications for a Short-Answer Test in Foods and Nutrition *

	Percentage of Items that Test Each Objective †			
Areas of Food and Nutrition	Knowledge of facts (25%)	Under-standing of concepts (30%)	Ability to apply principles (45%)	Per cent of items included
Nutrition and menu planning (30%)	5%	10%	15%	30%
Principles of cooking (25%)	10%	5%	10%	25%
Preparation and serving of foods and meals (25%)	0	10%	10%	20%
Selection (purchases of food (10%)	5%	5%	5%	15%
Care and storage of food (10%)	5%	5%	0	10%
Total	25%	35%	40%	100%

* Indiana Home Economics Association. *Evaluation in Home Economics.* Lafayette, Ind.: Purdue University, 1957, p. 6.

† Proposed percentages of items shown in parentheses; actual percentage shown without parentheses.

A second way of determining validity is by *comparison with outside criteria* (such as school marks, ratings of experts, or other tests covering similar objectives). Concurrent validity refers to the correlation between a test and assessment when both measures are taken at about the same time. When test results are compared with future ratings of success in college, homemaking, or employment outside of the home, you may gain helpful information about the predictive validity of your evaluation instruments.

2. RELIABILITY. Validity is closely related to the concept of reliability.

A valid test must be reliable; the reverse is not true, however, for a test can be reliable without being valid. A reliable test is one that yields accurate and consistent results.

Reliability is determined by a comparison of two measures obtained by: (1) retest; (2) comparable forms; or (3) a subdivided test. In the *retest* method, the same test is administered to the same individuals with sufficient time between the two tests for the students to forget what was covered. Even with a time interval between the two testings, one might find some increase in scores due to the practice effects. The *comparable forms* method consists of the use of two forms that are similar in content and difficulty. One is used on the first occasion and the other at a later time with the same students and under similar conditions. Using comparable forms provides a greater sampling of the items for measuring certain abilities. *Subdividing* (or the split-halves method) involves a single test used on one occasion. Two scores for each individual are obtained by subdividing the test. Usually one score is based upon the odd-numbered items and the other on the even-numbered items. The correlation of these two sets of scores is used to estimate the reliability that would result from the full-length test. Specific methods for computing test reliability may be found in the references at the end of this chapter.

As a beginning teacher, you should be concerned about ways of increasing the reliability of your tests. In general, increasing the length of a test makes it more reliable, providing the additional items are similar in difficulty and discrimination to those that were included in the shorter tests. Clear, simple directions and clear, concise items contribute to test reliability. Reliability is enhanced as the chances of guessing are reduced. In the case of objective items, four or five alternatives are more effective than only two alternatives in reducing the number of correct answers that can be obtained merely by guessing. Another means of increasing reliability is to develop accuracy and objectivity in scoring. An inflexible key, which lists the correct answers and any acceptable synonyms, can be used by two persons to yield identical results or can be used by the same person on two different occasions with consistent results.

3. USEFULNESS. The utility of an evaluation instrument depends a great deal upon its ease of use. One aspect that contributes to its usefulness is *ease of administration.* A test should contain clear and simple directions on the test itself, even though oral directions may be used to supplement them. When new or unfamiliar types of items are used, practice exercises or illustrations should be included. The weight, value and/or suggested time limits for each item or subsection should be indicated on the test.

Ease of scoring contributes to the usefulness of a test as well as to its reliability. Scoring errors are usually of two types: (1) constant errors, which may result from misunderstanding of the directions for scoring; and (2) variable errors, which may result from the introduction of the scorer's subjective judgment or his carelessness in computing scores. The use of strip keys and cut-out stencils makes possible accurate scoring that is simple, rapid, and routine.

Economy is a factor that may influence the ease of using a test. The length of time required for a test and the costs of test copies are two important considerations. Nevertheless, you can determine the true economy of a test only in terms of the degree to which it fulfills an important objective.

Principles of Test Construction

This portion of the chapter presents first some of the general principles of preparing a test and then some suggestions that are applicable to the construction of many types of test items.

Preparing a Test

The first step in preparing any type of evaluation instrument is to state your objectives and prepare a grid to guide you in covering all of the important outcomes of instruction with proper emphasis. One test cannot measure all of the outcomes of instruction, but it should include a large enough number of items to give an adequate representation of the student's ability and knowledge. As you clarify your objectives, try to think of the kinds of behavior a student should manifest if he is fulfilling each objective. For example, if your student has acquired the *knowledge* you have been teaching, what will he be able to do? You can list what he should be able to recall, recognize, or select. If he has developed an *understanding* in line with your objectives, what should he be able to explain, interpret, infer, generalize, summarize, or relate? Your next step is to decide on suitable ways of measuring progress in the kinds of behavior you have described.

When you are ready to start preparing items, allow sufficient time so that you can draft them early. At a later time you can appraise them more effectively than at the time of writing, particularly if you try taking the test yourself from the students' viewpoint.

Here are some suggestions for the selection and arrangement:

1. A major test should usually include more than one type of item, so as to hold the interest of the students and to provide an opportunity for individual students to show what they can do with a type of item they can handle.

2. Generally restrict a test to not more than three types of items, to avoid confusion in going from one set of directions to another.
3. All items of a particular type should be grouped together.
4. Within each group, progress from the easiest items to the more difficult ones, thereby encouraging every student to feel that he has a chance for success.
5. Test items should be arranged at random so the responses do not fall into a regular sequence.
6. Each item should be independent of the other items to prevent a person from obtaining an answer from another item.
7. Concise, yet clear and complete, directions should be included for each part of the test. The student should know what he is expected to do, how to proceed, and where to indicate his responses.
8. When a test is typed, all parts of a question should be placed on one page for easy reference.
9. Responses should be made in a simple and convenient manner, usually in columns provided by blanks beside the item numbers either at the left or right of the page.
10. An answer key and a simple method of scoring should be prepared in advance.

Construction of Test Items

A good practice, when writing test items, is to place each item on a separate card. Usually a 5 x 8-inch card is used because that size provides enough room for the objective, key, item analysis information, and notes on the effectiveness of the item.

Here are some specific suggestions for writing effective items:

1. Select a type of item that is best suited for the content and specific objective you wish to measure.
2. Use items that require the students to apply their learnings, not merely to recall or recognize information.
3. Select items that provide new situations in which the students can test their ability to apply their learnings. Statements that are taken directly from a text or reference book lack validity in measuring understanding and application of knowledge.
4. Make the entire content of an item homogeneous and plausible, so that the student will have to think before determining an answer.
5. The content of an item, rather than the form of statement or its wording, should determine the correctness of an answer.
6. Make items short and definite, including only one independent idea in each question.

7. Word the items simply, using language familiar to students.

8. Whenever possible, select items that include more than two choices, to reduce the possibility of guessing.

9. Make sure there is only one correct answer, unless the directions indicate some other procedure.

10. Use correct grammar, and do not give irrelevant clues to the correct answer (through the use of such words as "a" or "an").

11. Be sure to clarify any words that are qualitative or that have hidden meanings if such words are used.

Measuring Knowlege and Understanding

Knowledge includes the facts that one has learned about people, places, events, objects, principles, and practices. Understanding involves the ability to comprehend what is being communicated, evaluate its accuracy, relate it to other ideas, and structure these ideas into a suitable communication or plan of work. Knowledge and understanding can be measured in a variety of ways through essay, recall, or recognition items.

Essay

An essay item is one in which a student is free to develop his answer as he chooses. The principal advantages of essay tests are (1) emphasis on ability to organize knowledge and express ideas logically; (2) the necessity for a student to organize his knowledge into an integrated whole in order to interpret, compare, criticize, and/or defend a particular situation; (3) adaptability of questions to a variety of subject matter; (4) ease in construction and administration of tests; and (5) the permitting of a student to qualify his answer rather than make an unequivocable response.

A number of situations in which essay questions are suitable are listed below with brief suggestions as to how to use them:

1. ANALYZE THE CAUSE OR EFFECT.
   a. How might you account for_________(a given effect)_________?
   b. If you do_____(a given action—cause)_____, what might happen?
2. COMPARE TWO THINGS.
   a. On a specific point.
   b. In general.
3. CONTRAST TWO THINGS.
   a. On a specific point.
   b. In general.
4. CRITICIZE. On specific points such as adequacy, correctness, or relevancy.

5. DESCRIBE OR ILLUSTRATE. The application of a given principle.
6. EVALUATE. Selective recall.
   a. Discuss three important developments in ______________.
   b. Name three persons who had the greatest influence on _______.
7. EXPLAIN.
   a. The use of some object.
   b. The meaning of a word or phrase.
8. INTERPRET.
   a. Data contained in tabular or graphic form.
   b. Information given on a label.
   c. Newspaper articles or other writings.
9. OUTLINE.
   a. The major steps in a given procedure.
   b. The significant ideas in a movie, book, or magazine article.
10. RELATE.
   a. Decide whether two things are related.
   b. Explain the relationship between two things.
11. SUMMARIZE.
   a. Discuss the major ideas of a book or article.
   b. Discuss the author's purpose.
   c. Discuss the advantages and limitations of ______________.
   d. State the conclusion of ______________.

Gorow gave an example of an essay question built around a real-life situation. The students were shown a large colored picture of a furnished room. The problem was stated this way: "You have inherited your mother-in-law's house and plan to move in. This is the living room. Using the six principles of design, explain what is successful in the room as it now exists. What would you change and why?" [1]

The most serious limitation of essay questions is their *low validity*. Essay questions are limited in their sampling of course content and may be inadequate to show what a student has really learned. Furthermore, students may take advantage of the freedom to discuss as they see fit by bluffing or bringing in irrelevant information. Extraneous factors, such as handwriting, neatness, spelling, grammar, length of the answer, or organization, may have greater influence on the scorer than what the student has said. Another limitation of essay questions is their *low reliability* or subjectivity of scoring. "Constant" errors may result from the tendency of a teacher to be hard or easy in marking. Persons vary in their marking from time to time. The "halo effect" may cause a per-

[1] Frank F. Gorow, *Better Classroom Testing*. San Francisco: Chandler Publishing Company, 1966, p. 91.

son to rate an individual high or low in accordance with a general impression that carries over to specific ratings. The final limitation of essay tests is their *low usefulness.* Essay tests are time-consuming because they permit students to answer only a few questions, and because they take a long time to grade. They are difficult to evaluate statistically.

The following suggestions may help you to make effective use of essay questions:

1. Decide on the objectives you wish to measure.
2. To achieve a wider sampling of the course content, increase the number of questions but decrease the amount of discussion required for each question.
3. Teach the students how to answer essay questions.
4. Require all students to answer the same questions. When a choice is given among items, the students are actually taking different tests, which may have varying levels of difficulty.
5. Indicate the value and/or time limit of each question or part of a question.
6. Call for specific responses by providing an outline of the points to be discussed.
7. Prepare in advance a list of the important points and acceptable answers.
8. Grade one question on all of the papers before proceeding to the next question. This method of scoring has two advantages: (*a*) you can conceal the identity of the individual whose paper is being scored; and (*b*) you can increase the consistency of your scoring by concentrating your thoughts on one question at a time.
9. Answers may be scored by allowing one credit for each acceptable point that was covered. An alternate method is to read each answer and classify it as *excellent, good,* or *poor* (or *A, B, C, D,* or *F*). The papers in each classification should then be re-read to be sure that they represent similar levels of response.

Recall

Simple recall items are stated in the form of a direct question, requiring a single word or phrase as an answer. Completion items are in the form of a sentence in which a word or phrase has been omitted. Recall items have many advantages: (1) measuring retention of knowledge; (2) measuring application of certain types of knowledge; (3) adaptability to many subject areas; (4) wide sampling of the students' learnings; (5) demand for accuracy; and (6) ease of construction.

Here are examples of information for which recall items are suited.

1. COMPUTATION.
   a. Estimating amount of yardage necessary for clothing or home furnishing.
   b. Equivalent measurements.

Example: [2]

It is important to learn how to interpret a recipe. The biscuit recipe written below will serve *two* people. Enlarge the recipe to serve *six* people. Place the correct answer on the blank beside the item number.

Serves 2	*Serves 6*
1 c. flour	1. ______ c. flour
1/4 tsp. salt	2. ______ tsp. salt
1 tsp. baking powder	3. ______ tbsp. baking powder
1 tbsp. shortening	4. ______ tbsp. shortening
4 tbsp. milk	5. ______ c. milk

2. IDENTIFICATION.
   a. who—person
   b. when—date, time, or sequence in a procedure
   c. where—location of equipment, place to carry out an activity
   d. what—proper equipment or name

Example: [3]

The child who plays beside rather than with other children and who plays independently but with toys similar to those used by other children is displaying ____________________.

3. ANALOGY.
   a. Supply either the cause or the effect.
   b. Generalize or state a principle.
   c. Provide an example.

Example:

White is one neutral color; another is ____________________.

Recall items have certain limitations, particularly a tendency to overemphasize verbal facility, memorization, and the association of facts. Where short, clear answers are satisfactory, recall items have a place. However, students may find that recall items are time-consuming in their

[2] Betty Bradlyn, "Evaluation Devices for Homemaking at the Junior High School Level." Unpublished report, University of California, Los Angeles, 1956.

[3] Marjorie Brown and Jane Plihal, *Evaluation Materials For Use in Teaching Child Development*. Minneapolis: Burgess Publishing Company, 1966, p. 89.

demand for an exact word. You may find subjectivity entering into the scoring process because of the variety of answers that might be possible and because certain answers will be only partially correct. Recall items are used extensively and are easy to construct, but they do not always measure complete understanding.

The following suggestions may help you to construct and use recall items effectively:

1. Require problem-solving or the application of previous learning, not merely the retention of knowledge.
2. If possible, write statements in which only one correct response could be used. If more than one response is correct, all acceptable responses should be indicated on the scoring key.
3. Be specific in indicating the type of response desired. The item, "Rayon is a ________ fabric," does not indicate whether you are seeking an idea of its cost, fiber classification, physical properties, or some other factor.
4. Omit the *key word* rather than a trivial detail.
5. If more than one blank is included in a sentence, be sure that the meaning is clear and not lost in the mutilation of the sentence.
6. Avoid giving clues in the word preceding the blank ("a" or "an," "was" or "were").
7. When possible, have an omitted word at or near the end of the sentence.
8. Arrange the blanks in a column, usually at the right of the page, for ease in scoring.
9. Allow one credit for each blank. Avoid fractional credits and unequal weighting of items.
10. Minor misspellings are usually counted as correct answers unless the objective of the item is to measure spelling ability.

True-False

Probably everyone is familiar with the true-false item in its simplest form, in which a statement is given and the student reacts to its truth. Among their major advantages, true-false questions are easy to use. They are relatively easy to construct, familiar to the students, quick to answer, quick and objective in their scoring, and wide in their sampling of subject matter. They are useful in reviewing a previous lesson, promoting interest in a new topic, and introducing controversial points to stimulate discussion. Modified forms of true-false items can be used to measure judgment, recall, and complete understanding of a topic. They are somewhat realistic in that persons in everyday life are confronted with situations in which they must judge the truth or falsity of a variety of statements.

The basic types of true-false items include the following:

1. SIMPLE TRUE-FALSE OR YES-NO. Some people favor the question with a yes or no response, thinking that the student will not pick up or retain as much misinformation as he might from reading false statements.

Examples:

a. The return on savings in a savings and loan association is generally higher than the return on savings in a bank.	True	False
b. Is a month's income usually the minimum amount to keep as a reserve fund?	Yes	No

2. MODIFIED TRUE-FALSE. Modified true-false items require recall and therefore have advantages and limitations similar to those described above. Students may be directed to cross out the word that makes a statement false or to identify the word that makes a statement false and substitute a word to make it true.

3. CLUSTER TRUE-FALSE. An incomplete statement is given or a situation is described, and then several items must be considered as true or false in terms of the practical situation. These items measure understanding of a central idea.

Example: [4]

Whole grain cereals are valuable in the diet of a one-year-old because they

1. Provide energy 1. _____
2. Are rich in Vitamin D 2. _____
3. Aid in elimination 3. _____
4. Help him learn to chew his food 4. _____
5. Are relatively inexpensive 5. _____

4. INCREASED NUMBER OF CHOICES. Instead of forcing a student to decide whether a statement is absolutely true or false, a wider range of choices is sometimes given so that a student may rate each statement as follows:

T—Entirely True
GT—Generally True
GF—Generally False
F—Absolutely False

The quality of true-false items is often inadequate for measuring achievement. Many items tend to stress insignificant bits of information. Once you have tried writing true-false items you will realize the difficulty

[4] State High School Tests for Indiana, *Child Development,* Form A.

of writing statements that are completely true or false without being obvious. When the subject matter is controversial, this difficulty increases. From their frequent exposure to true-false questions, students have learned to detect irrelevant clues, such as grammatical construction or the choice of words. Questions having only two possible choices are conducive to guessing and therefore may not be as discriminating as other types of objective questions.

To overcome some of these objections, you might try the following suggestions when you write or select true-false items:

1. Restrict each statement to one central idea.
2. Make the point of the question clear. Avoid "trick" questions.
3. A false element should be part of the *reason* rather than the basic part of a statement.
4. In general, avoid the use of "specific determiners" that make an answer obvious. You might use them deliberately for statements in which the correct answer is the opposite of what is usually the case when such words are used. The following list contains the usual meanings of common "specific determiners":

Usually False		*Usually True*	
all	never	could	often
alone	no	frequently	should
always	none	generally	some
cause	nothing	may	sometimes
every	only	most	usually
everyone	reason		

5. Use quantitative rather than qualitative language. Avoid the use of such words as the following, which have different meanings for various persons:

few	great	many	principal
frequently	important	more	several

6. Keep the true and the false sentences approximately the same in length. You may find, as others have found, that you have a tendency to make the true statements longer than the false ones.
7. Approximately half of the statements should be true and half false, with these responses distributed at random so as not to form a regular sequence or a pattern.

Multiple-Choice

In a multiple-choice question the problem is presented in the form of a direct question, description of a situation, or an incomplete sentence.

Several possible answers are listed and the respondent is directed to choose the answer or answers most appropriate for that type of item. Here are some common types of multiple-choice items:

1. ONE RIGHT ANSWER. The respondent is directed to choose the one *correct* answer.

Example: [5]

The warp threads are threads running
a. diagonally across the material
b. lengthwise of the material
c. crosswise of the material
d. at right angles to the selvedge

2. BEST ANSWER. The respondent chooses the *correct* or *best* answer.

Example: [6]

Ruth, a high school girl, had completed her Child Care course in Homemaking and was working for the summer, taking care of Nancy, age 4. Nancy is independent, very often likely to dawdle, and insists on having her own way. She demands considerable attention. When Nancy has a poor appetite and plays with her food, Ruth might handle the situation in several ways. For each method suggested, choose *one* of the five possible effects which it might have on the development of good habits in a child:

A—May help to form a good habit that would be practiced regularly.
B—May handle the problem at the moment, but fail to correct the real cause of the difficulty.
C—May not be effective at this age level.
D—May interfere with learning by building up resistance.
E—May develop an undesirable habit.

1. Serve small servings; give seconds if she has eaten all the food on her plate. 1. ____
2. Plan a special dessert or a treat for a reward for "cleaning up" her plate. 2. ____
3. Let her eat when she is hungry. 3. ____
4. Urge her to eat, forcing her if need be so that she will have food. 4. ____
5. Remove her plate after 30 minutes and serve fruit juice in midafternoon. 5. ____

3. MULTIPLE-RESPONSE. Students may be directed as to the number of answers to select or they may simply be told to indicate the correct answer or answers for each item.

[5] State High School Tests for Indiana. *Clothing I,* Form A, p. 9.

[6] Adapted from Dorothy Rowe, *Test on Child Development—Routine Habits and Play,* Form A. Unpublished, Syracuse University, Syracuse, p. 3.

Example: [7]

Choose two cooking methods for preparing porterhouse, T-bone, and club steaks.

a. braising
b. broiling
c. cooking in water
d. pan broiling

4. REVERSE MULTIPLE-CHOICE. In this type of item, all but one of the responses is correct. The student is directed to select the *wrong* response. Since many situations have a variety of suitable solutions, a teacher may find it easier to write several correct answers than to think of plausible wrong answers. However, when such a reverse item is used, it should be separated from the regular type, and emphasis should be given to the negative quality of the item.

Example: [8]

Which of the following is *not* a suitable plaything for the three-year-old?

a. a small wheelbarrow
b. a soft ball
c. crayons and color book
d. scissors for cutting pictures

The reverse type of item may be combined with the multiple-response type. Respondents are directed to indicate the *best* answer and the *worst* answer for each question.

Multiple-choice items have many advantages: (1) versatility; (2) measuring the student's ability to recognize, which includes a wider range than what one can recall; (3) measuring the *identification of facts* such as definitions, the *understanding of principles* such as causes and effects or similarities and differences, and the *application of knowledge,* such as an evaluation of what is best for a given purpose and why, the sequence in which to achieve a given purpose, and reasons in support of controversial subjects; (4) students' familiarity with such items; (5) reducing opportunities for guessing, especially when four or five alternative choices are included; and (6) objective scoring.

In spite of their many advantages, multiple-choice items are subject to certain limitations. They may stress the memorization of facts rather than application of knowledge. It is difficult to write several relevant, plausible decoys. Another difficulty is experienced in keeping more than one response from being correct when only one is intended. Multiple-

[7] Wisconsin State Board of Vocational and Adult Education, *Homemaking Evaluation Devices.* Homemaking Series Bulletin No. HM 711, April 1950, p. 26.

[8] Clara B. Arny, *Minnesota Tests for Household Skills: Child Care.* Chicago: Science Research Associates, 1952, p. 3.

choice items are time-consuming to prepare and, also, to give because of the reading time required and the necessity of making fine discriminations among the alternatives.

As you select or construct multiple-choice items, you may find the following ideas helpful:

1. State the question first as a recall item and have the students write free responses. From their responses you can select relevant, plausible alternatives, and you will know how to word them in language that is familiar to the students. In this way you can gradually build a file of objective items for use with future classes.
2. An introductory statement should be complete and specific in defining the problem. Usually the stem, or introduction, is longer than the responses need to be.
3. The use of four or five alternatives reduces the possibility of obtaining correct answers by guessing. However, each alternative must seem plausible to someone who is not well-informed, or the item is no better than a two- or three-choice item.
4. A grammatically correct statement should be formed when each response is attached to the stem. Each response should follow a consistent style.
5. List responses on separate lines, not in paragraph form.
6. When figures or dates are used, arrange them in numerical order.
7. Correct and incorrect responses should be similar in length.
8. The position of the correct response should be scattered at random so as not to form a regular sequence.

Matching

Students are given two or more lists of items from which they are to select pairs. The same list of responses must be applicable to several items contained in the *stimulus* list. Matching items may involve *perfect* matching, consisting of the same number of items in each list, with each response used only once. These items are not likely to be very discriminating because of the possibility that a student can obtain the correct answers to the last few items merely on the basis of what is left after eliminating the ones that he knows.

Imperfect matching, which helps to overcome this problem, is of two types: (1) a few responses are included that do not match any item in the stimulus list; or (2) responses may be used more than once. The following is an example of imperfect matching: [9]

[9] Clara B. Arny et al., *Minnesota Tests for Household Skills: Cleaning*. Chicago: Science Research Associates, 1952, p. 1.

The kitchen in the average home needs a good deal of attention in order to keep it clean and orderly. Some of the cleaning jobs need to be done several times a day, some once a day, and others less often. In the answer column at the right of *each job* listed below, encircle the letter corresponding to the interval at which it should be done.

Interval of Time	*Cleaning Job*	
A. Several times a day	1. Clean sink	1. A B C D
B. Daily	2. Wash walls	2. A B C D
C. Monthly	3. Wipe top of stove	3. A B C D
D. Occasionally when needed	4. Wipe counter tops	4. A B C D
	5. Empty garbage can	5. A B C D
	6. Straighten and wipe out cupboards	6. A B C D

Compound matching, which involves the matching of items from the stimulus list with more than one response, is illustrated in the following problem.[10]

For each situation described below, select the best type of finish for the placket opening. In the blank in the column labeled "Choice," write the letter corresponding to the most appropriate finish; in the blank labeled "Reason," write the letter corresponding to the reason why it is desirable.

Types of finishes for placket openings	**Reasons for choosing**
A. Bias binding	E. Adapted for use of a zipper
B. Continuous-bound placket	F. Decorative
C. Fitted facing	G. Flat
D. Lap pocket	H. Produces a tailored effect

Choice	**Reason**	**Situations**
______ 1.	______ 6.	Neckline slash in a voile blouse.
______ 2.	______ 7.	Neckline slash in a wool crepe dress.
______ 3.	______ 8.	Slash in the bottom of a full sleeve gathered into a cuff, in a dress of heavy silk
______ 4.	______ 9.	Placket in a dart in a tight-fitting sleeve of rayon crepe.
______ 5.	______ 10.	Underarm seam in a wool gabardine dress which fits very snugly.

Listed below are some of the innumerable situations in home economics education that lend themselves to matching questions.

1. CAUSES AND EFFECTS.

   a. Causes of difficulties and the nature of sewing machine difficulties.

[10] Clara B. Arny, *Evaluation in Home Economics.* New York: Appleton-Century-Crofts, 1953, pp. 138–139.

   b. Nutrients in which a diet is deficient and the body conditions that may be due to these deficiencies.
2. EVENTS WITH DATES, PLACES, OR FREQUENCY. Interval of time for various cleaning tasks.
3. PERSONS AND THEIR CONTRIBUTIONS. Family members and their privileges or responsibilities.
4. PRINCIPLES AND SITUATIONS IN WHICH THEY APPLY.
   a. Color schemes and color combinations that illustrate them.
   b. Types of leavening and foods in which they are used.
   c. Nutrients and foods in which they are found.
5. PROBLEMS AND THEIR SOLUTIONS.
   a. Pattern corrections for various fitting difficulties.
   b. Procedures to remove specific stains.
   c. First aid needed for certain accidents or illnesses.
   d. Types of insurance suitable for various family situations.
6. SYMBOLS, ABBREVIATIONS, OR PARTS WITH THEIR PROPER NAMES OR EQUIVALENTS.
   a. Measurements and equivalent amounts.
   b. Abbreviations and what they represent.
7. WORDS AND THEIR MEANINGS.
   a. Fibers or fabrics and their characteristics.
   b. Names of finishes and the finishing processes.
   c. Definitions and names of cooking processes.

Matching questions are relatively easy to construct because of the variety of associations possible through such words as "who," "what," "when," "where," and "how." They can provide a wide sampling of students' information and understanding. Matching items minimize guessing (especially if lists of items are uneven), require little space on the test paper, are objective, and are easy to score.

Although many types of information can be covered in matching questions, they may tend to overemphasize the acquisition of facts and to be inadequate in measuring complete understanding or ability to apply knowledge. One of the major difficulties you may experience in writing matching items is in finding sufficient homogeneous items to make satisfactory lists. Phrases must be kept short and unintentional clues should not be given.

Among the aids that might help you prepare or judge matching questions are the following:

1. The basis for matching should be clear so the question measures the accuracy of matching rather than understanding of the basis for matching.

2. Restrict a stimulus list to *five* or *ten* items. If you wish to cover more than twelve items, use two separate questions.

3. Each column should contain only homogeneous material that is applicable to the items contained in the other list.

4. Include two or three extra responses, usually in the column that contains the shorter items, or permit the responses to be used more than once.

5. Items in the response column should be arranged in logical order, such as alphabetically or numerically.

6. Columns should be arranged close together for easy reference. When fairly long items are used in both lists, the response list may be placed above the stimulus list.

7. The entire question should be placed on the same page.

Application of Knowledge

Knowledge that is truly understood may be applied in a variety of ways such as making comparisons, determining causes and effects, seeing relationships, forming conclusions, and solving new problems. The possession of certain knowledge or skill does not guarantee that an individual will be able to apply it in solving a problem. However, a problem cannot be solved by a student who lacks the essential knowledge or skill.

Problem-solving situations may be drawn from such sources as newspapers, magazines, classroom experiences, or personal contacts. Whatever the source, the situation should be new to the students; yet it should present a familiar kind of problem that requires them to think about what they have learned and how it applies in this new situation.

Ability to apply knowledge can be measured through simple objective items such as those illustrated earlier in this chapter. Some of the more complex types of items are shown below:

1. FORMING A CONCLUSION.[11]

In the Harman household, the dinner hour provides the first opportunity of the day for the entire family to share each other's experiences. While the children were growing up, they enjoyed the chance to listen and be listened to. Having reached high school age, they are no longer willing to share in these discussions, showing resentment when their parents try to draw them out concerning their experiences at school and with their friends.

Do you consider it right of their parents to expect them to discuss their affairs this way? Circle YES or NO to indicate your answer.

Directions: Below are listed both good and poor reasons for your answer. Select three which you think apply to your answer and rank them from best

[11] Indiana Home Economics Association, *Evaluation in Home Economics.* Lafayette, Ind.: Purdue University, 1957, p. 33.

to poorest. Place the numeral 1 by the best; 2 by the second best; and 3 by the poorest reason.

_____ 1. You should realize that your parents are really interested in what you are doing and not just prying into your affairs.
_____ 2. If your parents are doing everything they can to make you happy at school and elsewhere, you should try to repay them by your actions.
_____ 3. You should go ahead and do what your parents expect of you even if you don't want to, rather than to hurt their feelings.
_____ 4. Parents are likely to make fun of your ideas and affairs so you hesitate to confide in them.
_____ 5. Sometimes you just feel like handling your affairs your own way and think you are entitled to your independence.
_____ 6. When you are of high school age your affairs are your own business.

2. JUDGING THE DESIRABILITY OF VARIOUS CHOICES.[12]

Mr. and Mrs. Jones have two children. Fifteen-year-old Judy is of average intelligence. Thirteen-year-old Bobby is mentally handicapped. Judy never brings any of her friends home because Bobby screams for a half hour at the sight of a strange face. Mr. and Mrs. Jones don't take Bobby anywhere because he becomes emotionally upset. Mrs. Jones is confined to their home because Bobby requires constant supervision so that he doesn't physically harm himself. Bobby does not respond to anyone's attention or affection. He is content to be left alone with his building blocks if he is not upset by unfamiliar people, places, or objects. Mr. and Mrs. Jones have taken Bobby to several doctors and psychologists but they all agree that nothing can be done to help him.

Considering the welfare of the entire family, what is the wisest action (not necessarily their preferred action) Mr. and Mrs. Jones could take?

_____ 1. Continue to search for a psychologist who is capable of helping Bobby through intensive therapy.
_____ 2. Arrange for Bobby's permanent care in a state or private institution for mentally retarded children.
_____ 3. Keep Bobby at home to be certain he receives the individual love and instruction that he requires.
_____ 4. Rebuild one room in their home that would be physically safe for Bobby and restrict him to this room.

Check the statements below that support your choice above.

_____ 1. Mentally retarded children, more than other children, need their parent's love and acceptance.
_____ 2. In making decisions, parents must consider each family member's individual needs that must be met.
_____ 3. New discoveries that are continually being made in the field of psychology give us hope that someday, perhaps soon, there will be a treatment for mental retardation.
_____ 4. Each family is responsible for the welfare of its members and

[12] Brown and Plihal, op. cit., pp. 66–67.

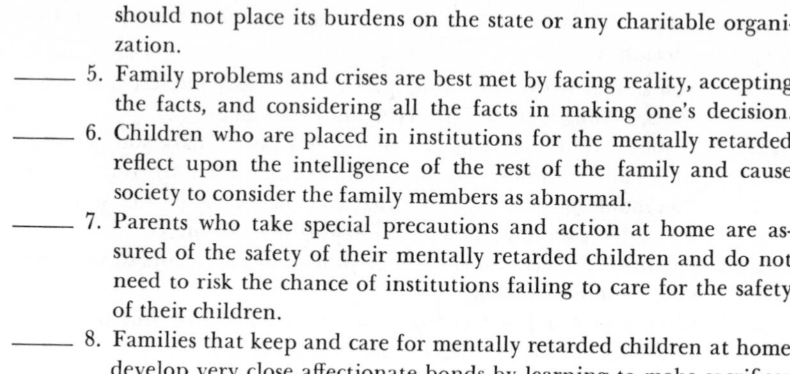

should not place its burdens on the state or any charitable organization.

_____ 5. Family problems and crises are best met by facing reality, accepting the facts, and considering all the facts in making one's decision.

_____ 6. Children who are placed in institutions for the mentally retarded reflect upon the intelligence of the rest of the family and cause society to consider the family members as abnormal.

_____ 7. Parents who take special precautions and action at home are assured of the safety of their mentally retarded children and do not need to risk the chance of institutions failing to care for the safety of their children.

_____ 8. Families that keep and care for mentally retarded children at home develop very close affectionate bonds by learning to make sacrifices for the retarded children.

Complex items such as these present problems of scoring. Does a student deserve credit for making the best choice if he does not check the proper reasons for his choice? Should he receive credit for reasons that are consistent with his choice, when his choice is not the best answer? You may find it possible to weigh the choices so the best answer receives the most credit, the next best answer receives some credit, and the poorest answer receives no credit. Perhaps you can set up a key to indicate which reasons should be given by students who check each of the possible choices. Then, a student who may not have checked the best answer can still receive partial credit for giving reasons that are consistent with his choice.

The use of pictures can be particularly effective in test items that require students to apply their learnings. Real photographs, diagrams, or small sketches help to simulate a natural situation better than words alone can do. Good pictorial items may convey their intent better than verbal items. They may reduce the number of words needed and thereby require less reading time. One of their major contributions is the interest they add to a testing situation.

Pictorial items are not always used to the best advantage. Remember that reproduced pictures must retain all the fine details of the originals (of course, the originals must be of high quality to be satisfactorily copied). As you select test items, keep in mind that (1) using a picture may or may not improve an item; and (2) some important subject matter simply cannot be pictorially represented.

Among the pictorial items that have been used are the following: (1) sketches of necklines to be matched with verbal descriptions of face shapes; (2) pattern layouts with questions pertaining to the effects of various pieces; (3) table-setting diagrams with questions pertaining to correct location of pieces; (4) various styles of cleaning brushes and the cleaning processes for which they would be most suitable; and (5) floor plans and the effects various changes would have on improving the plans.

Evaluating Behavior and Performance

Even though the utmost care has been exercised in preparing and selecting test items to measure students' knowledge and understanding, these tests may not enable one to predict with great accuracy what a student would do in a real-life situation. Behavior is complex, involving the interactions of motives, emotional balance, social acceptance, health, and the students' mental abilities. If you are to evaluate progress toward all of the goals that are important in home economics education, you will need to go beyond the administration of paper-and-pencil tests, and develop methods of observing behavior. Evaluating observed behavior has two aspects: the performance itself, and the quality of the finished product.

Performance Test

Performance testing involves a careful, systematic observation of progress in a controlled situation. If speed is a factor, the time devoted to the performance is recorded. The quality or accuracy of work is observed throughout the process, as well as at the conclusion of the test. Methods of performing the task are observed, including such aspects as the proper use of materials and equipment and the exercise of safety precautions. The student's confidence and self-assurance can be noted. Further, a group situation may give insight into the students' ability to cooperate with each other.

Since people tend to see only what they are looking for, a teacher may overlook important behavior unless her plan for observation includes a clear description of what to observe. Performance tests present difficulties because they are time-consuming, and a teacher can observe only a few individuals or groups at a time. Subjective factors may enter into the ratings: previous impressions may have a "halo effect," causing a teacher to look for evidence to support her earlier judgments. A student may be handicapped in performance tests because he does not work well under pressure.

The Performance Test on Family Meals is merely illustrative of the great variety of situations in home economics education in which a teacher might set up a real situation to evaluate the students' progress and to diagnose their difficulties.

Performance Test on Family Meals [13]

Objective: Ability to plan, prepare and serve well-balanced meals to the family with efficient use of time and within a limited cost allowance.

Suggestions for use: May be used as a pre-test and/or as an achievement test at end of the unit.

Directions: From the foods on the supply table (or in unit kitchen) prepare a low cost lunch. Two girls prepare for four.

Foods on table might include:

Potatoes	Can of green beans	Whole wheat bread	American cheese
Lettuce	Can of pineapple	White bread	Instant pudding
Carrots	Can of peaches	Cottage cheese	Soda crackers
Cabbage	Can of tomatoes	Peanut butter	Macaroni
Eggs	Can of tuna fish	Butter	Noodles
Milk	Can of milk	Mayonnaise	Tea bags

Give the other two girls a score card for the meal or give one a score card and ask the other to keep a record of unnecessary steps and motions. Summarize in the space below. Score as follows: 3 = Excellent, 2 = Good, 1 = Fair.

Score Card for Family Meal	Score	Record of Unnecessary Steps and Motions
1. Interesting and tasty menu	______	
2. Suitable for season of year	______	
3. Suitable for group	______	
4. Nutritionally good	______	
5. Both hot and cold foods	______	
6. Table properly set	______	
7. Prepared in time allotted	______	
8. Attractively served	______	
9. Food correctly served	______	
10. Pleasing contrast of textures	______	
11. Correct amount prepared	______	
12. Good work habits used	______	
Possible score is 36. Score of pupil		

[13] Indiana Home Economics Association, *Evaluation in Home Economics.* Lafayette, Ind.: Purdue University, 1957, p. 26.

In addition to the items listed above, the cost factor was stated as an objective and evidence should be collected with regard to it.

The *Minnesota Check List for Food Preparation and Serving,* shown in Table 10, not only suggests the points for a teacher to observe during a performance test but also describes three levels of achievement. If a student's performance most nearly corresponds to the excellent description, he would receive a rating of 5; if he is approximately average, his rating would be 3; if he does poor work, his rating would be 1; and if his performance falls somewhere between the levels that are described, he would receive a rating of 2 or 4.

Whether you devise your own performance tests, or adapt ideas that others have used, you may wish to apply the following suggestions:

1. Choose tasks that represent significant skills which you have emphasized.
2. Select a situation in which fundamental operations can be observed with objectivity and the conditions of work can be standard for all of the students.
3. Keep the cost as low as possible.
4. Restrict the test to one class period, but include a sampling of different tasks. In a foods class, the students may be told, the day before, the general meal pattern that is to be followed.
5. Directions for taking the test should be specific, giving a detailed description of the work that is to be performed.
6. A check list should be provided so the observer will have a clear picture of what to look for. The observer may be the teacher, another student, or both the teacher and a student.
7. Observations should be recorded immediately.
8. Results of observations should be used in helping students to strengthen aspects of their performance and also in evaluating the effectiveness of teaching.

Performance tests, in the formal sense, are of limited usefulness as compared with the daily opportunities for evaluating *student behavior.* Good teaching cannot be separated from evaluation. *Students who are given opportunity to develop their own plans, under guidance, and to evaluate themselves from time to time gain immeasurably. Two of the instruments that were developed by Webber to stress student self-evaluation are given below as examples of the relationship between good teaching and evaluation.*

TABLE 10 Minnesota Check List for Food Preparation and Serving *
University of Minnesota—Division of Home Economics (Revised Edition)

Devised under the Direction of Clara M. Brown by the Faculty and Graduate Students of the Division of Home Economics

Rating of __________ **Rated by** __________ **Date** __________ **Score** __________

<table>
<tr><th></th><th>1</th><th>2</th><th>3</th><th>4</th><th>5</th><th>Score</th></tr>
<tr><td>1. GROOMING</td><td>Untidy; hands or nails dirty; dress soiled or inappropriate, no apron; hair in disorder and unconfined.</td><td colspan="2">Reasonably well groomed; dress suitable; apron soiled or wrinkled; hair neat but not held in place.</td><td colspan="2">Immaculately clean; dress and apron fresh, unwrinkled and appropriate; hair held in place by band or covering.</td><td>1)</td></tr>
<tr><td>2. NEATNESS OF WORKING SPACE</td><td>No space to work; food spilled; table cluttered with dishes and utensils which are not put to soak or washed.</td><td colspan="2">Not very orderly but working space made available when needed; dishes and utensils fairly well cared for as used.</td><td colspan="2">Working space always available; clean and orderly; minimum number of dishes used; dishes and utensils properly cared for.</td><td>2)</td></tr>
<tr><td>3. EFFICIENCY IN USE OF TIME AND EFFORT</td><td>Few if any food supplies in desk; no plan for work or poor sequence; wrong equipment or utensils used; work not finished on time.</td><td colspan="2">A few food supplies in individual desks; plans sketchy; unnecessary steps taken or too many utensils used; is rushed at end of period.</td><td colspan="2">Staple supplies in desks; work schedule shows division of labor; suitable equipment used; efficient methods (such as use of utility tray); work finished on time.</td><td>3)</td></tr>
<tr><td>4. USE OF FUEL AND SUPPLIES</td><td>Burners or oven improperly regulated; oven door opened often; food burned, spilled, or thrown away.</td><td colspan="2">Burners on too long or too high; little food spilled or burned; supplies handled carefully.</td><td colspan="2">Burners and oven well regulated; no food spilled or burned; amounts prepared suitable for situation.</td><td>4)</td></tr>
<tr><td>5. ABILITY TO FOLLOW DIRECTIONS</td><td>Directions not followed; many questions asked or many mistakes made.</td><td colspan="2">Directions followed if explicit and stressed; few mistakes made.</td><td colspan="2">Directions followed carefully and without supervision; no mistakes made.</td><td>5)</td></tr>
<tr><td>6. SKILL IN WORKING</td><td>Awkward and slow or noisy.</td><td colspan="2">Skillful except in difficult operations.</td><td colspan="2">Expert even in difficult operations.</td><td>6)</td></tr>
</table>

7. SANITARY HABITS	Hands not washed before work is begun, wiped on apron; fingers dipped in food or soiled spoon used in tasting.	Hands washed before starting to work, wiped on towel; pans greased with fingers; spoon rinsed between tastings.	Hands washed frequently, dried on towel; fingers do not touch food; clean spoon used for tasting.	7)
8. SAFETY HABITS	Apron or towel used for pot holder; gas turned on before match is lighted; cutting tools handled carelessly.	Pot holder not always used; slight explosion when oven is lighted; cutting tools handled awkwardly.	Appropriate holder used when needed; burner turned on after lighting match; cutting tools used properly.	8)
9. CARE OF SUPPLIES AND EQUIPMENT AFTER USE	No system; things not washed clean, handled carelessly, misplaced or not put away.	Counter, stove, sink, and table clean and in reasonable order; towels not clean and hung carelessly.	All equipment and utensils clean, shining, and returned to proper places; towels clean and hung straight.	9)
10. SETTING OF TABLE	Wrong dishes, silver, or table cover used or arranged incorrectly; table looks crowded.	Dishes, silver, and table cover suitable and arranged correctly; centerpiece lacking or inappropriate.	Dishes, silver, table cover suitable and correctly arranged; decorations attractive.	10)
11. SERVING	Awkward or many mistakes made; unsuitable amounts served; food is messy.	Few mistakes made; correct amounts served; food is arranged neatly.	Serving correct and done with ease; proper amounts served; food is arranged attractively.	11)
12. TABLE MANNERS	Silver handled awkwardly; objectionable habits of eating; apron worn to table.	Occasional error in handling silver; eating is quiet and unobtrusive.	Silver handled expertly; good table manners shown in all respects.	12)
13. POISE	Ill at ease or nervous; little attempt at conversation.	Reasonably self-possessed except when things go wrong; conversation seldom lapses.	At ease, self-possessed; gracious; conversation interesting.	13)
	(To find score, divide by number of points checked.)		**Total** . . . . **Score**	____ ____

* Published by the University of Minnesota Press, copyright 1945.

Steps I need to take	Industry	Workmanship	My problems were...	I learned...
____1. to fit pattern. 				
____2. to lay out and pin pattern. 				
____3. to cut out, staystitch, pin, and stitch darts; press, pin side seams. 				
____4. to fit blouse. 				
____5. to stitch seams. 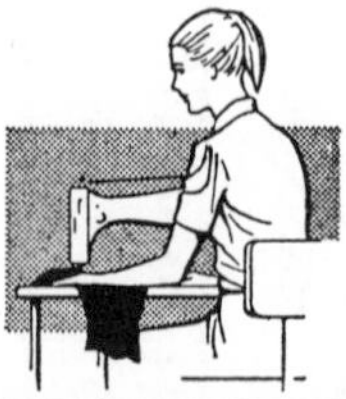				

____6. to finish neck opening; pin, baste, and stitch.				
____7. to complete sleeve; pin, baste, and stitch.				
____8. to complete lower edge of blouse.				
____9. to attach fastenings; final pressing.				

____10. to have a Blouse Beautiful!

Swatch: Sketch:

Pattern number: ____________

<u>Costs</u>

pattern price: ____________

thread: ____________

findings: ____________

total cost: ____________

1. THE STORY OF MY BLOUSE BEAUTIFUL [14]

As you complete the steps below,
The story of your blouse unfolds.
If each step with care is tried,
You will wear your blouse with pride!

Directions for using diagram (*pp. 376–377*).

a. Have the teacher check the blank to the left of the step number when the process is completed.

b. Grade yourself on *Industry* (How hard did I work?) and *Workmanship* (How well did I do the step?) according to the scale:
1. Best I have seen
2. Well done
3. Satisfactory, but could be improved

c. In the *Problems* column, describe the problems you encountered.

d. In the last column, describe what you *learned* from each step.

2. AM I DOING AS I SHOULD? [15]

Directions: After reading the question, decide first whether you *usually* do each item. Write *yes* or *no* in the first blank. Next decide whether you *should do* the procedure. Write *yes* or *no* in the second blank. The questions are to help you evaluate your knowledge and work habits. You will not be graded.

Do I:	**Should I:**	**A. Plan my time well?**
1. ____	1. ____	1. Have to be reminded to start sewing when the period begins?
2. ____	2. ____	2. Dash up to the sewing locker and put my box away ahead of other girls already in line?
3. ____	3. ____	3. Plan my work so that I do as much sewing as possible with one trip to the sewing machine?
4. ____	4. ____	4. Plan to do as much pressing as possible with one trip to the iron?
5. ____	5. ____	5. Have to be reminded to put my work away at the last minute?
		B. Have my sewing supplies neat?
6. ____	6. ____	6. Have my sewing box in the room each day?
7. ____	7. ____	7. Have all my sewing materials in my box?
8. ____	8. ____	8. Have my sewing box reasonably neat and in order?
9. ____	9. ____	9. Use only my portion of the table for my sewing supplies?

[14] Vivienne L. Webber, *Self-evaluation Devices for B7 Clothing*. Unpublished Paper, University of California, Los Angeles, 1957, pp. 36–39.

[15] Ibid., pp. 41–42.

Do I:	Should I:	C. Cooperate with others?
10. _____	10. _____	10. Visit with my neighbor so that neither of us accomplished what we should during the period?
11. _____	11. _____	11. Borrow supplies from my neighbor?
12. _____	12. _____	12. Assist another girl willingly when the teacher asks me?
13. _____	13. _____	13. Spend more time at the machine than is necessary?
14. _____	14. _____	14. Leave the machine neat, even if this means in better order than when I found it?
		D. Have good posture?
15. _____	15. _____	15. Bend over my work to see it better?
16. _____	16. _____	16. Rest my feet on the leg braces of my chair when I am sewing?
17. _____	17. _____	17. Hold my work very close to my face when I do hand sewing?
		E. Use my equipment properly?
18. _____	18. _____	18. Take my spool and bobbin to my table after finishing at the machine and keep them in a girl friend's box?
19. _____	19. _____	19. Keep my fingers several inches from the presser foot when sewing at the machine?
20. _____	20. _____	20. Unplug the iron after using it?
21. _____	21. _____	21. Leave the soleplate down on the ironing board after finishing with the iron?
22. _____	22. _____	22. Wear my thimble only when the teacher reminds me?
23. _____	23. _____	23. Wear my thimble for machine sewing?
24. _____	24. _____	24. Wear my thimble for all hand sewing?
25. _____	25. _____	25. Carry my scissors with the points toward other people?
26. _____	26. _____	26. Place my first two fingers in the larger handle opening when cutting with scissors?
27. _____	27. _____	27. Hold the fabric up in my hand when I cut it?

Object Tests

Actually there is much overlapping between the evaluation of performance and the product that results from the performance. Although both aspects are important, a home economics teacher should be concerned first with what happens to the students and to a lesser extent with the excellence of the product. Overemphasis on perfection in making a skirt can cause a girl to dislike sewing to the extent that she will never attempt to make anything beyond the projects required in her home economics class. Certainly standards of a finished product are important, but they can receive undue emphasis and prevent other significant goals from being accomplished.

Using real objects may increase the validity of a test and reduce the possibility of bluffing. Object tests have merit not only in measuring students' achievement, but also for diagnostic and motivational purposes. The following example of a score sheet illustrates the need for being specific in identifying the major characteristics and determining how to rate their fulfillment:

HORNBY SCORE SHEET FOR BISHOP-METHOD SKIRT [16]

Directions: Score each item, rating 10, 20, or 30 depending upon whether the quality corresponds to the description in the left hand column, or the right hand column, or falls between the two. Record score in the space provided for it. Total your scores. Analyze your next steps.

Item and Description		Score (in points)
Fabric		
1. Flimsy, loosely woven, harsh excess sizing.	Durable, closely woven, soft, free from excess sizing.	1. ____
2. Difficult to keep clean.	Easy to keep clean.	2. ____
3. Harsh, gaudy color, unsuitable.	Gay, yet less intense, suitable for skirt.	3. ____
4. Poor design, up and down, nap.	Good or suitable design—no up and down—no nap.	4. ____
Style and Design		
5. Restricts action.	Allows for action and growth.	5. ____
6. Overtrimmed; trimmings unsuitable to fabric; do not relate to garment lines.	Simple in design; trimmings suitable to fabric, follow lines of garment.	6. ____
7. Waistband too wide, too narrow, for design and figure.	Waistband adapted to design and figure.	7. ____
8. Placket, zipper, or fastening difficult to operate; buttons too small or too large.	Placket, zipper, or fastening easy to operate; buttons smooth, flat.	8. ____

[16] Adapted from Agnes Hornby O'Neill, *Hornby Score Sheet for Bishop-Method Skirt.* Agnes Hornby, Framingham State Teachers College, Framingham, Mass., 1952.

HORNBY SCORE SHEET, *continued.*

Item and Description		Score (in points)
Construction:		
Machine-stitching		
9. Evidence of uneven tension.	Tension even, stitches smooth.	9. ____
Staylines		
10. Evidence of no staylines or stitches against grainline and/or visible.	Evidence that staylines at waistband and placket even and close to seam line.	10. ____
Seams		
11. Seams less than ½"; uneven stitching (less than 10 or more than 16 per inch).	Seams ½"; consistently even stitching (10 to 16 per inch).	11. ____
12. Seams not finished; finish unsuitable for fabric.	Seams finished; suitable for fabric.	12. ____
Hem width		
13. Too wide or too narrow for fabric or style.	Hem width well adapted for skirt.	13. ____
14. Clean finish; too narrow or too wide; seam binding too close or too far from edge, stitched unevenly.	Even stitches ¼" from edge; seam binding not less than ¼" over raw edge; stitched close to selvedge.	14. ____
Completed hem		
15. Unevenly pleated fulness, uneven stitches showing on right side.	Fullness evenly arranged; stitches even, barely visible on right side.	15. ____
Placket		
16. Irregular stitching; uneven or stretched overlap; zipper showing; facing bulky; zipper tab more or less than ¼" from band.	Regular stitching; even overlap, neat, well covered, smooth; zipper tab ¼" from band.	16. ____
Fasteners		
17. Fasteners insecurely or improperly attached: (*a*) buttons sewed on without shank, poorly	Fasteners functionally placed, evenly and securely attached, not visible from right side.	17. ____

HORNBY SCORE SHEET, *continued.*

Item and Description		Score (in points)
Construction *(continued):*		
spaced; (*b*) hooks and eyes loosely sewed, poorly spaced; (c) snaps obvious from right side, unevenly attached, insecure.		
Buttonholes		
18. Improperly and poorly made: (*a*) worked stitches uneven, lack neatness; (*b*) machine-made stitches large, far apart, fuzzy.	Properly and well made: (*a*) worked out stitches even, neat on both sides; (*b*) machine-made stitches small, close together, no raveling.	18. ____
19. Length of buttonhole too short or too long.	Correct length.	19. ____
Waistband		
20. Final stitching not on seam line of waistline, shows unevenly on right side.	Final stitching (right or wrong side) on seam of waistline; shows evenly on right side.	20. ____
Final finish		
21. Loose threads or loop ends too short or not tied or fastened.	No loops or threads visible, threads fastened securely.	21. ____
General		
22. Lacks pressing; untidy, shows effect of ripping, restitching or folding wrinkles.	Clean, carefully pressed, clear lines of construction.	22. ____
Total Number Items Scored	__ + __ + __ = 22 10 20 30 All	

A series of objects may be set up and identified by number. Each student is assigned a given station as a starting point and then a signal is given for the students to advance to the next station. A student should not be permitted to return to any station. Of course, the stations must be planned so that the amount of time required is approximately the same at each station. The students are given a set of directions and a prepared answer sheet. A sketch showing the order in which the stations are arranged might be necessary. One or two sample situations may be provided as illustrations. The test should be administered in such a way as to prevent cheating and interference with other students.

Evaluating Appreciations, Attitudes, Interests, and Values

Students' achievement can be quite easily measured through the use of written tests, and teachers feel secure in basing their appraisals on the objective type of information that students supply on such tests. Furthermore, teachers usually find that they can give satisfactory ratings to the products that students prepare, and perhaps even to the performance of the students in prescribed situations. Nevertheless, even the most experienced teachers continually seek guidance to help them improve their evaluations of achievement and performance and to help them gain insight into ways of measuring the more intangible objectives dealing with students' appreciations, attitudes, interests, and values.

Appreciation

Appreciation connotes an emotional reaction or feeling of satisfaction obtained from a perception of the worth of an object or experience. In home economics education, students learn to appreciate food, clothing, homes, home furnishings, and many other aspects of the man-made environment. In addition, they gain appreciation of the natural environment as they study such topics as flower arrangement, foods, textiles, and color harmony. Growth in appreciation of children, siblings, parents, and friends is a major objective of home economics education. And finally, students learn to appreciate the process of performing the arts and skills of homemaking.

Appreciation is a highly personal matter. Students may not be willing or able to communicate this effectively to others. Teachers cannot establish precise standards for the students to strive toward.

Indirect methods are usually most suitable for a teacher to use in evaluating the appreciations of her students. These may be of three types:

1. Asking the students what they appreciate.
   a. check list or questionnaire for students to tell what they like
   b. discussion on how students spend their leisure time

Example [17]

Is it possible for you to empathize with the children of different social, economic, racial, and national groups? Can you understand why they might behave differently than you? Are there some things about them which are the

[17] Brown and Plihal, op. cit., p. 200.

same as you? Do children from different social, economic, racial, and national groups have special disadvantages to overcome which children of the majority group do not?

2. Providing opportunities for students to judge qualities.
   a. visit a museum
   b. visit a home
   c. judge pictures of rooms for such aspects as color harmony and furniture design
   d. choose appropriate accessories to wear on various occasions
   e. select tableware for certain settings
3. Observing activities in situations in which appreciations might be reflected in student behavior.
   a. curiosity a student shows about his environment or studies
   b. books and magazines a student reads
   c. creative efforts of students, in which they can apply ideas from what they have read or observed

These suggestions will provide indications of where your students are in appreciation. You can help them make judgments about their levels of satisfaction in these areas.

Attitudes

An attitude might be defined as a fairly consistent, learned tendency to behave in a certain way. Attitudes are dynamic. The individual is in a state of readiness to react toward people, situations, or objects. The manner in which one acts may be influenced by social pressures, specific characteristics of the particular situation, moral standards, emotions, or other complex elements. Attitudes may change as a person grows older, as he acquires knowledge, or as his environment changes.

Several dimensions of attitudes are important in their measurement: (1) *direction*—for or against something; (2) *degree*—the extent to which one is for or against it; (3) *strength* or *intensity*—the strength of this belief as compared with his other beliefs (motivational and emotional aspects that might become a basis for action); (4) *salience*—the freedom with which one gives vent to his attitudes (refers to the centrality of the attitude within the individual and cultural permissiveness); and (5) *coherence* or *consistency*—the ordering or integration of attitudes, maintaining that attitude under different situations.[18]

You will find it much easier to change a student's choice of dessert than to change his commitment to the value of a family or to his own way of

[18] S. Stansfield Sargent and Robert C. Williamson, *Social Psychology* (3rd ed.). New York: The Ronald Press, 1966, pp. 246–247.

life. Ego-involved attitudes are intimately felt and cherished. Behavior gives some indication of a person's attitudes, but a teacher cannot be satisfied with this outward manifestation for two reasons: (1) A student may act contrary to his professed attitudes when he feels pressures from his social group. (2) A student may behave in a manner inconsistent with his expressed attitudes without realizing that he is inconsistent.

When constructing or selecting attitude scales, a teacher should remember that attitude scores are not valid for grading purposes. Statements should be applicable for the cultural group in which they are used and they should be debatable. Persons with differing views should respond differently. Statements that are poorly phrased, that contain unfamiliar words, or that are subject to more than one interpretation will not differentiate satisfactorily between persons with opposing views. The most desirable choice should vary in position—part of the time it might be a statement with which the students should agree, while part of the time it should be one with which they should disagree.

Several methods of measuring attitudes might be useful in home economics education. A few of the common approaches are illustrated:

1. METHOD OF EQUAL-APPEARING INTERVALS. Herrington developed a series of five attitude scales on family living using the Thurstone method of equal-appearing intervals. Hundreds of statements expressing various beliefs regarding personal, family, and community relations were written by teachers. Selected items were submitted to forty-five judges who placed each statement in one of eleven piles, ranging from the most favorable to the least favorable attitudes toward family and community living. If the judges varied considerably in their ratings, an item was discarded as ambiguous. The median of the judges' ratings became the scale value of an item. Items illustrating the various scale positions from Herrington's *Standards of Home Life* include: [19]

10.4	1. Jealousy among family members is stimulating.
9.0	4. A child should always obey his parents without question.
7.6	20. A young child should always obey older members of the family.
6.0	16. Older people in the family are too free with their advice to the younger members.
5.0	41. A family which is self-supporting, law-abiding, and friendly with neighbors, is a united family.
3.8	46. Every mother should stay home and take care of her own children.

[19] Evelyn Herrington, *Standards for Home Life: An Attitude Scale.* Syracuse: Syracuse University Press, 1948. (*See also* Carolyn R. Wickes, "A Study of the Attitudes of Three Groups of Married Couples." Unpublished master's thesis, Syracuse University, Syracuse, 1956.)

2.4 51. Brother and sister quarrels are to be expected sometimes, but should not be too frequent or too prolonged.

1.0 21. Children should be made to feel that they are a part of the family group by having certain home responsibilities.

In responding to this type of scale, a student checks only the items with which he agrees. If the instrument is valid and the individual's beliefs are consistent, his responses will represent items of similar scale values. If an individual's responses are scattered over several scale positions, his attitudes probably are not well crystallized or the attitude scale is not functioning well for him.

2. RATING SCALE.

a. One type of rating scale presents a group of statements and the students indicate the extent to which they agree or disagree with each item.

Example: Attitudes Toward Personal and Family Living[20]

Directions: We are attempting to find out how you feel about yourself, your family, and your friends. Your answers will be treated with the strictest confidence, so please feel free to give honest replies. . . . You are to indicate the extent to which you agree with each statement. Read each statement and decide how *you* feel about it. Then mark your answer on the space provided on your answer sheet. . . .

	1	2	3	4	5
If you *strongly agree,* blacken the space under 1.	▮				
If you *agree,* blacken the space under 2.		▮			
If you are *undecided or uncertain,* blacken the space under 3.			▮		
If you *disagree,* blacken the space under 4.				▮	
If you *strongly disagree,* blacken the space under 5.					▮

Examples of Statements

	1	2	3	4	5
1. Children should be paid for work they do around the house.					
2. A devoted mother has no time for her social life.					

b. Remmers and Stedman simplified this approach in their attitude inventory, *Bringing Up Children.* Their directions were as follows:[21]

[20] *Attitudes Toward Personal and Family Life.* Texas Cooperative Youth Study, 1956. (CYS—Part I. Consists of approximately 100 statements similar to these.)

[21] H. H. Remmers and Louise A. Stedman, *Bringing Up Children: An Inventory of Attitudes.* Chicago Science Research Associates, 1954, Form A.

On the back of this booklet, you will find 45 statements that describe different things children do, and different ways of handling children. Read each statement very carefully to decide whether you agree or disagree with it.

If you agree with the statement, mark an X in the box under YES.

If you do NOT agree with the statement, mark an X in the box under NO.

Try to mark either YES or NO for each statement.

If you really don't know whether you agree or disagree, mark an X in the box under the question mark.

1. A child should be given an opportunity to assist in the selection of his clothing.
2. Praise is more effective than blame in dealing with children.

c. Another type of evaluation asks the students to express their attitudes about the effectiveness of various ways of handling a problem: [22]

Six-year-old Judy is afraid of the dark. She will cry if the light is turned off in her bedroom before she goes to sleep, and she will not go into a dark room.

What do you think of these methods of treating the problem?

	Good	Fair	Poor
1. Let her cry in the dark until she gets used to it.	_____	_____	_____
2. Treat her fear lightly as unimportant.	_____	_____	_____
3. Talk to her about why she is afraid.	_____	_____	_____
4. Force her to go into dark rooms to get accustomed to the dark.	_____	_____	_____
5. Scold and shame her for being so silly.	_____	_____	_____
6. Let her take a flashlight to bed with her.	_____	_____	_____

3. INCOMPLETE SENTENCES. Incomplete sentences are particularly effective when you are teaching areas of family life and child development. Their use is based on the assumption that a student reveals his thoughts, fantasies, and emotional conflicts as he completes the sentences. Direct questioning would very likely be more threatening than incomplete sentences. As you select phrases for students to complete, try to control their responses as little as possible and use a broad range of stimuli. You may include such areas as the family, childhood, drives, goals, and reactions:

I feel proud of . . .
My greatest ambition . . .
My father . . .
I am afraid . . .
My future husband . . .
I pity . . .
Most people . . .
I wish . . .
I feel hurt when . . .
Mothers who work outside the home . . .

[22] Ralph H. Ojemann, "Attitudes Regarding Child Development." Unpublished report, The State University of Iowa, Iowa City.

In interpreting responses, be sure to notice those that are given by very few students. Also, responses that are used by the same individual in responding to different items may be significant. Among the themes that secondary school students bring out in personal and family life are conflicts with parents, shyness or antagonism toward members of the opposite sex, fears of the future, attitudes of indifference, and preoccupation with moral demands.

4. PICTURE-STORY. Pictures or cartoons may be used as a stimulus for the students to develop a story. The pictures should present a fairly unstructured situation and may involve relationships between an adult and a child, two young children, or an adolescent and a young child. The students write a story about what has happened prior to what is shown in the picture, how the people feel about the situation, and what the outcome will be.

The projective technique may be used to study social conflict. For example, ambiguous figures in a shabby-looking room might bring out a variety of attitudes regarding laborers, government's role in looking after poor families, and racial problems.

5. OBSERVATIONS AND SELF-REPORTS. The use of observations and self-reports, described in Chapter 5, is also helpful in studying the attitudes of students. However, since the usual method of writing anecdotal records is very time-consuming, you might like to try an adaptation. One suggestion is to have the students write anecdotes of their own behavior and attitudes. The teacher might suggest *critical incidents* that she feels would reveal the students' behavior and feelings. Examples of questions that might be used in a clothing class are: [23]

1. Do you ever sew at home? If so, tell what you have made.
2. Describe an incident in which you observed safety rules.
3. Describe the way in which you began work when you entered the classroom yesterday.
4. Describe a situation and your reaction to it in which you had to rip some stitching out, or had to start over on some phase of a sewing project.
5. What do you do when you do not understand a step in the sewing procedure of the project on which you are working? Describe a particular incident.

Interests

Interest is a reflection of pleasant feelings, of liking or enjoying something. The difference between attitudes and interests has been summarized in this way: "Interests merely indicate the degree to which an individual prefers to hold an object before his consciousness, whether he

[23] Marla Stone, *Evaluation in B7 Clothing*. Unpublished report, University of California, Los Angeles, 1957.

reacts approvingly or disapprovingly toward it, whereas attitudes indicate his reaction in terms of its direction, pleasantness or unpleasantness, agreement or disagreement." [24]

Knowledge and interest are related from two standpoints: (1) people tend to be interested in something about which they have some knowledge; and (2) interest may stimulate a person to seek further knowledge about something.

Many of the methods for measuring attitudes can apply also to the evaluation of interests. Much can be learned from informal techniques such as student writings (asking the student to tell what activities he enjoys most), check lists, and questionnaires. These may be unreliable because the student may not know how he really feels or may be unwilling to express interests that are characteristic of lower socioeconomic levels. Direct observation and reports on hobbies are other means by which interests are made manifest. Standardized inventories are used widely.

1. INTEREST, KNOWLEDGE, AND NEED. A check list for planning the home economics program encourages the students to broaden their interests as well as to deepen them. All areas of home economics education have been included in the one prepared by Michigan State University but only a few statements are shown here for illustrative purposes: [25]

> Following is a list of some of the things which are studied in home economics classes. In the first column to the right, labeled, *Have studied,* write "X" if you have already studied it and write "O" if you have not. In the second column, labeled, *Want to study,* write "X" if you want to study it this year, and write "O" if you do not want to.
>
> You may want to learn more about some of the things you have studied before, but you will want to study new things, too.

Child Care and Guidance

Home Economics Can Help Me to Do These Things	Have studied	Want to study
1. Understand the duties of a baby sitter.	__________	__________
2. Construct suitable play material for children.	__________	__________

Perhaps this type of check list would be more useful if one additional point were emphasized. Students *need* to learn certain things, whether or not they *want* to study them. When presenting this check list to a group,

[24] H. H. Remmers, N. L. Gage, and J. Francis Rummel, *A Practical Introduction to Measurement and Evaluation* (2nd ed.). New York: Harper & Row, 1965, p. 308.

[25] Meta Vossbrink, *Homemaking Education, A Checklist for Planning the Program*. Professional Series Bulletin No. 17. East Lansing: Michigan State University, 1956, pp. 4–5.

you might stress that the students should consider what they *need* to be able to do in their present home living and what their future needs might be when they have responsibility for a home and family. As they check items that they "want to study," they should interpret this to include both interests and needs. An alternative approach would be to add a third column as follows: "Have studied," "Want to study," "Need to study."

2. OPPORTUNITY, INTEREST, AND INFORMATION. Another check list was devised to help students analyze their activities and determine their needs from three standpoints: [26]

> What do you do that interests you? In what ways do you want this course to help you? Perhaps you can get a fairly good idea, if you read carefully the following invoice to decide the opportunities, interests, and information you already have in the field.
>
> Answer each question according to your degree of opportunity, interest, or information. Place the *number only* on your answer sheet. Finish all three answers to each question before proceeding to the next one.

Opportunity	*Interest*	*Information*
3—I have much	3—I have much	3—I have much
2—I have some	2—I have some	2—I have some
1—I have little	1—I have little	1—I have little
0—I have no	0—I have no	0—I have no

MARKETING

Do I:

1. Buy at chain stores?
2. Buy meat?
3. Select fresh fruits?
4. Read labels on canned goods?
5. Know kinds of cereals?
6. Buy frozen foods?

An important evaluative criterion is the student's carry-over or continuing interest. For example, after studying consumer economics, does the student listen to financial and economic news on the radio or television? Does he read economic items in newspapers and magazines? Does he enter into discussions about these matters?

Values

Values are motivating forces that influence the choices one makes. They represent striving toward a given goal. They are related to attitudes

[26] Anonymous, *Home Economics Activity Invoice*. Unpublished report, Syracuse University.

and are projected upon other persons, objects, and situations. Generally, we think of values in terms of general goals and enduring clusters of wants. The teacher should endeavor to be sensitive to the values a student holds and to respect these values. At the same time, she should help the students determine the relative importance of their values on their conduct and see the consequences of cherishing certain ideas or possessions. As a teacher, you may help your students to set values consistent with a workable philosophy of life.

Cutler's study of personal and family values influencing the selection of a home used the technique of *paired comparisons*. She introduced ten basic home values: "beauty, comfort, convenience, location, health, personal interests, privacy, safety, friendship activities, and economy."[27] In the first part of the test, the respondents (who were adults) placed the ten values in rank order on the basis of the "first thought" or verbalized pattern of values. Then the respondents read a description of each value, such as the following:

> This is a beautiful home. It has nice colors and good design. It is good to look at both inside and outside, and fits in with the surroundings. You may not have much chance to carry on your hobbies and may not have much privacy but it is very beautiful.

Following this, each word was paired with each other word and the individual was asked to indicate his preference in each of the 45 pairs. For example:

> 1—is the *beautiful* home. It has nice colors and good design. It is good to look at both inside and outside.
> 10—is the *inexpensive* home. It won't cost much to operate and will suit the family income.

When this part of the test was completed, a score was obtained for each of the values indicating the individual's "functional pattern of values."[28]

Dyer's *forced choice* values test has been used by Paolucci to help college students identify their value clusters and rankings:[29]

[27] Virginia F. Cutler, *Personal and Family Values in the Choice of Home.* Cornell University Agricultural Experiment Station Bulletin, November 1947, pp. 6–21. (Out of print.)

[28] Ibid.

[29] Developed by Doris Dyer and adapted for classroom purposes by Beatrice Paolucci, in "Students' Wives' Values As Reflected in Personal and Family Activities." Unpublished master's thesis, Michigan State University, 1963.

Forced Choice Values Test

Following you will find several descriptive stories about homemakers. You will find that one of the stories best describes your idea of what a homemaker ought to be or do.

Read all nine stories. Put a "1" in front of the story that best meets your desires. Put a "2" in front of the one that is *next best.* Check (√) the one that is *least desirable.* You may have trouble deciding on these three stories but remember that no story is apt to be perfect nor is one apt to be directly contradictory to your desires.

_______ 1. Mrs. C. likes to do things that build mutual understanding and loyalty within her family. She thinks it is important for parents and children to work and play together. Mrs. C. feels her job is to keep the family going, to please them, and to be aware of the needs of everybody in her family. Mrs. C. is very apt to start dinner early in the afternoon so more time is available to play with the children during their "cross time" in late afternoon. She bakes special goodies to please the tastes of her family. She'd choose to go picnicking with the whole family rather than to go out for a restaurant meal with her husband alone. Mrs. C. likes to be visited by relatives and enjoys family reunions a great deal. Mrs. C. refuses to involve herself in community activities because she's needed at home.

_______ 2. Mrs. H. believes that a healthy family is the key to a happy family. She protects her family members so as to avoid situations that might lead to physical fatigue, ill health, or accidents. She arranges activities in which the family can get lots of fresh air and sunshine. She doesn't approve of children devoting lots of time to television viewing because they become less physically active. Mrs. H. plans on the children getting adequate rest, and avoids activities that interfere with their nap time. She arranges nutritious meals because good diets are essential to good health.

_______ 3. Mrs. E. believes that children should know that most things cost money, and therefore, there is a limit to what they can have. She arranges to make clothes for herself and the children because the finished product is made better and you can get so much more for your money. Mrs. E. doesn't habitually use cake mixes because they are too expensive. She plans to shop from a grocery list because it helps keep her food bill down. She shops for bargains. Mrs. E. feels that extra time in a do-it-yourself project is time well spent to save money for something the family wants more. She feels that families should be self-supporting, even when in school. Too many of Mrs. E's friends are not good money managers because they know that their parents are standing by ready to help them financially, with no arrangements for systematic repayment.

_______ 4. Mrs. F. likes to sleep later in the morning than she's able to do with the demands of her family. She arranges time for herself and enjoys getting out of the house for awhile, alone. Mrs. F. takes long leisurely baths and when relaxing she just sits—hoping not to be interrupted by needs of others. Mrs. F. sees definite advantages in vacations separate from her husband and family. She believes such a vacation would be quite refreshing. If Mrs. F. could do what she wanted to do, she would go someplace for a few hours by herself. She'd like to spend money and time in ways for which she would not have to account to anyone.

_______ 5. Mrs. A. likes a tidy house. She keeps things where they belong and feels uncomfortable if she lets the dusting go. Still, Mrs. A's house has its cluttered places. The children's walls exhibit their artistic expressions with crayons, paints, and soap suds pictures. She feels that children should learn to appreciate art and music, and plans piano and dancing lessons for her children. The children are encouraged to express themselves artistically. Mrs. A. selects children's books that are attractive and reads the traditional childrens' classics to them. Mrs. A. has started a collection of the great musical works so her family can come to know and enjoy them. She plans trips to the theater and Sunday afternoon concerts so that the whole family can attend. Mrs. A. enjoys arranging flowers, likes table centerpieces, and recently dyed a bedspread so it would blend with the wall color.

_______ 6. Mrs. P. thinks that the opinions of her friends and neighbors are important. She continually cautions the children against behavior that would meet their neighbors' disapproval. She strives to keep the children well-dressed and she herself attends the beauty shop regularly to have her hair done. She subscribes to fashion and decorating magazines. She likes to be the first in the neighborhood to try out a recipe or wear a high style dress. She manages her money in order to belong to the country club. Mrs. P. plans on the children having nice playmates and is pleased to know that their school district is in an area where people of similar social class live. If she were to have a choice of activity today, Mrs. P. would have some friends in for tea and bridge.

_______ 7. Mrs. S. likes her friends. She feels that without friends one has little in this world. She arranges to have her neighbors in for coffee because it allows her to get together with them. Mrs. S. thinks that children can learn to be friendly, and most of this learning comes from watching and imitating their parents. She thinks it is important for children to arrange their activities to include their friends. Mrs. S. plans vacations so that friends may be visited along the way. Mrs. S. arranges her home to be open to friends who need a place to eat or stay overnight, and includes them in the family breakfast the next morning. Mrs. S. would like to have more time to visit friends whom she hasn't seen for awhile. She spends much time writing friends in other places. She would leave everything if a friend called who needed her.

_______ 8. Mrs. R. and her family attend church regularly. She feels that the teachings of their religion are the foundation of the family. Mrs. R. believes that she should put all her effort into making religion the power of daily life. The family members say grace at meal time and prayers daily. Mrs. R. participates in the church choir. Her husband serves on the governing committee. Mrs. R. believes that formal religious education is important for her children, the oldest of whom is already participating. Mrs. R. thinks her beliefs should govern her life in helping others, being honest and kind. She hopes that her example will represent her religion and help others to learn about their God.

_______ 9. Mrs. D. thinks that education should never stop. She reads to extend her learning and broaden her interests. She sets aside time for reading the newspaper nightly so she'll know what's going on in the world. Mrs. D's husband is a full-time student. Mrs. D. plans time to discuss classes, papers, or problems with him. She is always willing to take the time to help him review for exams. Mrs. D. plans to re-enroll to finish her degree. It will necessitate leaving three preschool-age children with a baby sitter four days each week. She maintains that her education level should equal that of her husband and is willing to sacrifice many things toward this end. Mrs. D. plans time to teach her children to help with little chores of the house. She buys and helps them with numerous educational toys. She arranges quiet times for them when her husband is home studying.

Key to values test:

1. Family-centeredness	4. Freedom	7. Friendship
2. Health	5. Aesthetic interests	8. Religion
3. Economy	6. Prestige	9. Education

Brown and Plihal gave an example of an essay question that measures a student's understanding of values and the effects of parents' values on their children: [30]

Hypothesize as to the effect upon a child's development of creative abilities if his parents hold the values and possess the characteristics of the general

[30] Brown and Plihal, op. cit., p. 158.

society and consequently promote the development of these values and characteristics in their child. Give three specific examples to support your hypothesis.

USING EVALUATION DATA

The ways in which you might use evaluation data depend upon your purposes in gathering the information, the validity of your techniques, and the accuracy with which you record and interpret the results. As a beginning teacher, you will not be expected to carry out all of the many types of evaluation that have been described. However, you should be careful to select a variety of appropriate methods that will help both your students and you secure information for evaluating progress. Among the ways in which evaluation can serve you are the following:

Curriculum Planning

You may give pretests or check lists of interests and knowledge to help determine what subject matter should be included at each grade level. Individuals and classes vary in their needs and abilities; evaluation data can help you plan a program that is suited to their grade level and at the same time adapted to their interests and capabilities.

Motivation of Students

You may also use pretests to stimulate students to want to learn and to develop responsibility for their own learning. But, as a teacher, you should use the results to gain a better understanding of how much to expect of a student and what goals are realistic for various individuals.

Through diagnosing the specific learning difficulties of individuals, you can learn the areas in which a student needs further help. Also, through discovering the successes of an individual and giving commendation for the student's effort and success, you can stimulate further effort.

Diagnostic teaching requires that you be aware of your students' skills and that you can see evidence of competence or lack of it, in behavioral terms. From a diagnostic study of the class performance, you can determine what areas should be given extra attention. When the majority of the class does not come up to your expectation, you may want to revise and improve your teaching methods.

You may be very subtle in stimulating students to learn merely by using a rigid evaluation program. Students tend to work harder for teachers who demand that they learn and apply their learnings. They also have tendencies to study particularly those things on which they expect to be evaluated. They tend toward creative thought when self-direction is encouraged.

Effective Grouping

By using a variety of evaluation techniques, you can learn specific ways in which your students differ. Your assessment should help you value and maintain the diversity of your students. For some phases of instruction you might wish to divide the class into small groups, with students of similar ability working together. Then you can adjust the instruction to the ability level of each group, and thus accommodate students of all ability levels.

On certain occasions, you might find that students can learn more effectively if they have an opportunity to work with others of somewhat different background or ability. From a careful study of sociometric and other types of data, you can determine which grouping might be most functional.

Student Self-Evaluation

If you believe that students should share in planning the aims for their home economics courses, you should also permit them to share in evaluating their progress. Students who are given the opportunity to use self-checking devices may gain interest in improving and begin to grow in the ability to direct their own learning. The feedback an individual receives from evaluation determines what his next steps will be. If he experiences success, he is likely to move forward with the next task. Failure may affect not only that individual's adjustment but also the functioning of the rest of the class and the teacher.

In their self-evaluation, some students may use their own level of aspiration as a standard. Individuals frequently set goals that are unrealistic for them to attain. To prevent continuous feelings of failure, these students must learn to compare their achievement with the standards of others.

A difficulty that you may encounter in using self-evaluation techniques is that students may have little insight into their own behavior. They may tend to rate themselves too high on desirable qualities and too low on undesirable qualities. Personal traits are closely related to a student's self-ratings. Some students consistently overrate themselves, while others lack confidence to rate themselves as high as they deserve.

Like other forms of evaluation, self-evaluation is a process of making meaning from experiences. Your responsibilities as a teacher include (1) instructing the students about the proper use of self-evaluation techniques; (2) recognizing that student judgments may not be valid when compared with your judgment; (3) discovering which students consistently overestimate their ability and which ones consistently underestimate their ability; and (4) guiding students to a realistic appraisal of their achievement.

Improvement of Evaluation Instruments

In order to measure relative achievement among a group of students, their scores must be dispersed as widely as possible. Spread of scores results from using test items of appropriate difficulty and high discriminating power. An item analysis of a test provides useful feedback information, enabling you to find out which points still need to be mastered before students are ready for the next step. In addition, it gives a picture of how well each item measures the same thing as does the total test of which it is a part. Elaborate statistical procedures are not necessary or applicable where the number of students is relatively small. Nevertheless, an analysis and evaluation of each of your tests will help you to improve your teaching and make your evaluation effective.

The *difficulty* of an item can be determined by finding the percent of students who answered it correctly. No fixed percents can be stated as standards for an acceptable item. In fact, programmed instruction is demonstrating that nearly all students can attain mastery if given enough time. Generally, an item is regarded as too easy to function effectively if 90 percent or more of the students answer it correctly. However, certain facts are so basic that nearly everyone must master them. An easy test may provide encouragement to students for whom learning is difficult. It may indicate that students can do more than they had been expected to achieve. However, too many easy items cause a test to lack discriminating power. When an item is so difficult that 20 percent or less of the students can answer it correctly, you should try to discover why. Was the item poorly designed? Did you assume the students already had certain skills or comprehension? Was your method of instruction inadequate? Before using that item again, you should improve it or revise your teaching methods.

An ideal, albeit seldom attained, is for the average difficulty level of test items to be approximately 50 percent, or midway between a score that might be obtained by chance guessing and the highest possible score. If you used a multiple-choice test with five options for each question, a student would have one chance in five of guessing the correct answer. When you subtract 20 percent from a perfect score of 100 percent, the middle difficulty level would be 60 percent. For this test, you should strive to have most items answered correctly by about 60 percent of your students.

An item is considered to be *discriminating* if those who answer it correctly tend to score higher on the total test than those who have a wrong answer. In general, the use of positively discriminating items tends to spread out test scores. Item discrimination is harder to estimate with small groups than it is with groups of a hundred or more. You may obtain a rough estimate by taking the following steps:

1. Arrange the papers in order from the highest to the lowest total scores.
2. Select the upper and lower groups by using approximately 25 to 35 percent of the highest and lowest scoring papers. For a group of 25 to 40 students you may use the highest 10 and lowest 10 papers.
3. Count the correct responses of each person in the upper group, as shown in Column 1 of the Item-Analysis Worksheet. (See p. 399.)
4. Count the responses of each person in the lower group (Column 2).
5. Convert the number of correct responses to percentages of the total group of students (Columns 3 and 4).
6. Subtract the percentage for the lower group from the percentage for the upper group (Column 5).
7. Obtain a *rough* estimate of the discriminating ability of the items as follows (Column 6):

Acceptable: When the students with high scores generally obtain a correct answer and the students with low scores generally answer incorrectly, an item has high discriminating ability. The difference between the two groups should be over 15 or 20 percent for items to be considered acceptable. (See items 2 and 4.)

Weak: If an item was answered correctly by less than 15 or 20 percent more of the students in the high group than in the low group, it has little discriminating value and should be examined for ambiguity, extreme difficulty or easiness, or an incorrect key. (See item 5.)

Not discriminating: If the same percent of students in the high and low groups answered an item correctly, the item does not discriminate between students who possess the knowledge and those who do not. (See item 1.)

Negative: If a higher percent of the students in the low group than in the high group answered an item correctly, the item is poor—it is operating in reverse. (See item 3.)

8. Estimate the difficulty of an item by taking the average of Columns 3 and 4. (See Column 7.)

Machine-scoring and analysis of tests can be of real assistance as you attempt to improve your tests. A simple count of how many students chose each possible answer shows whether each distractor is functioning.

Item-Analysis Worksheet

	(1)	(2)	(3) Percent Correct	(4)	(5) Percent Difference	(6) Discrim-ination	(7) Diffi-culty
Item	H *	L †	H	L	H − L		
1	10	10	100	100	0	0	100
2	9	6	90	60	30	+	75
3	6	8	60	80	−20	−	70
4	8	5	80	50	30	+	65
5	4	3	40	30	10	0	35

* H = number of the highest 10 scoring students who answered this item correctly.
† L = number of the lowest 10 scoring students who answered this item correctly.

Still more effective is to count the responses to each possible answer by the students who obtained the highest scores and by those with the lowest total scores. Summaries such as the following can be helpful:

	Responses					
Item 4	A	B	C *	D	E	Omit
Highest 10 students	1	0	8	1	0	0
Lowest 10 students	3	2	5	0	0	0

* Correct response.

One distractor (E) for item 4 was not working at all for this group of students. Sometimes a distractor is more attractive to the better students than to the low-scoring students (see D); it is said to function in reverse.

Grades and Report Cards

You can be much fairer in assigning grades if you use letter grades or just a few categories rather than percents, since you will have to distinguish only about five levels of ability rather than 100 levels. Even then you need to think about what the grade stands for. Does it represent effort regardless of whether the student accomplished something? Does it compare the student's accomplishment with an absolute standard? Is the student's status evaluated in relation to the rest of his class? Or, is each student's progress considered in relation to his own ability? It is impossible to know whether a "B" grade represents an "A" student who did not work to capacity, a "B" student who made normal progress, or a "C" student who pushed himself to achieve beyond normal expectations.

A final grade that is based on objective tests may be obtained by combining all of the raw scores. The tests need not be weighted, since scores from the longer tests tend to be dispersed more than the others. Absolute standards, such as Nunnally proposed, might be applied to the combination of raw scores from several tests:

1. A—about 85 or 90 percent of the items were correct.
2. F—about 40 or 45 percent of the items were correct.
3. The number of items between the A and F zones might be divided into three approximately equal parts for the B, C, and D zones.[31]

Another way of determining the final grades is simply to average the grades from each unit, providing each unit was independent of the others—that is, they could have been presented in any order; the content of one unit does not require the student to have already learned what is in another of the units. If there is a hierarchy of knowledge (with each unit building upon a previous one), the final exam is the best measure of a student's accomplishment.

The approach with which many college students are familiar can be applied in determining grades at other levels as well. Grade points might be assigned to letter grades in a manner such as this: A = 4 points, B = 3, C = 2, D = 1, F = 0. To save having to convert letter grades to grade points, numerical ratings from 4 to 0 are sometimes used. Each basis for determining a final grade is rated and assigned the corresponding number of points. The determiners may carry different weights, as in the following example, where the tests count twice as much as the other factors. The total number of grade points divided by the number of weighted determiners (4 in the example) gives the grade point average. This is how a teacher's record book might look:

Name of Student	Written Classwork	Laboratory Work	Tests	Total Grade Points	Grade-Point Average	Grade
Weights	1	1	2			
Ames, Evelyn	A 4	B 3	C 4	11	2.8	B—

Home economics teachers usually find that no single standard can be set as an absolute requirement for all students to meet. Standards are multiple—superior students should be expected to attain higher stand-

[31] Jum C. Nunnally. *Educational Measurement and Evaluation.* New York: McGraw-Hill, 1964, p. 159.

ards than those reached by the less able students. Students in higher grades should be expected to produce higher quality work than inexperienced or immature students can do. Therefore, the teacher must establish varying standards, and she must also determine the minimum level that each student will be expected to achieve before he goes on to a new grade level.

There is a trend toward simply giving "credit" or "no credit" for a course, with a "C" or "2" rating required to receive credit. "No credit" does not count against a student as a "D" or "F" would. Such an approach relieves the pressure on students but may cause some students not to work as hard as they would if levels of satisfactory performance were being recorded. Whatever approach you use, try not to overevaluate the students and be sure that the grades you assign have a rational foundation.

Marks should not be used to stimulate a student to do something in which he sees no purpose. Their primary purpose is to facilitate the educational development of each student in relation to his ability. When a student is achieving at a low level, you might cooperate with a counselor in studying possible causes and taking remedial action. The student may be from a culturally-deprived home, may be a slow learner, may have a personality conflict with you or a classmate, or there may be other factors causing his low achievement.

Marks are also used to inform the parents of the progress being made by their children. The teacher has an obligation to college admissions offices and prospective employers to enable them to have confidence in the validity of her grades when used along with other grades and test data in making predictions about the future success of her students.

Evaluation of Your Teaching

The final chapter of this book will discuss, at greater length, the importance of your self-evaluation. Evaluation is a tool that helps you to improve your teaching. One of the best ways to determine whether you are doing a good job of teaching is to think in terms of how well your students are achieving the goals of home economics education as you have defined them for your own situation. Information that you collect in relation to specific home economics teaching gives you the necessary data for making judgments about the degree of goal attainment. Also, a well-planned evaluation program enables you to assemble facts showing the contributions that a stimulating and broad home economics curriculum makes to your community and its families.

Selected References

Adams, Georgia Sachs, *Measurement and Evaluation in Education, Psychology and Guidance.* New York: Holt, Rinehart and Winston, 1964, pp. 367–395, 401–425.

Ahmann, J. Stanley, and M. D. Glock, *Evaluating Pupil Growth* (2nd ed.). Boston: Allyn and Bacon, 1963.

American Psychological Association, *Standards for Educational and Psychological Manuals.* Washington, D.C.: American Psychological Association, 1966, pp. 12–32.

Arny, Clara B., *Evaluation in Home Economics.* New York: Appleton-Century-Crofts, 1953.

Brown, Marjorie, and Jane Plihal, *Evaluation Materials for Use in Teaching Child Development.* Minneapolis: Burgess Publishing Company, 1966.

Downie, N. M., *Fundamentals of Measurement: Techniques and Practices* (2nd ed.). New York: Oxford University Press, 1967, pp. 213–225.

Gorow, Frank F., *Better Classroom Testing.* San Francisco: Chandler Publishing Company, 1966, pp. 72–84.

Green, John A., *Teacher-made Tests.* New York: Harper & Row, 1963.

Jorgensen, Gary O., et al., *Interpersonal Relationships: Factors in Job Placement.* Salt Lake City, Utah: Graduate School of Social Work, Rehabilitation Research Institute, Bulletin Number 3, 1968. (excellent check lists)

Lyman, Howard B., *Test Scores and What They Mean.* Englewood Cliffs, New Jersey: Prentice-Hall, 1963.

Mager, Robert, *Developing Attitudes Toward Learning.* Palo Alto, California: Ferrin Press, 1968.

Nunnally, Jum C., *Educational Measurement and Evaluation.* New York: McGraw-Hill, 1964, pp. 14–27, 77–88, 158–165.

Remmers, H. H., N. L. Gage, and J. Francis Rummel, *A Practical Introduction to Measurement and Evaluation* (2nd ed.). New York: Harper & Row, 1965.

Stodola, Quentin, and Kalmer Stordahl, *Basic Educational Tests and Measurement.* Chicago: Science Research Associates, 1967, pp. 130–162, 254–300.

Tyler, Leona E., *Tests and Measurements.* Englewood Cliffs, N.J.: Prentice-Hall, 1963.

Wood, Dorothy A., *Test Construction.* Columbia, Ohio: Charles E. Merrill, 1961.

13

Evaluating the Setting for Learning Experiences

In every area of the curriculum and at every level of teaching, the classroom environment and organization can contribute to effective teaching. Home economics education benefits particularly from an appropriate setting—one that provides a homelike atmosphere and is in keeping with the socioeconomic levels of the community. Since the needs of various communities differ, no single set of standards can be established for evaluating the home economics department. Schools in some communities should come close to fulfilling most of the ideals discussed in this chapter if they are to meet the needs of the growing number of families in the upper-middle or high income brackets. However, schools in communities that are less privileged should strive for goals that are realistic for their communities.

This chapter will present suggestions for evaluating the space and equipment for teaching home economics courses, the management of the business affairs of the department, and the student behavior that contributes to the accomplishment of the departmental goals.

THE EFFECTIVENESS OF THE PHYSICAL ENVIRONMENT IN PROMOTING LEARNING

The space and equipment that are provided for the teaching of home economics contribute to or detract from the attainment of the departmental goals. Simple, attractive, and up-to-date furnishings can stimulate interest in taking home economics. Satisfying experiences in a convenient and attractive room may help students to develop appreciation for beauty and encourage them to try to make their homes more livable and attractive. Students may be able to see ways of carrying over their school instruction to their homes if the standards set by the school seem possible for them to achieve.

Umbach pointed out wisely that the primary purpose of home economics instruction "should be the improvement of people rather than the production of things." The home economics teacher needs to understand and make clear to her administrator and community members that the home economics department is not intended to be a "model of perfection" but is rather a "setting for learning." With this basic philosophy, the teacher should guide each class in making some contribution to the "aesthetic enjoyment" of the department.[1]

In evaluating the setting of your home economics department or room, you might consider four major factors: (1) how effectively it lends itself to various teaching purposes and techniques; (2) how flexible it will be as new needs arise in the future; (3) whether its standards are attainable in the community; and (4) how well it presents a homelike atmosphere. The following questions will guide you in evaluating the present status of your department and in determining possible directions in which to work for improvement.

How Well Does the Physical Environment of the Home Economics Department Contribute to Effective Teaching?[2]

1. IS THE LOCATION OF THE DEPARTMENT SUITABLE?
   a. Is the department located conveniently for the delivery of supplies and equipment?
   b. Is the department accessible for school and community groups who need to use the facilities?
   c. Are all of the rooms in the department adjacent or housed as a unit?
   d. Is the department located near the other school activities?
2. ARE ADEQUATE SPACE AND EQUIPMENT PROVIDED?
   a. Are the facilities adequate for the size of classes that will be using the rooms?
   b. Are there enough rooms for the number of home economics teachers and classes who will need classrooms?
   c. Are the work areas large enough, with free passage between them, but no traffic through them?
   d. Are all of the important areas of home economics education provided for?
   e. Is preparation for wage-earning possible for students who need it?
   f. Are most of the facilities used effectively a large portion of the time?
   g. Are the rooms flexible and expandable to provide for more teachers and varied patterns of teacher utilization?

[1] Dorothea Umbach, "An Apartment in Homemaking Teaching." *Journal of Home Economics,* **46**:21–23, January 1954.

[2] Adapted in part from *Space and Equipment for Homemaking Education* (rev. ed.). Sacramento: California State Department of Education, Bureau of Homemaking Education, 1954, pp. 13–17.

h. Are the facilities suited to the age levels that will be served in the school and community?

3. DOES THE DEPARTMENT HAVE A HOMELIKE SETTING?
   a. Are the rooms well-proportioned?
   b. Do the rooms have attractive, well-chosen background colors?
   c. Are the walls and ceilings clean and in good repair?
   d. Are the finishes suitable for the various work centers?
   e. Do the rooms and their furnishings demonstrate good use of color, line, form, and texture?
   f. Are the furnishings durable and easy to care for under hard and constant use?
   g. Does the department provide for flexibility in the arrangement and use of the space and furnishings?
   h. Is the department in keeping with the economic levels of homes in the community?
   i. Is a living-and-dining center provided to accommodate an entire class for experiences in home furnishing, care of the home, and social and family living?

4. IS A HEALTHY AND SAFE ATMOSPHERE MAINTAINED IN THE DEPARTMENT?
   a. Is the natural and artificial lighting adequate for all activities?
   b. Are the windows shaded to prevent glare?
   c. Are screens and outside doors used where they are necessary?
   d. Are the ventilation and heating easily controlled?
   e. Are the heating and fresh air evenly distributed?
   f. Is the hot water supply sufficient?
   g. Are running water, soap, paper towels, and a waste basket available in each classroom where students carry on activities?
   h. Are the floors comfortable to stand on, quiet when people walk, easy to clean, and kept in good repair?
   i. Are the chairs comfortable for students of various sizes?
   j. Are the rooms soundproofed?
   k. Is adequate provision made for the refrigeration of food and sanitary disposal of garbage?
   l. Are there adequate facilities for washing and drying towels, aprons, and other materials used in the classroom?
   m. Are the heights of working surfaces, tables, and chairs suitable for students of different heights?
   n. Have safety precautions been taken?
   o. Is a regularly serviced fire extinguisher of adequate size available readily in all parts of the department?

5. DOES THE DEPARTMENT PROVIDE A SITUATION THAT IS CONDUCIVE TO GOOD TEACHING?
   a. Are the chalkboards and bulletin boards adequate in size, located where all students can see them, and of good background color?
   b. Are open shelves and decorative centers provided as centers of interest?
   c. Is a display center available in the corridor and/or home economics room?

d. Is audiovisual equipment readily available and can the rooms be darkened satisfactorily?

e. Is space available for independent study or individualized programmed instruction?

f. Are books, magazines, and pamphlets easily located and accessible to the students?

g. Are the electrical outlets well-placed and sufficient in number?

h. Are movable tables and comfortable chairs available for each class?

i. Are various types of equipment, representing different cost levels, provided to broaden the students' experiences?

j. Is all equipment checked regularly and kept in proper working condition?

k. Is a teacher's work center provided with a desk, chair, and files?

l. Can supervision be given easily to each work area?

m. Is a demonstration center provided?

n. Is space provided for teacher-student conferences and for discussions by small groups of students?

o. Is a discussion area available for an entire class?

p. Is an outdoor living area provided, where practical?

q. Is a laundry center, with a washing machine and drier, provided?

r. Does the clothing center provide:

1. a unit arrangement of equipment including a work table with tote trays, sewing machine, and ironing equipment?
2. a private dressing area?
3. a full-length triple mirror and space for instruction on fitting garments?

s. Does the food and nutrition center provide:

1. a unit arrangement for meal planning, preparation, and service including a range, counter space, cabinets, sink, table, chairs, and equipment for family meals?
2. a demonstration unit equipped with a mechanical dishwasher, garbage disposal, and refrigerator with adequate space for frozen foods?

t. Are arrangements possible for a play school to be set up in the home economics department or for experiences with young children to be obtained elsewhere?

6. IS ADEQUATE AND WELL-PLANNED STORAGE SPACE PROVIDED?

a. Does the teacher have storage space for her personal belongings, such as wraps, personal articles, and files?

b. Is adequate storage space available for students' personal belongings, such as wraps, books, and purses?

c. Can instructional materials be filed easily where they are readily accessible? (*Examples:* books, pamphlets, magazines, charts, exhibits, models, posters, flannel board, film strips, and slides.)

d. Has well-planned and readily accessible storage space been provided for cleaning equipment and supplies? (*Examples:* brooms, mops, dust pans, dust cloths, wax, polish, and vacuum cleaner.)

e. Is storage space provided for materials that are used in *child study*? (*Examples:* toys, layette, bassinet, bathing and feeding equipment, construction materials, play equipment, chairs, tables, cots, blankets, and easels.)

f. Are the supplies for the study of *clothing and textiles* stored conveniently? (*Examples:* swatches of fabrics; illustrative material showing steps in clothing construction; garments under construction; finished garments; pressing equipment—portable ironing boards, irons, pressing boards, cloths, distilled water; small sewing equipment; and supplies.)

g. Has storage space been planned for the supplies and equipment necessary to teach *food and nutrition*? (*Examples:* refrigeration for fresh and frozen foods; ventilated bins for citrus fruits and root vegetables; large containers for staples; seldom-used equipment—large kettles, canning equipment, ice cream freezers, punch bowls and cups, tea and coffee service, trays, electrical appliances, and pressure saucepan; extra equipment as replacements for unit kitchens; garbage can and/or disposal; table linens and paper goods; and aprons.)

h. Has provision been made for storing the materials used in teaching *home care of the sick*? (*Examples:* bed; bedding, pillows, and linens; and first aid kit and/or medicine cabinet.)

i. Are the *home furnishings* supplies and equipment included in the storage space? (*Examples:* tools, work bench, and saw horses; springs, batting, and webbing; paints, removers, stains, brushes, and sandpaper; furniture being renovated; curtain, drapery, and upholstery fabrics; samples of floor coverings, wall paper, and wood finishes; and art objects, pictures, and flower containers.)

j. Has provision been made for the equipment needed in the study of *social and family living*? (*Examples:* card tables and folding chairs; dining table leaves; hassocks and/or cushions for additional seating space; and guests' wraps.)

As you examine your department in the light of the preceding standards, you will very likely realize that it is far from perfect. Even one of the newer departments, which seems to be ideal in providing everything that might be desired, must change as the home economics program grows. One mark of an alert teacher is a changing department. As new needs arise, she rearranges or adds to her department. A well-planned department is the result of cooperative efforts of many people over a long period of time. Adding something new to the department because it is fashionable shows a lack of understanding of the need for long-range planning. Techniques of good management, which will be presented in the following section, enable a teacher to evaluate and plan for present and future needs.

MANAGEMENT FOR EFFECTIVE TEACHING

Management is a process of intelligent decision making on the allocation of human and material resources toward the realization of the home economics department's goals. As the teacher and students work out plans for managing the various aspects of the home economics department, they need to think through what their goals really are. Perhaps the teacher will find that her values are different from the values cherished by her students. The Map of Values in Table 11 shows some of the major values that were held by college students, those held by teachers, and those held jointly by teachers and students. As you work with students at the junior and senior high school levels, you may discover that other values are important to them.

TABLE 11 Map of Values *

Values held by college students	Values held jointly by both	Values held by faculty members
"Belonging"	Ambition to improve one's position	Efficiency
Curiosity	Beauty	Enjoyment of work
Effectiveness	Comfort	Order
Entertainment	Contribution made by the homemaker	Planning
Fairness	Cooperation	Self-evaluation
Novelty	Democratic family as means of fulfilling individual needs	Skills
Social status	Family tradition	
Spontaneity	Health	
	Importance of the individual	
	Knowledge	
	Love and affection	
	Professional tradition	
	Recognition	
	Recreation	
	Security	

* Adapted from Elizabeth W. Crandall, "Home Management and a Theory of Changing." *Journal of Home Economics,* **51**:345, May 1959.

Effective management of the home economics department is necessary if students are to realize the importance of management in the home and have experience in carrying out the various management processes. Most departments have limited resources; thus, choices must be made to insure that these resources are used to obtain the maximum goal attainment with the least expenditure of human and material resources. Choice-making is complex because teachers and students may hold different values, may be motivated toward expressing the same value through different kinds of goals, or may consider different kinds of alternatives. Then, too, students and teachers vary as to the amount of a resource they are willing to allocate to a home economics class goal and as to the degree of responsibility they are willing to assume concerning the consequence of a particular choice.

Social forces affecting family life exert their influence toward and against change, adding a further complicating factor as a teacher tries to develop effective ways of managing a home economics department. For example, technological advances affect the equipment and products that are used in homes; yet, the school may have made previous heavy investments in equipment and appliances. Changing concepts of men's and women's roles are evolving; yet, the home economics teacher may be confronted with perfectionist standards. She may feel that becoming flexible in standards leads to informality, and that this may be interpreted as laziness. Just as the homemaker finds that her role expectations are no longer clear-cut, so does the home economics teacher. Although American society is willing to accept and, in fact, promotes change in material aspects, change in home practices that are a part of an underlying value system is not as easily accepted. Because the home economics teacher is more concerned with the intangible aspects of family living than she is with the material aspects, managing her teaching environment to achieve these goals presents a challenge. These and other forces, which were outlined by Crandall, must be taken into consideration as a teacher makes decisions that will affect the management of the home economics department.[3]

The home economics teacher is the chief decision maker in her realm of operation—the home economics classroom. Although some decisions, such as just what resources are available to her and how they will be allocated, are determined by other school authorities, she generally makes the crucial decisions of managing the teaching environment for her students during the times they are in her classes. Whether or not she participates in the "doing" aspects of operating her classroom, she does "manage" so that particular learnings do take place.

Paolucci's study of "Decision-making in Relation to Management in Classes of Home Economics by Beginning Teachers" revealed that beginning teachers varied in the number of decisions with which they were

[3] Elizabeth W. Crandell, "Home Management and a Theory of Changing." *Journal of Home Economics,* 51:347, May 1959.

confronted, but that their decisions centered around similar types of problems. Included among their managerial decisions were "how to teach," "care and use of room, materials, and equipment," "use of time," "money," "interruptions," "discipline," and "what to teach." Ease in reaching a closure was determined by the amount of knowledge, skill, information, and past experience of the teacher as well as by the number of possible alternatives and the certainty of consequences afforded by the situation. Factors that contributed to satisfaction in decision-making were "recognition, approval, achievement, conformity, efficiency, and success." Dissatisfaction was experienced when decision-making resulted in "disapproval, inefficiency, inequality, lack of achievement, lack of success, and uncertainty." [4]

A number of the problems that were mentioned by this group of beginning teachers have been discussed previously in this book. The remainder of the section points out some of the factors to consider as you evaluate the care of the home economics room and its equipment, the financial management of the home economics department, and the filing of materials used in instruction and guidance of the students.

Care of the Home Economics Room and Its Equipment

As you consider with the students the housekeeping needs of your department, you will need to work out plans for two important aspects: cleanliness and orderliness. You might work out a general plan with your students, using the following questions as a guide:

1. *What* needs to be done?
2. *Why* should it be done? Is it really necessary?
3. *Who* will be responsible for doing it?
4. *When* should it be done?
   a. Should it be done daily, weekly, or only occasionally?
   b. When tasks are done on the same day, in what sequence should they be accomplished?
5. *How* can it be done most effectively?
   a. What equipment is essential?
   b. Is the necessary equipment up-to-date and in good repair?

In developing these plans, the teacher should realize the need for being flexible and adjusting the plans when necessary. She should help each class to feel that the care of the department is the responsibility—in part,

[4] Beatrice Paolucci, "Decision-making in Relation to Management in Classes of Home Economics by Beginning Teachers." Unpublished doctor's dissertation, Michigan State University, 1956. (As abstracted in *Journal of Home Economics*, **49**:225, March 1957.)

at least—of the class. The more mature classes should be given opportunity to develop increasingly difficult skills and assume increased managerial responsibilities. The teacher plays an important managerial role when she directs the students and others in creating an environment that is attractive, orderly, efficient, flexible, and conducive to work, and in this role she helps students learn to set standards, to try out alternatives, and to assume responsibility. In fulfilling her managerial role, the teacher supervises the carrying out of a number of routine tasks that are necessary parts of everyday living at school as well as at home.

Cleanliness

Before working out plans with the students for maintaining the cleanliness of your department, you should obtain a clear picture of the janitorial services that your rooms will receive. Perhaps the major cleaning of floors and walls can be done perodically by the custodians while they are cleaning the rest of the school. Even though such services are available, each class should be responsible for leaving the room clean for the students who use the classroom next. In addition to leaving the floor clean, the class should pay attention to tables, desks, chairs, sewing machines, shelves, drawers, cupboards, chalkboards, and window sills. Dish towels and small equipment such as kitchen utensils should be cleaned before they are stored. Even a frost-free refrigerator should be cleaned regularly. Leftover foods should be used and perishables thrown away. The garbage can should be kept clean and free from odors. Water faucets should be in good condition, so that they can be shut off completely, and are not left dripping.

Special attention should be given to cleanliness and protection of furnishings immediately before vacation periods. Silver should be stored where it will be safe. Furniture should be protected. Draperies should be cleaned and stored. Foods that will keep should be placed in glass or metal containers.

Other suggestions that might help to prevent unnecessary cleaning and to maintain high standards of cleanliness in the department are the following:

1. Use plastic trays, since they are easy to clean when used as sewing supply drawers.
2. Have a dispenser full of paper cups placed beside each sink, to eliminate an accumulation of used drinking glasses.
3. Try to have duplicate equipment, so that housekeeping routines can be done quickly.

4. Replace worn parts or equipment promptly, so as to prevent serious damage to the equipment and/or room.
5. Have screens on all windows and doors; these contribute to health and sanitation in rooms where food is prepared.

Orderliness

Three guides for maintaining an orderly department are: (1) provide a definite place for every article; (2) keep everything in its place; and (3) place supplies and equipment near where they will be used. These guides apply not only to the large, movable equipment and furnishings but also to small equipment and illustrative materials.

In evaluating the degree to which your home economics department is orderly, you might consider such points as the following:

1. Are containers labeled and arranged systematically?
2. Is a place provided near the door for students to leave their supplies from other classes?
3. Do you have a screen to conceal supplies and equipment needed for special projects, so as to eliminate getting them out and putting them away?
4. Do you plan units of instruction so that more than one class can use special equipment while it is out?
5. Do you provide a place to keep instructional materials as they are received, and are they filed regularly?
6. Is a large, attractive pin cushion hanging near the bulletin board for pins that are picked up?
7. Is all of the kitchen equipment from one unit kitchen marked as belonging to that unit (such as with colored handles or special paint to identify the unit)?
8. Are the alphabet letters for bulletin boards filed systematically?

Your students can help you work out ways for keeping the home economics room attractive and ready for teaching at all times. Together you may want to work out a rotating system for accomplishing the little tasks that can be accomplished quickly when all help—straightening chairs, returning materials to proper places, caring for plants, checking out reference materials, and the like. Being able to make accurate judgments about what can be accomplished during a particular class period will be an important managerial skill for you to achieve. This will require ability on your part to establish time norms, assess the work capacity of your class both as individuals and as a whole, and set realistic goals.

Managing the Finances of the Department

Financial management of the home economics department might be divided into four major aspects: (1) making a financial plan; (2) keeping financial records; (3) preparing accounts; and (4) taking inventory. The following questions will help you to know what factors to consider as you develop your financial plans and as you attempt to evaluate your progress toward sound business procedures.

1. In making the financial plan for the year, did you consider the:
   a. opportunity for students to have a practical experience in financial management by sharing in the planning?
   b. total amount of money available and its adequacy for meeting the needs of the department for the whole year?
   c. expeditures of the previous year (or years)?
   d. size of each class?
   e. grade level of each class?
   f. nature and goals of each course?
   g. supplies and equipment already available for teaching each course?
   h. upkeep of the department—needs for maintenance, repair, and replacement?
   i. need for illustrative material and magazine subscriptions?
   j. possibility of equalizing the expenditures throughout the year by purchasing illustrative materials at times when other expenditures, such as the food purchases, are relatively low?
   k. need for providing teaching materials for *all areas* of the home economics program?
   l. future needs of the department for additions or improvements?
2. Do you *keep financial records* that show for each purchase:
   a. the nature of the purchase?
   b. the amount that was purchased?
   c. the date of purchase?
   d. from whom the purchase was made?
   e. by or for whom the purchase was made?
   f. a receipt indicating the date of payment, the person who made the payment, and the method of payment?
   g. the amounts spent for care and repair?
3. Do you *prepare accounts* periodically to show the:
   a. funds that were available at the beginning of the period?
   b. amount that was budgeted for various purposes?

c. actual expenditures that were made in each category?
d. balance on hand at the end of the period?

4. Do you keep a "running file" on each article in the department and *take inventory* periodically to show the:
   a. name of each article purchased?
   b. amount or quantity of each article that was purchased?
   c. date of each purchase?
   d. location of each article in the department?
   e. amount or quantity that is on hand at the time of inventory?
   f. date of the inventory?

Filing Instructional Materials

The term *instructional materials,* as used in this chapter, includes the illustrative materials that are used with or by the students, the records of individual and class activities, and the reports on enrollment and accomplishments of the department. School systems differ in the kinds of records they require of home economics departments. The size of a home economics department itself may also be a factor in determining the quantity and categories of records that are needed. Furthermore, individual home economics teachers differ in their interest in record keeping, and in their ability to keep up an elaborate system of filing instructional materials and reports.

The four main goals of each home economics teacher should be: (1) a system of filing instructional materials that will be simple, clear, and convenient; (2) complete records available at all times; (3) promptness and accuracy in the preparation of all records and reports; and (4) assumption by the students of management responsibility (this you accomplish by letting them share as much as possible in the planning and utilizing of the instructional materials).

Instructional materials may be filed in a variety of containers such as manila folders, large envelopes, letter-file boxes, cardboard cartons, library-bulletin boxes, and sectional filing cases. The durability and expense of the containers and the ease of using the filed materials are factors that should be considered in selecting the method of filing.

Illustrative Materials

You will need to develop a system of headings that will be most useful for your department. Ostler and Carleton found the following list suitable for classifying materials on consumer education, which is a field that cuts across the major areas of home economics. You may be able to adapt ideas from this list as you develop a flexible system to meet the needs of your school: [5]

- Child Care
- Clothing
- Clothing Construction
- Consumer Economics
- Credit
- Fabrics
- Foods:
  - Breakfast, breads, cereals, and flours
  - Desserts and candy
  - Fruits, vegetables, and salads
  - Meat, fish, eggs, and poultry
  - Milk and milk products
  - Nutrition, menu planning, and purchasing
  - Preservation
  - Seasonings and sugars
  - Special
- Gift Suggestions
- Good Grooming
- Health and Home Nursing
- Home Furnishings
- Home Management
- Home Safety
- Home Wiring
- Household Equipment
- Housing
- Marriage and Family Living
- Money Management
- Sewing Equipment
- Table Setting
- Travel

As you evaluate how effectively your department is handling its illustrative materials, you might seek answers to these questions:

1. Are the students sharing the managerial experiences connected with the preparation, filing, and use of the materials?
2. Are helpful materials from magazines clipped and filed?
3. Are materials discarded if they are unimportant, lacking in authenticity, unsuitable for the grade level, or out of date?
4. Are books that are soiled or worn replaced or repaired?
5. Are there on hand enough copies of books and pamphlets for efficient use by the class—neither too few nor too many copies?
6. Has an efficient system been arranged for the circulation of books?
7. Has suitable filing and storage space been provided for charts, models, pictures, posters, projection equipment, and films?

Student Records

Two major types of instructional records should be kept in the home economics department. Your *classbook* provides a permanent record of the names of students enrolled in each course, their attendance, grades on various projects through the semester, and final grade in the course.

A *personal data folder* for each individual student should be con-

[5] Ruth-Ellen Ostler and Frederica B. Carleton, *Free and Inexpensive Consumer Education Teaching Materials*. Syracuse, N.Y.: Syracuse University, Bureau of School Services, 1956, table of contents. (Out of print.)

veniently filed, so that you have immediate access to the information about the student and her family. Chapters 4 and 5 described the types of materials that you might include in these files. Basically, these records will be of two types:

1. TEACHER RECORDS. Any information that you obtain from school records, home visits, conferences with the student, or observation should be filed in the student's personal folder. Such facts as the parents' names and occupations, home address, number and ages of brothers and sisters, and health information should be included.

2. RECORDS PREPARED BY THE STUDENTS. In addition to the records that the teacher fills out, she should include helpful materials prepared by the student. These might include records of her home experiences, questionnaires or check lists that were completed by the student, and a sampling of the student's written classwork.

Annual Reports

Periodic reports, perhaps even more frequent than the annual reports, may be necessary for a variety of reasons. Schools that are reimbursed by the State and Federal governments for their vocational home economics programs will need to show evidence that the reimbursement is justified in terms of the State Plan for Vocational Education. Other reports may be required on occasion by the local school board, the school principal, and/or the head of the home economics department. Such reports should not be treated lightly. The financial condition and reputation of the school may be influenced considerably by the content and accuracy of teacher-made reports.

Since reports serve a variety of purposes, no specific guides can present a complete picture of what should be included or how the reports should be presented. You should strive to make your reports interesting, to highlight the significant accomplishments of your department, and to present the facts accurately. As you evaluate your annual report, you might see if you have presented a clear picture of the following points.

1. Total enrollment during the year.
2. Number who dropped the various courses during the year.
3. Courses offered and the enrollment in each course.
4. Objectives and content covered in each course and the length of time devoted to each phase.
5. Types of home and/or community experiences completed by the students.

6. Number of homes visited by the teacher and evaluations of these visits.
7. Projects that were undertaken cooperatively with other groups in the school or community.

Remember that long after you have left a school your personality and effectiveness as a home economics teacher will live on through the records and reports of the home economics department. Reports have a far-reaching influence beyond the school and immediate community. People who may never see your department will make judgments about it on the basis of the reports that you and other teachers submit to your local school board, to the State Department of Education, and to the United States Office of Education. You can help to build a good reputation for your department and for the profession of home economics by having worthwhile accomplishments to report and by reporting them truthfully, effectively, and on time.

GUIDING STUDENT BEHAVIOR TOWARD DESIRABLE GOALS

Until now this chapter has been concerned with methods for managing the physical environment so as to make it conducive to learning. Another very important part of the learning environment is the social setting. Student behavior must be directed toward desirable goals, or the most elaborate physical environment will be wasted. "Discipline" is listed frequently as one of the major problems for a beginning teacher. Even experienced teachers feel that they could spend a larger portion of their time in effective teaching if they did not have to spend so much time handling problems of misbehavior that interfere with the education of the entire class. This chapter is not designed to give you "tips" or ready-made solutions for handling specific types of disciplinary problems, but, through reading this section, you should develop a better understanding of the meaning of "preventive discipline," a philosophy about classroom control, and general principles of guiding student behavior toward the accomplishment of class objectives. As you apply this basic philosophy in your teaching, you can evaluate how successful you are in preventing or dealing with a variety of behavior problems that might interfere with the attainment of home economics objectives.

Hymes has pointed out that children want discipline. Basically they are social beings who need the good will and respect of others. Their eagerness to conform is shown in their continuous imitation. Although they want discipline, Hymes stressed that they also want freedom. These two wants present rather conflicting situations: "Children must think *and* obey. Children must fit in *and* break out. They must follow accepted paths *and* branch out on their own." [6]

Good student behavior, or discipline, has several functions in the home economics classroom: (1) helping to create and maintain classroom conditions that are conducive to the attainment of the class objectives; (2) promoting favorable attitudes toward doing what is appropriate for the accomplishment of desirable objectives; (3) guiding students in the development of self-control and the ability to cooperate in meeting their daily responsibilities; and (4) instilling within students respect for authority in promoting the welfare of society.

Good student behavior is learned from a variety of specific experiences, often over a long period of time. Results of good disciplinary techniques may be difficult to observe quickly or objectively. However, some of the evidences of success in discipline may be seen in student growth toward acceptance of responsibility, compliance with school regulations, kindness, promptness, respect for property, self-control, and honesty.

Shostrom's philosophy is that the teacher who maintains *control* over students is reducing "human beings to the status of things." Techniques such as detention, sarcasm and ridicule, isolation, or sending a student to the office are negative, controlling, and fostering of conformity. A teacher should actualize student interests by encouraging inventiveness, innovation, and productivity. In this sample of classroom dialogue, he contrasts the teacher's actualizing behavior with controlling behavior: [7]

MARY: I'd like to put this design on the border of a play skirt for my little sister.

TEACHER A: Would you care to see if you could do some sewing in your crafts class?

TEACHER B: This is a class in art, not sewing.

As you strive to maintain the kind of student behavior that will make possible the attainment of desirable home economic goals, you take many precautions that help to prevent disciplinary problems. Probably the most successful teacher would admit, however, that she has never succeeded in eliminating discipline problems completely. An understanding of preventive discipline can help you to reduce the number and types of problems that arise, to reduce the seriousness of many of the misbehavior problems, and to handle problem situations effectively from the stand-

[6] James L. Hymes, *Behavior and Misbehavior*. Englewood Cliffs, N.J.: Prentice-Hall, 1955, pp. 5–8.

[7] Everett L. Shostrom, *Man, the Manipulator*. Nashville: Abingdon Press, 1967, pp. 157–160.

point of both enforcing class regulations and promoting the development of student self-control.

As you think back over the kinds of disciplinary problems that you have observed or with which you have been confronted during your student-teaching experiences, you can probably classify the causes of most of these problems in one or more of the following groups: (1) teacher or student personality factors, or a conflict in human relationships; (2) factors inherent in the classroom environment; and (3) the methods of planning or teaching that were used.

In evaluating your effectiveness in guiding student behavior and enforcing necessary classroom controls, you may find that the following questions will help you to eliminate undesirable factors in human relationships, in the classroom atmosphere, and in the teaching methods, and thereby prevent many problems from arising.

Teacher-Student Relationships

The rapport that a teacher has with her students can be judged from at least two standpoints: (1) what specific behaviors and techniques the teacher applies in her classroom and in her informal contacts with students; and (2) how the students view the teacher's personality and behavior.

1. IN YOUR DEALINGS WITH YOUR STUDENTS, DO YOU TRY TO:
    a. determine social blocks to learning?
    b. provide ways for students to achieve recognition other than through self-display?
    c. build up the ego of each student by giving special jobs, honors, or compliments?
    d. avoid situations in which students feel they have to tell lies?
    e. use personal comments and praise rather than criticism?
    f. help to maintain the morale of the group?
    g. refer individual students to the proper source of help to correct health problems, physical defects, or nervous instability?
    h. take time to listen to their side of the story and their reasons for the behavior?
    i. obtain all the facts before drawing a conclusion?
    j. be consistent in your actions day after day?
    k. be impartial and fair to all?
    l. work out goals and objectives cooperatively with your students?
    m. reject irresponsible behavior and teach better ways of behaving?
    n. help the students develop self-discipline?
    o. put aside your own work to help students with their problems?

2. IN THEIR RELATIONSHIPS WITH YOU, DO YOUR STUDENTS FIND THAT YOU:
   a. are tolerant, friendly, and sincere?
   b. maintain an adult reserve and formality while showing personal interest in each individual?
   c. show enthusiasm for your subject?
   d. are energetic and possess vitality?
   e. give attention to maintaining your own good physical condition?
   f. have overcome annoying mannerisms?
   g. have cultivated a good sense of humor?
   h. use an effective speaking voice—one that is low, with rich tones and a wide range of pitch?
   i. are active, walking around the room and talking pleasantly with individual students?
   j. are courteous, and consistent in treating students with respect?
   k. exercise self-control?
   l. are firm, but reasonable?
   m. are fair and willing to admit when you make a mistake?
   n. accept students as they are and understand their feelings?
   o. help students when they seek or need help?
   p. have time and interest to really get involved in increasing the students' feelings of self-worth?
   q. show initiative and resourcefulness?
   r. use good leadership techniques?
   s. appear self-confident?
   t. are alert to what is happening in all parts of the room?
   u. are prepared and know your subject matter?
   v. use a variety of techniques and educational media in presenting material so that interest is high?
   w. provide for the varying abilities and talents of each individual student?
   x. are receptive to their creative, positive suggestions for improving classroom instruction?

Classroom Environment

Since the importance of the physical environment was discussed earlier in this chapter, it will be mentioned here merely to point out its contribution toward the development of good student behavior. Maintaining an attractive room, with an arrangement of tables and chairs that provides for congenial social groups may help to prevent discipline problems from arising. Letting students share responsibility for adjusting the physical conditions of the room for their comfort may prevent problems that might stem from improper heating, lighting, and ventilation. Another technique for guiding student behavior into wholesome channels is to let them create an interesting room, giving special attention to books, magazines, pictures, flowers, bulletin boards, and exhibits.

Planning and Teaching

The training you have for teaching, the preparation you make for each class, your effectiveness in carrying out a variety of sound teaching methods, and your professional attitude and conduct are additional factors that influence student behavior. You must work to achieve that balance of discipline and freedom that will permit optimum learning in your classroom. As you guide students toward desirable goals, you might evaluate your planning and teaching by answering such questions as the following:

1. Do I have mastery of the concepts I will be teaching and am I flexible enough to incorporate new or conflicting information into this body of knowledge?
2. Do I prepare thoroughly the aims, motivations, and content for each class period? Do I show how these concepts relate to other subject areas?
3. Do I expect students to be in class with a desire to learn?
4. Do I expect the class to come to order when I give a quiet signal, such as standing at the front of the room?
5. Do I begin classwork promptly?
6. Am I teaching students something worthwhile and challenging?
7. Do I use methods that enable students to see the relationship between what they are learning and their lives outside of school?
8. Do I explain concisely and clearly what I expect of the students?
9. Do I present instruction at the proper level—neither too advanced nor too elementary?
10. Do I plan work in the proper sequence so that it is not too difficult or too fatiguing?
11. Do I show respect for the routine daily tasks, and never assign them as punishment for misbehavior?
12. Do I make the course interesting and gear it to the abilities and needs of the students?
13. Do I readjust the classwork if necessary or individualize the course?
14. Am I willing to permit orderly conversation?
15. Do I let the students help plan rules when they are needed and help to maintain an orderly classroom?
16. Am I showing consistency in enforcing classroom and school regulations?
17. Do I observe and check the beginnings of discipline problems (such as lack of interest, discontent, and misbehavor) before they grow into serious problems?

18. Do I always first determine the cause of misbehavior and take action that is consistent with the cause and suited to the individual students?

19. Do I often compliment students for their cooperation and contributions to classwork?

20. Do I let students make decisions?

21. Do I encourage discussions on such topics as getting along with others, being liked, and leadership?

22. Do I let discussions take the direction the students' own thinking suggests and help students reach sounder conclusions by raising other alternatives for them to think about?

23. Do I provide opportunities for direct observation and for audio-visual experiences?

24. Do I give students opportunity to participate in group projects, demonstrations, oral reports, dramatizations, panel discussions, or class-room management responsibilities?

25. Do I show respect for the student's effort?

26. Am I using a fair system of evaluation and grading?

In summary, a home economics teacher may be able to provide an effective learning environment for her students by giving attention to both the physical setting and the social-psychological atmosphere. The adequacy of space and equipment can be assured through a long-range plan and sound financial management. Cooperative planning and sharing of responsibility for the maintenance of a homelike atmosphere are important factors in guiding students toward desirable behavior and the attainment of the goals of the home economics department. The provision of necessary teaching materials and a plan for storing them where they will be convenient to use are important in the prevention of student misbehavior problems that might result from boredom or inappropriate illustrative materials. To provide an appropriate learning environment, then, involves careful management of the department's resources, adequate facilities, and guidance of student behavior in ways that will permit effective use of the department and provide for the development of student responsibility.

Selected References

Brembeck, Cole S., *Social Foundations of Education*. New York: John Wiley and Sons, 1966, pp. 61–117.

Burke, William J., "View from a Back-Row Seat." *National Education Association Journal* 57: 19–22, April, 1968.

Coon, Beulah I., *Home Economics Instruction in the Secondary Schools.* New York: The Center for Applied Research in Education, 1965, pp. 89–97.

Glasser, William, *Reality Therapy.* New York: Harper & Row, 1965, pp. 154–166.

Hall, Olive A., "Facilitating Change" in *The Adventure of Change.* Washington, D.C.: American Home Economics Association, 1966, pp. 31–40.

MacLennan, Beryce W., and Naomi Felsenfeld, *Group Counseling and Psychotherapy with Adolescents.* New York: Columbia University Press, 1968.

Parody, Ovid F., *The High School Principal and Staff Deal With Discipline.* New York: Teachers College Press, Columbia University, 1965.

Rogers, Carl R., *On Becoming a Person.* Boston: Houghton Mifflin, 1961, pp. 31–57, 107–124,273–278.

Schooler, Ruth, and Mary Mather, "Planning Homemaking Departments." *Illinois Teacher of Home Economics.* Vol. IV, No. 7.

Shostrom, Everett L., *Man, the Manipulator.* Nashville: Abingdon Press, 1967, pp. 157–168.

Thorpe, Louis P., *The Psychology of Mental Health* (2nd ed.). New York: The Ronald Press, 1960, pp. 402–413.

Walker, Beulah, and Mary Mather, "Innovations in Space and Facilities for Homemaking Departments." *Illinois Teacher of Home Economics.* Vol. V, No. 5, January, 1962.

14

The Teacher's Self-Evaluation

As you begin your teaching career, you will be entering a new phase of your life where each day's experiences have three-fold significances. (1) What you do as a teacher will be influenced by the values and attitudes you have developed and the previous experiences you have had. (2) Your attitudes, values, interests, and knowledge will have an influence upon your students and associates. (3) Your reactions to situations that arise in your daily teaching will help to determine the direction of your professional activities in the future. One way that you can insure a successful career in education for yourself is to be willing to evaluate yourself sincerely and periodically, considering what your goals really are, what resources you have, and what choices you must make in order to attain your goals.

To make an honest self-evaluation, you need to be aware of what can reasonably be expected of a beginning teacher. During your first year or two of teaching you will have to make many adjustments. Besides working out your own personal and family needs, you must adjust to the needs of your students, their parents, and your professional colleagues. As you gain teaching experience, your self-evaluation should be focused upon the challenges that await the mature and experienced teacher. If you continue to evaluate yourself in terms of what was acceptable when you first entered the teaching profession, you will do a great injustice to yourself and to your profession. This chapter should help you to clarify your goals as a beginning teacher, to understand what you should expect as you gain teaching experience, and to see the relationship between your individual growth and the future of the home economics teaching profession.

GOALS FOR A BEGINNING TEACHER

A beginning teacher might think about her goals from four standpoints: her students, her community, her professional colleagues, and her personal goals. These are by no means placed in the order of their importance; in fact, educators very likely would disagree as to their relative importance. One point that should be stressed, however, is that these four aspects are closely related. For example, a teacher may consider her personal life to be entirely her own business; but, in reality, her relationships with her students and colleagues may reflect her personal happiness or feelings of frustration. Likewise, the satisfactions and successes she gains from her work contribute to her own personal and emotional adjustment.

Goals in Working with Students

As you evaluate your effectiveness in helping students develop, you might consider first how well you *understand the students* and then how *skillfully you plan* experiences to meet their needs. The following questions are merely suggestive of those that you might seek to answer honestly as you rate yourself:

1. UNDERSTANDING OF STUDENTS.
   a. Do I consider each student a person of worth and dignity?
   b. Do I provide for their individual differences in planning learning experiences?
   c. Am I sensitive to the feelings of my students?
   d. Am I effective in helping students satisfy their social and emotional needs?
   e. Do I recognize the reasons why certain students have difficulty in learning?
   f. Am I developing in my students a feeling of security?
   g. Am I helping my students to develop wider interests?
   h. Am I friendly, but not "chummy," in my relationships with my students?
   i. Am I teaching my students to think for themselves?
2. SKILL IN PLANNING LEARNING EXPERIENCES.
   a. Am I effective in stimulating within my students a desire to learn?
   b. Do the students have opportunities to share in planning and evaluating their learning experiences?
   c. Am I resourceful in selecting and using instructional materials?
   d. Do I provide constructive leadership for the class activities?

e. Are decisions made in such a way that they are accepted by members of the class?

f. Are the students interested and busy with worthwhile activities?

g. Does the home economics curriculum for my classes develop competence in the following aspects of family living? [1]

> family relationships and child development
> consumption and other economic aspects of personal and family living
> nutritional needs and the selection, preservation, preparation, and use of food
> design, selection, construction, and care of clothing, and its psychological and social significance
> textiles for clothing and for the home
> housing for the family and equipment and furnishings for the household
> art as an integral part of everyday life
> management in the use of resources so that the values and goals of the individual, the family, or of society may be attained.

h. Are my assignments made as a part of a coordinated plan with other instructors?

Community Relationships

A beginning teacher who wishes to attain good relationships with the citizens of her community should remember that her dealings with students in her classroom are of utmost importance. A teacher who sends her students home each day with a sense of accomplishment and a knowledge of what they have achieved is building good public relations with her community.

An understanding of families and family problems, as presented in Chapter 4, is basic to building a program that meets the needs of the community. A beginning teacher, as well as an experienced one, can learn much about her community and, at the same time, help others learn much about the home economics program by inviting members of community organizations to functions where they can observe the learning experiences of the students. A word of caution might be given at this point. Home economics teachers often use "staged performances," such as fashion shows, teas, and luncheons, for occasions when the public is invited to the department. Such experiences give the public a narrow conception of what is done in home economics classes. Remember that

[1] *Home Economics—New Directions: A Statement of Philosophy and Objectives.* Washington, D.C.: American Home Economics Association, 1959, p. 4.

the focus of home economics is on families. As you plan ways of relating your program to the community, try to draw upon your resourcefulness and vast fund of knowledge so that community members may see the broad picture of home economics education in its natural setting.

In addition to your obligations as a teacher to develop a program suitable to your community, you have responsibilities as a citizen. Your professional education qualifies you to work with other citizens for the improvement of home and family life in your community. You should be willing to accept your share of community responsibilities, particularly those in which you are especially capable of making a contribution. In your enthusiasm to become acquainted with your community and to obtain recognition from the community leaders, you need to evaluate which responsibilities are most important for the improvement of home life and to determine how you can make your most effective contribution to the community. If you accept heavy responsibilities in your community, you may find that you do not have adequate time to prepare for your daily teaching. Both you and your students may suffer if you allow yourself to become physically or emotionally fatigued from out-of-school activities.

Among the prescriptions for happy teaching given to teachers entering the Parma Public Schools was the admonition: "Freedom is everybody's job. You don't have to register. You don't have to vote. But what would you do if you couldn't? . . . Non-voting is a symptom of civic sleeping sickness—evidence of anemic unconcern on the part of the patient for his own well-being." [2] As a citizen who is well educated and respected in your community, you have a responsibility to set an example by your concern for the preservation of democracy.

Relationships with Professional Colleagues

To the members of your community the word "teacher" stands for certain characteristic behaviors which they may have observed in their former teachers or in teachers who live in their community. From your very first day as a teacher, you will be helping to shape the image of a teacher in the minds of the members of your community. You have a responsibility to your colleagues to represent them in a wholesome manner that will enable the public to develop fair concepts of teachers.

Exhibit pride in your school and your profession! A beginning teacher is fundamentally a learner. You should be aware of the great contributions your colleagues make to your success. Just as you are influenced permanently by the standards and techniques of the teachers with whom

[2] Carl C. Byers and Arch S. Brown, *Prescriptions for Happy Teaching*. Cleveland: Parma Public Schools, 1954, p. 41.

you have student teaching experiences, so will your teaching career continue to be affected by the philosophy and methods of those with whom you share your first years of teaching. Truly great teachers recognize that success is not merely the product of their own efforts but is the result of assistance given by many of their colleagues.

Other teachers may be able to give you insight into the behavior of individual students whom you cannot seem to understand. However, whenever you talk about school problems, you should be discreet in your conversation. Gossip about students, parents, teachers, or administrators should not be part of your conversations with colleagues, whether in school or outside of the school.

Personal Goals

In spite of the shortage of teachers, the teaching profession is becoming a highly selected group. Undoubtedly you have already taken standardized tests and you may have had personal interviews designed to help a committee determine your suitability for teaching. The individuals who have selected you as a promising candidate for the teaching profession had faith that you would continue to maintain the desirable qualities that you possess now and that you would strive to develop certain characteristics that might be weak. Among the qualities that deserve your attention as a beginning teacher are: personal appearance, sincerity, pleasant and effective voice, vigorous health, resourcefulness, emotional stability, self-confidence, wholesome philosophy of life, integrity, commitment, enthusiasm, good social adjustment, consistency, a good sense of humor, and interest in helping others, especially young people. Learning to accept your own mistakes and those of others is an important part of your adjustment.

Home economics teachers have the advantage of studying about personal and home management as they are preparing to teach. The importance of practicing sound management cannot be overemphasized for the beginning teacher. You should devote a full work week to your teaching position; you are not entering a part-time profession or one that makes few demands on your time. At the same time, you need to remember that a satisfactory time plan provides for balancing your work hours with time for play, cultural development, spiritual refreshment, and social interests. You could easily spend most of your time preparing for your first year's classes, but you will be a more interesting and interested teacher if you learn to manage your resources and live a well-balanced life.

Good teaching is a sharing of yourself with others. It is only when you feel adequate yourself that you will be able to assume that others are adequate, responsible, loyal, and work-oriented. As a leader of students, you will communicate feelings of trust or distrust, permissiveness or control, and self-confidence or fear. Make yourself available to your students as a *person,* not as someone who is playing the *role of teacher.*

Home economics teachers have had considerable opportunity to develop broad cultural interests during their college years. As you enter the teaching profession, you must become self-directing. You have the choice of concentrating your interests on your area of specialization or of broadening your cultural understanding. Of course, you will need to master the subject matter that you will be teaching. Nevertheless, you may become so highly specialized that you do not see the relationship of home economics to other fields. A broadening of your interests may help you to converse intelligently with your colleagues and to make rich contributions to the lives of your students.

GROWTH WITH EXPERIENCE

Although the preceding section gave you points to consider in evaluating yourself during your first few years of teaching, you should realize that individual teachers differ. Occasionally, a teacher in her first year is much more mature and accomplished as a teacher than one who has had many years of teaching experience. No one can make a definite list of personal qualities and teaching experiences that should be required of every beginning teacher. Neither can we determine an exact cutoff point at which a teacher stops being a beginner and should be expected to measure up to standards for an experienced teacher. The emphasis in this chapter is on teacher self-evaluation. Only *you* will be capable of determining your strengths and weaknesses at any given time. *You* alone must accept the challenge to continue and direct your intellectual growth. But *you,* in cooperation with your colleagues in home economics and in the teaching profession, have a responsibility to advance your profession and to provide competent teaching for America's children.

Teaching Competence

As you gain experience in teaching, you will realize that each year brings new intellectual challenges and opportunities for growth in human relations. Ten years of teaching should be ten years of new and challenging experiences rather than one year's work taught over again ten times. An experienced teacher may need to guard against becoming bored, being careless about discipline, talking too much, using personal experiences excessively, reusing lesson plans without evaluating them and bringing them up to date, continuing to use familiar products when there are new and more effective ones, and covering a topic too rapidly.

A committee of educators and laymen in California formulated a statement of Factors in Teaching Competence that sets a high standard by which an experienced teacher might evaluate herself. These factors have been adapted slightly so that you can ask yourself how competent you are becoming: [3]

1. As a *director of learning,* do I
   a. adapt principles of child growth and development to planning of learning activities?
   b. plan my teaching-learning situation in accord with acceptable principles of learning?
   c. demonstrate effective instructional procedures?
   d. utilize adequate evaluation procedures?
   e. maintain an effective balance of freedom and security in the classroom?
2. As a *counselor and guidance worker,* do I
   a. utilize effective procedures for collecting information about each student?
   b. use diagnostic and remedial procedures effectively?
   c. help the student to understand himself?
   d. work effectively with the specialized counseling services?
3. As a *mediator of the culture,* do I
   a. draw on a scholarly background to enrich cultural growth of students?
   b. direct individuals and groups to appropriate significant life application of classroom learning?
   c. design classroom activities to develop student ability and motivation for finding democratic solutions to current social problems and recognizing and identifying key problems?
   d. direct students in learning to use those materials from which they will continue to learn after leaving school?
   e. help students develop attitudes and skills necessary for effective participation in a changing democratic society?
   f. help my students acquire the values realized as ideals of democracy, such as mutual respect, willingness and ability to cooperate in the solution of problems and the use of intelligence in problem solving, goals, and standards for effective living in our culture?
4. As a *link with the community,* do I:
   a. utilize available education resources of my community in classroom procedures?
   b. secure cooperation of parents in school activities?
   c. assist lay groups in understanding modern education?
   d. participate in definition and solution of community problems relating to education?

[3] Commission on Teacher Education, *Teacher Competence; Its Nature and Scope.* San Francisco: California Teachers Association, 1957, pp. 32–41.

5. As a *member of the staff,* do I:
   a. contribute to the definition of the over-all aims of the school?
   b. contribute to the development of a school program to achieve its objectives?
   c. contribute to the effectiveness of over-all school activities?
   d. cooperate effectively in the evaluation of the school program?
6. As a *member of the profession,* do I:
   a. demonstrate an appreciation of the social importance of the profession?
   b. contribute to the development of professional standards?
   c. contribute to the profession through its organizations?
   d. take a personal responsibility for my own professional growth?
   e. act on a systematic philosophy, critically adopted and consistently applied?

Microteaching

One of the promising recent developments used in the preservice training of teachers can be a significant means of self-evaluation and growth for an experienced teacher also. Although many variations are possible, microteaching involves having the trainee stress one technical skill as he teaches a short lesson to a small group of students. First, the trainee might watch a model teacher demonstrate good techniques on video tape. Then the trainee teaches a group of perhaps five students for about five to eight minutes. The session is recorded on video tape so he has an opportunity to see and hear himself. He may also receive constructive criticism from other trainees or a supervisor. He reteaches the same lesson to a different small group and evaluates the improvement in his performance.

The heart of microteaching lies in the idea of analyzing teaching into the component technical skills. Bush formulated the following list of instructional techniques and procedures for which microteaching has been used to demonstrate a specific skill:

Establishing set (cognitive rapport and immediate involvement in the lesson)

Establishing appropriate frames of reference (organizing and teaching the material from several points of view)

Achieving closure (pulling together the major points to provide a cognitive link between past knowledge and the new learning)

Using questions effectively (asking provocative, answerable, and appropriate questions)

Recognizing and obtaining attending behavior (noting indications of interest, boredom, comprehension, bewilderment)

Control of participation (practicing techniques which encourage interaction)

Providing feedback (eliciting feedback from students and modifying the lesson accordingly)

Employing rewards and punishments (reinforcing desired student behavior)

Setting a model (improving their ability to analyze and imitate teaching models) [4]

Advanced Study

An important part of your program for self-advancement is your plan for continuing your education throughout your career. Nothing can be more deadening for students than to have a teacher who graduated from college several years ago and who considers her education complete. Actually your present knowledge is only tentative. If you are to keep up with the rapid changes that affect home and family life and if you are to be familiar with improved ways of working with students, you will need to plan for graduate study. In-service education might be done in several ways, depending upon your objectives and resources. You might choose to travel. You might attend professional workshops or meetings of professional associations. You might take further college courses to broaden your interests or help overcome areas of weakness. You might plan your graduate program toward a master's or doctor's degree. An advanced degree might be taken in some subject matter specialty, in home economics education, or in education.

The home economics profession needs qualified persons for positions of leadership. As you gain teaching experience, you may find that you have definite ideas as to where you would like to be vocationally 5 or 10 years hence. Perhaps you will be happy to continue as a junior or senior high-school home economics teacher, either in the same school where you began your teaching career or in a different community. Perhaps you would like the challenge of supervising student teachers while you continue as a secondary-school teacher. Maybe you would like to take over administrative duties and become the head of your department. You might find counseling or a vice-principal's position of interest. Supervision of teachers for a city, county, or state school system provides another opportunity for you to advance. Teachers, research workers, and extension leaders are needed for international service. The need for college home economics teachers and administrators continues to expand. You will find outstanding positions in these and other fields are open to experienced home economics teachers who have completed an appropriate graduate program.

[4] Robert N. Bush, "The Science and Art of Educating Teachers," in *Improving Teacher Education in the United States*. Bloomington, Indiana: Phi Delta Kappa, 1967, pp. 41–48.

An important decision as you plan a graduate program is the choosing of the college or university that is best for you. The American Home Economics Association has recommended that, as you write to graduate schools and study their catalogues, you should consider such information as the following: [5]

1. How well prepared are the faculty members?
2. Are there good library facilities at and near the college or university you are considering?
3. Are the laboratories adequate in size and are they relatively up to date?
4. How much home economics research is being carried on? Is there concern for learning about new findings?
5. How much teaching and research work is offered in fields related to home economics education—in statistics, education, psychology, and sociology?
6. What is the reputation of the school's undergraduate program in the area in which you are interested?
7. Are suitable housing facilities provided for graduate students?
8. What are the graduates of the school doing? Are they making significant contributions either in research or administrative positions?

Another decision is whether to continue toward your master's degree immediately after you have received your bachelor's degree or to wait until you have had some teaching experience. Considerations on both sides were presented in a *Journal of Home Economics* article. Owens summarized her reasons for taking her master's degree immediately: [6]

1. Since my college courses were a basic preparation for graduate work, I did not want to give myself time to forget the technical knowledge I had acquired.
2. I felt that I was still geared to the routine of school life and would have fewer mental and emotional adjustments to make than I would have after a few years.
3. I did not want to waste time on a second-choice position when, after additional study, I might be doing what I really wanted to do.
4. I was afraid that I might find it difficult later on to part with the financial security of a job in order to return to school.

Scruggs waited awhile before taking her master's degree because:

Teaching was the logical culmination of my undergraduate experiences. I wanted and needed to teach. There were many opportunities to learn on the job. Teaching experience is a basic requirement of most positions in home

[5] Adapted from *Wanted: Home Economists with Advanced Degrees.* Washington: American Home Economics Association, 1956 (folder).

[6] Betsy Owens, "Why I Took My Master's Degree Immediately after My Bachelor's." *Journal of Home Economics,* **49**:120, February 1957.

economics education. To be of most benefit, graduate study in home economics education needs to be based upon understanding gained from experience.[7]

If you choose to work toward a master's degree, you might major in home economics education, or you might prefer to specialize in one of the subject areas of home economics. Home economics education courses provide excellent background if you wish to continue teaching at the secondary level, enter college teaching, become an administrator, or supervise other teachers. In preparing yourself, however, you would want to strengthen your background in one or more subject areas of home economics. If you find that your major interest is in college teaching or research, you may want to specialize in a subject area of home economics or in a related basic discipline such as economics or psychology. In this age of specialization you need to be cautious about overspecializing. You might examine college catalogues and talk to administrators about the combinations of subjects that a college teacher might be required to teach. A well-qualified, versatile teacher is an asset to a home economics department.

Regardless of whether you obtain a degree in home economics education or in an area of specialization, you should plan to include courses in statistics to increase your understanding of research methods and research findings. Research is basic for the improvement of home economics as well as other professional fields.

Many colleges and universities that offer graduate programs in home economics have scholarships, fellowships, or teaching assistantships for which you might qualify. Information may be obtained directly from the institutions of your choice. The *Journal of Home Economics* gives a biennial list in February of the opportunities for assistantships, scholarships, and fellowships. Application must usually be made in the early part of the spring semester. Once you have been a full-time teacher on regular salary you may hesitate to become a full-time graduate student or even to have the reduced income offered to a graduate assistant. However, the experience you could receive while studying part-time and serving as an assistant to university faculty members is invaluable.

Some school districts provide for sabbaticals whereby you might teach six years and spend the following year in graduate study or travel. If you have such an opportunity, use it to strengthen your professional competence. You might work for a master's degree, you might study abroad, or you might combine study and travel.

[7] Marguerite Scruggs, "Why I Waited to Take My Master's Degree." *Journal of Home Economics,* **49**:121, February 1957.

Even if you do not have opportunity for a sabbatical or for full-time graduate study, you can enrich your teaching by attending summer sessions or by taking work during the school year at a nearby college or university. Short workshops and meetings of your professional association will help to inform you about the recent developments affecting your field. If you are unable to participate in group meetings, you still have the obligation to keep informed and up to date through reading, professional books and journals, and educational television.

Experimentation to Improve Teaching

Experienced teachers who are alert will think of different ways of studying the needs and interests of their students, and of increasing the effectiveness of their teaching methods and materials. School systems often encourage teachers to try out promising new techniques. A term that is sometimes applied when teachers engage in studies dealing with their own school situations is *action research.* Corey defined action research as "the process by which practitioners attempt to study their problems scientifically, in order to guide, correct, and evaluate their decisions and actions." [8] Action research provides a way for teachers to examine what they are doing and to try out new methods. Problems that are of immediate practical concern to classroom teachers are identified and attacked creatively through action research.

One characteristic of action research is that the problem is of immediate concern to the individual teacher or group planning and conducting the study. The purpose of action research is to have an impact on the researcher; in this case, to help the teacher develop new and more effective ways of working with her students. When teachers themselves are guided in the selection and solving of their own problems, they are more likely to change their educational practices than if they were merely informed of recommendations based upon research carried out by "experts."

The design of an action research study is often developed cooperatively and is subject to modification as the study progresses. Although an individual can plan a study alone, action research frequently develops in a cooperative setting with a group of teachers and research consultants working together. The process of working together in solving problems of common interest can be as rewarding an experience as that of reaching conclusions based upon the research data. A better study often results because of the greater variety of talent directed toward it and the moral support each person gains from knowing that others support the basic ideas.

[8] Stephen M. Corey, *Action Research to Improve School Practices.* New York: Teachers College, Columbia University, 1953, p. 6.

The value of action research is measured by improved practice in the particular situation. Since the basic purpose of action research is to enable teachers to solve their own problems, this goal is fulfilled when a teacher discovers an improved way of dealing with an educational problem and then changes her practices in this direction. Ultimately, similar improvements may be made in other communities also.

Lippeatt outlined the procedures that a home economics teacher or group of teachers might follow if they wished to use action research as a basis for improving home economics programs: [9]

1. Identify the problem area.

   Example: We need to discover or evolve some effective ways to promote group operation in classrooms, Future Homemakers of America activities, and elsewhere.

2. Clarify the specific problem within the problem area with which she is concerned.

   Example: What leadership techniques produce demonstrable feelings of individual and group responsibility?

3. Decide upon a possible solution and state the hypothesis to be tested.

   Example: If the group leader (teacher, Future Homemakers of America officer, etc.) uses techniques of cooperative planning, the participants (pupils, members, etc.) will show feelings of responsibility toward the group and for the results of group effort.

4. Plan how to test the hypothesis and keep records of what happens (taking into account insofar as possible all pertinent variables).

   Example: How shall techniques of cooperative planning be described? Articles and studies may be reviewed and practices surveyed to identify some techniques.

   How shall those which seem desirable for the study be identified and selected? A study of techniques previously used by teachers, or identification of techniques used by others, or new proposed techniques. Decisions concerning desirable learning experiences to be tried out based upon hunches about what will be most effective (selection of study topic, use of time, possible outcomes, group participation, etc.).

   What kinds of data are needed as evidence of items being tested or questioned in the hypothesis? How will these data be collected (data related to techniques of cooperative planning; feelings and evidence of responsibility of participants toward group effort and group productivity)? Prepare appropriate instruments to be used by:

   Group Observer—logs and observation techniques.

   Participants—check lists and score cards.

[9] Selma Lippeatt, *Adventuring in Research to Improve School Practices in Homemaking Programs.* Misc. 3512—I: An Individual Approach. Misc. 3512—II: A Group Approach. Washington, D.C.: United States Department of Health, Education, and Welfare, Office of Education, Vocational Division, 1956 (folders).

Teachers—anecdotal records.

What time limit shall be considered and accepted as reasonable for the study?

5. Collect evidence as the study progresses.
6. Evaluate results and draw conclusions or inferences.

   Study the findings. . . .

   A. Have findings indicated what solutions seem to produce feelings of responsibility?
   B. How can conclusions be stated so that they may be used as a guide in future work?
   C. Have findings shown a need for other experiments that should be tried?
   D. How far can generalizations be made from conclusions?
7. Retest.

   Retest the hypothesis in new situations. The findings of one experiment will not necessarily apply in other situations or even in identical situations. . . .

   A. Would the conclusions reached hold true at other grade levels? With classes in succeeding years?
   B. What would happen to the conclusions in other school or community situations?

Among the problems that Taba suggested might be studied by action research are the following: [10]

1. Selection and organization of curriculum content: development of sequences of learning, implications of social class structure for learning, implications of psychological life needs, and guides to curriculum content.
2. Interpersonal relations, grouping and leadership: patterns of grouping, impact of psychological climate on learning.
3. Meeting heterogeneity: varying content and standards of achievement to meet needs of heterogeneous groups (socially, culturally, intellectually), adequacy of program for slow learners, challenge for faster and creative learners.
4. Forms of control in classroom: methods of nondisciplinary group control, developmental levels of group controls, cultural factors in styles of effective controls.

Participation in Professional Associations

As you gain experience and evaluate your plan for self-advancement, you should keep in mind that your own growth and the advancement of your profession must go hand-in-hand. If your major goals center around

[10] Hilda Taba and Elizabeth Noel, *Action Research: A Case Study*. Washington, D.C.: Association for Supervision and Curriculum Development, National Education Association, 1957, pp. 3–5.

personal ambitions, such as a high income or working hours that fit conveniently with your family schedule, the professions of home economics and of education will suffer. With the rapid changes that take place in our society, a profession that stands still will, in reality, be losing ground. Even a beginning teacher has an obligation to become an active member of professional associations, particularly in her local district, but also in state and national associations. Of these associations, at least one should have as its primary interest the total aspects of education and at least one should be concerned with home economics. An experienced teacher may choose to widen her membership to include several professional associations, but she should also assume an active role in helping to set the direction of the association's goals, membership requirements, programs, code of ethics, or other aspects that will influence the future of home economics education.

Members of professional associations receive many personal benefits. Sometimes the benefits are in proportion to the amount of time and effort a member gives to active participation in the group. National organizations can exert influence for legislation that is beneficial to society and to the profession. They work for public recognition and support of their programs. In addition, individual members receive copies of professional journals, bulletins, and research reports that present the latest information and expert opinions on current issues. Members who participate actively in local, state, or national meetings find fellowship, inspiration, and new ideas.

Among the organizations to which a home economics teacher should belong are the following:

1. AMERICAN HOME ECONOMICS ASSOCIATION.[11] AHEA is an association of home economics graduates whose purposes are stated as follows:

> The purposes of the Association shall be to further education and science in home economics. Without in any way limiting the foregoing, but in expansion thereof, the Association shall improve and strengthen education in home economics; establish and improve standards of service and scientific research in the public interest in home economics; sponsor and otherwise support seminars, debates, symposia, conferences, and similar professional discussion in home economics; state and disseminate policy for professional guidance at the national and international levels concerning the public interest in home economics; identify and study social, economic, and psychological changes having implications for home economics programs, and bring these changes to the attention of the home economics profession and the pub-

[11] "Bylaws of the American Home Economics Association," *Journal of Home Economics*, **60**: 589, September, 1968.

> lic; encourage and promote a sufficiently full and fair exposition of the pertinent facts involving legislation affecting home economics and the improvement of home and family life as to permit an individual or the public to form an independent opinion or conclusion; and promote liaison and other cooperative professional activity with groups having related concerns in behalf of the public interest in home economics.

Each home economics teacher can benefit from the work of the AHEA's *subject-matter* sections: Art; Family Economics—Home Management; Family Relations and Child Development; Food and Nutrition; Home Economics Teacher Education; Housing, Furnishings, and Equipment; Institution Administration; and Textiles and Clothing. The *professional sections* are: Colleges and Universities; Elementary, Secondary, and Adult Education; Extension Service; Health and Welfare; Home Economists in Business; Home Economists in Homemaking; Research; and College Chapters.

The work of its *committees* is varied and has a far-reaching influence for the improvement of homes as well as the prestige of the profession. Recent concerns and the direction for future plans of AHEA are evident in such committees as Accreditation; Consumer Interests; Future Development; Graduate Recruitment; Headquarters Development; International Program; Legislation; and Public Relations.

Representatives of the Association work cooperatively with groups having *related interests,* such as the American Public Welfare Association; Associated Organizations for Teacher Education; Council of National Organizations for Adult Education; Future Homemakers of America; National Conference on Social Welfare; National Council on Family Relations; and National Health Council.

2. HOME ECONOMICS EDUCATION ASSOCIATION. Membership in the Home Economics Education Association is open to persons who are "actively engaged in teaching, supervision, or administration of home economics in schools or colleges."

> The purpose of the Association is to improve the quality of home economics instruction in our nation's classrooms through:
>
> 1. Representing home economics as an integral part of the total educational program.
> 2. Informing educators and others of the value of home economics in educational programs.
> 3. Bringing together educators in the field of home economics for the promotion of studies and discussion of questions pertaining to home economics in school programs.

4. Engaging in and encouraging research concerning home economics education, and disseminating findings to educators and others interested in education including the members.
5. Acting as a liaison between other groups dedicated to these purposes or to the improvement of education generally.[12]

3. HOME ECONOMICS EDUCATION DIVISION OF THE AMERICAN VOCATIONAL ASSOCIATION. Educators and persons employed in business and industry join together in the American Vocational Association to help people enter the world of work or make progress in it, according to their capabilities and desires. As a reflection of the broad mandates for vocational education, the Association is composed of Divisions as well as Departments. The Divisions are concerned with Agriculture, Business and Office, Distributive, Home Economics, Industrial Arts, Trade and Industrial, New and Related Services, Guidance, Health Occupations, and Technical Education. Departments represent levels of instruction such as Adult, Secondary, and Post-Secondary; or functions such as Supervision and Administration, Research and Evaluation, Teacher Education, and Related and Special Programs (serving persons with academic, socioeconomic, or other handicaps that prevent them from succeeding in the regular vocational education programs).

The purposes of the Home Economics Division are:

> To work for improved support, especially at the national, regional, and state level, in order that a more effective total program of home economics education will be achieved.
>
> To provide professional service to home economics educators.
>
> To improve the image of home economics education.[13]

Code of Ethics

Along with the many ways in which professional associations work for the improvement of society and for the benefit of individual members of the profession, another important goal is to raise the status of the profession. Both home economics and education have faced serious challenges to their professional status. If they are to attain the recognition of which they are worthy, individual members of the profession must accept their responsibility for professional conduct.

[12] "Bylaws," Home Economics Education Association (formerly Department of Home Economics, National Education Association), February, 1969.

[13] Excerpts from the pamphlet, "Home Economics Education," the bulletin "AVA Dialogue" (page 14), (both published in Washington, D.C. by the American Vocational Association) and *American Vocational Journal,* 44: 17, March 1969.

When you become a graduate home economist, you accept certain responsibilities that have been listed concisely in the Code of Ethics of the American Home Economics Association: [14]

A member of the home economics profession and the American Home Economics Association shall:

Support the objectives of the American Home Economics Association.

Contribute to the development of the Association through being well-informed and participating in its programs.

Maintain the highest standard of professional performance and level of service, acting with responsibility, loyalty, and enthusiasm.

Recognize as an obligation the upgrading of personal professional competence.

Advance public awareness and understanding of home economics as a profession in its broadest sense.

The National Education Association has prepared a *Code of Ethics of the Education Profession,* applicable to all subject areas and levels. Any code must be reviewed continuously. You will notice that this code expresses explicit standards of conduct: [15]

PRINCIPLE I—Commitment to the Student

The educator measures his success by the progress of each student toward realization of his potential as a worthy and effective citizen. The educator therefore works to stimulate the spirit of inquiry, the acquisition of knowledge and understanding, and the thoughtful formulation of worthy goals.

In fulfilling his obligation to the student, the educator—

1. Shall not without just cause restrain the student from independent action in his pursuit of learning, and shall not without just cause deny the student access to varying points of view.
2. Shall not deliberately suppress or distort subject matter for which he bears responsibility.
3. Shall make reasonable effort to protect the student from conditions harmful to learning or to health and safety.
4. Shall conduct professional business in such a way that he does not expose the student to unnecessary embarrassment or disparagement.
5. Shall not on the ground of race, color, creed, or national origin exclude any student from participation in or deny him benefits under any program, nor grant any discriminatory consideration or advantage.
6. Shall not use professional relationships with students for private advantage.

[14] American Home Economics Association Code of Ethics, October, 1966.

[15] *Code of Ethics of the Education Profession.* Adopted by the NEA Representative Assembly, July, 1968.

7. Shall keep in confidence information that has been obtained in the course of professional service, unless disclosure serves professional purposes or is required by law.
8. Shall not tutor for remuneration students assigned to his classes, unless no other qualified teacher is reasonably available.

PRINCIPLE II—Commitment to the Public

The educator believes that patriotism in its highest form requires dedication to the principles of our democratic heritage. He shares with all other citizens the responsibility for the development of sound public policy and assumes full political and citizenship responsibilities. The educator bears particular responsibility for the development of policy relating to the extension of educational opportunities for all and for interpreting educational programs and policies to the public.

In fulfilling his obligation to the public, the educator—

1. Shall not misrepresent an institution or organization with which he is affiliated, and shall take adequate precautions to distinguish between his personal and institutional or organizational views.
2. Shall not knowingly distort or misrepresent the facts concerning educational matters in direct and indirect public expressions.
3. Shall not interfere with a colleague's exercise of political and citizenship rights and responsibilities.
4. Shall not use institutional privileges for private gain or to promote political candidates or partisan political activities.
5. Shall accept no gratuities, gifts, or favors that might impair or appear to impair professional judgment, nor offer any favor, service, or thing of value to obtain special advantage.

PRINCIPLE III—Commitment to the Profession

The educator believes that the quality of the services of the education profession directly influences the nation and its citizens. He therefore exerts every effort to raise professional standards, to improve his service, to promote a climate in which the exercise of professional judgment is encouraged, and to achieve conditions which attract persons worthy of the trust to careers in education. Aware of the value of united effort, he contributes actively to the support, planning, and programs of professional organizations.

In fulfilling his obligation to the profession, the educator—

1. Shall not discriminate on the ground of race, color, creed, or national origin for membership in professional organizations, nor interfere with the free participation of colleagues in the affairs of their association.
2. Shall accord just and equitable treatment to all members of the profession in the exercise of their professional rights and responsibilities.

3. Shall not use coercive means or promise special treatment in order to influence professional decisions of colleagues.
4. Shall withhold and safeguard information acquired about colleagues in the course of employment, unless disclosure serves professional purposes.
5. Shall not refuse to participate in a professional inquiry when requested by an appropriate professional association.
6. Shall provide upon the request of the aggrieved party a written statement of specific reason for recommendations that lead to the denial of increments, significant changes in employment, or termination of employment.
7. Shall not misrepresent his professional qualifications.
8. Shall not knowingly distort evaluations of colleagues.

PRINCIPLE IV—Commitment to Professional Employment Practices

The educator regards the employment agreement as a pledge to be executed both in spirit and in fact in a manner consistent with the highest ideals of professional service. He believes that sound professional personnel relationships with governing boards are built upon personal integrity, dignity, and mutual respect. The educator discourages the practice of his profession by unqualified persons.

In fulfilling his obligation to professional employment practices, the educator—

1. Shall apply for, accept, offer, or assign a position or responsibility on the basis of professional preparation and legal qualifications.
2. Shall apply for a specific position only when it is known to be vacant, and shall refrain from underbidding or commenting adversely about other candidates.
3. Shall not knowingly withhold information regarding a position from an applicant or misrepresent an assignment or conditions of employment.
4. Shall give prompt notice to the employing agency of any change in availability of service, and the employing agent shall give prompt notice of change in availability or nature of a position.
5. Shall not accept a position when so requested by the appropriate professional organization.
6. Shall adhere to the terms of a contract or appointment unless these terms have been legally terminated, falsely represented, or substantially altered by unilateral action of the employing agency.
7. Shall conduct professional business through channels, when available, that have been jointly approved by the professional organization and the employing agency.
8. Shall not delegate assigned tasks to unqualified personnel.
9. Shall permit no commercial exploitation of his professional position.
10. Shall use time granted for the purpose for which it is intended.

A LOOK TOWARD TOMORROW'S HOME ECONOMICS PROGRAM

No one can truly predict what the future will be like for a home economics teacher. Social, economic, and technological developments now unforeseen can have a marked effect on what and how home economics courses will be taught. What you do each day as you begin your teaching career and as you become an experienced teacher will also help to determine the future for yourself as well as for those who follow you in preparing to be home economics teachers. On the basis of what you have learned in this book and what experts predict for the future, you might enjoy speculating a little about what you think might, or should, lie in the future for a home economics teacher. You can compare your ideas with those presented in the remainder of this chapter. Use your imagination, though, and try to come up with new approaches that will be in keeping with the very latest trends right in your own community.

To guide your thinking about tomorrow's programs, we describe briefly the learning environment that seems to be emerging, the differentiation of teacher roles, and the expansion of programs whereby adults will continue their education.

The Learning Environment

For much too long, educators have assumed that learning takes place only in the classroom. Now we realize that physical presence may or may not mean that learning is taking place. Likewise, before students come to our classrooms, many of them have already learned much of what we were planning to teach. If they can really be motivated while they are with us, they can make fruitful use of their summers and free time during the school year. As more home economics programs become available, students will be learning from educational television, programmed instructional materials, computer centers with controls in dormitories, and perhaps home learning centers. Home economists will need to develop new and effective ways of evaluating cognitive objectives and performance of skills so as to enable students to move forward rather than take courses they may not need.

Changes will be evident in the classroom environment also. *Flexible-modular scheduling* has changed our concepts of class periods in the school day. Gradually educators are thinking in terms of modules, perhaps 20 minutes in duration with about 21 modules as divisions for each day. Instead of having a class that meets at the same time every day and for the same number of minutes, flexibility is being introduced. A class may meet at various times during the week, in various sizes, with varying numbers of teachers, and for different lengths of time. Students are not committed to the classroom, but they can spend their time in the library, conferring with a teacher, working in the laboratory, or discussing with a small group of fellow students. For example, a student taking a college course in family relations might spend 40 minutes a week with about 100 students for lectures, 60 minutes a week in section meetings with a group of 20 or 25 students, and 20 minutes in a seminar where 10 or 12 students can discuss family relations with a professor.

Closely related to the flexibility of the learning environment is the emphasis on a *responsive environment.* In an age when people are often identified by numbers, they are seeking opportunities for personal involvement and interaction. Television programs will be encouraging more listener involvement. Programmed instruction will gain importance over traditional books because of the opportunities for students to interact while studying. Small-group discussions and seminars will provide for interaction with other students as well as with teachers. Movable partitions in the classrooms will permit individual study or work in small groups.

In recent years we have come to accept the "discovery method" as having merit. McLuhan and Leonard pointed out that this method simply leads students to "standard perceptions and approved solutions." Students must be encouraged to "seek their own solutions" to problems that have never been solved and perhaps not even conceived as problems. To do this demands that teachers "train the senses and perceptions rather than stuff the brain." [16]

The educational program must give more attention to the desires of minority groups to increase their knowledge of themselves and their positions in society. New curricula will bring interdisciplinary focus to Afro-American history, developments, and progress. Home economics teachers may become involved in such aspects as the "Preparation of Soul Food," "Human Relations in the Black Community," "Arts and Ideas of Afro-American Culture," and "Personal and Social Adjustment of Afro-Americans." [17] Whether or not special courses are offered, home economics teachers must be creative in fostering better understanding of other races and cultures through various learning experiences and instructional media.

Leadership studies have revealed that teachers who have the opportunity to take part in the formation of general school policies may be

[16] Marshall McLuhan and George B. Leonard, "The Future of Education: The Class of 1989." *Look,* **31**: 23–25, February 21, 1967.

[17] Doris A. Meek, "Black Power and the Instructional Council." *Junior College Journal,* **39**: 13, October, 1968.

less autocratic in their classrooms than those who feel they are under a dictator. In addition, teachers must be willing to express their opinions. Someone has said that it is just as undemocratic to be submissive as it is to require submission. Teachers must learn to talk over their areas of disagreement if they hope to provide a democratic classroom environment in which their students can grow.

Role Differentiation of Teachers

Several approaches, which are already being used by some school districts, will undoubtedly be expanded in an effort to utilize teacher talent more effectively. One such approach, *team teaching,* gives recognition to the fact that teachers differ in competency and interests. When two or more teachers plan, instruct, and evaluate cooperatively, the team can take advantage of each member's special competence. A teacher who has depth of interest in a particular subject area and who can communicate her knowledge clearly and interestingly might instruct a large group of students. Teachers might alternate in leading the large groups, specializing in a particular area of study. Students might meet in smaller groups with teachers whose special competence is bringing students out in small-group discussion. Not only do the students benefit from contacts with more than one teacher, but the teachers have the opportunity to specialize and thereby improve their performance. Potential dangers that need to be guarded against are the possibility that teachers might push their own specializations with little attempt to interrelate knowledge about various aspects of home and family living. Also, a unique teaching style, which is not suited to a team arrangement, may be squelched. On the more positive side, the team approach can provide invaluable growth opportunities for a beginning teacher as well as challenge for the more mature teacher.

Closely related to the team concept is that of providing support personnel for teachers. College students sometimes serve as paid *teacher aides.* The "New Careers" concept has encouraged the placement of impoverished people in low-level classroom jobs as nonprofessional aides.[18] While these positions may be terminal, there are opportunities to work toward eventual professional status. A number of tasks that were formerly done by professional educators can be assigned to people without a college education but with insights that might be important. As they gain experience and formal education, they can climb the "career ladder." The professional is freed to do the things he is equipped to do. At

[18] Arthur Pearl and Frank Riessman, *New Careers for the Poor: The Nonprofessional in Human Service.* New York: The Free Press, 1965, pp. 57–62.

the same time, he can learn to understand his students better as he talks with the aide who is a product of the social problems in that community. The students benefit from having a teacher aide who can take time to listen to them and give extra attention where most needed. Duties of the teacher aide might include clerical work, maintaining supplies and equipment, and assisting with laboratory preparations. An individual who lacks a degree may qualify as a teacher aide. Nearby colleges might give credits for on-the-job activities.

Another level of support personnel is a *teacher assistant* who has had two years of college preparation. The assistant might prepare instructional materials, correct test papers and other assignments, organize supplies for demonstrations, evaluate laboratory work, and assist in small-group instruction.

Some proposals have carried the role differentiation of teachers still further, designating those who have bachelor's degrees as *teacher associates.* These persons would hold positions that could qualify for tenure. They would be under the direction of a supervising teacher. This plan would make all beginning teaching positions of a junior-level responsibility. Persons who are really committed to career teaching would pursue the extensive demands leading to a truly professional position.

In line with this trend is that of requiring all teachers to complete five years of college study. These fully-credentialed persons would be called *teachers* and they would be released from routine chores in order to take on the role of a true professional. Teachers at this level would need training in making effective use of assistants.

The title *supervising teacher* or *instructional manager* would give recognition to teachers whose achievement has been outstanding. Supervising teachers would be familiar with the duties of the aide, assistant, and associate, and offer individual help when needed. They would have special training for supervising and evaluating teachers at the other levels. They would serve on teams with other certified teachers.

Continuing Education

Education has become the major business of industry, military service, government, arts, and sciences. Not only has technology created a need for new education, but it has also opened vast opportunities for fulfilling this need. Some industries have responded to the challenge by cooperating with educators on adapting various media of instruction to the demands of schools. Some have engaged in innovative programs to train the hard-core unemployed for jobs. Many have encouraged their employees to keep growing by offering reimbursement for costs incurred while taking college courses that should improve their job performance.

The trend toward lifelong education can be expected to gain momentum. An important part of this trend is the "new careers" emphasis designed to enable disadvantaged persons to obtain jobs and receive their training while they work. Even if relatively few of these persons ever attain professional standing, an important goal will have been fulfilled just by giving them the opportunity for work and advancement.

The major emphasis in home economics will continue to be on educating individuals—boys and girls, men and women—for family living. As the roles individuals assume in families change over time, home economics too will change. Where in the past, emphasis was placed on assisting individuals in their housekeeping role, today emphasis is placed on the managerial, consumer, and relationship roles.

Home economics education will continue to place occupational preparation among its goals. Expanded offerings must be made available to young people who might otherwise drop out of school prior to high school graduation, as well as to those who have dropped out while lacking skills for obtaining a job. Homemakers who are entering the job market for the first time will need training, and home economics should offer them opportunities to capitalize on the skills they have developed in their own homes. Adults whose training is outdated and those who wish to upgrade their level of employment will be seeking guidance on opportunities related to home economics.

Community colleges will play an increasing role in meeting needs for job training as well as for general education of youth and adults. They have been recognized for many years as contributing effectively to the students who wish to take the first two years of college in their own local communities before transferring to a four-year college. They are uniquely qualified to give vocational education because of their close ties to the local communities that support them. Advisory committees composed of home economists and potential employers of graduates can be very helpful in identifying the need for particular programs, planning curricula, interpreting and supporting the programs, and evaluating their effectiveness. Occupational preparation must be designed to meet local needs, but in our mobile society, it must not neglect supporting courses in the liberal arts, particularly oral and written communication skills, American history and government, and breadth courses in such areas as the humanities, social sciences, and natural sciences.

Home economics must be recognized as providing opportunities for creative pursuits. The homemaker who feels trapped with "little people and lots of housekeeping chores" will be looking toward community colleges and adult education programs to help her achieve self-actualization through creative expression in personal and social achievements.

As we stand here and look toward tomorrow's home economics program, we have mixed feelings. Of course, we are anxious to see changes that will be in keeping with social, economic, and technological advances. Nevertheless, we may be reluctant to give up something that has become a traditional part of the home economics program, such as the emphasis on skills in foods and clothing. Yet, we must realize that, as something new is added, something that is no longer needed must be dropped to make room for the new. The needs of modern society point to intellectual experiences in all phases of the home economics curriculum, with major emphasis on human development, management, and family dynamics.

Undoubtedly most of us question whether we are capable of carrying out the kind of home economics program that is best for our community. Indeed, this questioning is probably a healthy sign, for a person who has no hesitation about her ability is not likely to have a full concept of what she should be doing. The job of a home economics teacher is large and changes continually, bringing a constant challenge to try another approach that may be more effective in helping students to improve their home and family living. As a home economics teacher, you can face the future confidently, knowing that you have been selected carefully, you have received effective preparation for your present teaching position, you will have resources provided for you to continue your professional growth, and you will have the strength of professional organizations in home economics and education to support and guide your work. Herbert Hoover gave a helpful suggestion for facing the future when he said: "Wisdom consists not so much in knowing what to do in the ultimate as in knowing what to do next."

Selected References

Beggs, David W., III (Editor), *Team Teaching: Bold New Venture.* Indianapolis: Unified College Press, 1964.

Biddle, Bruce J., and William J. Ellena (Editors), *Contemporary Research on Teacher Effectiveness.* New York: Holt, Rinehart and Winston, 1964.

Cottrell, Donald P., "Teacher Competences Required for Emerging Educational Programs." (Précis of an address for the National Association of Teacher Educators of Home Economics, December, 1967.)

Garrett, Pauline G., *Post-Secondary Education in Home Economics.* Washington, D.C.: American Vocational Association, 1967.

Goodlad, John I., "Learning and Teaching in the Future." *National Education Association Journal* 57: 49–51, February, 1968.

Home Economics in Institutions Granting Bachelor's or Higher Degrees 1963–64. Washington, D.C.: American Home Economics Association.

Home Economics Research Abstracts. Washington, D.C.: American Home Economics Association. (Request the most recent year's reports on masters' theses and doctoral dissertations completed in Family Economics—Home Management; Institutional Administration; Textiles and Clothing; Art—Housing, Furnishings, and Equipment; Home Economics Education; and Family Relations and Child Development.)

Lippeatt, Selma F., and Helen I. Brown, *Focus and Promise of Home Economics*. New York: Macmillan, 1965.

McGrath, Earl J., and Jack T. Johnson, *The Changing Mission of Home Economics*. New York: Teachers College, Columbia University, 1968.

McGrath, Earl J., "The Imperatives of Change for Home Economics." *Journal of Home Economics* **60**: 505–514, September 1968.

Michael, Donald N., *The Next Generation: The Prospects Ahead for the Youth of Today and Tomorrow*. New York: Random House, 1965.

National Commission on Teacher Education and Professional Standards, *The Real World of the Beginning Teacher*. Washington, D.C.: National Education Association, 1965.

National Commission on Teacher Education and Professional Standards, *Remaking the World of the Career Teacher*. Washington, D.C.: National Education Association, 1966.

Pearl, Arthur, and Frank Riessman, *New Careers for the Poor: The Nonprofessional in Human Service*. New York: The Free Press, 1965.

"Toward the Year 2000: Work in Progress." *Daedalus* **96**: 639–1002, Summer 1967.

Index